Studies of the Max Planck Institute Luxembourg for
International, European and Regulatory Procedural Law

edited by
Prof. Dr. Dres. h.c. Burkhard Hess
Prof. Dr. Hélène Ruiz Fabri

Volume 20

Hélène Ruiz Fabri | André Nunes Chaib | Ingo Venzke
Armin von Bogdandy (eds.)

International Judicial Legitimacy

New Voices and Approaches

Nomos

Max Planck Institute
LUXEMBOURG
for Procedural Law

Coverpicture:
Title: Surreal faces in clouds | Image ID: 67247012
Media Type: Stock Photo | Copyright: Bruce Rolff

The Deutsche Nationalbibliothek lists this publication in the Deutsche Nationalbibliografie; detailed bibliographic data are available on the Internet at http://dnb.d-nb.de

ISBN 978-3-8487-6762-5 (Print)
978-3-7489-0866-1 (ePDF)

British Library Cataloguing-in-Publication Data
A catalogue record for this book is available from the British Library.

ISBN 978-3-8487-6762-5 (Print)
978-3-7489-0866-1 (ePDF)

Library of Congress Cataloging-in-Publication Data
Ruiz Fabri, Hélène / Nunes Chaib, André / Venzke, Ingo / Bogdandy, Armin von
International Judicial Legitimacy
New Voices and Approaches
Hélène Ruiz Fabri / André Nunes Chaib / Ingo Venzke / Armin von Bogdandy (eds.)
300 pp.
Includes bibliographic references and index.

ISBN 978-3-8487-6762-5 (Print)
978-3-7489-0866-1 (ePDF)

1st Edition 2020

Published by
Nomos Verlagsgesellschaft mbH & Co. KG
Waldseestraße 3-5 | 76530 Baden-Baden
www.nomos.de

Production of the printed version:
Nomos Verlagsgesellschaft mbH & Co. KG
Waldseestraße 3-5 | 76530 Baden-Baden

Printed and bound in Germany.

ISBN (Print): 978-3-8487-6762-5
ISBN (ePDF): 978-3-7489-0866-1

DOI: https://doi.org/10.5771/9783748908661

Onlineversion
Nomos eLibrary

Preface

This book is the outcome of two workshops, mostly between members of the Max Planck Institutes from Heidelberg and Luxembourg (April 2015 and September 2015), in which they reacted to the publication "*In Whose Name? A Public Law Theory of International Adjudication*" by two of the editors. Following the workshops, the outcomes of our inter-institutional discussions were taken further in writing. Generally speaking, the topic of our discussions was not all-together new, to be sure. The legitimacy of international institutions, more specifically international courts, to conduct their business has been scrutinized for quite a while. However, our volume is particularly interesting because it showcases a variety of new approaches, mostly from younger scholars, on how to tackle the issue.

Initially, our discussions and texts on the legitimacy of international courts were framed as a direct reaction to arguments put forward in the book "*In Whose Name?*". The subjects ranged from a comparison between international organizations and international courts and how they can contribute to democratize international law to assessing the democratic legitimacy of international human rights courts.

As our debate progressed, a variety of different approaches to international judicial legitimacy emerged. Certain issues became central points treated across all chapters in this volume. At first, the present volume may seem like just another attempt to raise questions about the legitimacy and authority of international courts, but in fact it goes beyond that. Not only are we looking at the theoretical foundations of authority as a concept informing political action, but also as an analytical category, and how it has been employed in different ways by authors and scholars in the various social sciences. We are also looking at how such a concept allows one to properly gauge the very elements that justify the legitimacy of international courts. Considering the difference between the texts, a decision was made to extend the scope of the edited volume and include contributions that do not necessarily respond directly to *In Whose Name?*, but that rather discuss its general topic of the legitimacy of international courts. This allowed for the identification of a few lacunae in the treatment of such courts and a number of younger authors were invited to contribute to the volume.

The focus of the project also changed over time. Instead of remaining a simple reaction to *In Whose Name?*, it became an opportunity to debate and elaborate on the potential justifications for the legitimacy of specific international courts; and also to investigate how, given the importance of issues being dealt with by international courts, particular elements of legitimacy ought to be brought into discussion. The result was an astonishing collection dealing with both theoretical and practical questions regarding the legitimacy of international courts and how such problems relate to fundamental problems of our times.

Armin von Bogdandy, Heidelberg,
André Nunes Chaib, Maastricht,
Hélène Ruiz Fabri, Luxemburg,
Ingo Venzke, Amsterdam

Table of Contents

Introduction

Prof. Hélène Ruiz Fabri[*] */ Dr André Nunes Chaib*[**]

The everyday presence and impact of international law in our lives has probably never been felt as much as it has in the last hundred years. International law, and its associated rules and institutions, has effected changes in social and political structures that now often determine the way public and private entities conduct their affairs. Amongst these many institutions, international courts are some of the most important, but also potentially most contentious. International courts' decisions have begun to greatly affect the lives of peoples everywhere, ranging from redefining maritime limits of States and thereby affecting the economic activities of fisheries, to determining that domestic public authorities ought to compensate individuals for violations of individual and social human rights.

These courts have become more than just *legal* institutions and have rearranged the general global *political* scenario. They can no longer be considered mere deciders of cases between parties. In doing so, international courts have also repositioned themselves within the broader international political and social spectrum and their activities have, in many cases, been contested as acting beyond their original powers. The increase in the impact of international court decisions over peoples' lives derives from them having both the *authority* and the *legitimacy* to do so. These two concepts are central and integral to better understand the position of international courts in both the international and domestic legal, political and social scenario and are the fundamental elements discussed in the chapters of this volume. This introduction will sketch out some of the main issues that bind the various chapters of this volume.

* Director, Max Planck Institute Luxembourg for Procedural Law; Professor of International Law, University Paris 1 Panthéon-Sorbonne.
** Assistant Professor in Globalization and Law, Maastricht University.

The central issues at stake

A discussion about the legitimacy and authority of international courts must begin with some conceptual clarification. We shall begin with "authority". Nowadays, social sciences generally rely on the concept of authority provided by Max Weber at the beginning of the 20th century — a concept that serves not only as a descriptive formula but also allows one to make sense of the various political mechanisms put in place in different societal spheres.[1] It also does not consider the *loss* of authority an absolute event but instead acknowledges the different ways that authority exists and can be exercised.[2] Weber's concept of authority has been so influential that authors such as Alaisdair MacIntyre have gone as far as to assert that there is no modern conception of authority that is not Weberian in its core.[3] In this respect, this volume looks at the exercise of public authority by courts and assesses the extent to which various public law theories may be used to create a democratically oriented framework that seeks to legitimize these courts' activities.

However, in this context another central problem appears. Even though international courts make law, the question whether their acts need to be "democratically" justified remains. As compared to other international institutions, it could be said that international courts should not need to seek democratic legitimacy if they focused on exercising their counter-majoritarian function. Their primary aim should be to guarantee their functional and normative legitimacy instead.[4] Nevertheless, the process of institutionalization of the international legal order greatly relies on the work of international courts. And if institutionalizing the international legal order means guaranteeing the minimum means of redress for violations of rights or mechanisms to protect rights, then one must investigate how such courts can be legitimized vis-à-vis those who may make use of them. This is clearly shown by the fact that international courts have determined many of the basic understandings of what has come to constitute crucial rules of international law. Examples would be the *Brazilian Loans*

---

1 Weber, M. (1980), *Wirtschaft und Gesellschaft* (5th ed.). Tubingen: Mohr Siebeck, 123.

2 Authority is given specific characteristics according to the mode in which is exercised: *Ibid.*, 124.

3 MacIntyre, A. (2007), *After Virtue. A Study in Moral Theory*. (3rd ed.). Notre Dame: University of Notre Dame Press, 109.

4 For instance, von Bogdandy, A. and Venzke, I. (2014), *In Whose Name? A Public Law Theory of International Adjudication*. Oxford: Oxford University Press.

Case[5], the *Serbian Loans Case*[6], and the *Oscar Chinn Case*[7]. An important contextual question here is whether international courts have the same potential to not only *institutionalize* international economic law but also to create public and democratic generalities in the international sphere. Some authors have argued that, at the international level, international courts are not only capable of effecting such changes but are also voices in the name of "peoples and citizens"[8].

For this purpose, one cannot only look at democratic theories. The concept or principle of democracy must be fundamentally internalized and operationalized through a larger, more comprehensive legal framework. Applying a public law theory to the activities of international courts would make sense, insofar as it has the potential to effectively create the conditions for the development of a democratic generality that affects decision making. Public participation and transparency, amongst other principles, could indeed reinforce the process of "politicization" these institutions are going through.

Yet for such a public law framework to be applicable, an attempt to define the contours of what, in fact, *the public* of such a framework would be needs to be made. One fundamental aspect about the determination of a public for international institutions – and the future application of a public law framework to serve the principles that guide their action – is represented by the idea of a potentially existing democratic generality at the international level.[9] This "generality" is no longer only represented by States as legal subjects in international law, but also consists of individuals, singularly and collectively considered (the "peoples") as well as other types of private actors, such as non-governmental organizations, multinational enterprises, etc. All of these entities, just like States, have acquired sufficient autonomy at the international level, which pushes them towards a

---

5 *Brazilian Loans*, Judgement 15, PCIJ, Series A, 12 July 1929. Similar to the Serbian Loans Case, in this decision, the PCIJ strengthened the process of stabilizing and reinforcing the institution of diplomatic protection, which would be instrumental to the development of international investment arbitration.

6 *Serbian Loans*, Judgement 15, PCIJ, Series A, 12 July 1929.

7 *Oscar Chinn*, Judgement 15, PCIJ, Series A/B, 12 December 1939. The Oscar Chinn case was also instrumental in providing further legal and political content to the institution of diplomatic. It went beyond that, however, and provided a legal justification for free trade in the beginning of the 20th century.

8 Von Bogdandy and Venzke, *supra* note 4, 213.

9 *Ibid*., 134.

movement of self-determination as free legal subjects.[10] Because they also constitute entities that form part of those affected by international courts' activities, the fact that they strive to guarantee their right to existence and action both at the domestic and international level creates a tension between individual self-determination (of these entities as legal subjects) and democratic self-determination.[11]

If public law, in accordance with the liberal-democratic tradition, is understood as a system that protects individual freedom and makes collective self-determination possible, and not merely as a political jurisprudence,[12] every act with repercussions for these normative principles must come under scrutiny to the extent that these repercussions are significant enough to raise justified doubts about the legitimacy of an act.[13] This is fundamentally grounded on an idea that the reason why international courts are capable of imposing changes on other entities is because of their authority. That this authority might be sociologically grounded alone, that is it does not need to be based on a particular set of positive norms, raises the question as to whether the normative legitimacy of these courts becomes necessary.

To assess how a public law framework ought to drive the work of international courts, it becomes vital to distinguish points of international *public* law from those elements of private law in the global sphere. This attempt to identify principles governing such public law is also an attempt to determine this public law itself in the international sphere.[14] The identity of this international *public* law is crucial for the justification of its principles.[15] Most public law theories attempting to consolidate principles that guarantee not only a simple justification for international courts but to also further a *democratic* justification, rely on two fundamental concepts: public authority and democracy. Democracy, as previously observed, is

10 Möllers, C. (2005), *Gewaltengliederung. Legitimation und Dogmatik im nationalen und internationalen Rechtsvergleich*. Tübingen: Mohr Siebeck, 28.

11 For a fundamental explanation of this tension, see *Ibid*., 29–30.

12 Loughlin, M. (2010), *The Foundations of Public Law*. Oxford: Oxford University Press, 159. See also, Möllers, *supra* note 10, III.

13 Von Bogdandy and Venzke, *supra* note 4, 169.

14 Grimm, D. (2012), *Das öffentliche Recht vor der Frage nach seiner Identität*. Tübingen: Mohr Siebeck, 43.

15 *Ibid*., in particular 48–57.

hard to define, in particular when considering the international sphere.[16] Such concepts are, as Armin von Bogdandy once stated, *prima ballerinas* for the understanding of modern public law, and need to be discussed and well developed before tackling and crafting new terms, such as those of governance and accountability.[17] In domestic law, the public authority of institutions is usually granted the coercive means to enforce their decisions[18] and will most likely find its grounding in a normative instrument, usually a national constitution.[19] The three most prominent theories attempting to provide such a framework combining these two concepts are well-known today: global administrative law, global constitutionalism, and the international public authority project. They attempt, though, to reconcile in different ways the ideas of public authority and democracy to offer a proper set of principles within which one can control and retain accountable international institutions. Also, in reaction to a model of international law based on *consent*, a public law framework should provide the necessary means to constrain, but also to enable the exercise of the various social agents' freedom.[20]

In this context, normative legitimacy is no longer an issue because public authority should be considered as an "actor's capacity" and should not require any further justification.[21] As has been argued, public authority within domestic law has grown "in the context in which the state, legitimate means of coercion, sovereign control over territory, politics, policies, and public law all coincided"[22]. However, given these same conditions are not present in the global sphere, the concept of public authority applied within the domestic law context cannot be simply transposed to the international. Here public authority ought to be defined more broadly and

---

16 As Manfred Schmidt observes, many of the concepts of what one refers today as democracy depend not only on ancient and modern theories of democracy, but also of the content attributed to this concept by national constitutions (Schmidt, M.G. (2006), *Demokratietheorien. Eine Einführung* (3rd ed.). Wiesbaden: VS Verlag für Sozialwissenschaften, 20). The same difficulty can be also found at the international level. See also for this, Cartledge, P. (2016), *Democracy. A Life.* Oxford: Oxford University press, 283–304.

17 Von Bogdandy, A. (2013), "Foreword", *Transnational Legal Theory* 4(3), 313–314.

18 Von Bogdandy and Venzke, *supra* note 4, 111.

19 *Ibid.*, 112.

20 Von Bogdandy, A. *et al.* (2008), "Developing the Publicness of Public International Law: Towards a Legal Framework for Global Governance Activities", *German Law Journal* 9(11), 1375–1400, 1376.

21 Von Bogdandy and Venzke, *supra* note 4, 112.

22 *Ibid.*, 113.

should, in fact, be taken as the "capacity, based on legal acts, to impact other actors in their exercise of freedom"[23]. This definition provides for the scope of public law to be enlarged, which would allow it to encompass acts of domestic, supranational and international institutions. After all, as the authors argue, the previous conception of public authority fails to grasp that institutions beyond the state are also capable of influencing political self-determination and social interactions.

Nevertheless, the question as to whether there are ways of constructing mechanisms of democratic governance beyond the state has given rise to an interesting debate in international legal scholarship. Some authors have gone as far as to claim the existence of an "emerging right to democratic governance"[24]. Debating whether or not there is such a right is essential, but does not plumb the depth of the problem. International law has functioned and continues to operate regardless of it being democratic or not.[25] Not to mention, also, that for as much as contemporary international lawyers like to do away with it, consent is still a vital element in legitimizing international law and institutions.[26] Evidence of how little importance is attached to the idea of democracy in international law is the fact that there is absolutely no consensus about its definition in international law,[27] even if there have been efforts by the UN in that sense.[28] This "second-order view" problem remains unresolved precisely because there is no answer to the "first-order view'" question: is democracy a necessary value for international law and relations? The fact that despite the lack of any answers in this regard, international law continues to exist and function goes to show that, at this point, it remains moot as to whether democracy constitutes a fundamental aspect of international life.

In this regard, justifying the public authoritativeness of the acts of international courts is crucial for understanding how courts can function within a democratic-oriented public law framework that transcends the boundaries of States. Through a reconceptualization of public authority

---

23 *Ibid.*, 112.

24 See for this Franck, T. (1992), "The Emerging Right to Democratic Governance", *American Journal of International Law* 86(1), 46–91.

25 Crawford, J. (2013), "Chance, Order and Change: The Course of International Law", *Collected Courses of the Hague Academy of International Law* 365, 275.

26 Krisch, N. (2014), "The Decay of Consent: International Law in an Age of Global Public Goods", *American Journal of International Law* 118(1), 1–40, 2.

27 Crawford, *supra* note 25, 277–278.

28 Charlesworth, H. (2015), "Democracy and International Law", *Collected Courses of the Hague Academy of International Law* 371, 99–100.

and the establishment of certain criteria for democracy based on a particular set of positive laws, some authors have attempted to precisely delineate a public law framework for international courts.[29] At the European level it may be even easier to identify a "democratic generality". At the international level, as noted above, this identification is more problematic. For instance, already in the beginning of the 20th century, the PCIJ saw that its function ought to be limited to the parties and that its effects ought to be restricted to them. This meant that rules of international law were the only normative basis for PCIJ decisions and no recourse to principles outside of this normative sphere could be taken.[30]

The structure of the book

The present volume has two parts. The first part centers on the more theoretical issues arising from the debate about the work of international courts. Instead of specifically tackling the activities of individual tribunals, it looks at the fundamental challenges posed by modern theories intended to either bolster or demolish the legitimacy and authority of international tribunals. Central to this part are the critiques – not criticisms – of the use of public law theories to justify the work of courts or the need to construe mechanisms to expand their "democratic legitimacy".

Therefore, the first part starts with a reflection by Alain Zamaria on the potentialities and limits of public law theories to explain or frame the activities of international courts and regulatory agencies. Mr Zamaria looks at how courts as "non-majoritarian institutions" are increasingly empowered and thereby require limitations on the basis not only of rules of law, but of principles of public law. Following Mr Zamaria's reflections on public law and international court more broadly, we have Prof. Aida Torres Pérez' chapter on how international courts in fact speak in the name of "nobody". Challenging a growing conception that international courts ought to be "democratically" legitimized, Prof. Pérez' chapter tries to show how integral to the proper exercise of their function is the retention of their counter-majoritarian position. In this respect, they correctly ought *not* to speak in the name of anyone. The third chapter, from Ms Parvathi

29 Von Bogdandy and Venzke, *supra* note 4; also, Grossmann, N. *et al.* (eds) (2018), *Legitimacy and International Courts*. Cambridge: Cambridge University Press.

30 *Serbian Loans*, *supra* note 6, 19. "From a general point of view, it must be admitted that the true function of the Court is to decide disputes between States or Members of the League of Nations on the basis of international law."

Menon, builds on the topic raised by Prof. Pérez, but goes in another direction. By taking recourse to a TWAIL approach, Ms Menon tries to show how international courts often- if not mostly – ignore the differences existing between States and participants' positions in the northern and southern hemispheres. Chapter four, by Dr. Lorenzo Gasbarri, adopts an interesting perspective and focuses on how courts work out their own "language" in order to create their own justificatory space. The last chapter of the first part, by Dr. André Nunes Chaib, takes on the issue of democracy and democratic generalities and questions whether such principles should be in fact applied to international courts. To justify their limited applications to international tribunals, Dr Nunes Chaib, compares the ways in which such principles can be used by courts and international organizations.

The second part is of a more practical nature. Instead of focusing on specific theoretical questions, it delves into the experience of a few specific courts or courts dealing with specific topics that may generate questions of legitimacy and authority. For instance, Chapter six, by Dr Cecily Rose, looks into how questions of legitimacy have been raised at the International Court of Justice (ICJ), by focusing on the issues raised in the Croatia vs. Serbia Case. Chapter seven, by Dr Lan Nguyen, challenges traditional notions of legitimacy often applied to the International Tribunal for the Law of the Sea (ITLOS). Dr Antoine Duval, in Chapter eight, concentrates on how the legitimacy of international – or transnational – courts governing the world of sports can offer interesting reflection points on how to rethink the way in which democracy, legitimacy and authority of courts can be rethought. In Chapter nine, Dr. Geraldo Vidigal offers a novel approach to examining how the principle of democracy can be used to look into the work of the WTO dispute settlement body. In Chapter ten, Prof. Rene Urueña discusses and critiques the use of particular democratic principles in the work of the Inter-American Court of Human Rights. In Chapter eleven, Dr Freya Clausen looks at the work of the European Court of Justice from a public law perspective and questions the extent to which the idea of democracy is really necessary to grant the Court's work legitimacy. Finally, in Chapter twelve, Prof. Armin von Bogdandy and Dr Laura Hering discuss how the democratic legitimacy of the European Court of Human Rights can be said to be based on the fact that they speak *in the name of the European Club of Liberal Democracies*.

The complex, but coherent, set of chapters contained in this volume should provide the reader with a wide array of novel information and approaches as to how one can discuss and tackle the issues of the legitimacy and authority of international courts. We hope to see this not as the conclusion of the debate, but as a reimagined spark to constantly and continuously stimulate thinking about the best ways in which we can reaffirm the importance of, or challenge, the work of such international courts.

Democratic Legitimacy and Non-Majoritarian Institutions: Reflections on the Functional and Democratic Legitimacy of International Adjudicative Bodies and Independent Regulatory Agencies

Alain Zamaria[*]

Introduction

The growing role of international adjudicative bodies, regulatory agencies driving public policies in areas such as telecommunications, health, energy and antitrust, and independent central banks running monetary policies are among the numerous signs of the empowerment of non-majoritarian institutions ("NMIs") that carry out public policy without being accountable to the people through electoral and political processes.[1] Despite being subject to tighter procedural rules, their development is increasingly raising questions of legitimacy as they are, just like "conventional" political authorities, blamed for not having delivered the promises that justified their creation.

In *In Whose Name? A Public Law Theory of International Adjudication*, Armin von Bogdandy and Ingo Venzke reconsidered the basic purposes of one particular type of NMIs: international jurisdictions.[2] Claiming that neither the original consent nor the functional goal is sufficient to settle their legitimacy and representation concerns convincingly, the authors tried to find universal standards for the democratic legitimacy of these institutions. The frontier between universalism and skepticism being thin,[3] "any contribution that purports to be conceived as universal should be

* Research Fellow, Max Planck Institute Luxembourg for Procedural Law.

1 Majone, G. (1999), "The Regulatory State and Its Legitimacy Problems", *West European Politics* 22(1), 1–24, 10.

2 Von Bogdandy, A. and Venzke, I. (2014), *In Whose Name?: A Public Law Theory of International Adjudication*. Oxford: Oxford University Press.

3 On the search for a common ground between universalism and skepticism, see Philips, M. (1994), *Between Universalism and skepticism: Ethics as social artifact*. Oxford: Oxford University Press.

viewed with suspicion"[4]. As Armin von Bogdandy pointed out, "in view of the political, ideological, and cultural fragmentation of global society, every claim to be writing from a global or universal point of view strikes us as potentially hegemonic and guilty of hubris"[5]. To avoid succumbing to the "apologetic temptation" of using functional arguments to justify institutions[6] or to the utopian appeal for abstract and general norms, the authors used the broad notions of representation, transparency, deliberation, and participation found in the Treaty on the European Union in order to tackle the legitimacy and democratic deficit of international adjudicative bodies and "chart a path between utopia and apology"[7].

Democracy, one of the three building blocks of the public law theory of international adjudication (hereafter referred to as the "public law theory"), alongside multifunctionality and international public authority, is one of the most controversial topics discussed in the book. Unlike decisions from international courts and tribunals exercising public authority ("ICTs"), judicial decisions from domestic courts have a clear democratic dimension as they are rendered "in the name of the people". The public law theory came in a particular context: the eloquent growth of international adjudication in the last two decades,[8] and the fact that ICTs now perform numerous functions beyond the settlement of disputes in individual cases, such as "the stabilization of normative expectations", "law-making" and "the control and legitimation of public authority"[9].

This context and the shifting of the source of legitimacy from domestic courts to ICTs have far-reaching ramifications that could recall the questions raised by independent and semi-independent regulatory agencies ("IRAs"). Regulatory agencies appeared in the United States at the end of the nineteenth century in order to regulate rail transport (through the Interstate Commerce Commission) and then to tackle all the subjects that are technically, legally, or politically complex or sensitive. Later, with the development of interventionist states in the 1980s, they started proliferat-

4 Von Bogdandy, A. (2013), "The Democratic Legitimacy of International Courts: A Conceptual Framework", *Theoretical Inquiries in Law* 14(2), 361–379, 363, available at https://www7.tau.ac.il/ojs/index.php/til/article/view/138, accessed 11 February 2020.

5 Bogdandy and Venzke, *supra* note 2, 26.

6 *Ibid.*, 6.

7 *Ibid.*, 151.

8 "Since 2002, international courts have rendered more judicial decisions every single year than was the case from time immemorial up to 1989", see *Ibid.*, 1.

9 *Ibid.*, 8.

ing in Europe as the need for "political credibility in an increasingly interdependent world"[10] became clear. Since then, democratic institutions have progressively delegated public authority to these agencies that claimed to produce faster and expertise-oriented decisions and quickly gained autonomy.

If there are practical reasons to justify these trends in a purely functional manner – i.e. the specific needs of regulation or the rising international challenges – such a legitimization would remain unsatisfactory. For the purpose of this contribution, the paper will not discuss the current developments involving all the NMIs but investigate, based on the public law theory of Armin von Bogdandy and Ingo Venzke (hereafter referred to as "the authors"), some of the most acute legitimacy problems that impact both contemporary international adjudication and domestic regulation. Although NMIs take various institutional forms, including ICTs, supranational and international organizations, IRAs, specialized constitutional courts, and central banks, this paper will mostly focus on ICTs and IRAs. It will study the solutions advanced for legitimising ICTs and the prospect to respond to the democratic deficit by some form of input or procedural legitimacy. Two concepts will be mainly considered in this study: the concept of "domestic analogy" and the concept of "delegation", as public authority is being transferred from national democratic institutions to NMIs.

While the public law theory can be conceived as a specific legitimation theory for the specific context of international adjudication, the paper aims at (i) contextualizing the public law theory to understand how domestic analogy is used for legitimizing ICTs, (ii) mapping the public law theory to understand how it articulates with other proposals that developed in the last decades, (iii) and testing the public law theory for the legitimacy concerns of regulatory agencies. A reflection on the democratic legitimacy of NMIs seems indeed very timely as populism is spreading across the world, and non-electoral legitimacy is under pressure.

I. Domestic Analogy and the Legitimacy of International Adjudicative Bodies

The public law theory found in domestic law the legal tools to provide legitimacy to international courts and tribunals exercising public authority, hence trying to resolve one of the most controversial challenges in interna-

10 Majone, *supra* note 1, 11.

tional law in a manner that could be described as either ambitious or utopian (A). The main obstacle for implementing a public law theory and a viable democratic framework in an international setting lies in the lack of *demos* at the global level (B).

A. *Domestic Analogy and the International Order*

From Analogy to Utopia?

Along with several proposals formulated since the creation of the League of Nations, the public law theory aims at transferring domestic legal and political principles to the international realm. This reasoning is based on a domestic analogy. A domestic analogy means that the principles sustaining order within national states can reproduce order at the international level based on the presumption that national and international phenomena share the same conditions of order.[11] The domestic analogy is problematic when considered not only as a potentially emulating experience but as a universal ideal to strive for in the long term. Indeed, "[the] conditions of an orderly social life, on this view, are the same among states as they are within them: they require that the institutions of domestic society be reproduced on a universal scale"[12], an assumption that is highly debatable.

The quest for world order and unity at large can be criticized for its utopian nature. In an article on "The Mystery of Global Governance", David Kennedy analyzed a contradiction between the "purposive bias [...] against the concept of disorder" and the fact that disorder is a reality of any social life.[13] More specifically, criticism comes from those who regard international law as a system of law *sui generis* – especially authors from the late nineteenth and the early twentieth century – and International Relations ("IR") scholars who conceive IR as "dependent on, but separated from Politics"[14]. There are other grounds for being skeptical in this respect: the

11 Suganami, H. (1966), *The Domestic Analogy and World Order Proposals*. Cambridge: Cambridge University Press, 1.

12 Bull, H. (1966), "Society and anarchy in international relations" In: H. Butterfield and M. Wight (eds), *Diplomatic investigations.* Oxford: Oxford University Press, 35–60.

13 Kennedy, D. (2009), "The Mystery of Global Governance" In: J.L. Dunoff and J.P. Trachtman (eds), *Ruling the World?*. Cambridge: Cambridge University Press, 37–68.

14 To see Manning's criticism: Suganami, *supra* note 11, 10.

impression that analogy is less scientific than deductive reasoning, the assumption that states need to be considered differently from individuals, and the rejection of legalism or cosmopolitanism.[15] Analogy has nonetheless been repeatedly used as a tool to conceptualize the international legal order.

In the *Leviathan*, Thomas Hobbes assumed that the conditions of an orderly social life for individuals differed from conditions of order among states. In a Hobbesian perspective, the invention of political sovereignty puts an end to the anarchy between individuals (or the "state of nature"), which leads to a "war of all against all"[16]. Hobbes drew a parallel with the anarchical international order but he did not consider the feasibility or the necessity of an international social contract. Therefore, it is not clear whether the idea of a global sovereign to solve interstate conflict was "in the very logic of his argument" or if it was instead a lacuna that could either be left unexplored or bring explanations on the reasons why states' anarchy does not lead to a state of war.[17] Hedley Bull, a critic of the domestic analogy who engaged with the lacuna, claimed that, according to Hobbes, the anarchy between individuals who are threatening each other in the state of nature would be fundamentally different from the risks incurred by states. As sovereigns would then belong to the state of nature, the "Hobbesian view" is still considered by numerous political scientists as the realistic position,[18] and it is usually opposed to the liberal approach of IR, associated with Immanuel Kant.

Unlike the English philosopher, Kant clearly drew an analogy between individuals and states, stating in the *Metaphysics of Morals* that "states, like lawless savages, exist in a condition devoid of right" in the international state of nature.[19] A few years later, he pushed the analogy further: "[no]

---

15 *Ibid., 16.*

16 Hobbes, T. (1996) [1651], *Leviathan*. Cambridge: Cambridge University Press, Chapter 13.

17 Grewal, D.S. (2016), "The Domestic Analogy Revisited: Hobbes on International Order", *Yale Law Journal* 125(3), 618–680, 628–630, available at https://www.yalelawjournal.org/essay/the-domestic-analogy-revisited-hobbes-on-international-order, accessed 11 February 2020.

18 Morgenthau, H. (2005), *Politics Among Nations*. New York: McGraw-Hill Education; for a critique of the confusion between the Hobbesian and the realistic view and a reflection on Hobbes as 'a theorist of international peace', see Grewal, *supra* note 17.

19 Kant, I. (1797), *Die Metaphysik der Sitten* ("*Metaphysics of Morals*"), as translated by Nisbet, H.B. (1991), *Kant's political writings* (2nd ed.). Cambridge: Cambridge University Press, 131–175, 165.

where does human nature appear less admirable than in the relationships which exist between peoples"[20]. Progressively, after World War I, this Kantian image of sovereign states forming legal subjects within an international community, just like individuals in the domestic order, started influencing international lawyers and legal theorists.[21]

The Legitimacy of International Institutions

At the heart of the concept of domestic analogy as it is used today, lies the question of the international government, or to quote Kant, of a "federation of nations" – *Völkerbund*. The relevance of domestic analogy is called into question by the fact that, in the domestic sphere, the existence of the body politic universally depends on the "harmonious action of the three factors, legislation, adjudication and execution", whereas no such equivalent exists at the international level.[22] Following the concept of separation (or "distribution") of powers commonly credited to Montesquieu, "[these] three powers should naturally form a state of repose or inaction. [...] They are forced to move but still in concert"[23]. As there is no legislative power at the world stage, it seems impossible to reproduce the *check and balance* system with one or two of the three instruments of the concert missing on the international stage, resulting in a major problem of legitimacy.[24] In this regard, the case law of the Court of Justice of the European Union ("CJEU") is quite specific as it performs as a "true third branch", in harmony with "a European legislator and a European executive which can respond to the decisions of the court"[25]. Unlike international courts, the CJEU is functioning within a centralized political framework that displays a unique example of dual legitimation (the European Parliament representing the EU citizens on the one hand; the Council of the EU and the European Council representing EU Member States on the other hand). Therefore, the authors chose not to include it in their study.

---

20 *Ibid.*, 91.

21 Koskenniemi, M. (2005), *Global Legal Pluralism: Multiple Regimes and Multiple Modes of Thought*. Cambridge: Cambridge University Press, 22.

22 Lorimer, J. (1884), *The institutes of the law of nations* (2 vols). Edinburgh: William Blackwood and Sons.

23 Montesquieu, C. (1758), *De l'Esprit des Lois*, Livre XI, Chapitre VI.

24 See the contribution of Aida Torres for a discussion on the different "democratic pedigree" of international courts and tribunals.

25 Bogdandy and Venzke, *supra* note 2, 25.

As for the functioning of other international courts, Hidemi Suganami found three grounds for criticism against the principle of compulsory jurisdiction into international law that show how flawed the design of international institutions may be.[26] First, while law can "give an answer to every dispute, not all disputes can be resolved thereby" since the contestants of an international legal dispute may never respect a legal settlement (as in a hypothetical case where the US and the USSR would be part of an international legal dispute just to "test their respective strengths"). Second, a poor system of sanctions of international judicial decisions makes compulsory jurisdiction unlikely to fill its role. Suganami mentions the "excessive confidence in the capacity of law" of Lauterpacht's argument according to which "the absence of centralized sanctions would reduce, but not substantially impair, the function of the judiciary endowed with compulsory jurisdiction". Third, ineffective compulsory jurisdiction is worse than the absence of compulsory jurisdiction as it explicitly shows the bad faith of the party that fails to comply with the decision and potentially aggravates political conflicts.

Domestic analogy precisely served as the "background framing" of global governance proposals that are meant to correct the deficiencies in the system of sovereign states.[27] As state consent and procedural fairness cannot suffice to ground the legitimacy of ICTs and other global institutions, theories on democratic legitimacy, global accountability and constitutionalism are indeed among the topics discussed by legal scholars to try solving their legitimacy deficit in the absence of a *demos*.

B. Democratic Legitimacy and the Demos

The approach of the authors aims at getting closer to the reality of judicial law-making by challenging the "private-law inspired foundation of international law"[28]. Their reason to do so is that the state-consent approach does not reflect the dynamic of the international judiciary, as the example of the World Trade Organization's ("WTO") institutional development clearly demonstrates.[29] The authors' theory is not only descriptive but also constructive: they present their work as "a principled reconstruction of the law

26 Suganami, *supra* note 11, 171–177.
27 Grewal, *supra* note 17, 628.
28 Bogdandy and Venzke, *supra* note 2, 3.
29 See *ibid.*, 35 for an extensive description of this example.

of international courts [...] informed by political theory and practical philosophy"[30].

A European Agenda

In the section on the *Agenda and Objectives*, the authors acknowledged their particular vantage point and the fact that their work was shaped in Amsterdam and Heidelberg, from 2008 to 2013 by two Europeans who are influenced by "a specific tradition of thinking and the context of contemporary debates on the democratic legitimacy of international institutions"[31]. None of these disclosed facts is a reason to blame the authors for an alleged Eurocentrism. However, behind their technocratic ambition to use European provisions may lie a utopian European project.

The goal of the authors is to use the provisions on the democratic principles from the TEU to frame the democratic legitimation of international courts: "in Articles 9–12 TEU we find a framing of democracy for institutions beyond the state that is neither utopian nor apologetic, but plausible and viable"[32]. The public law theory thus becomes a means to universalize principles proclaimed in the TEU. Yet, even if we put aside the internal problems of the EU, its democratic deficit and its growing discontent,[33] what gives legitimacy to "fair weather institutions"[34] may not be credibly replicated elsewhere. Such an agenda can nevertheless be understood in the light of the European trend of German public law.

30 *Ibid.*, 22.
31 *Ibid.*, 26.
32 *Ibid.*, 136.
33 As Armin von Bogdandy put it himself, it is "not a democratic showcase". Bogdandy, *supra* note 4, 362.
34 Expression borrowed from the French sociologist Hassner, P. (1995). *La violence et la paix*, Paris: Esprit, 375–376.

The promotion of the ius publicum europaeum

While authors from the nineteenth century tried to expose German public law as "a set of rules establishing and regulating the workings of the institutions of government"[35], the endeavour now seems to aim at promoting these rules and principles across Europe.[36] The Max Planck Institute for Comparative Public Law and International Law may well be today's epicenter of this movement, as it is hosting the *ius publicum europaeum* project. Put in its national and historical context, the *ius publicum europaeum* project can be related to the German trend of framing constitutional authority at a supranational level to alleviate the concerns raised by the lack of unity of international law.[37] The fact that different attempts to legitimize international jurisdictions emerged in Germany is by no means incidental. Indeed, the *belle époque* of the *ius publicum europaeum*[38] is a result from the evolution of German public law. The *ius publicum europaeum* project aims at redefining national concepts of the EU member states in light of a new reality: the European legal order. Unlike the French tradition of public law, which is state-centered and focused on the public service or the *puissance publique*, the project presupposes that it is no longer relevant to consider states as the only purpose of public law theories.[39] The European Union could ideally serve such a purpose as it is a

35 Loughlin, M. (2013), "The Nature of Public Law" In: C. Mac Amhlaigh, C. Michelon and N. Walker (eds), *After Public Law*. Oxford: Oxford University Press, 11–24.

36 *Ibid.*

37 Walker, N. (2009), "Multilevel Constitutionalism: Looking beyond the German debate", *LSE 'Europe in Question' Discussion Paper Series (LEQS)* 8, 1–30.

38 Jouanjan, O. (2014), "Remarques sur l'Histoire du droit public en Allemagne (1800–1914) : pourquoi lire Michael Stolleis en France?", *Jus Politicum* 12, 1–6, available at http://juspoliticum.com/article/Remarques-sur-l-Histoire-du-droit-public-en-Allemagne-1800-1914-pourquoi-lire-Michael-Stolleis-en-France-886.html, accessed 15 January 2020: "*Seule une connaissance approfondie de la doctrine allemande du XIXe siècle permet de comprendre la « belle époque » du droit public européen, et spécialement la construction de la grande doctrine française, à travers cet affrontement politiquement conditionné, mais scientifiquement productif qui a fait naître les œuvres majeures du droit public français. Le droit public allemand de la fin du XIXe siècle est un peu « l'envers de l'histoire contemporaine » du droit public français.*"

39 Xifaras, M. (2012), "Après les Théories Générales de l'État : le Droit Global?", *Jus Politicum* 8, 1–57, available at http://juspoliticum.com/article/Apres-les-Theories-Generales-de-l-Etat-le-Droit-Global-622.html, accessed 11 February 2020.

supranational democracy that displays a dual legitimation (from states and from the European citizens), and reflects "*une idée d'oeuvre commune*"[40].

An unachievable common project?

The *ius publicum europaeum* project and the public law theory share a similar rationale and are both strengthening the principles at the core of the European Union. This might be problematic considering the political theory debates on the existence of a "European identity"[41]. Indeed, conflict and consensus are necessary elements of democracy, as well as a sense of collective self-identification and a common project. The sense of belonging to a common project is usually shaped by a confrontation with other existing projects. Like identity, democracy develops in a symbolic framework of emotions and rejections. It is often shaped by sacrifices, wars and hatred. The fact that these common experiences do not exist at the international level partly explains why democracy has never been successfully practiced at a supranational level so far. The Habermassian project to frame a European constitutional patriotism may be too "dry and abstract" to resolve the European identity issues and the lack of a European homeland.[42] To face the current heterogeneity at the European level, the *ius publicum europaeum* project seeks to offer concrete solutions, such as educating lawyers to provide them a better understanding of European national legal systems and better promote mutual acquaintance between European citizens, a way to strengthen the European identity and improve the *ius publicum europaeum* science, which is still in embryonic state.

---

40 Azoulai, L. (2015), "Solitude, désœuvrement et conscience critique", *Politique européenne* 50(4), 82–98.

41 On this issue of European identity, see for example Keulman, K. and Koós, K.A. (2014), *European Identity: Its Feasibility and Desirability.* Maryland: Lexington Books.

42 Meny, Y. (2011), "Can Europe be Democratic? Is it Feasible? It is Necessary? Is the Present Situation Sustainable?", *Fordham International Law Journal* 34(5), 1287–1303, 1302, available at http://ir.lawnet.fordham.edu/ilj/vol34/iss5/6, accessed 11 February 2020.

Several competing proposals aimed at tackling the deficit of legitimacy of international institutions and the alleged need for unity and order. We have come to a point where it is rather a "disorder of orders" [43] that comes out of these unifying attempts.

II. Proposals to Legitimize International Adjudicative Bodies – A Disorder of Orders?

As a result of the fragmentation of the international order, which is itself caused by globalization and the emergence of new institutions and particular regimes, international lawyers try to find appropriate responses using the language they know and "the gift of vocabulary that gives sense to plurality"[44]. The public law theory provides to this plurality of institutions and rationalities an analytical framework and fits into the ambitious proposals that have emerged in the past two decades to seek solutions to the legitimatory concerns raised by the development of international adjudication. The main proposals forming the backbone of this general framework are global constitutionalism (A) and multilayered governance approaches (B).

A. Constitutionalist approaches

The issue of the applicability of constitutionalism to the international order covers a broad range of positions that differ from one author to another. Armin von Bogdandy and Ingo Venzke share with constitutionalist authors "the conviction that the stock of principles of the democratic constitutional state is important to international law"[45]. However, they differ regarding the "step too far" that constitutionalists cross when they attribute constitutional functions to existing institutions indistinctly. Some organizations fulfil functions that can be interpreted as constitutional, as in the WTO legal order. Yet, the treaties founding such organizations only

---

43 Walker, N. (2008), "Beyond boundary disputes and basic grids: Mapping the global disorder of normative orders", *International Journal of Constitutional Law* 6(3–4), 373–396.

44 Koskenniemi, *supra* note 21, 4.

45 Bogdandy and Venzke, *supra* note 2, 123.

provide "micro-constitutionalizations"[46] at best.[47] Other approaches are even more holistic and utopian: among them is the project to conceive the United Nations Charter as the constitution of the international community,[48] which may ultimately reinforce the institution that reflected the distribution of power after World War II,[49] or the Habermasian foundational constitutionalism conceptualized in the European framework.

Two constitutionalist "dangers" are mentioned by the authors of the public law theory. First, the fact that the constitutionalist argument not only "expands" the concept but "dilutes" it, giving room for any interpretation of international law from any international court to have a constitutional function.[50] Anne Peters anticipated this reproach: "if all (international) law is somehow constitutionalized, then nothing is constitutional"[51]. The constitutionalist agenda seems less about describing the reality than conceiving the international legal order in a new light, through a comprehensive approach with an assumed moral and ideological bias. Its relevance lies in the "symbolic-aesthetical dimension inherent in national constitutional law"[52]. Far from being a mere set of norms, a constitution is also the mythological result of conflicts that have had a historical and foundational meaning, as in the French and American traditions. In one word, a Constitution is "owned" by a people.[53] Knowing the intricacies of

46 However subtle, this term is not paradoxical: it presupposes a rejection of the "myth" of the unity of constitution and the refusal to consider that the concept of "constitution" necessary relates to state constitutions. See Peters, A. (2009), "The Merits of Global Constitutionalism", *Indiana Journal of Global Legal Studies* 16(2), 397–411, 402.

47 Peters, A. *et al.* (2011), "The Constitutionalisation of international trade law" In: T. Cottier and P. Delimatsis (eds), *The Prospects of International Trade Regulation. From Fragmentation to Coherence.* Cambridge: Cambridge University Press, 69–102. For a more ambitious approach of WTO's constitutionalism, see Petersmann, E.-U. (1992), "National Constitutions, Foreign Trade and European Community Law", *European Journal of International Law* 3(1), 1–35.

48 Fassbender, B. (1998), "The United Nations Charter as Constitution of the International Community", *Columbia Journal of Transnational Law* 36(3), 529–619.

49 Krisch, N. (2009), "Global Administrative Law and the Constitutional Ambition", *LSE Legal Studies Working Paper* (10), 1–22, available at https://papers.ssrn.com/sol3/papers.cfm?abstract_id=1344788, accessed 11 February 2020.

50 Bogdandy and Venzke, *supra* note 2, 131.

51 Peters, supra note 46, 403.

52 Peters, A. (2006), "Compensatory Constitutionalism: The Function and Potential of Fundamental International Norms and Structures", *Leiden Journal of International Law* 19(3), 579–610, 582.

53 Peters, *supra* note 46, 400.

the constitutionalist project, Anne Peters based her theory on a radical project of refoundation of international law. She ousted the principle of sovereignty from its cardinal position to replace it with the principle of humanism.[54] She also supplanted the principle of state consent with majoritarian decision-making so that "world citizens" can be viewed as the ultimate reference points of democracy, not states. Even if the public law theory does not rest on the same assumptions, it remains confronted with the same problem, albeit to a lesser extent. Like a constitution, public law is also embodying a political community, which is itself rooted in a democratic framework.

B. *Multilayered governance approaches*

The global administrative law project

Despite the overlaps, the public law theory is more modest and less utopian than the constitutionalist project. A comparison with global governance approaches seems more appropriate as they claim to be different from top-down constitutionalist approaches. The very existence of global administrative law shows that international courts' activities can no longer be seen as sporadic dispute resolution as they must be conceived as *administration*.[55] Instead of using a foundational source of legitimation similar to constitutionalists', global administrative law ("GAL") advocates are inspired by administrative law; the field of law that governs the administrative agencies of government. GAL aims at making global administrative bodies accountable for the tasks that states used to perform themselves, such as the administration of public property. However, unlike similar approaches, GAL does not necessarily reuse the tools of domestic administrative law for institutions of global governance. Administrative law is less used by analogy than as a source of inspiration and contrast.[56] Indeed, it is more of a sociological project, whose goal is to be closer to the reality of the global world, and of practical use in the global governance space.

---

54 Peters, A. (2009), "Humanity as the A and Ω of sovereignty", *European Journal of International Law* 20(3), 513–544.

55 See Bogdandy and Venzke, *supra* note 2, 82, and Kingsbury, B., Krisch, N. and Stewart, R.B. (2005), "The emergence of global administrative law", *Law and Contemporary Problems* 68(3–4), 15–61.

56 Domestic administrative law is used "as a background rather than as the basis for prescription". See Krisch, *supra* note 49, 13.

The public law theory and global projects

The practical goals of the public law theory often converge with the constitutionalist literature and global governance approaches: the procedural standards about the publication of decisions and transparency, the need for substantiated rulings, and the possibility to appeal. However, it has been shown that the limited ambitions of global governance are not as limited and practical as portrayed.[57] The GAL project and the public law theory not only have common features, they also share philosophical underpinnings, *publicness* being the common basis for both approaches. A rule produced by a global actor is related to GAL only if it complies with the inherent qualities of public law. The criteria of these inherent qualities of public law are the general principles of public law: "legality", "rationality", "proportionality", "the rule of law" and "human rights". Here lies a bridge between constitutional law approaches and the authors' theory.

A brief cross-analysis of the differences and similarities between the proposals leads us to wonder if the authors are providing an alternative to the existing projects or if it is rather a synthesis aiming at fixing shortcomings in both theories. On the one hand, these projects look similar and complementary as they are all using the public law language as a strategy for legitimization. On the other hand, the public law theory might also combine issues raised by the competing proposals. In sum, it appears increasingly difficult to "disentangle the administrative from the constitutional"[58] as questions of legitimacy persist.

The article "Developing the Publicness of Public International Law" helps understanding why the authors felt the need to fill the lack of legitimacy through a public law approach to international law in their book.[59] Analyzing the discourse on global governance, Armin von Bogdandy explicitly found it "deficient from a public law perspective"[60]. In his opinion, a public authority is legitimate only if constituted and limited by pub-

57 See "*Le constitutionnalisme processuel, un projet modeste… revu à la hausse*" in Martineau, A.-C. (2016), *Le débat sur la fragmentation du droit international. Une analyse critique*. Bruxelles: Bruylant, 117–172; Kingsbury, B. (2009), "The concept of 'law' in global administrative law", *European Journal of International Law* 20(1), 23–57; and Krisch, *supra* note 49.

58 *Ibid.*,16.

59 Von Bogdandy, A., Dann, P. and Goldmann, M. (2008), "Developing the Publicness of public international law: Towards a legal framework for global governance activities", *German Law Journal* 9(11), 1375–1400, available at http://papers.ssrn.com/sol3/papers.cfm?abstract_id=1348809, accessed 11 February 2020.

60 *Ibid.*, 2.

lic law. The problem the authors had to face is that the concept of public law does not seem to fit the categories of global governance, especially so when the measures are non-coercive, informal or not related to the public sphere. Global governance covers topics such as health, human rights, environment, trade, education, and finance. The concept can be used for the impact of the Pisa rankings made by the Organisation for Economic Co-operation and Development on educational policies as well as for the role the credit rating agencies played in the American subprime crisis of 2007–2008. Therefore, it seems impossible to understand the emergence of global governance fully, let alone find its source of legitimacy: "[we] do not know how power is put together on the global stage let alone how its exercise might be rendered just or effective"[61].

Therefore, unlike GAL advocates, the authors decided to narrow the focus on international courts that exercise authoritative acts of public authority. However, the different language used shows that the authors are thinking within a public law framework as if using public law was a necessary condition for legitimizing any act of authority: "[we] suggest the shift towards the exercise of international public authority in order to better identify those international activities that determine other legal subjects, curtail their freedom in a way that requires legitimacy and *therefore* a public law framework"[62]. The idea that publicness and a public law framework are required to ensure legitimacy is at the core of the author's demonstration. In legal and political terms, using a public law framework is less ambiguous and more familiar than the global governance vocabulary.[63] However, the fact that GAL thinkers prefer using another paradigm instead of more traditional concepts such as "public law" or "democracy" appears more in line with the diffused nature and object of global governance. Such a concept also gives ground to the legitimization of domestic regulatory agencies.

61 Kennedy, *supra* note 13, 828.

62 Bogdandy, Dann and Goldmann, *supra* note 59, 1381 (emphasis added).

63 Ambiguity is inherent in Global Administrative Law, see Finkelstein, L.S. (1995), "What Is Global Governance?", *Global Governance* 1(3), 367–372, available at http://www.jstor.org/stable/27800120?origin=JSTOR-pdf, accessed 11 February 2020.

III. The Democratic Legitimacy of Independent Regulatory Agencies

To conceptualize their public law theory, the authors used Articles 9–12 of the Treaty on the European Union, considering that these articles could help theorize the democratic credentials of ICTs. The principles that underlie these articles are about citizenship, representation, participation and transparency. They are all very similar to the principles put forward by a French historian and sociologist, Pierre Rosanvallon, to investigate the legitimacy of regulatory agencies.[64] While these institutions feature a peculiar institutional design as non-majoritarian institutions that increasingly take political decisions (A), they raise legitimacy concerns similar to the challenges faced by international adjudication (B).

A. The institutional design of regulatory agencies

Non-identified political objects

Whether they are specifically called "*Non-departmental Public Bodies*" in the UK, "*Independent Regulatory Agencies*" in the US, or "*Autorités administratives indépendantes*", as in France, they are characterized by a hybrid model: they are executive authorities that combine legislative and adjudicative functions. Initially created in the US at the end of the nineteenth century to depoliticize key sectors of the economy (such as the US railway), their supposed benefits made them popular worldwide and democratic institutions progressively "lost terrain vis-à-vis non-majoritarian institutions, due to resources restrictions and policy complexity"[65]. Yet, their conceptualization as specific political forms has proved challenging, even in France where a strong tradition of codification exists. No effort has been made to codify the law of independent authorities or reflect on them as if preserving a pragmatic approach was preferred over their conceptualization.[66] The organic law n°2017–54 and the ordinary law n°2017–55 enumerated a list

---

64 Rosanvallon, P. (2010), *La légitimité démocratique*. Paris: Point; see P. Rosanvallon translated by Goldhammer, A. (2011), *Democratic legitimacy: Impartiality, reflexivity, proximity*. Paris: Points.

65 Biela, J. (2014), "What Deficit? Legitimacy and Accountability of Regulatory Agencies", Working Paper prepared for the 42nd ECPR Joint Sessions, Salamanca, 1–22, available at https://ecpr.eu/Filestore/PaperProposal/c294ff37-abb7-4aff-8583-868a1fa3b227.pdf, accessed 11 February 2020.

66 Rosanvallon, *supra* note 64, 160.

of 26 agencies (19 *autorités administratives indépendantes* and 7 *autorités publiques indépendantes*, the latter having legal personality) and stated that the legislator was the only body competent to create these two types of agencies. Interestingly, the law provides no definition of what constitutes one of these agencies as a mere enumeration was preferred. Being established *ex nihilo* or recognized *ex post facto*, these agencies propagated with no vision and coherent agenda. It is mainly the output legitimacy of IRAs, i.e. their ability to effectively respond to their policy outcomes, that accounts for their development across Europe.

The rise of the unelected

While legitimacy in a modern democracy should be established via elections, according to the principles of representative democracy and the sovereignty of the people, the fact that increasing important policy-making powers are transferred from the administration and the democratic institutions (government and parliament) to non-elected agencies constitutes an acute challenge to democratic legitimacy. These agencies that form the "regulatory state" are part of the United States model of democracy and illustrate its pragmatic way to correct the deficiencies of the market. Their decision-making process articulates within the checks and balances system.[67] Instead, in the European tradition – setting aside the United Kingdom and Scandinavian countries – it was more common to assign new ministerial powers and reorganize government departments rather than contravening the idea of state's unity representing the public interest with agencies detached from the state and exercising public authority.

Regulatory agencies in Europe

Unlike in the United States, IRAs in EU Member States were mostly imposed by EU constraints, especially regarding the liberalization of telecom, banking and postal industries. To enforce transparent competition and prevent state-owned historical operators from benefiting from their monopolistic position, independent regulatory agencies became necessary

---

67 Frison-Roche, M.-A. (2011), "Les autorités administratives indépendantes : distorsion ou réforme de l'État?" In: J.-P. Betbèze and B. Coeuré (eds), *Quelles réformes pour sauver l'État?*. Paris: Presses Universitaires de France, 125–130, 125–126.

tools in countries that decided, as in the case of France, not to immediately privatize their public operators, for reasons related to public services.[68] As they are contrary to the unity of the state and alter the way the separation of powers is perceived in the continental tradition, they are accepted but often seen as dismantling of the state (*démembrement de l'État*). As a result, politicians often interfere in the decisions of national and EU regulators, especially when they acquired "habits [...] of pervasive state interventionism", making them less independent "*de facto* and generally also *de jure*" than their American counterparts.[69]

Regulatory agencies in the US

In the United States, all the American federal agencies, even the ones which are not independent, are commonly described as a "fourth branch of government"[70] fully embedded in the check and balances system, and allowing to restrict the political powers and "impede the tyranny of the majority"[71]. The 1946 Administrative Procedure Act stated how agencies could establish regulations under the control of federal courts and played a role as the main source of the US administrative law. Thus, the powers of executive agencies (government departments, Federal Bureau of Investigations, Central Intelligence Agency, *etc.*) are subject to the political will of the US President, while those of independent agencies (Federal Communication Commission, Securities Exchange Commission, Federal Reserve Board, *etc.*) are independent of his or her political ideas and have statutory guarantees of independence.[72] But it is only due to a transatlantic misunderstanding that agencies are seen strictly independent from the political power. As Posner stated in 1974, "the agency's head is answerable both to the legislative and (if he desires promotion or reappointment) to the execu-

68 *Ibid.*, 127.
69 Majone, *supra* note 1, 11.
70 Brownlow, L. *et al.* (1937), *Report of the Committee, with Studies of Administrative Management in the Federal Government*. Washington: U.S. Government. Print, 38–39.
71 Maggetti, M. (2010), "Legitimacy and Accountability of Independent Regulatory Agencies: A Critical Review", *Living Reviews in Democracy*, 1–9, 2–3, available at https://ethz.ch/content/dam/ethz/special-interest/gess/cis/cis-dam/CIS_DAM_2015/WorkingPapers/Living_Reviews_Democracy/Maggetti.pdf, accessed 11 February 2020.
72 Zoller, E. (2004), "Les agences fédérales américaines, la régulation et la démocratie", *Revue française de droit administratif* (4), 751–771.

tive branches"[73]. Moreover, agencies are independent only when needed for reasons related to their functions (i.e. following the principle of independence of the judiciary power, an agency can only have a sanctioning power if its adjudicative power is insulated to an organ independent from the agency) or depending on the sector concerned, once the political authorities decided that this sector should be independent of the influence of political parties.[74] In sum, American agencies have variable degrees of independence, but they have more independence and a more refined structure of accountability than at the EU level.[75]

B. *Output and Input Legitimacy of Regulatory Agencies*

The output legitimacy of regulatory agencies

NMIs in general, and IRAs in particular, are usually established for two main reasons. First, as they do not rely on representative bodies but on neutral experts, they can implement policies in an efficient and effective way, their independence allowing them to be insulated from the arena of day-to-day politics[76]. The delegation of power to experts allows agencies to produce more effective results and lower decision-making costs: since legislators and government executives save precious time and resources avoiding to "[refine] legislation", they get more policy leeway to introduce new legislation or carry out a broader political agenda.[77] Second, the development of NMIs comes from the opportunistic "blame-avoidance hypothesis" and the interest to have responsibility for policy-failures shift from legislators to other decision-makers. NMIs may be convenient tools to avoid the political cost of unpopular decisions and release the regulation of key sectors from the short time horizon of electoral politics and the expectation of alternation, which cause a lack of credible commitments.[78] Their functional advantages come from their procedural features.

73 Posner, R.A. (1974), "Theories of Economic Regulation", *The Bell Journal of Economics and Management Science* 5(2), 335–358, 338.

74 Zoller, *supra* note 72.

75 Such generalization can, of course, be nuanced, considering for instance how the ECB enjoy an exceptionally high degree of independence, for reasons related to the reputation of the Euro and the need to fight inflation.

76 Majone, *supra* note 1, 21.

77 *Ibid.*, 3.

78 *Ibid.*, 4.

The delegation of public authority

Delegation is defined by Mark Thatcher as "an authoritative decision, formalised as a matter of public law, that (a) transfers policy making authority away from established, representative organs (those that are directly elected, or are managed directly by elected politicians), to (b) a non-majoritarian institution, whether public or private"[79]. As it has become one of the primary modalities of public policy, delegation is problematic when the objectives of the agents differ from their principals. The non-delegation doctrine, theorized by John Locke in his *Second Treatise on Civil Government*, implied that policy-making powers cannot be delegated as legitimacy cannot be transferred: "The legislature cannot transfer the power of making laws to any other hands". However, this theory has been "repealed by long-established constitutional practice"[80] and the influence of American "contractual political theory"[81]. As far as the paper is concerned, the logic of delegation is raising legitimacy issues due to the gap between the functions and the impact of IRAs and ICTs and their initial delegations. If "international tribunals [were] practical devices for helping states to resolve limited disputes when the states are otherwise inclined to settle them," as evoked by Richard Posner in a chapter on "adjudication in anarchy"[82], there would be no real issue of legitimacy. But ICTs have become problematic agents of states, just like regulatory agencies.

The independence of non-majoritarian institutions

NMIs' independence from the "politico-administrative state hierarchy" constitutes the main part of their input legitimacy and the source of their output legitimacy. It allows them to apply public authority in a distinct form of political power, which is called "regulatory power"[83]. IRAs have a rationale which is often "exogenous" to states. Regulatory matters, especially in finance, are usually sensitive, complex and have international consequences, hence the need for discretion and distance from governments.

79 Thatcher, M. and Stone Sweet, A. (2002), "Theory and Practice of Delegation to Non-Majoritarian Institutions", *West European Politics* 25(1), 1–22, 3.
80 Majone, *supra* note 1, 7–8.
81 *Ibid*.
82 Posner, R.A. (2009), *The Perils of Global Legalism*. Chicago: University of Chicago Press, 129.
83 Maggetti, *supra* note 71.

Moreover, markets that need to be regulated can be "more powerful than states", as a result of their global scale and of the mobility of economic actors.[84] This is particularly the case for financial regulation matters. The need to have non-elected bodies implement policies has also been clearly established for a particular kind of NMIs, central banks. The reason why numerous financial experts, politicians and economists advocate for the independence of central banks is that they should be free from political interference to be able to keep inflation low and perform their functions. In other words, as is the case for IRAs, central banks obey a legitimization narrative that stresses the need to limit input legitimacy – by limiting the involvement of democratic institutions and the accountability of central banks officials – for achieving output legitimacy.[85] Apart from their independence, the efficiency of NMIs results from their demanding procedural accountability. Like ICTs, IRAs have a specific democratic pedigree as they are required to use their decision-making powers in a more transparent, open and lawful way than bureaucrats and elected politicians.[86]

Therefore, there seems to be a negative correlation between input and output legitimacy: democratic legitimacy (and elections in particular) may form an obstacle to deliver better outcomes.[87] However, instead of sacrificing institutions that could be useful and "effective" – a concept all the more delicate as effectiveness may contradict the desires of the citizens – to government policy, substitutes to electoral legitimacy may be found. As summarized by Scholten, "'Input legitimacy' does not equal 'elections'; rather, democratic input legitimacy = authorization + safeguards + accountability"[88]. Therefore, she investigated in line with Pierre Rosanvallon on how democratic legitimacy could be implemented out of an electoral framework.

---

84 Frison-Roche, *supra* note 67, 127.

85 Majone, G. (1997), "Independent Agencies and the Delegation Problem: Theoretical and Normative Dimensions" In: B. Steunenberg and F. van Vught (eds), *Political Institutions and Public Policy: Perspectives on European Decision Making*. Dordrecht: Springer, 139–156.

86 Maggetti, *supra* note 71, 3.

87 Scholten, M. (2015), "Democratic Input Legitimacy of IRAs: Proposing an Assessment Framework", *Utrecht Law Review* 11(2), 64–77, 65.

88 *Ibid.*, 77.

Procedural accountability: the road to input legitimacy

Instead of doing careful scrutiny of the functioning of different agencies, Pierre Rosanvallon chose to refer to an *idéal-type* and tried to identify a set of procedural rules that would make these institutions legitimate. Quite similarly to the authors of the public law theory, he questioned the way in which institutions are deemed legitimate. Noting that regulatory agencies enjoy "secondary legitimacy" ("*légitimité dérivée*") since the law established them, Pierre Rosanvallon considered that this cannot be a unique and satisfactory source of legitimacy as these bodies are non-elected and yet increasingly powerful.

Just as the authors of the public law theory refused to regard functionalist approaches as the only source of legitimation of ICTs, Pierre Rosanvallon pointed out that functional advantages should not be the only source of legitimacy of IRAs. Functionalism can explain the rising power of international courts or regulatory agencies, not justify it. To go beyond a functionalist reasoning, Pierre Rosanvallon based the democratic legitimation of regulatory agencies not only on their independence, but also on impartiality and transparency.

Legitimacy through impartiality and transparency

The traditional and widely-accepted procedure to choose the representatives is the election. Questioning the existence of representation without elections, he conceptualized representation through impartiality ("*la représentation par l'impartialité*"). Rosanvallon's inspiring reflections and his references to Hannah Arendt's *Lectures on Kant's Political Philosophy* give an interesting account on impartiality. Adopting Kant's point of view, according to whom impartiality means "adopting all conceivable points of view," Arendt considered that "active impartiality" was not achieved by detachment but via a "reflective immersion" in the word.[89] Instead of an electoral understanding of representation, based on the idea that the rule of the majority stands for the will of the whole, representation can consist of seeking out minority perspectives. This analysis of impartiality, which allows to draw a parallel with the democracy-oriented conception of inter-

89 *Ibid.*, 142.

national adjudication described by the authors of the public law theory,[90] gives room to a democratic theory that does not depend on elections.

Concerned about the need for democratic involvement, Pierre Rosanvallon gives much importance to transparency, as the "democratic appropriation" of agencies can only be possible if their composition and their functioning are transparent. Their activity must be subject to public reporting and lead to public debate; the problems they encounter must be discussed publicly; the parliament should play a constant role in determining their missions, and they must allow citizens to challenge their decisions. In other words, IRAs should be made accountable to both their principals – top-down accountability to the political institutions that grants their democratic legitimacy – and their stakeholders – bottom-up accountability to the organized interests and the public opinion at large.[91] Legitimacy through impartiality, as it is shown, is an endless fight ("*une légitimité* [...] *sans cesse à conquérir*"). Indeed, NMIs must make decisions in the public interest, and it is crucial that they interact with the general audience to avoid that their political independence came at the expense of democratic accountability.

While the scope of the competences of IRAs needs to be predefined, agencies should later commit to the policy objectives that are assigned to them "to enforce accountability by results" and strictly and transparently follow the procedures that have been defined.[92] Otherwise, their independence would lead to arbitrariness instead of being a bulwark against it. The extent to which democratic institutions such as the parliament could interfere in their action is complex and varies depending on the political and legal culture and the degree of expertise that the topic requires (e.g. privacy issues and data protection laws are technical subjects that still need public debates). As for the importance that Pierre Rosanvallon grants to the issue of public involvement, this seems much less feasible when the *demos* in question is diffused at the international level.

90 See section on "Pathways of Democratic Legitimation" in Bogdandy and Venzke, *supra* note 2, 161, for the quotation of Hersch Lauterpacht: "impartiality [...] is in the last resort a personal quality of intellect and conscience. [...] It presupposes on [the judges'] part the consciousness of being citizens of the world".

91 Maggetti, *supra* note 71, 4.

92 Majone, *supra* note 1, 15.

Democratic legitimacy beyond the state

Paraphrasing Robert Dahl, one could wonder if a theory of democratic legitimation is not a mere attempt to "clothe [international courts] in the mantle of democracy simply in order to provide them with greater legitimacy"[93]. The main difference between the conceptions of democratic legitimacy brought by Rosanvallon and the one used for the public law theory is about the democratic deficit prevailing in the international legal process. Using democratic legitimation in the international realm causes inextricable situations in all the legitimation proposals mentioned above. Global constitutionalism provides an illustration of such inadequacy. While constitutions protect the differences between law and politics[94] and reflect the existence of a set of rules existing above *everyday politics*, global constitutionalism tends to be apolitical, unless law and politics are considered so "deeply intertwined" that they cannot be conceived separately.[95] As constitutional law is in its essence a "political law",[96] replacing such a framework at the international level seems hardly conceivable.

Conclusion

"Democratic regulation" or "procedural democracy" represents a key element of democracy, but not a sufficient one, according to Pierre Rosanvallon. Westminster democracy embodies and institutionalizes this conflictual dimension as it rests on the rule of the majority and the existence of two competing political parties. Assuming that there is a populist component intrinsic to democracy and that no international or cosmopolitan *demos* can have a strong feeling of its own identity, then no form of con-

---

93 Dahl, R. (1999), "Can international organizations be democratic? A skeptic's view" In: I. Shapiro and C. Hacker-Cordón (eds), *Democracy's Edges*. Cambridge: Cambridge University Press, 19–36, 32.

94 Möllers, C. (2012), "Les Gardiennes d'une séparation : Les constitutions comme instruments de protection des différences entre le droit et la politique", *Jus Politicum* 7, 1–16, available at http://juspoliticum.com/article/Les-Gardiennes-d-une-separation-Les-constitutions-comme-instruments-de-protection-des-differences-entre-le-droit-et-la-politique-462.html, accessed 11 February 2020.

95 Peters, A. (2009) "Conclusions" In: A. Peters, G. Ulfstein and J. Klabbers (eds), *The Constitutionalization of International Law*. Oxford: Oxford University Press, 342–352, 349.

96 Avril, P. and Le Divellec, A. (2010), *Ecrits de théorie constitutionnelle et de droit politique*. Paris: Presses Universitaires de Paris-Nanterre.

flictual democracy would be conceivable in the international realm. As shows the problematic of a European identity, consensus and conflict appear consubstantial to democracy and yet impossible to combine in any form of international legitimation. The prospects for legitimizing ICTs are, therefore, deeply connected to reflections on transnational or cosmopolitan citizenship.

As for NMIs that can be accountable to their people, the introspection on their democratic legitimacy is challenging but indispensable in times of populism. As any political institution, NMIs have taken political decisions that benefited to certain economic players and harmed others. They have sometimes failed to fulfil their general interest and often became unpopular. Therefore, they should be neither isolated nor dependent from the political process. It could be acceptable to be free from direct political control, but not to be free from public accountability.[97] It is only by dispelling the illusion that they are composed of distant experts that these agencies could be appropriated by the *demos* and that "their democratic history" could really start.[98]

97 Majone, *supra* note 1, 11.
98 Rosanvallon, *supra* note 64, 166.

In Nobody's Name: A Checks and Balances Approach to International Judicial Independence

Aida Torres Pérez[*]

I. Introduction

By sharply posing the question "In whose name do or should international courts decide?"[1], Armin von Bogdandy and Ingo Venzke have singled out one of the most pressing challenges in current debates regarding international courts (ICs): the source of their legitimacy.[2] The proposed answer -the peoples and citizens- puts democratic legitimacy at the center of the inquiry at a time in which there is an increasing concern accompanying the current rise in power and number of ICs.

At the domestic level, state courts can claim to speak in the name of the people to the extent that their authority derives from the constitution, which encapsulates the will of the people as the constituent power. Also, domestic courts are bound to apply the law, as the expression of the will of majority in parliament. Their democratic legitimacy indirectly derives from the application of the law, and only the law, to the resolution of cases brought before them, with exclusion of influences or pressures from others actors, or their own preferences. Indeed, the main objective served by the principle of judicial independence is securing the rule of law.

---

* Professor of Constitutional Law, Pompeu Fabra University (Barcelona). I would like to thank Professor von Bogdandy for the ongoing discussion about this topic and for helping me to refine my own ideas. The manuscript was submitted in June 2017.

1 Von Bogdandy, A. and Venzke, I. (2014), *In Whose Name? A Public Law Theory of International Adjudication.* Oxford: Oxford University Press, 5.

2 Follesdal, A. (2013), "The Legitimacy Deficits of the Human Rights Judiciary: Elements and Implications of a Normative Theory", *Theoretical Inquiries in Law* 14(2), 339–360.

Still, the fact that domestic courts can invoke the people as the source of their authority does not conceal at least two important reasons for concern over the democratic character of the judiciary.[3] Let us begin with judicial discretion. Montesquieu's syllogism that limited the role of the judge to "no more than the mouth that pronounces the words of the law" has long been gone.[4] No one argues that the law is completely determinate or that interpretation does not leave any room for discretion; and there is thus a risk that judges read their own values into the law. The second concern involves judicial law-making. It is possible for judges to contribute to the creation of norms through adjudication.[5]Moreover, courts are often vested with the power to review and set aside or annul legislation outright. The so-called "counter- majoritarian difficulty"[6]refers to this capacity to control or even make law. In order to confront this democratic concern, a myriad of interpretive, procedural, or institutional theories have been put forward to justify and constrain the power of courts.[7]

When von Bogdandy and Venzke claim that ICs make their decisions "in the name of the peoples and the citizens," this dual formula reveals the difficulty of identifying the democratic source of authority for ICs. "Peoples" refers to the states in their democratic dimension, and "citizens" to individuals from a transnational or cosmopolitan perspective.[8]In addition to the inner tension between the two sources, the hurdles of a transnational or cosmopolitan citizenship reflect the lack of a global political community or a global legislator, as well as the democratic deficit of international governance more broadly. In this vein, Besson argued that in order to confront the democratic legitimacy of ICs, and in the absence of

3 Besson, S. (2014), "Getting over the *Amour Impossible* between International Law and Adjudication" In: C.P.R. Romano, K.J. Alter and Y. Shany (eds), *The Oxford Handbook of International Adjudication*. Oxford: Oxford University Press, 413–433.

4 Pasquino, P. (2003), "Prolegomena to a Theory of Judicial Power: The Concept of Judicial Independence in Theory and History", *The Law and Practice of International Courts and Tribunals* 2(1), 11–26, 18.

5 Von Bogdandy and Venzke, *supra* note 1, 12–14; Besson, *supra* note 3, 420–426.

6 Bickel, A.M. (1986), *The Least Dangerous Branch: The Supreme Court at the Bar of Politics*. New Haven: Yale University Press.

7 Among many others, Ely, J.H. (1980), *Democracy and Distrust: A Theory of Judicial Review.* Cambridge: Harvard University Press; Ackerman, B. (1991), *We The People: Foundations.* Cambridge: Harvard University Press; Friedman, B. (2009), *The Will of the People*. New York: Farrar, Straus and Giroux; Ferreres Comella, V. (1997), *Justicia Constitucional y Democracia*. Madrid: Centro de Estudios Políticos y Constitucionales.

8 Von Bogdandy and Venzke, *supra* note 1, 209–214.

an international legislature representing the international community, the only way forward is greater institutionalization of ICs at the international level.[9]

Given the current structure and limits of international law, instead of expecting ICs to speak in the name of all political communities and citizens, this paper will contend that ICs should speak in nobody's name and will shift the focus to judicial independence as a necessary (but not sufficient) condition for the legitimacy of international adjudication.[10]Adjudication consists in applying the law to specific disputes brought before the court through a binding decision reached in accordance with the corresponding procedural rules.[11]In doing so, judges should not act on the behalf or speak in the name of any specific actor. Precisely, judicial independence is at the core of what defines any court, including ICs.[12]

This approach does not require surrendering to formalism, since no one disputes that ICs are often presented with cases that leave room for discretion in identifying and interpreting the law, or that the functions of ICs are no longer limited to dispute- resolution, but also include law-making and monitoring state action.[13]Thus, just as any authority that exercises public power, ICs must be constrained. Judicial independence cannot therefore be understood in terms of the courts' insularity and appropriate constrain-

---

9 Besson, *supra* note 3, 430–433: "In the absence of other institutions and especially of a legislature to interact with, and, more generally, of a political community to represent, the judiciary cannot play its interpretive and judicial law-making role. It is neither checked by nor accountable to any institution or community. [...] It is important, as a result, to explore ways of developing an international institutional order besides courts. [...] It requires building a set of institutions outside courts but also around and including them, whether at the same level of governance or across levels of governance in connection with domestic courts and institutions."

10 Benvenisti, E. and Downs, G.W. (2011), "Prospects for the Increased Independence of International Tribunals", *German Law Journal* 12(5), 1057–1082, 1058.

11 Besson, *supra* note 3, 417.

12 Romano, C.P.R., Alter, K.J. and Shany, Y. (2014), "Mapping International Adjudicative Bodies, the Issues, and Players" In: Romano, Alter and Shany, *supra* note 3, 3–26; Jouannet, E. (2010), "Actualité des Questions d'Indépendance et d'Impartialité des JurisdictionsInternationales:LaConsolidationd'unTiersPouvoirInternational?" In: H. Ruiz Fabri and J.-M. Sorel (eds), *Indépendance et Impartialité des Juges Internationaux.* Paris: Pedone, 271–302, 271–272.

13 Besson, *supra* note 3, 419–423, argues that the problems arising from judicial discretion and judicial law- making are magnified in international adjudication due to the limited number of sources of international law; the indeterminate nature of certain sources of international law; international legal pluralism; and norms in certain regimes, like international human rights law, that are necessarily abstract.

ing mechanisms ought to be put in place. The forms of appropriate constraints upon courts might be understood as sources of interdependence that advance their overall legitimacy from the perspective of the checks and balances doctrine.

While the interest and concern regarding international judicial independence is a relatively new phenomenon, the amount of doctrinal analysis of the independence of domestic courts is so abundant that it is tempting to apply a domestic frame of reference to the international sphere. First, I will therefore reflect upon the differences between domestic and international courts in framing a notion of judicial independence adequate for the international sphere. Hereinafter, I will flesh out the notion of judicial interdependence and map the actors that might provide appropriate constraints following a checks and balance approach to the institutional design of ICs.

II. From the National to the International Judiciary

Mackenzie and Sands, in their seminal article on the independence of the international judiciary, put forward the following question: "Is it appropriate to treat the independence of the international judiciary as one would that of national judges, or is there something qualitatively different about international law and courts such that different (lesser) standards should apply in the international setting?"[14]Unfortunately, they left it unanswered.

Given the diverging institutional and political frameworks of domestic and ICs, it is argued that the principles developed at the domestic level cannot be automatically transposed to the international one.[15]In that regard, how might the differences between domestic and international judiciary affect the way judicial independence is conceived and implemented?[16]

---

14 Mackenzie, R. and Sands, Ph. (2003), "International Courts and Tribunals and the Independence of the International Judge", *Harvard International Law Journal* 44(1), 271–285, 275–276.

15 Crawford, J. and McIntyre, J. (2012), "The Independence and Impartiality of the "International Judiciary"" In: S. Shetreet and F. Forsyth (eds), *The Culture of Judicial Independence*. Leiden: Nijhoff / Brill, 187–214, 191, 205–206, claimed that "the increased intermingling of politics and law, and the fragility of the institutions, might seem to demand more rather than less stringent application of these principles".

16 Mahoney, P. (2008), "The International Judiciary – Independence and Accountability", *The Law and Practice of International Courts and Tribunals* 7(2), 313–349, 317.

A. The Pervasiveness of State Consent

Domestic courts are one of the three branches of power provided for in the constitution. The constitution usually lays down the main principles regarding the structure and composition of the judiciary. Domestic courts enjoy compulsory jurisdiction and coercive powers to enforce their decisions.

To the contrary, the creation of ICs, their jurisdiction, and enforcement of their decisions are conditional upon state consent.[17]Hence, at least from an institutional perspective, ICs are largely dependent on the states that created them. Several authors have pointed out that dependence and demanded enhanced protection for the judicial independence of ICs. For instance, Mahoney declared that: "This dependence, when coupled with the fact that in the international arena the interplay between law and politics is necessarily more heightened than at national level, makes the position of the international judge more uncomfortable."[18]As a consequence, his argument goes, "far from pointing to the inapplicability or reduced applicability of the ordinary principles of judicial independence, the international context rather highlights the need to immunize international judges against interference if the notions of justice, fair trial and the rule of law are to be maintained in relation to their work"[19].

In what follows, we will take a closer look at the argument premised on state consent to argue that the role of state consent is sometimes overstated; that the relevance of state consent varies across courts; and that the dominance of state governments requires, rather than isolation or higher standards of independence, mechanisms to shield ICs from direct governmental pressures or control that reflect the context in which they operate.[20]

17 Crawford and McIntyre, *supra* note 15, 190–191.
18 Mahoney, *supra* note 16, 317–318.
19 *Ibid.*,318.
20 *Ibid.*,191.

1. The origin and the design of ICs

As the authors of international treaties, the creation and design of ICs is determined by state parties. That state parties be responsible for creating independent ICs poses a puzzling problem from the perspective of state sovereignty has not escaped scholarly attention.[21]

Indeed, Posner and Yoo argued that dependent ICs were more effective than independent ones.[22]In response, Helfer and Slaughter strived to explain why independent ICs might be in the states' interest.[23]Relying on political science literature, they held that delegating authority to independent international courts serves the interests of the states to the extent that such delegation enhances the credibility of the states' international commitments.[24]They argued that states choose independent tribunals over dependent ones when they face multilateral, as opposed to bilateral, cooperation problems, which would be the case, for instance, for treaties that create rights for private parties.[25]Yet they also pointed out that states face a second level of design decisions where they might set up control mechanisms in order to exert some influence over the courts.[26]Helfer and Slaughter formulated a theory of "constrained independence", according to which "states establish independent international tribunals to enhance the credibility of their commitments in specific multilateral settings and then use more fine- grained structural, political, and discursive mechanisms to limit the potential for judicial overreaching"[27]. The authors offered a typology of mechanisms in which they distinguished between formal and political mechanisms for state control (ex ante and ex post), and also diverse constraints coming from the global community, more loosely identified.[28]

21 Moravcsik, A. (2000), "The Origins of Human Rights Regimes: Democratic Delegation in Postwar Europe", *International Organization* 54(2), 217–252, 219; Helfer, L.R. and Slaughter, A.-M. (2005), "Why States Create International Tribunals: A Response to Professors Posner and Yoo", *California Law Review* 93(3), 899–956, 932.

22 Posner, E.A. and Yoo, J.C. (2005), "Judicial Independence in International Tribunals", *California Law Review* 93(1), 1–74.

23 They also challenged the variables and data used by Posner and Yoo.

24 Helfer and Slaughter, *supra* note 21, 33–34.

25 *Ibid.*, 41–42. Moravcsik, *supra* note 21, 226, in the context of human rights courts, has argued that the reason is to lock in particular preferred domestic policies in the face of future political uncertainty.

26 Helfer and Slaughter, *supra* note 21, 943.

27 *Ibid.*, 899.

28 *Ibid.*, 945–955.

They emphasized that this does not mean that the system becomes a "system of judicial dependence in disguise", since those mechanisms might be difficult or costly to exercise for several reasons, and may not be sufficiently effective in practice.[29]

Their work is very valuable since it shows how it can be in the states' interests to create independent ICs, particularly in multilateral regimes, along with mechanisms to ensure a measure of control. This is not to mean that judicial independence is doomed, but must be understood as constrained. At the same time, the authors focus overtly on state governments, and their approach towards a theory of constrained independence is descriptive rather than normative. As it will be argued, some constraining mechanisms might respond to the need to counterbalance the power of ICs using the principle of checks and balances, and allow for a more diverse set of actors that might constrain the action of ICs. Moreover, the effectiveness of those mechanisms in practice might vary over time as the political and institutional context evolves.

2. *Compulsory jurisdiction*

One of the main differences between the national and international judiciary is that while the jurisdiction of domestic courts is compulsory, in the sense that the consent of the defendant is not needed to file a lawsuit, the jurisdiction of ICs is usually conditioned upon state consent.[30] Nonetheless, as Romano has argued, there has been a paradigm shift from consensual to compulsory jurisdiction. While the principle of state consent still stands, its significance in practice has been reduced: "The expression of consent has become so removed in time and substance from the exercise of jurisdiction that one may question whether consent continues to serve a significant function in the international order."[31]

At present, for several ICs, acceptance of the jurisdiction of these courts is a pre- requisite to joining a certain international organization or legal regime, and thus all state parties are subject to the compulsory jurisdiction of the corresponding court, such as the European Court of Human Rights

---

29 *Ibid.*, 43.

30 Romano, C.P.R. (2007), "The Shift from the Consensual to the Compulsory Paradigm in International Adjudication: Elements for a Theory of Consent", *International Law and Politics* 39(4), 791–872, 792.

31 *Ibid.*,795.

(ECtHR),[32]the Appellate Body of the World Trade Organization (WTO AB), the Court of Justice of the European Union (CJEU), the Andean Tribunal of Justice (ATJ), and the Caribbean Court of Justice (CCJ), among others.[33]In other cases, states may decide after becoming parties to an international organization whether they accept the jurisdiction of the corresponding court through an additional protocol or declaration. This is the case, for instance, of the Inter-American Court of Human Rights (IACtHR). Most of the states who ratified the Inter-American Convention on Human Rights (IACHR) accepted the jurisdiction of the Court.[34] According to Romano, Alter, and Sebregondi, at present, most ICs possess compulsory jurisdiction.[35]Alter has documented a trend from "old-style" ICs – ICs that lack compulsory jurisdiction where access is limited to the states' parties – to the "new- style" ICs, whose compulsory jurisdiction is far-reaching and where access by non-state actors is possible.[36]

Describing domestic courts, Shapiro argued that the relevance of judicial independence is linked to the shift from arbitration to adjudication as a model for conflict resolution.[37]In the arbitration model, where jurisdiction is not compulsory and the parties have a choice regarding the arbitrators, institutional independence is not especially pressing from the perspective of legitimacy. However, in multilateral and compulsory jurisdiction courts, structural safeguards to shield the court from external influence become crucial for those subject to its jurisdiction. Similarly, at the international level, the shift from arbitration to adjudication has increased the concern over and demands for the independence of ICs.

32 At first, the jurisdiction of the ECtHR and the authorization to file individual complaints before the Commission were dependent on state consent. Protocol 11, which entered into force in 1998, merged the Commission and the Court, made the jurisdiction of the Court compulsory, and allowed individual complaints.

33 See Alter, K.J. (2014), *The New Terrain of International Law: Courts, Politics, Rights*. Princeton: Princeton University Press, 84.

34 Out of 25 States that ratified the convention, only four did not accept the jurisdiction of the court: Dominica, Grenada, Jamaica, and Trinidad and Tobago. In addition, Venezuela denounced the Convention in September 2012, which became effective one yearlater.

35 Romano, C.P.R., Alter, K.J. and Sebregondi, F. (2014), "Illustrations: A Reader's Guide" In: Romano, Alter and Shany, *supra* note 3, 27–39, 32.

36 Alter, *supra* note 33, 81–85, points out that out of 27 ICs, 21 have mandatory compulsory jurisdiction.

37 Shapiro, M. (1981), *Courts. A Comparative and Political Analysis*. Chicago: University of Chicago Press.

3. *Enforcement and compliance*

ICs do not enjoy coercive powers to enforce their decisions and thus compliance depends on state acceptance.[38] The risk of political backlash, in terms of non- compliance, treaty or legislative override, or other consequences of withdrawal might constrain the decisions of ICs.[39]One could view the decision of the Grand Chamber of the ECtHR in *Lautsi*[40]as a reaction to the opposition by several governments and pressures to reverse the Chamber's decision, which had condemned Italy for the display of crucifixes in public schools.

Nonetheless, sometimes the enforceability difference between the domestic and the international judiciary is also overstated. In order to enforce judgments coercively, domestic courts actually need the collaboration of the executive branch. Shetreet warns against the preemption of the enforcement of judicial decisions by actions of the executive. While the executive has a duty to enforce court decisions, in practice the expectation of compliance is not always fulfilled. Also, this author indicates that the failure to enforce judgments is not always intentional, and that there might be practical or material limits for expeditious enforcement of judgments.[41]

At the international level, despite the fact that IC judgments are binding, ICs do not have the means to coercively compel state authorities to comply or to directly annul legislation or quash national court decisions. Nonetheless, there are more and more mechanisms through which national and international authorities can strengthen the enforcement of IC judgments. At the international level, supervisory bodies might enhance the effectiveness of ICs decisions through diplomatic and other means, such the Committee of Ministers within the Council of Europe.[42]

38 Dzehtsiarou, K. and Coffey, D.K. (2014), "Legitimacy and Independence of International Tribunals: An Analysis of the European Court of Human Rights", *Hastings International and Comparative Law Review* 37(2), 271–322, 279.

39 Ginsburg, T. (2014), "Political Constraints on International Courts" In: Romano, Alter and Shany, *supra* note 3, 484–504.

40 *Lautsi v. Italy*, ECtHR Application No. 30814/06, Judgment of 18 March 2011 (Grand Chamber).

41 Shetreet, S. (2012), "Creating a Culture of Judicial Independence: The Practical Challenge and the Conceptual and Constitutional Infrastructure" In: Shetreet and Forsyth, *supra* note 15, 15–67, 55-56.

42 Protocol 14 has enhanced the role of the Committee of Ministers in that regard by providing for an action before the ECtHR in case of non-compliance (Article 46 ECHR).

In addition, enforcement might be secured through the collaboration of various state authorities, such as domestic courts. For instance, the petition for preliminary reference has offered the CJEU a means to ensure the enforcement of its judgments through the action of state courts. National courts have also played relevant roles in other contexts for the enforcement or broader effectiveness of IC rulings, in particular involving the ECtHR and the IACtHR.[43]

In any event, the lack of enforcement powers, the risk of non-compliance, treaty or legislative override, or more broadly, a political backlash, must be taken into account in evaluating ICs' independence.[44]

B. *The Isolation and Diversity of ICs*

While the domestic judiciary consists of a system of permanent courts hierarchically organized, the international judiciary tends to be composed of single, specialized courts pertaining to diverse legal systems where jurisdictions might partly overlap.[45]The absence of a vertically or horizontally integrated judiciary has raised concerns involving the ensuing fragmentation of international law.[46]In addition, ICs are diverse in terms of structure: some are permanent, others are ad hoc courts; some are inter-state courts and others grant individual standing. Subject-matter (from human rights, economic and political integration, to criminal responsibility)[47]and functions (from dispute settlement, securing norm-compliance, monitoring the exercise of national and international authority, to law-making)[48] are also

---

43 Nollkaemper, A. (2014), "Conversations among Courts: Domestic and International Adjudicators" In: Romano, Alter and Shany, *supra* note 3, 523–549, 530-535, regarding the role of national courts in implementing ICs' judgments.

44 Carrubba, C.J., Gabel, M. and Hankla, C. (2008), "Judicial Behavior under Political Constraints: Evidence from the European Court of Justice", *American Political Science Review* 102(4), 435–452; Stone Sweet, A. and Brunell, T.L. (2012), "The European Court of Justice, State Noncompliance, and the Politics of Override", *American Political Science Review* 106(1), 204–213.

45 Crawford and McIntyre, *supra* note 15, 190–191.

46 Dupuy, P.-M. and Viñuales, J.E. (2014), "The Challenge of 'Proliferation': An Anatomy of the Debate" In Romano, Alter and Shany, *supra* note 3, 135–157, 143–149.

47 Romano, Alter and Shany, *supra* note 12, 12–14.

48 Shany, Y. (2009), "No Longer a Weak Department of Power? Reflections on the Emergence of a New International Judiciary", *The European Journal of International Law* 20(1), 73–91; von Bogdandy, A. and Venzke, I. (2013), "On the Functions of

various. All of these elements should be considered in determining the appropriate model of judicial independence to apply.

The purpose here, after all, is not to argue that there exists a single model of judicial independence that will fit all international courts, just as no single model for judicial independence exists at the domestic level. The principle of judicial independence is key in any well-functioning democracy, but the ways in which it is implemented vary across countries and legal cultures. Moreover, the same legal arrangements might operate differently according to the broader socio-legal and political context.[49]

In addition within the same country, the differing functions performed by certain courts might pose specific challenges for the notion of judicial independence and, accordingly, diverse institutional arrangements might be put in place. For instance, constitutional courts, where they exist, perform the function of reviewing the constitutionality of legislation, and might also be vested with the function of solving disputes regarding the territorial allocation of powers and protecting fundamental rights. Given the politically charged issues under their jurisdiction, their independence from other political bodies becomes a matter of concern. Often the mechanism for judicial appointment differs from the selection of judges for the ordinary courts. Whereas in civil law countries judges tend to be recruited through merit-based bureaucratic methods, constitutional court judges are appointed by political bodies, such as parliament and government.[50] While political appointment might undermine the perception of the court's independence, that might be justified in terms of the added accountability that results, in light of the role that constitutional courts play in monitoring legislation.[51]

In any event, Seibert-Fohr, on the basis of the findings of a transnational research project on judicial independence, argues that shared normative denominators regarding judicial independence do exist and identified

International Courts: An Appraisal in Light of the Burgeoning Public Authority", *Leiden Journal of International Law* (26) 49; von Bogdandy and Venzke, *supra* note 1, 5–17.

49 Jackson, V.C. (2012), "Judicial Independence: Structure, Context, Attitude" In: A. Seibert-Fohr (ed.), *Judicial Independence in Transition*. Berlin/Heidelberg: Springer, 19–86, 60.

50 *Ibid.*, 69.

51 Ferreres Comella, *supra* note 7.

common concerns and strategies which have become transnational, variations in implementation notwithstanding.[52]

Indeed, at the international level, various nongovernmental and intergovernmental organizations have developed common standards for judicial independence, which have in turn made significant contributions to domestic rules,[53] one example being the Mt. Scopus International Standards on Judicial Independence.[54] In addition, international human rights organizations have also had an important impact in setting common rules. For instance, within the framework of the Council of Europe, several resolutions and recommendations on judicial independence have been adopted, such as the Magna Charta of Judges,[55]and there is an advisory body, the Consultative Council of European Judges for issues related to the independence and impartiality of judges, composed exclusively of judges. Furthermore, the ECtHR case law has also been very relevant in setting some minimum requirements and criteria for assessing judicial independence. Although the interest is preserving the right to a fair trial, and a wide margin of discretion for the institutional design of the judiciary is assigned to the states, ECtHR decisions have had an impact upon the institutional dimension of independence.[56]

With regards to the independence of ICs, there has also been an effort to identify common standards, as shown by the Burgh House Principles On The Independence Of The International Judiciary, according to which independence requires that: "The court and the judges shall exercise their functions free from direct or indirect interference or influence by any per-

52 Seibert-Fohr, A. (2012), "Judicial Independence – The Normativity of an Evolving Transnational Principle" In: Seibert-Fohr, *supra* note 49, 1279–1373, 1279–1281, held that "conceptualizing judicial independence as a functional principle which provides for an obligation of result rather than of means helps to identify it as an international norm which nevertheless gives room for diverse and context-specific implementation".

53 Shetreet, S. (2009), "The Normative Cycle of Shaping Judicial Independence in Domestic and International Law: The Mutual Impact of National and International Jurisprudence and Contemporary Practical and Conceptual Challenges", *Chicago Journal of International Law* 10(1) 275–332,275–276.

54 *Mt. Scopus Revised International Standards of Judicial Independence*, 19 March 2008, approved by the International Association of Judicial Independence and World Peace, available at https://www.jiwp.org/#!mt-scopus-, approved on 10 March 2008.

55 Recommendation CM Rec (2010) 12.

56 See the latest decisions in *Oleksandr Volkov v. Ukraine*, ECtHR Application No. 21722/11, Judgment of 9 January 2013; *Baka v. Hungary*, ECtHR Application No. 20261/12, Judgment of 27 May2014.

son or entity."[57] In formulating a normative theory of international judicial independence and identifying a common core of what judicial independence means and requires,[58] several considerations must be made for the specificities of the international setting in which ICs operate and the great diversity of ICs that exist, since the optimal degree of independence and the adequate mechanisms must surely vary across courts. Indeed, the comparative analysis of several ICs might offer valuable insight into institutional design and practice.

C. *Separation of Powers*

At the domestic level, the emergence and evolution of the notion of judicial independence occurred hand in hand with the doctrine of separation of powers.[59] As has been put, "[t]he culture of judicial independence can only exist in a system which is based on the doctrine of separation of powers"[60].

The classic formulation of the doctrine of separation of powers corresponds to Montesquieu, who argued for separating the judicial function from the legislative and the executive functions to protect liberty: "There is no liberty, if the judiciary power be not separated from the legislative and executive. Were it joined with the legislative, the life and liberty of the subject would be exposed to arbitrary control; for the judge would then be the legislator. Were it joined to the executive power, the judge might behave with violence and oppression."[61] Montesquieu further conceived the role of judges as limited to no more than the "mouth that pronounces the words of the law". The tripartite vision of the principle of separation of powers

57 The *Burgh House Principles On The Independence Of The International Judiciary* were formulated by The Study Group of the International Law Association on the Practice and Procedure of International Courts and Tribunals, in association with the Project on International Courts and Tribunals.

58 Mackenzie and Sands, *supra* note 14, 285, suggested that despite their diversity, "it is both possible and desirable to identify certain common core guidelines for judicial independence applicable to all international judges, regardless of the tribunal on which they sit".

59 Pasquino, *supra* note 4, 14–15; Zimmermann, D. (2014), *The Independence of International Courts*. Baden-Baden: Nomos, 55.

60 Shetreet *supra* note 41, 19.

61 Montesquieu, *The Spirit of the Laws*. Cambridge: Cambridge University Press, 157.

still persists, although it is no longer understood as a pure model of separation (if it truly ever was).[62]

In the American tradition, courts were understood as political actors, involved in lawmaking and in controlling both the legislative and the executive. Thus, their independence has been understood in light of the doctrine of checks and balances,[63] which is addressed to prevent institutions from overstepping their powers.[64] Ferejohn developed an argument according to which the roots of judicial independence are found in the structural protections afforded by the Constitution, which instituted a complex set of interdependencies among the major departments of government so that "political intrusions on judicial terrain depend on the capacity of politicians to achieve sufficiently high levels of coordination to overcome the checks and balances imposed by the Constitution"[65].

To what extent might the doctrine of checks and balances be transposed to the international sphere and in particular to the interplay between ICs and other political actors as a normative guiding principle? Clearly, the political and institutional framework in which ICs operate is very different from the domestic framework, and the tripartite separation of powers does not apply. According to constitutional doctrine, all power derives from the people and is allocated among the constituted powers through the constitution. At the international level, sources of power are diverse and the institutions pertaining to overlapping systems are not regulated by a single, ultimate norm. One might by consequence conclude that the principle of separation of powers is not helpful in the international sphere. Nonetheless, the more dynamic and flexible principle of checks and balances should not be excluded as a normative framework for the organization of

62 Carolan, E. (2009), *The New Separation of Powers: A Theory of the Modern State.* Oxford: Oxford University Press; Möllers, C. (2013), *The Three Branches. A Comparative Model of Separation of Powers.* Oxford: Oxford University Press; Shetreet, *supra* note 41, 51–52.

63 Ferejohn, J. (1999), "Independent Judges, Dependent Judiciary: Explaining Judicial Independence", *Southern California Law Review* 72, 353–384, 362: "the dependence of the judiciary on the political branches is not a constitutional accident. Rather, it fits within the broader federalist scheme of making the major departments of government interdependent rather than establishing a strict separation of powers".

64 Shetreet, *supra* note 53, 302, argues that the doctrine of checks and balances is "based on the concept that no function of one branch of government should be exercised by another branch and that each branch should function as a check on any improper use of power by the otherbranches".

65 Ferejohn, *supra* note 63, 356–357.

power, even if using it would require greater nuance in order to capture the interaction among national, supranational, and international institutions from a multilevel perspective, as the national and the international grow increasingly intertwined.[66]

Although ICs tend to be presented as isolated, the principle of checks and balances places them in a broader institutional setting and enables a critical examination of the constraining mechanisms already in place. In practice, one finds that there are already several mechanisms for legally and politically constraining ICs, which tend to be in the hands of state governments.[67] At the same time, the constraints placed on the executive by constitutions are virtually absent in the international sphere.[68]

In sum, although the domestic and international judiciaries differ in many respects, sometimes those differences are overstated,[69] particularly when we focus on multilateral courts with compulsory jurisdiction. Independence is at the core of what defines a court. Nonetheless, the conceptualization of international judicial independence, and particularly its implementation, is made difficult by distinct challenges: the dominance of state governments; the diversity across courts in terms of institutional setting; and the need to reconceptualize the principle of separation of powers at the international level.

III. From Judicial Independence to Interdependence

A. Why Interdependence?

From the outset, one might distinguish between two meanings of judicial independence: independence in the sense of the judge's neutrality vis-à-vis the parties to the case; and in the sense of the independence of the judiciary from the other branches of political authority to perform its func-

---

66 Torres Pérez, A. (2015), "How can judicial selection secure judicial independence? A checks and balances approach to international courts" In: Bobek, M. (ed.), *Selecting Europe's Judges: A Critical Review of the Appointment Procedures to the European Courts*. Oxford: Oxford University Press, 181–201, 187.

67 Ginsburg, *supra* note 39.

68 Bohlander, M. (2012), "Separation of Powers and the International Judiciary – A Vision of Institutional Judicial Independence in International Law" In: Shetreet and Forsyth, *supra* note 15, 269–280.

69 Ginsburg, *supra* note 39, 486.

tion.[70]The former could be captured under the concept of impartiality, whereas the latter conveys a notion of institutional independence. Both notions are related, but here we will focus on the institutional dimension of judicial independence. In this sense, independence might be understood as the amount of space for adjudication that is free of undue influence from external actors.[71]

To the extent that adjudication is not limited to the automatic application of the law, and that ICs engage in law-making and sometimes enjoy a wide margin of discretion in interpreting the law, their increasing power and influence coupled with the lack of accountability raises serious concerns over their democratic nature. Indeed, absolute independence is neither feasible in practice nor desirable in normative terms.[72] Judicial independence must therefore be conceived as a relative concept.[73] The notion of interdependence refers to constraining mechanisms coming from other actors to prevent the court from overstepping its powers.[74] Interdependence responds to the rationale of the checks and balances principle applied to the action of ICs in their interplay with other authorities.

Drawing the line between proper and improper influences or constraints is thus necessary, albeit difficult, from a normative perspective. As Ferejohn pointed out, "[t]here is a line, sometimes quite fine and hard to discern, that separates appropriate forms of institutional dependence from objectionable interferences with the execution of the judicial power"[75]. Indeed, the mechanisms to check the power of courts might be abused in order to advance self-interest. In the international sphere, those mechanisms and their operation will have to be evaluated in the context of each court. The next section will broadly map the actors that might provide mechanisms of interdependence under the principle of checks and balances.

70 Pasquino, *supra* note 4, 14–15.

71 Voeten, E. (2013), "International Judicial Independence" In: J.L. Dunoff and M.A. Pollack (eds.), *Interdisciplinary Perspectives on International Law and International Relations.* Cambridge: Cambridge University Press, 421–444, 421–422.

72 Crawford and McIntyre, *supra* note 15; Zimmermann, *supra* note 59.

73 Jouannet, *supra* note 12, 288–289.

74 Zimmermann, *supra* note 59, 64: "if [the judiciary] does have some real power, then its independence must be flanked by some degree of interdependence in order to prevent an abuse of isolated independence".

75 Ferejohn, *supra* note 63, 356.

B. Interdependence between Whom?

In the international sphere, courts might be influenced or constrained by a variety of actors. Indeed, the relevant actors and the level of their influence might easily differ across courts. Note that these actors might exert influence or pressure that undermine independence, yet still provide adequate constraints through interdependence.

Several theoretical approaches to courts and international adjudication focus on specific actors and sources of influence. From the perspective of realists and principal-agent theories, the main threat to ICs comes from state governments, since the states create international courts and retain some control through different mechanisms. Neofunctionalist and other sociological approaches emphasize the influence of other actors and the broader social environment and observe how courts might obtain autonomy from governments by seeking the support of other actors, such as domestic courts or civil society organizations.[76]In this way, diverse sources of interdependence might be established and independence from state governments might actually be gained through increased dependence on other actors.

From this perspective, the relevant actors might be categorized under three main groups: political institutions (domestic and international); courts (domestic and international); and public opinion. Since our approach takes the principle of checks and balances as a guiding principle, public opinion will be set aside.[77]A better analysis of the potential constraints coming from the public opinion, it would seem, would derive from the notion of accountability and the tenets of sociological legitimacy.

1. State governments

The main threat to the independence of the international judiciary comes from state governments, since they are responsible for the design of ICs, and they have the power to amend the constitutive rules of ICs. In addition, they might retain control mechanisms, such as those for the selection and reappointment of judges. Furthermore, states might defy the authority of ICs by refusing to comply with IC judgments, voicing discontent with

76 Voeten, *supra* note 71, 426.

77 Voeten, E. (2013), "Public Opinion and the Legitimacy of International Courts", *Theoretical Inquiries in Law* 14(2), 411–436.

specific decisions, or even threatening to withdraw,[78]as evidenced by the UK's stance towards the ECtHR and the saga of cases about prisoners' voting rights.[79]

Some of the existing control mechanisms might be understood as constraints under a checks and balances approach. If abused, they might pose a threat to independence, but their actual impact in practice might be overemphasized, since some of the mechanisms are costly to activate, require the cooperation of other states, entail reputational costs, or might generate opposition from other states or other international or domestic actors,[80]and, in the end, their effectiveness depends on contextual factors.

For instance, let us take the example of judicial selection.[81]This is usually regarded as one of the primary mechanisms through which state governments might influence ICs and rein in their independence, as governments might be tempted to appoint judges who are political allies. In courts with one judge per member state, such as the ECtHR or the CJEU, state governments have more leeway in selecting their candidates, while in courts with fewer judges than states, such as the International Court of Justice (ICJ), the International Criminal Court (ICC), or the IACtHR, state governments need to seek the support of other governments for their candidate to be selected so campaigning and vote-trading have become common practices.[82]In both, the system of selection is highly politicized and obscure.

Yet, granting the power of judicial selection to state governments might be conceived of as a mechanism to promote interdependence under the principle of checks and balances. To the extent that ICs are granted the

78 Ginsburg, *supra* note 39.

79 *Hirst (n° 2) v. the United Kingdom*, ECtHR Application No. 74025/01, Judgment of 6 October 2005 (Grand Chamber); *Greens and M.T. v. the United Kingdom*, ECtHR Applications Nos. 60041/08 and 60054/08, Judgment of 23 November 2010; *Firth and Others v. the United Kingdom*, ECtHR Application Nos. 47784/09, 47806/09, 47812/09, 47818/09, 47829/09, 49001/09, 49007/09, 49018/09, 49033/09 and 49036/09, Judgment of 12 August 2014; *McHugh and Others v. the United Kingdom*, ECtHR Application No. 51987/08, Judgment of 10 February 2015.

80 Helfer and Slaughter, *supra* note 21, 44.

81 See Torres Pérez, *supra* note 66.

82 Mackenzie, R. *et al.* (2010), *Selecting International Judges: Principle, Process, and Politics*. Oxford: Oxford University Press, 100–128; Faúndez Ledesma, H. (1998), "La independencia e imparcialidad de los miembros de la Comisión y de la Corte: paradojas y desafíos" In: J. Méndez and F. Cox (eds.), *El futuro del sistema Interamericano de los Derechos Humanos*. San José: Instituto Interamericano de Derechos Humanos, 185–210, 187.

power to monitor state action (even when resulting from democratic processes), judicial selection by the states to be bound by the ICs' decisions might constitute a warranted check on ICs.

Moreover, the motives for selecting judges vary greatly, and governments look at much more than only talent or political affinity.[83]Then, once appointed, the capacity of governments to influence judges,[84]and the capacity of those judges to influence court decisions, both depend on a wide set of factors, including term length, the possibility of re-appointment, the composition of the court, and the collegiate nature of ICs.

To the extent, however, that selection power is concentrated in the hands of state governments, the process risks abuse by governments tempted to nominate loyal judges who will defend their interests. Instead of de-politicizing the selection process, further checks on the action of governments may instead be introduced, such as advisory expert panels that assess the suitability of candidates in terms of their expertise and independence; and/or more transparent procedures both at the national and international level.[85]Following Voeten, appointment procedures should offer states opportunities "to shape the overall direction of the court, but minimize opportunities for governments to influence judges on individual cases"[86].

2. *International political institutions*

ICs might also be constrained by the political institutions and other bodies of the international organizations in which they operate. The role of specific bodies, such as the Inter-American Commission of Human Rights with regard to the IACtHR, or of international prosecutors in criminal courts should also be considered.

International organizations in which ICs operate commonly include an intergovernmental institution that represents the state parties, such as the Committee of Ministers of the Council of Europe; the General Assembly of the OAS; the Assembly of States Parties for the ICC; or the UN General

---

83 Voeten, E. (2009), "The Politics of International Judicial Appointments", *Chicago Journal of InternationalLaw* 9(2), 387–405, 389, 391–392.

84 *Ibid.*, 403: "Understanding if and how governments influence judicial behaviour requires an understanding both of government motives and of the institutional opportunities to act upon these motives."

85 See Bobek, *supra* note 66.

86 Voeten, *supra* note 83, 405.

Assembly and the Security Council for the ICJ. Intergovernmental bodies offer state governments another avenue to exert influence on ICs in coordination with other states. Indeed, Benvenisti and Downs have indicated that inter-state competition is an important contextual factor that enhances the independence of ICs.[87]Several forms of constraint might derive from the competences attributed to these bodies in terms of judicial selection (as mentioned above), or the regulation of aspects related to the court's functioning or financing.

For instance, the reform process for the so-called "enhancement" of the Inter- American system[88]was launched by several states who were unhappy with certain decisions of the Commission.[89]Proposals for reform included the amendment of several articles of the Statute of the Inter-American Commission. According to Art. 22 of the Statute, the Statute may be amended by the General Assembly. However, a large group of scholars argued against the unilateral amendment of the Commission Statute by the General Assembly.[90]They held that Art. 22 of the Statute should be read together with Art. 39 of the American Convention, which provides that "[t]he Commission shall prepare its Statute, which it shall submit to the General Assembly for approval" and held that the Statute may not be modified without the proposal for reform being initiated within the Commission itself.[91]They concluded that "[i]n the case of the Commission, it is clear that its position would be weakened if the reform of the Statute was decided unilaterally by the Member States of the Organization"[92]. Eventu-

87 Benvenisti and Downs, *supra* note 10, 1073, indicate that "[i]nterstate competition occurs at the level of an international organization where state parties compete for power and are divided on policies".

88 Regarding the process of reform, see http://www.reformasidh.org/.

89 Notably Brazil, with regard the interim measures ordered in *Belo Monte*; and Ecuador and Venezuela, with regard the activities of the *Relatoría Especial para la Libertad de Expresión.*

90 *The legal limits to amendments of the Statute of the Inter-American Commission on Human Rights (IACHR),* March 2013.

91 Also, they argued that the current proposals to reform the powers of the Commission could not be achieved through the amendment of the Statute. Instead, the Convention and the Commission's Rules of Procedure would need to be modified.

92 *The legal limits to amendments of the Statute of the Inter-American Commission on Human Rights (IACHR),* March 2013, para. 67.

ally, in March 2013, the General Assembly accepted the proposals by the Commission to amend the Rules of Procedure.[93]

Another control mechanism is budgetary, for "every international court is highly dependent on one crucial aspect: the money and resources that it takes for it to function"[94]. The possibility to tamper with judges' salaries is one way of pressuring a court. The Burgh House Principles point out the relevance of remuneration and conditions of service: "4.1. Judges' essential conditions of service shall be enumerated in legally binding instruments. 4.2. No adverse changes shall be introduced with regard to judges' remuneration and other essential conditions of service during their terms of office. 4.4. Conditions of service should include adequate pension arrangements".

According to Article 50 of the ECHR, the cost of the Court is to be borne by the Council of Europe. At present, the Court does not have a separate budget, but is part of the general budget of the Council of Europe. As such, it is subject to the approval of the Committee of Ministers in the course of their examination of the overall Council budget.[95]

In addition, it is for the Committee of Ministers to set the salary of judges.[96]Until 2009, the Strasbourg Court was the sole major international court without a pension plan for judges. This situation, however, changed after the Committee of Ministers' Resolution CM/Res(2009)5, which

---

93 At the same time, the dialogue about the reform was left open in order to reach an agreement with the States that had pushed for deeper reforms, which actually sought to weaken the regional monitoring system. See AG/RES. 1 (XLIV-E/13), *Resultado del proceso de reflexión sobre el funcionamiento de la Comisión Interamericana de Derechos Humanos para el fortalecimiento del Sistema Interamericano de Derechos Humanos*, 22 March 2013.

94 Terris, D., Romano, C. and Swigart, L. (2007), *The International Judge: An Introduction to the Men and Women who Decide the World's Cases.* Oxford: Oxford University Press, 160.

95 http://www.echr.coe.int/Pages/home.aspx?p=court/howitworksandc=#newComponent_1346157778000_pointer, accessed 27 December 2017. The Council of Europe is financed by the contributions of the 47 member States, which are fixed according to scales taking into account population and gross national product.

96 Resolution CM/Res(2009)5 on the status and conditions of service of judges of the European Court of Human Rights and of the Commissioner for Human Rights.

granted judges a pension scheme equivalent to that which already existed for staff members of the Council of Europe.[97]

A recent document entitled Reinforcement of the independence of the European Court of Human Rights, issued by the PACE Committee on Legal Affairs and Human Rights, expressed concerns regarding issues such as the social security and pension entitlements and post-retirement status of judges.[98]Mahoney, former Registrar and current Judge of the ECtHR, expressed concerns regarding the relationship of the political bodies of the Council of Europe and the Court and its operational independence, pointing out "revived attempts by the executive arm of the Council of Europe to assume ultimate responsibility, in place of the Court, for staff appointments and structures, for budgetary preparations, for internal working methods, and so on"[99].

Powers attributed to the political bodies of the corresponding international organization might serve as political checks on the IC from an institutional perspective. Some arrangements might be inherently problematic as a matter of design, and others might risk abuse in practice. Whether balance is achieved will be determined by the extent to which those powers are used to encroach upon the court's independence, or to fulfill their role as a potential check on the court.

3. Domestic courts

Domestic courts might influence the decision of ICs in several ways and thus contribute to counterbalancing their power. Sociological and neo-functionalist approaches have emphasized the role of domestic courts in the context of enforcement of international judgments and effectiveness more broadly. Alliances with domestic courts might help shield ICs from governmental control, while creating a new source of dependence. In this context, Benvenisti and Downs have emphasized how inter-branch compe-

97 Committee on Legal Affairs and Human Rights, "Need to reinforce the independence of the European Court of Human Rights: Introductory Memorandum", AS/Jur (2013) 34, 12 November 2013, para. 18, available at http://www.assembly.coe.int/CommitteeDocs/2013/ajdoc34_2013.pdf, accessed 27 December 2017.

98 PACE Committee on Legal Affairs and Human Rights, *Reinforcement of the independence of the European Court of Human Rights*, 26 May 2014.

99 Quoted in Dzehtsiarou and Coffey, *supra* note 38.

tition within a state might contribute to enhance the independence of ICs vis-à- vis state governments.[100]

For the CJEU, the collaboration of state courts through the preliminary reference has been crucial. CJEU decisions are encapsulated in domestic court judgments, which are more difficult for state governments to ignore.

In the context of the ECtHR, a recent case offers a good example of how the collaboration of domestic courts might overcome governmental reluctance. In Del Río Prada v. Spain[101], the ECtHR condemned Spain for violation of the right to liberty and the right to no punishment without a law subsequent to the retroactive application of a judicial doctrine according to which sentence remissions were no longer to be applied to the maximum term of imprisonment (thirty years), but successively to each of the sentences imposed (the so-called Parot doctrine). Consequently, the ECtHR ordered the release of a convicted terrorist who had fulfilled her prison sentence. Despite the reluctance of the Ministers of Justice and Internal Affairs,[102]not only did the competent domestic court decide to release the applicant, but also to extend the effects of the judgment to other convicted terrorists in the same circumstances.

In turn, the need for support by domestic courts might also have an effect upon ICs' decisions and promote doctrines of deference or self-restraint. For example, the CJEU, on occasion, limits itself to issuing guidelines regarding the rights and freedoms or general interest in conflict and defers the application of the proportionality principle to the referring court.[103]

For its part, the ECtHR has developed the well-known and long-disputed margin of appreciation doctrine. The notion of consensus among the states parties is key in the application of the margin of appreciation; but the action of domestic courts is also relevant in determining the scope of the margin left to the states. As such, the ECtHR's review is not as intense when domestic courts have demonstrated that they apply the crite-

100 Benvenisti and Downs, *supra* note 87, 1075.

101 *Del Río Prada v. Spain*, ECtHR Application No. 42750/09, Judgment of 21 October 2013 (Grand Chamber).

102 “Estrasburgo revisará la anulación de la doctrina Parot”, *El Mundo*, 23 October 2012,available at https://www.elmundo.es/elmundo/2012/10/23/espana/1350981928.html, accessed 27 December 2017; “El Tribunal de Estrasburgo tumba la ‘doctrina Parot’”, *El País*, 21 October 2013, available athttps://elpais.com/politica/2013/10/08/actualidad/1381229761_719630.html, accessed 27 December 2017.

103 For instance, *Familiapress*, Case 368/95, Judgment of 26 June 1997, ECLI:EU:C:1997:325 *Alokpa*, Case 86/12, Judgment of 10 October 2013, ECLI:EU:C:2013:645

ria previously developed by the Strasbourg case-law regarding the balance between rights in conflict.[104]

4. International courts

The forms in which ICs might influence each other should also be taken into consideration. References to the case-law of other ICs might contribute to mutually reinforce their authority vis-à-vis states parties. Also, cross-citation and judicial dialogue might promote coherence and contribute to counteract fragmentation in the international sphere. At the same time, references to other ICs might create forms of epistemic dependence[105]that could undermine its position vis-à-vis other actors.

In the context of human rights law, cross-citation is quite common, but the patterns vary. For instance, while the IACtHR often quotes the ECtHR, the ECtHR makes a more selective use of the IACtHR case-law, to better ground, for instance, a shift of previous doctrine.[106]While the reference to the more consolidated Strasbourg case-law might have bolstered the authority of the IACtHR, the perception of a Court too dependent on the European understanding of fundamental rights might prove to be counterproductive.

104 See the *von Hannover* saga, regarding the conflict between the right to privacy and the freedom of the press: *von Hannover v. Germany*, ECtHR Application No. 59320/00, Judgment of 24 June 2004; *von Hannover v. Germany No. 2*, Applications Nos. 40660/08 and 60641/08, Judgment of 7 February 2012 (Grand Chamber).

105 Helfer, L.R. and Slaughter, A.-M. (1997), "Toward a Theory of Effective Supranational Adjudication", *Yale Law Journal* 107(2), 273–391; Saldías, O. (2012), "¿Refugiándose enredes epistémicas? El Tribunal de la Comunidad Andina y la independencia judicial" In: M. Hernández Ramos *et al.* (eds.), *Tribunales en Organizaciones de Integración: MERCOSUR, Comunidad Andina y Unión Europea* (2012). Cizur Menor: Thomson Reuters Aranzadi, 51–66.

106 Burgorgue-Larsen, L. and Montoya Céspedes, N. (2013), "El diálogo judicial entre la Corte Interamericana de Derechos Humanos y la Corte Europea de Derechos Humanos" In: G. Galindo, R. Urueña and A. Torres Pérez (eds.), *Protección Multinivel de Derechos Humanos*. Barcelona: Red de Derechos Humanos y Educación Superior, 187–210, available at https://www.upf.edu/dhes-alfa/materiales/docs/PMDH_Manual.pdf, accessed 27 December 2017.

IV. Concluding remarks

When domestic courts claim to speak in the name of the people, they employ a rhetorical formula that conveys their submission to the rule of law under the principle of judicial independence. Given the lack of a single global community, ICs cannot invoke the people as the source of their authority and international law does not have the same "democratic pedigree" as national law and cannot provide the same sort of democratic legitimacy, but they are still bound to apply the law under the principle of judicial independence. The differences between domestic and ICs might lead to a different implementation of judicial independence, but independence remains at the core of what defines a court.

The concern for the antidemocratic nature of judicial discretion and law-making that has long existed at the national level is magnified in the international sphere. The adjudicative power wielded by ICs therefore needs to be constrained, although those constraints must also be compatible with the principle of judicial independence. The analysis of ICs from the perspective of checks and balances could be fruitful in this regard.

Indeed, ICs do not operate in isolation, but are embedded in a complex institutional setting. Their adjudicative power is constrained by different national and international actors. They are institutionally dependent on other public authorities for their creation, composition, functioning, and compliance. As argued, existing constraints do not necessarily undermine judicial independence; rather, some might be justified under the checks and balances principle to prevent ICs from overreaching their powers. It is essential to understand how those mechanisms are operationalized in practice. Some, such as non-compliance, might prove costly, and risk generating opposition from other institutions or groups, others, such as treaty amendments, cannot be activated unilaterally, and still others, such as judicial selection, might not be ultimately effective. In turn, the existence of these mechanisms and the capacity to activate them might eventually lead to judicial self-restraint.[107] Similarly, the predominant role of state governments vis-à-vis ICs might be counterbalanced by other actors. The proper balance to be reached for each IC and whether it is attained must be investigated from a diachronic perspective. In the end, the notion of interdependence captures both the need to ensure decision-making free of undue

107 Ferejohn, J.A. and Kramer, L.D. (2002), "Independent Judges, Dependent Judiciary: Institutionalizing Judicial Restraint", *New York University Law Review* 77(4), 962–1039.

external pressures and influences and maintain adequate power constraints according to the principle of checks and balances.

Not in the Name of the "Other": The Democratic Concept of International Adjudication through the Looking Glass

Parvathi Menon[*]

I. Introduction

International lawyers and institutions today, charged with a cosmopolitan ethos, demonstrate the desire to project a technicality that they hope will bring legitimacy to their projects. Pushing states to the background as mere intermediate stages in the rise of a global federation under the rule of law, they portray international law as the saviour of individual human rights against the marked politics of state sovereignty[1]. The "technisization" of different regimes in international law has enabled the fragmented fields to push against each other's specialization as a means to prioritize their own agendas, leaving open the perennial question: who has jurisdiction? In other words, who can decide? While a clash of jurisdictions playing out the political choice making at the international institutional level has received much attention already, von Bogdandy and Venzke turn the question on its head in their book and ask "In Whose Name" do these institutions decide?

Shifting the focus from the jurisdictional question to the space of representational politics[2] raises umpteen questions and concerns. In the current international legal sphere of innumerable courts and tribunals, with each

---

* Researcher, Erik Castren Institute of International Law and Human Rights, University of Helsinki.

1 This theme has been discussed in detail by Koskenniemi, M. (2005), *From Apology to Utopia: The Structure of International Legal Argument, Reissue with a New Epilogue.* Cambridge: Cambridge University Press, and later mapped in: Koskenniemi, M. (2002), *The Gentle Civiliser of Nations. The Rise and Fall of International Law 1870–1960.* Cambridge: Cambridge University Press. See also: Lauterpacht, H. (1933), *The Function of Law in the International Community*. Oxford: Clarendon Press.

2 While using the term "representational politics", I do not equate representation with democracy, albeit I use the phrase alluding to the space of democratic politics the authors von Bogdandy and Venzke refer to, in which representation can occur. See: Ernesto L. (1996), *Emancipation(s)*. London: Verso. See also: Laclau, E. & Mouffe, Ch. (2001), *Hegemony and Socialist Strategy*. London: Verso, where they describe a representation of interests as one where there is a transparent relation-

institution having their own internal hierarchies and schemas, to speak in the name of the people begs the question who those people are, to avoid projecting a homogeneity on the "represented", and which people get excluded when we make such determinations. Would refugees or *sans papier* migrants fit within the category of people in whose name international courts speak? Furthermore, this would require an understanding of whose agenda the court is advancing and whether that agenda continues to have a Westphalian bias, primarily. Nonetheless, even within the Westphalian contours, the heterogeneity of the "people" begs the question whether institutions like the International Criminal Court are speaking in the name of the Africans they target, or the Western world they mostly refrain from targeting. Whether the European Court of Human Rights speaks in the name of all Europeans or merely in the name of a Western European ethos they believe will help civilize the Eastern Europeans. At the same time, would transposing a representative element onto these institutions run counter to their depoliticized frameworks? Lastly, the "in whose name" question downplays the importance of the decision maker, because it suggests that no matter which court ends up having jurisdiction, what eventually matters is that they speak in the name of the people.

Resolving these tensions necessitates zooming both in and out. Von Bogdandy and Venzke idealize the "unique possibility of giving a voice to individuals who are affected by the actions of a foreign state", or one's own State. Yet, they remain pragmatic in recognizing the limits of such a possibility, deeming it "indispensable to the legitimation of every court that it operates at a distance from political processes"[3]. Portraying international courts as "beacons of humanity" that place limits on states' exercise of power based on a "universal community of values", they cater to what has become a standard trope among international law scholars: of the international's rescue from state authoritarianism. Treating the international as a means to ameliorate cases of democratic exclusion domestically, such a stance affords international courts the opportunity to set right flagrant violations occurring domestically, whilst ignoring completely whether these courts themselves can perpetuate the exclusion they sometimes prevent. Courts as "actors of international public authority" can be a useful premise, given the competition between functional regimes.[4] How-

---

ship between the representative and the represented, wherein the former promotes the interest of the latter.

3 Von Bogdandy, A. and Venzke, I. (2014), *In Whose Name?: A Public Law Theory of International Adjudication*. Oxford: Oxford University Press, 19.

4 *Ibid.*, 100.

ever, that would also require an international political society that is capable of determining the jurisdiction and extent of such public authority. Not unlike the inter-war liberal internationalism, the public theory of adjudication rests upon the managerial underpinnings of a global federation idea that was rife during that period. Yet, in the absence of such a federation of global legislative mechanism, it is perhaps a worthy reminder that we are in fact in a world of competing hegemonic ideas, and not the global constitutionalism that such an international public authority is deemed to create.[5]

On the other hand, while zooming in, it seems perturbingly obvious that many of the suppositions of international equality and humanitarianism, which have become the signposts of a liberal idea of legality, rest on the technicalities of procedural guarantees. These guarantees, on a closer inspection, reveal the structural biases that aid greatly in the determinations of fairness or other standards that lend the system its legitimacy. By focusing on whom these guarantees safeguard, problematic as they already are, the theory ignores who chose them as the hallmark of universal standards, and what those choices entail in allowing an enduring legacy of a constitutionalism resembling empires of the 18th and 19th centuries. Questioning whether procedural systematization accounts for the diversity within the international community or its distribution of resources will foster an understanding of the field as one that is full of contestable and contested choices.

In this paper, I focus on two different sides of the relationship between international adjudicatory mechanisms and the democratic inclusiveness they project onto the international: an external and an internal perspectives. In the external perspective, I shall pan out to examine whether the democratic ideal of the international adjudicatory bodies engages with the history of the field, its undemocratic origins, and the contestations that currently reproduce its asymmetrical beginnings. The external allows me to demonstrate how the power structures at play embolden a type of exclusionism and particularity in the name of inclusion and universalism in international courts and tribunals. Thereafter, the internal view will close in on some of the specific guarantees or standards that define democratic legitimacy of courts. Standards such as impartiality and independence of

5 See: De Wet, E. (2006), "The Emergence of International and Regional Value Systems as a Manifestation of the Emerging Constitutional Order", *Leiden Journal of International Law* 19(3), 611–632. *Cf.* Koskenniemi, M. (2007), "International Law: Constitutionalism, Managerialism and the Ethos of Legal Education", *European Journal of Legal Studies* (1), 1–18.

judges or, more generally, a procedural fairness, I argue, discount the actuality of the issues plaguing the international system. Whether procedural fairness can ensure substantive fairness in these international courts and tribunals that were built on uneven playing fields will form the second part of my analysis. In gauging the (internal) relationship between international courts and people, this paper shall examine the substantive and procedural mechanisms stated to enable such representation; whether concepts such as fairness, in relation to judges (i.e., impartiality) along with its procedural guarantees, expose international law's conflicting reality will form the basis of the examination. In other words, this paper will study the implications of the democratic ideology that has long pervaded international law by relying on examples of its perpetuation of the North-South "dynamic of difference"[6].

II. Europe vis-à-vis the Rest: Democracy and Its Discontents in International Adjudication

When the effort towards democratization was made in relation to states, it brought about a wave of ambition, implicitly forcing states to re-model and restructure in order to meet the prescribed standard to be worthy of membership into the international community.[7] Democracy was becoming the basis for governmental legitimacy in international law, evidenced by the work of Thomas Franck.[8] Political theorists like Hanna Pitkin treaded more cautiously because of the various meanings she ascribed to democratic representation—delegation, trusteeship, descriptive and symbolic representation—arguing that representation does not mean democracy (and most often runs counter to any real democracy).[9] Scholars like von Bogdandy and Venzke, but also others like Richard Bellamy who engage with the question "who represents whom and how" allow representation to pivot on the existence of formal democratic processes of authorization and accountability to ensure democratic values are being pro-

6 Anghie, A. (2005), *Imperialism, Sovereignty, and the Making of International Law.* Oxford: Oxford University Press.

7 Franck, T. (1992), "The Emerging Right to Democratic Governance", *American Journal of International Law* 86(1), 46–91.

8 Marks, S. (2011), "What has become of the Emerging Right to Democratic Governance?", *European Journal of International Law* 22(2), 507–524.

9 Pitkin, H. (1967), *The Concept of Representation*. Berkeley: University of California Press.

moted.[10] Although von Bogdandy and Venzke explicitly refrain from attributing any real representational quality to judicial institutions, they allude to the election of judges as an example of what representation can entail in such bodies.[11]

The marriage between democracy and legitimacy became the clarion call for the international community to recalibrate its expectations towards states seeking membership into its hallowed institutional circles. If we look at the debate that arose after Thomas Franck published his influential piece on democracy, there was a clear shift from the community to the individual: the kind of serious individualism that mirrored the universality it celebrated.[12] Equally, there was also an emerging cosmopolitanism that celebrated the "context-dependent variety of legitimate actions, of lawyers and courts, not through judicial technique, but rather through the intuitive application of good sense"[13]. This good sense, it was imagined, united people like the logic of the market. Democracy implied such good sense, or vice versa.

While democracy has been prescribed as the preferred process to bridge the legitimacy gap in international courts and institutions, scholars opine, "an institution is legitimate if its power is justified in terms of moral and other socially embedded beliefs, and if those subject to its rule recognize that it should be obeyed"[14]. If we presume the democratic process to be one of such belief, there is no doubt that its fulfilment would grant international courts its requisite legitimation. Yet, this presumption overlooks two aspects: firstly, is democracy as desirable as its endorsement reflects? Secondly, if yes, is international law itself a product of such a democratic process that can grant legitimacy according to the thesis put forward by the authors?

---

10 Bellamy, R. and Castiglione, D. (2011), "Democracy by Delegation? Who Represents Whom and How in European Governance", *Government and Opposition 46*(1), 101–125.

11 Von Bogdandy and Venzke, *supra* note 3, 148.

12 Koskenniemi, M. (2002–2003), "Legal Cosmopolitanism: Tom Franck's Messianic World", *NYU Journal of International Law and Politics* 35, 471–486, 481. Von Bogdandy and Venzke refer to the Treaty of the European Union as embodying such individualistic approaches, tracing it back to a Kantian or Hobbesian idea. Von Bogdandy and Venzke, *supra* note 3, 140.

13 *Ibid.*

14 Zaum, D. (2013), "International Organizations, Legitimacy and Legitimation" In: D. Zaum (ed.), *Legitimating International Organizations*. Oxford: Oxford University Press, 3–25, 9.

From the liberal democratic theory to deliberative democracy and other discursive approaches, the history of the democratic tradition has seen a variety of descriptions. Even if the history has not been without turbulence,[15] scholars—both Western and otherwise—have praised the universal appeal and value of democracy.[16] Its practice, however, has degenerated from a concept of direct citizen participation to one that has become only indirectly plausible. Citizen participation in the decision-making process, as one of the ideals of democracy, has been hardly met by modern states.[17] In fact, the concept of democratic decision-making has been reduced to the individuals' right to vote, evincing the disappearance of "the more radical association of democracy with popular power" in Western thought.[18] Despite the dissonance, the dissonance, international law has implicated notions of democracy.

The evolution of democracy within the context of international law has met with strong opposition with regard to its credentials, historically, as being a "product of the interests and practices of imperial powers"[19]. International law and its initiative to bring about "good governance" began (re)colonizing through the language of globalization. "The concept of good governance, in turn, generated more specific programs focusing on how international law and institutions could promote democratic governance and legitimate governance."[20] Antony Anghie focuses on institutions that have higher impact on the peoples of the Third World, like the IMF and the World Bank, in order to demonstrate how "despite the opportunities and advantages it is supposed to create, [it] has intensified inequalities between the West and the Third World" through the use of the concept of governance. Much like the mantra of global governance, myriad legal prin-

---

15 Charlesworth, H. (2014), "Democracy and International Law", *Collected Courses of the Hague Academy of International Law* 371, 54–69. For example, the fall of the Berlin Wall in 1989 was thought to be the turning point, a "possible end point in mankind's ideological evolution and the universalization of Western liberal democracy as the final form of human government" (Fukuyama, F. (1992), *The End of History and the Last Man*. New York: Free Press, 4).

16 See: Sen, A. (1999), "Democracy as a Universal value", *Journal of Democracy* 10(3), 3–17. See also: Ibrahim, A. (2006), "Universal Values and Muslim Democracy", *Journal of Democracy* 17(3), 5–12.

17 Dahl, R. (1956), *A Preface to Democratic Theory*. Chicago: Chicago University Press. See also: Dahl, R. (1989), *Democracy and Its Critics*. New Haven: Yale University Press.

18 Charlesworth, *supra* note 15, 60.

19 *Ibid.*, 70–95.

20 Anghie, *supra* note 6, 246.

ciples in international law bear the burden of European thought and history. Tracing the genealogies of any of them would lead us to seeing the shaping of the world from a very Eurocentric point of view.

The public theory of adjudication comes with its own guilt of presuming how the European solution could be fitted and adjusted to other jurisdictions. Whether it may be possible or not does not form the basis of my argument, but the presumption that it is an ideal worth pursuing based entirely on the European experience calls for criticism, similar to those levied by scholars against the European origins of international law.[21] The liberal theory of democracy, despite its undemocratic creation, has brought about a formulaic approach to the requirements that must be met in order to increase the prospects for peace under international law.[22] Anne-Marie Slaughter argues that international law makes no difference between liberal and non-liberal states under the law; yet, there is an inherent perception that the liberal state is the Gold Standard. If we adopt the same stance in the case of the democratic theory of adjudication, we find that the criteria listed out as the measures to meet in order to fulfil the liberal ambition carries forward the implicit desire to impose the European expectation onto non-Western experiences.

When it came to international organizations, the model of democracy was considered as aspirational as it was in the case of states. Albeit, as explicated by Robert Dahl in his chapter on democratic functioning of international organizations, popular control in democratic countries was admittedly difficult, making the case of international organizations (or courts, in this case) an aggravated problem.[23] Relying on the difficulties that arise from the epistemic limits, cultural diversity and procedural factors, Dahl portrays the farfetchedness of any type of control that a people can exert on decision-making in international organizations. With respect to the procedural factors, specifically, he maintains that the substantive and pro-

---

21 See: *Ibid.*; Koskenniemi, M. (2001), *Gentle Civilizer of Nations: The Rise and Fall of International Law, 1870–1960*. Cambridge: Cambridge University Press.

22 Marks, S. (2000), The Riddle of all Constitutions: International Law, Democracy, and the Critique of Ideology. Oxford: Oxford University Press, 43; *Cf.* Slaughter, A.-M. (1992), "Towards an Age of Liberal Nations", *Harvard International Law Journal* 33(2), 393–495, 403.

23 Dahl, R. (1999), "Can International Organizations be Democratic? A Skeptic's View" In: I. Shapiro and C. Hacker-Cordoj (eds), *Democracy's Edges*. Cambridge: Cambridge University Press.

cedural hurdles to realize "public good", as in the case of governments, become more pronounced when exported into the international sphere.[24]

Von Bogdandy and Venzke use the Treaty of the European Union (TEU) as a point of reference to elucidate the concept of democracy for institutions beyond the state.[25] They consider citizenship (Article 9), representation (Article 10), deliberation, participation, transparency, responsiveness and control (Article 11) and a reorientation of domestic parliamentarianism (Article 12) as the pillars of democratic engagement. Transposing these values from the TEU onto the international judicial framework presumes the efficiency of the values in delivering the "democratic" end product within the context of the European Union, even if clearly stated that it does not offer an exemplar of ideal democratic governance. The TEU, considered the result of democratic politics via the Lisbon Treaty, it is said, carries the legitimacy that comes with such a long process of deliberative and elaborate procedures. However, requiring democratization to legitimize governance or (public) authority in its move from the local to the universal has standardized the democratic expectation, and therefore reduced its engagement with ground realities. Reducing the differences, whilst normalizing the (democratic) expectation, creates an illusion of homogeneity, even in the European context, let alone beyond the European borders. Thus creating a concept of "international democracy" leaves much to be desired.[26]

Von Bogdandy and Venzke, while claiming that "political representation is indispensable", are also clear that "it does not exhaust the democratic idea". Relying on the Treaty of the European Union, they believe that "Article II of the TEU contains further guidelines for more inclusiveness. Transparency, the involvement of affected individuals, and dialogue—the cornerstones of Article II—are of particular importance for an international judiciary, because they identify strategies by which courts can contribute to their democratic legitimation"[27].

Equating participating in the "political process" to emancipation or political inclusion is one of the well-known critiques against democracy. I can see how a politically emancipated population/citizens, through very localized institutional mechanisms for example, can probably feel a part of

24 Benhabib, S. (2014), "Democratic Sovereignty and Transnational Law: On Legal Utopianism and Democratic Skepticism", *APSA 2014 Annual Meeting Paper,* 1–52, available at https://ssrn.com/abstract=2455436, accessed 7 February 2020.

25 Von Bogdandy and Venzke, *supra* note 3, 136.

26 *Ibid.*, 139.

27 *Ibid.*, 152.

a vertically upward legitimation process, but it is unclear how positive law from above can emancipate the disenfranchised groups at the bottom, using techniques that involve reinforcements of rights they barely possess. This begs the question: how does one relate binding every public authority by these human rights to the "bureaucratic vocabulary human rights have become, available for defending whatever interests or preferences the speaker wants to defend"[28]. A right is one thing, but the expediency of the right could be quite another.

A. *Democratic Inclusion and Exclusion*

The conundrum surrounding the failure of the democratic objective in adjudicatory bodies leaves us with the oft-asked question: what are the other alternatives? In the engagement between courts and the people approaching its corridors, as I argued above, the depoliticization of law has been the primary reason for the court's inability to go beyond the sophistry of the law. What once used to be achievable through political recourse today is inhibited by a technicization of the means to achieve it. Yet, the persisting problem with the liberal idea of legality is exactly that: the projection of a neutral formula that does not submit itself to the vagaries of politicking. The public theory of international adjudication falls prey to such excessive legalization, within the realm of international law, when it espouses that positive law can form the basis of a democratic concept of the judiciary's workings. In this section, I will rely on the jurisprudence of two courts: one, which von Bogdandy and Venzke credit with a high degree of "democratic legitimation": the European Court of Human Rights (ECHR), and two, which the scholars admit lacks sufficient democratic quotient: the International Criminal Court (ICC). I argue that while both these courts work differently and pursue different agendas, they both project an inclusive and exclusive ideal, contesting the characterization of their varied levels of democratic legitimacy. Such an approach helps establish two aspects: one, that the democratic quotient of the human rights language as protecting communities from domestic exclusion is flawed, much like that of the ICC, which has received its fair share of criti-

28 Koskenniemi, M. (2006), "Human Rights Mainstreaming as a Strategy for Institutional Power", *Humanity: An International Journal of Human Rights, Humanitarianism, and Development* 1(1), 47–58, available at https://muse.jhu.edu/article/394857/pdf, accessed 7 February 2020.

cism for its selection of cases. Two, even if the democratic legitimacy rests upon a procedural approach of representativeness, the substantive asymmetries project the ethnocentrism procedural guarantees try to avoid.

The ECtHR employs what von Bogdandy and Venzke call the "community-based approach", reflecting the "European consensus". The "thick layer of legal normativity over domestic constitutions" that the ECtHR lays down is understood as stabilizing the normative expectations.[29] Created to address complaints by individuals against their State, the ECtHR demonstrates an equality that brings out through its inclusiveness a type of rational cosmopolitanism that goes beyond kind of "self-other" distinction endemic to international law more generally.[30] Such cosmopolitanism may even become convincing to the detractors of universalism to be a reality they must accept. Yet, what we see in the jurisprudence coming from the court is a range of diverse notions of how discrimination looks, for example.

In a set of cases, where the court dealt with the meaning and import of Article 14, it has prevented discriminatory acts based on the individuals' identities as Roma, Jewish, Turkish origins etc. The court has also maintained that the right to practice one's own religion and manifest it is *unconditional* and *absolute* under Article 9.[31] Equally, the same court issued a series of decisions allowing Turkey, France, and Belgium to ban headscarves or veils, as not being in violation of Article 9. Starting with *Leyla Şahin v. Turkey* (2004), the court persistently upheld that the banning of scarves did not violate the European Convention on Human Rights (Convention). Following the Turkish case, the ECtHR went on to uphold its decision in *S. A. S v. France* (2014) and in the twin cases of *Dakir v. Belgium* and *Belcacemi and Oussar v. Belgium* (2017). Describing the veil ban cases as those where the court took into account the domestic contexts, it was held that "the choice of the extent and form such regulations should take must inevitably be left, up to a point, to the State concerned". The cosmopolitanism of the court and its European consensus thus reverted to the

29 Von Bogdandy and Venzke, *supra* note 3, 70.

30 The Third World Approach to International Law (TWAIL) highlights the distinction to enumerate how international law continues to uphold the civilizational discourse between the Global North and the South, using it as a mechanism to exercise control whilst projecting a type of faux sovereign equality. See: Anghie, *supra* note 6. See also: Said, E. (2014) [1979], *Orientalism.* London: Penguin.

31 *Ivanova v. Bulgaria,* ECtHR Application No. 52435/99, Judgement of 12 April 2007, para 79; *Mockute v. Lithuania,* ECtHR Application no. 66490/09, Judgement of 27 February 2018, para 119.

State, after all, in the name of maintaining public order. The ECtHR sacrificed its community-oriented approach at the altar of security concerns of a state-oriented world. Such conflicting rights are at the very core of human rights adjudication, thus making any cosmopolitan aspiration merely a cover under which the status quo remains. If the community-oriented approach constantly clashes with its state-oriented surroundings, confronting its own limits, the possibilities of the 'international' pushing the States to provide for a domestic inclusive community fails before it even begins. At the same time, requiring international adjudicative bodies to foster inclusion in domestic societies equally presupposes a clarity surrounding what individual identity means and its treatment in the most unidimensional manner. Thus, in the words of Koskenniemi, the liberal idea of legality continues in the pragmatic space of the in-between: a little more than positive law and a little less than morality.[32]

The pragmatism accompanying what we today herald as democratically legitimate spaces of international adjudication becomes more precarious in fields such as international criminal law. Openly admitting to its struggle between individual criminal responsibility and its need for State cooperation to prosecute international crimes, the international criminal court in all its cosmopolitan fervour deems its agenda as rising above all differences, given the *ius cogens* nature of the crimes it wishes to prosecute. Fighting impunity implies that all victims and the "interests of justice" remain paramount to the court, until it faces its own boundaries when it wants to investigate the crimes committed by the US armed forces in Afghanistan. Determining that such an investigation would not be in the "interests of justice", the Pre-Trial Chamber enunciates "interests of justice" from an extremely pragmatic point of view. In the words of the presiding judge, Justice Mindua, "an investigation can hardly be said to be in the interests of justice if the relevant circumstances are such as to make such investigation not feasible and inevitably doomed to failure"[33]. Any kind of radicalism that may have been attributed to the court finally investigating the hegemon turned into a case of the Emperor merely wearing new clothes, even if it was not the only basis of the court's decision. Nonetheless, the clash between a variety of cosmopolitanism ushered in by the international criminal court and its pragmatic view of justice as something to be pur-

32 Koskenniemi, M. (1997), "Lauterpacht: The Victorian Tradition in International Law", *European Journal of International Law* 8(2), 215–263.

33 *Decision Pursuant to Article 15 of the Rome Statute on the Authorisation of an Investigation into the Situation in the Islamic Republic of Afghanistan*, ICC Pre-Trial Chamber II, 12 April 2019, para 90.

sued only if "feasible" is a glaring reminder of the limits of international adjudication and a welcome step towards its acceptance. At the same time, the court in a prior case of *Prosecutor v. Jean Pierre Gombo Bemba*[34] chose the technicalities of the law ("rule of law")[35] in favour of what some scholars called the "interests of the victims"[36]. A case of competing universalisms, scholars on both sides of the debate argued whether procedural justice or substantive justice satiated their appetite for inclusiveness. Choosing the former means that the excessive technisization shrouds the real purpose of the court: to fight impunity. The latter implies a disservice to the processes the court must uphold: fair trials and equality of arms.[37] Beyond the struggle of the ICC between these competing interests, the question that has loomed large over the court has been whether in the quest for procedural fairness while fighting impunity, the court's "radar for racism is permanently broken"[38].

What I describe as substantive justice, which demands that victims feel vindicated, does not take away from the larger asymmetries that plague the court, or courts more generally. Whether it is the exclusion of the Muslim "other" or the African "other", the courts do not shy away from imposing in the name of procedural guarantees and rule of law what is an inherent Eurocentrism upon the rest of the world. Who that includes and who that excludes may not be immediately discernible in courts other than the ICC, but a closer look into their workings reveal that no court, not even the one with the highest democratic quotient, is free from its European bias.

---

34 Case No ICC-01/05–01/08–3636-Red (Official Case No) ICL 1849 (ICC 2018).

35 Heinze, A. (2018), "Some Reflections on the Bemba Appeals Chamber Judgment", *Opinio Juris*, 18 June, available at http://opiniojuris.org/2018/06/18/some-reflections-on-the-bemba-appeals-chamber-judgment/, accessed 7 February 2020.

36 See: Sadat, L. (2018), "Fiddling While Rome Burns? The Appeals Chamber's Curious Decision in Prosecutor v. Jean-Pierre Bemba Gombo", *EJIL: Talk!*, 12 June, available at https://www.ejiltalk.org/fiddling-while-rome-burns-the-appeals-chambers-curious-decision-in-prosecutor-v-jean-pierre-bemba-gombo/, accessed 7 February 2020; Amman, D.M. (2018), "In Bemba and Beyond, Crimes Adjudged to Commit Themselves", *EJIL: Talk!*, 13 June, available at https://www.ejiltalk.org/in-bemba-and-beyond-crimes-adjudged-to-commit-themselves/, accessed 7 February 2020.

37 See: Koskenniemi, M. (2002), "Between Impunity and Show Trials", *Max Planck Yearbook of United Nations Law* 6(1), 1–35.

38 I thank Sundhya Pahuja for this phrasing.

B. *Who is the Fairest of Them All? The Legitimating Force of Impartiality and Independence*

The book written by von Bogdandy and Venzke presents a very bold thesis of, *inter alia*, re-imagining the premise of international adjudication through the lens of a democratic process through their public law theory of adjudication. Looking at international courts as more than mere dispute settlers, the book suggests a renewed understanding of judiciaries at the international level. They argue a popular sovereignty thesis: that courts draw their legitimacy not just from the consent of the states, the international community, the parties to the dispute or the regimes they are a part of, but from the people and the citizens they were (indirectly) constituted by. When investigating into the conceptual frameworks within which such a democratic theory functions, it is prudent to begin at the level of its aspirations. Etymologically concerned with the role of people in governance, democracy aspires to consult these people and enable their participation in the process of making choices.[39] What this consultation entails and how limited these choices may be, are aspects that throw light on the relationship between international courts and the "people". Thereby linking political transformations with socio-economic justice, it is my argument that examining democratic principles against the (in)ability of judicial authorities to ensure such justice exposes the pitfalls of the democratic veil that attempts to equalize even in the face of inherent inequalities. In a Hegelian sense, international institutions created through democratic processes do not bridge the gap between private and communal interest; on the other hand, they decrease the scope for mutual recognition.[40]

The legalisation of the international order and its subsequent bureaucratization become aspects such legitimacy claims miss, and ardently support. The judicial processes and procedures, if anything, relegate political participation to the margins. In doing so, a thesis that lays as its foundation the democratic legitimacy of international adjudication must ironically bemoan the call to politicize. The contradiction that emanates from such a characterization, I argue, is precisely why the idealism related to adjudication's democratic quotient deserves questioning. Two aspects bear import here. First, why does depoliticization remain at the core of judicialization?

39 Franck, T. (1995), *Fairness in International Law and Institutions*. Oxford: Oxford University Press, 83.

40 Ferro, B. (2019), "Hegel, Liberalism, and the Pitfalls of Representative Democracy", *Hegel Bulletin* 40(2), 215–236.

Depoliticization renders the democratic concept wanting, and forces us to revisit the implications of foisting its idealism upon international courts and tribunals. Second, the legalization of the international order in turn maintains the "dynamic of difference" between the Global North and the South, rendering in its democratic quotient what Susan Marks calls the dominant ideology, subsumed in the judicial processes.

Furthermore, it is important to remember that nation-states create international adjudicatory bodies, whether as part of or separate from an international organizational structure. These international or supranational bodies are further removed from political mobilization than nation-states. At the same time, we should exercise caution with regard to such an approach. Supranational or international institutions are, equally, an extension of the nation-states that constitute them. Relying largely on procedural mechanisms to entrench the so-called democratic quotient into the adjudicatory model perhaps alludes to the illusion that irrespective of the differences between states and people, procedural safeguards are an equalizer, and desirably so. This supposition is inherently problematic for two reasons. One, the procedural guarantees to ensure reasonableness, impartiality, equality etc., presume clarity of the standards, and how they must be met; two, even if the standards are admitted as variable, the procedural fairness—through transparency and a democratic functioning—in its imperviousness to the particularity and variability of the people it applies to, tends to defeats its very purpose. The age of human rights and individualization of the rights language has preferred to ignore the differences, in the attempt to achieve equality. The resolution of this dilemma by means of a distinction between form and content, substance and procedure saw the regulation of the interaction of individuals through the domain of formal and procedural rules, devoid of any content or particularity; blind to particularities such as religion and race.[41]

The Treaty of the European Union, upon which the authors base their procedural mechanisms, opts for an individualistic approach, enshrining fundamental civil and political rights as individual rights. "All citizens shall receive equal attention from its institutions, bodies, offices and agencies."— notwithstanding the paternalistic tone, this provision is said to enshrine the principles of civil equality as the guiding democratic princi-

41 Seth, S. (2012), "The Limits of International Relations Theory: A Postcolonial Critique", *E-International Relations*, 24 August, available at https://www.e-ir.info/2012/08/24/the-limits-of-international-relations-theory-a-postcolonial-critique/, accessed 7 February 2020.

ple. "Rights are a key element in the universalization projects of ideological intelligentsias of all stripes. A universalization project takes an interpretation of the interests of some group, less than the whole polity, and argues that it corresponds to the interests or to the ideals of the whole. Rights arguments do this: they restate the interests of the group as characteristics of all people."[42] The individualization of the rights paradigm has systematically undone the concept of a collective, in its attempt to equalize everyone, beyond their differences. Much like the concept of sovereign equality as enshrined in the United Nations Charter, the universal human rights project does a disservice to the diverse needs of people, either as a collective or as an individual.

Article 9 reinforces, according to the authors, the conceptions of democracy for the international level without positing or requesting the formation of a new people or a new nation, but by relying on the idea of a cosmopolitan or transnational citizenship. Authors believe that this doctrine of a transnational or cosmopolitan citizenship might be relevant to courts based on individual rights, like the European Court of Human Rights, the Inter American Court of Human Rights, and even the International Court of Justice. The basis for this citizenship was individual rights that flowed from supranational sources that can be enforced against domestic and supranational acts that impinged upon them. In Western liberal democracies, public authority requires legitimation through one principal source: the citizens of the polity. The deepest, most clearly engraved hallmark of citizenship in these democracies is that power vests in citizens, to enable institutions that will exercise governance on behalf of, and for, the citizens. However, citizens/individuals are subjects only in the effect of the law, and the ability to go to court and enjoy a right does not emancipate them. "Citizenship should reflect not merely the politics of public authority, but also the social reality of peoplehood and the identity of the polity"[43]; the theoretical framework within which the international public authority speaks in the name of its democratic subject does not reflect that reality.

One of the touchstones of the positive law upon which von Bogdandy and Venzke base their thesis, is that of the courts creating or reflecting popular will, more specifically the "international representativeness" of the

---

42 Kennedy, D. (2002), "The Critique of Rights in Critical Legal Studies" In: W. Brown and J. Halley (eds), *Left Legalism/Left Critique*. Durham: Duke University Press, 178–227.

43 Weiler, J.H. (1998), "To Be a European Citizen: Eros and Civilization", *Working Paper Series in European Studies* (spring), 1–52, available at https://core.ac.uk/download/pdf/148847645.pdf, accessed 7 February 2020.

bench—a concept whereby the authors claim the judges can fulfil the *democratic mandate* entrusted to them, if they render their decisions independently, impartially and expertly. Relying on these high-values in the international sphere, whilst not enunciating an ethnocentrism, is much like Thomas Franck's resort to a procedural gateway to universal values.[44] Franck describes fairness as a "human, subjective, contingent quality which merely captures in one word a *process of discourse, reasoning, and negotiation* leading, if successful, to an agreed formula located at a conceptual intersection between various plausible formulas for allocation"[45].

The concept of legitimation serves particular interest in this context. Considered as the process by which authority is seen as "*valid and appropriate*", the dark side of legitimation is often obscured by the affirmation it provides.[46] Max Weber observed that power and legitimation, often derived from the consent of those subjected to it, depends either on the tradition, on the personal traits of the leader, or the legality of the rules laid down.[47] That this leads to the most "legitimate" means to dominate often goes unheeded. International courts, like any other institution, wield power that determines how precedents are created and how the normative world is shaped. Their deriving legitimacy through a means that may be democratic does not necessarily avoid the relations of domination they are able to maintain, by virtue of the functional importance they possess. The halo over democratic functioning, as asserted by liberal theorists, is often misguided to the point of heralding representativeness, impartiality and independence of the judiciary as the hallmarks of its success. The theory of democratic adjudication of international courts, by putting forth such a viewpoint, normalizes such expectation and equalizes the (diverse) people it claims to represent. The lack of popular will is imaginably apparent, although the existing procedure, process and the rule of law that are present are all components of the Liberal theory of democracy.[48]

---

44 See: Tasioulas, J. (2002), "International law and the Limits of Fairness", *European Journal of International Law* 13(4), 993–1023. In this article, the author compares Franck's approach to that of the Italian philosopher, Danilo Zolo, in how they tackle ethnocentrism and universal values. While Zolo injects into any type of a universal an inherent ethnocentrism, Franck deflects the criticism by resorting to a procedural mechanism.

45 Franck, *supra* note 39, 14.

46 Marks, *supra* note 22, 20.

47 Weber, M. (1965), *Politics as a Vocation*. Philadelphia: Fortress Press.

48 Kennedy, D. (1997), *Critique of Adjudication*. Cambridge: Harvard University Press.

The idea that the judges, through their "democratic" selection, impartiality and independence, can bring about the representativeness within the workings of their court, devoid of any partiality, is perhaps an idealistic supposition. Whilst perceptions of partiality are subjective, the conception of impartiality mandates an objectively plausible view of the law and its application.[49] I think of judges as part of the political system/State they come from, not just as "appliers" of law made by someone else, but also as formers of the sentiments that express themselves in their decisions, and in treaties or other legal instruments. Without underestimating the judicial contribution to gradual formation of consensus in favour/against something, it still might be simplistic to denounce this process as "undemocratic". There is no "private" sphere in which the will of the people could form without contamination by all the various sources of authority in society. It is equally simplistic to sanitize this authority through the theory that judges reflect changing social ideas and customs. They do indeed reflect them, but in their diversity and above all in their contradictions.[50] This is not to say that the court does not shape or reshape the demos, but that the judges these days think of themselves as social entrepreneurs or constitutional activists is perhaps indicative of the shift from their previous role of laying foundations of judicial review, a model of rule of law and of adjudication, and guiding of colonial lawyering into a constitutional profession. In their previous role, they were mindful of the wider question of social legitimation of the founding instrument, be it of their court or the demos. Equally, it is important to take note of the dilemma of the judges who, through their election/selection domestically, oscillate between the paradox of increasing the representativeness of the bench because of the state they come from and the decreasing standard of impartiality if they were found not to distance themselves from that state. The basis for this conundrum stems from the hypothesis that the bench can be reconstructed through a democracy-oriented approach.

The fairness of judicial proceedings or the bench evades the incoherence and instability of the meaning of fairness, again. Whom do the judges owe fairness to in the case of an international criminal trial, for example, as the one I outlined above? One of the basic tenets of international criminal law is the right to a fair trial. As Rigney writes, "there appears to be a dedica-

49 Megret, F. (2015), "In Search of International Impartiality", *ESIL Reflections* 4(8), 1–6, available at https://esil-sedi.eu/wp-content/uploads/2015/10/ESIL-Reflection-Frederic-Megret_0.pdf, accessed 7 February 2020.

50 Kennedy, *supra* note 48, 40.

tion to fairness amongst international legal practitioners", that it is considered a legitimating force.[51] Yet, positing how much of the trial must aspire for fairness, Judge Van Den Wyngaert states in the *Katanga* case: "in order for a court of law to have the legal and moral authority to pass legal and moral judgment on someone, especially when it relates to such serious allegations as international crimes, it is essential (...) to scrupulously observe the fairness of the proceedings and to apply the standard of proof consistently and rigorously. It is not good enough that most of the trial has been fair. All of it must be fair."[52] Here the reference to the court of law implies the role of the judges as the bearers of the authority reposed in the institution they speak in the name of, and from these fallible beings is expected a clear and shared understanding of fairness, as stipulated in the statutory responsibilities.

The acquittal by the Appeals Chamber in *Prosecutor v. Jean Pierre Gombo Bemba*[53] and later the ICC's Pre Trial Chamber's decision regarding authorizing investigation of the situation in Afghanistan as being against the "interests of justice"[54] were questioned and challenged by those who believed the judges were not speaking in the name of the victims. Both cases demonstrated to scholars a failure of the judiciary to aid the prosecutor's case.[55] What fairness was expected of these judges? Or were they recognized as mere cogs in a system that was ready to put another name on its list of sentenced criminals? What becomes unclear in this case is which of the two choices would increase the legitimacy of the court: one that puts more people away in prisons, or one that defers to the rule of law and processes even at the cost of acquittal? It becomes clear that the international community does not know the answer to that question. Therefore, to suppose that factors such as fairness of procedural guarantees is the way forward is to oversimplify the debate.

---

51 Rigney, S. (2015), "'That a Trial is Fair': The Centrality and Incoherence of Fairness in International Criminal Trials" In: A. Savarian *et al.* (eds), *Procedural Fairness in International Courts and Tribunals*. London: British Institute of International and Comparative Law, 119–134.

52 *Prosecutor v. Katanga Judgment (Minority Opinion of Judge Christine Van Den Wyngaert)*, International Criminal Court, Trial Chamber II, Case No ICC-01/04–01/07, 7 March 2014, Judge Van Den Wyngaert, 311.

53 Case No ICC-01/05–01/08–3636-Red (Official Case No) ICL 1849 (ICC 2018).

54 ICC, *Decision Pursuant to Article 15 of the Rome Statute on the Authorisation of an Investigation into the Situation in the Islamic Republic of Afghanistan*, Pre-Trial Chamber II, 12 April 2019.

55 See: Sadat, *supra* note 36; Amman, *supra* note 36; Heinze, *supra* note 35.

III. Conclusion: The Road to Inequality is Paved with Democratic Intentions

Whether the international courts offer the possibility of giving a voice to individuals who are affected by actions of a foreign state towards ameliorating problems of democratic inclusion, is a proposition that deserves further probing. Notwithstanding the absence of these individuals in the creation of the courts, can their representation be ensured by a procedural fairness that guarantees its legitimacy? As Aida Torres Pérez mentions in the previous chapter, should international courts (pretend to) speak in the name of anyone at all, other than the parties to the dispute?[56] However, that falls short too, when we take into account the asymmetry of the parties. The individuals that the authors believe the international courts can shape the freedoms of often suffer from the very lack of freedom to access the court, or to participate in the transnational or global publics with which the authors claim they can engage critically.[57] Not to suggest that international courts are entirely incompetent to provide for such rights and freedoms, but that they remain a distant recourse for many whose basic guarantees fail for reasons owing to the hierarchical structures, whether locally or globally. The discourse must first attend to the structural deficiencies of the system of international courts that exclude the groups who could best benefit from its power. The belief that the courts speak in the name of the people, even if indirectly, is more of an assuaging argument about an institutional mechanism that is here to stay, with all its shortcomings, and less a critical reflection that challenges our normative assumptions.

While I challenge the main hypotheses of courts and their democratic legitimacy, I admit that there are important victories won by various courts, especially the ECHR, that are able to limit the authoritarianism of States. Yet, it is necessary that we contest its contributions at every opportunity it appears deficient. For centuries, hegemons have created institutional frameworks that have appeared to work for the cause of the vulnerable, or the voiceless, against the authoritarianism of the existing systems, whilst in reality advancing their own causes and agendas. Several critical scholars like Anghie have exposed the underlying biases and interests that have continued to be at play in the guise of a humanitarianism. To ignore those biases in order to restore faith in the international system would at best be

56 *Cf.* the chapter written by Aida Torres Perez: "In Nobody's Name: A Checks and Balances Approach to International Judicial Independence".

57 Von Bogdandy and Venzke, *supra* note 3, 212.

a disservice to those who continue to rely on them for their piece of the pie. The competing interests along with the competing agendas of various courts and jurisdictions do not simplify the answer to the question "in whose name do the courts speak?". If anything, it exposes the complexity of the system of international adjudication, which remains a political project with very long genealogical roots.

Courtspeak: A Method to Read the Argumentative Structure Employed by the International Court of Justice in its Judgments and Advisory Opinions

Lorenzo Gasbarri[*]

I. Introduction

It is intuitive that a persuasive judgment has more chances to achieve compliance, to set a precedent and to influence the authority of a court generally.[1] It is more difficult to identify the writing tools that create its rhetorical structure. This paper focuses on the relation between text and context in order to describe the role of writing techniques in judicial argumentation and to propose a method to examine the argumentative structure of judgments issued by the International Court of Justice. The analysis of the text allows for the digging up of the contextual factors that are beyond the control of international judges and affect the authority of a court.[2]

"Courtspeak" is a neologism that gives a name to the language of international courts and to the role of rhetoric in international judicial practice. The term recalls "doublespeak", or "newspeak", invented to express the capacity of a speaker to deliberately obscure, disguise and distort the meaning of words.[3] This is traditionally associated with political language and the bias against rhetoric, intended as the art of disguising the truth for the

---

* Research Fellow, Bocconi University. The author would like to thank the Max Planck Institute for Comparative Public Law and International Law and iCourts (University of Copenhagen) for funding the periods of research during which this paper was written. Special thanks for their valuable comments and fruitful discussions on the first draft go to Andrea Bianchi, Anne Lise Kjær, Martti Koskenniemi, Momchil Milanov and Niccolò Ridi.

1 Bianchi, A. (2017), "International Adjudication, Rhetoric and Storytelling", *Journal of International Dispute Settlement* 9(1), 23–44.

2 Alter, K.J *et al.* (2016), "How Context Shapes the Authority of International Courts", *Law & Contemporary Problems* 79(1), 1–36.

3 Orwell, G. (2006), *Politics and the English Language*. Peterborough: Broadview Press; see also Moretti, G. and Pestre, D. (2015), *Bankspeak: The Language of World Bank Reports, 1946–2012*. Stanford: Literary Lab, available at https://litlab.stanford.edu/LiteraryLabPamphlet9.pdf, accessed 7 February 2020.

purpose of the speaker.[4] Differently, this paper uses an anti-foundationalism approach, and it contends that claiming the existence of "the Truth" is only an argumentative attempt to claim superiority of the method.[5] Thus, "courtspeak" relies on the capacity of an actor to impose its semantic authority to find acceptance for an interpretative claim.[6] The power of the text is created by an artisanal activity that reflects the contextual sources of authority. The relationship between text and context defines what makes a judgment persuasive. The characteristics of the international legal system make the development of "courtspeak" a fundamental element to measure the success of a court. This paper provides a method to analyse the rhetorical structure of judgments in order to describe how the text reflects and cannot be distinguished from its context. The following sections will describe "courtspeak" relying on the elements of the text that have been first identified by literary criticism.

The method to rely on literary theory to describe the rhetorical structure of judgments and advisory opinions of the International Court of Justice stems from an analogy between legal formalism and the formal analysis of the text.[7] In particular, this chapter employs the method invented by a group of literary theorists commonly known as "Russian formalists".[8] Russian formalism was a school of literary theory that emerged in Moscow and Saint Petersburg from the 1910s to the 1930s, around two different movements: the OPOJAZ (society for the study of poetic language) and the Moscow Linguistic Circle.[9] The scientific activity of the Russian formalists aimed at analysing the formal rules that regulate "literary facts". The text is the only object of their research, refusing interpretations based on psychology, philosophy or sociology. Their primary intent was to discover what makes a text literature through a process of subtraction that eliminates all the elements that are considered "superfluous". Under this framework, the meaning of the work does not come from the biographical ana-

4 Perelman, C. (2012), *L'Empire rhétorique* (2nd ed.). Paris: Vrin.

5 Fish, S. (2016), *Winning Arguments*. New York: HarperCollins.

6 Venzke, I. (2016), "Semantic Authority" In: J. D'Aspremont and S. Singh (eds), *Fundamental Concepts of International Law*. Cheltenham: Edward Elgar.

7 The analogy is intuitive, but not arbitrary. For instance, compare (1) Kennedy, D. (2001), "Legal Formalism" In: N.J. Smelser and P.B. Baltes (eds), *Encyclopedia of the Social & Behavioral Sciences*. Amsterdam/Paris/New York: Elsevier, 8634–8638, and (2) Eichenbaum, B. (2001), "La théorie de la 'méthode formelle'" In: T. Todorov (ed.), *Théorie de la littérature. Textes des Formalistes russes*. Paris: Seuil, 29–74.

8 Jakobson, R. (2001), "Vers une science de l'art poétique" In: Todorov, *supra* note 7, 7–11.

9 *Ibid*.

lysis or from the social background of its author. The purpose of the Russian formalists was to discover the origin of the literary work in scientific and technical terms. This is achieved through a concrete analysis of the form.

The method employed to define "courtspeak" is based on the relevance of rhetoric in judicial argumentation and on the consequent role of the community of interpreters in identifying the rules that govern its language.[10] The following pages will empirically appraise the relevance of literary criticism in describing five rhetorical elements found in the machinery of judgments.[11] First, the element called "Motivation" explains how every argument must find its justification in the unity of the judgment. Second, the distinction between the "*Fabula*" and the "*Syuzhet*" describes the role of the plot in the construction of the judgment. Third, the Heroes refer to the development of legal arguments as characters of the judgment. Fourth, the "Voice" is the element of the text that represents the point of view narrating a judgment. Finally, the "Theme" of the judgment represents the sum of all the formal elements of the work and describes the literary existence of the judgment.

II. The Motivation

The literary machinery of the judgment is composed of a variable number of motifs, defined as the single thematic unity whose sum creates the theme of the judgment as literary work. Motifs are "raisons de fait ou de droit" that justify the dispositive.[12] Every motif must find its justification in the argumentative unity of the judgment. Every motif must have its purpose. Chekhov said: "remove everything that has no relevance to the story. If you say in the first chapter that there is a rifle hanging on the wall, in the second or third chapter it absolutely must go off. If it's not going to be

10 Bianchi, A. (2015), "The Game of Interpretation in International Law" In: A. Bianchi *et al.* (eds), *Interpretation in International Law*. Oxford: Oxford University press, 34–51.

11 Tomaševskij, B. (1928), *Teorija literatury. Poetika*. Moscow/Leningrad. I will use the French translation: Tomaševskij, B. (2001), "Thématique" In: Todorov *supra* note 7, 267–303.

12 Cahin, G. (2008), "La motivation des décisions de la cour internationale de justice" In: H. Ruiz Fabri and J.-M. Sorel (eds), *La motivation des décisions des juridictions internationales*. Paris: Pedone, 9–90.

fired, it shouldn't be hanging there."[13] The Russian formalist Tomasevskij contends that the motifs in the text are functionally justified when they answer to a motivation that can be compositional, realist and aesthetic.[14]

The compositional motivation prepares the reader by introducing fundamental motifs outside their context and paragraphs before their actual use. It answers to the principle of economy and necessity, and frequently adopted in judgments. For example, in paragraph 58 of the *Jurisdictional Immunities* case, the judges, without any apparent link to its immediate context, state that: "immunity is essentially procedural in nature"[15]. It is the first time in which judges introduce this fundamental motif that will resolve the legal question at paragraph 93.

The compositional motivation is a powerful argumentative tool, useful to emphasize common values. If the writer states at the beginning of the work that the earth is flat, the reader is ready to accept that at the end the hero falls from its borders. The writer needs to prepare the terrain for its interpretative activity and even the ICJ uses this rhetorical tool in multiple occasions. Besides the *Jurisdictional Immunities* case, many other examples can be provided. In paragraph 25 of the 2012 Advisory Opinion on the *Judgment n. 2867 rendered by the Administrative Tribunal of the International Labour Organization*, the Court, dealing with jurisdiction, "takes the opportunity to emphasize" a fundamental motif that will resolve a delicate problem paragraphs later.[16] In paragraph 27 of the *Legality of the Use of Force*, the Court stressed the "new fact" of the acceptance of the Federal Republic of Yugoslavia as a new member of the United Nations.[17] Dealing with jurisdiction in paragraph 68 of the question relating to the obligation of prosecute or extradite, the Court does not lose the chance to introduce the fundamental motif of *erga omnes* obligations.[18] In paragraph 17 of the *Wall* Advisory Opinion, the Court "would observe" the competence of the General Assembly related to "any questions and any matters", and in particular

---

13 Rayfield, D. (1997), *Anton Chekhov: A Life.* Evanston: Northwestern University press.

14 Tomaševskij, *supra* note 11.

15 *Jurisdictional Immunities of the State case (Germany v. Italy: Greece Intervening)*, Judgment, ICJ Reports 2012, 99, para 58.

16 *Judgment No. 2867 of the Administrative Tribunal of the International Labour Organization upon a Complaint Filed against the International Fund for Agricultural Development*, Advisory Opinion, ICJ Reports 2012, 10, 22, para 25.

17 *Legality of Use of Force (Serbia and Montenegro v. United Kingdom)*, Preliminary Objections, Judgment, ICJ Reports 2004, 1307, 1320, para. 27.

18 *Questions relating to the Obligation to Prosecute or Extradite (Belgium v. Senegal)*, Judgment, ICJ Reports 2012, 422, 449, para. 68.

on "the maintenance of international peace and security"[19]. In the *Whaling* case, paragraph 83 discusses the use of lethal methods and the relevance of the resolutions issued by the International Whaling Commission, in connection with paragraph 137.[20]

The realist motivation deals with plausibility. The audience expects from the text an elementary illusion, which creates the feeling of being involved in real facts. Concerning the judgment, this form of motivation is based on the use of motifs that reflect the social environment in which the disputes arose. The chronology of the proceeding, the historical background, the submission of the parties, the use of footnotes or the reference to the work of the International Law Commission have this function in the textual dynamic of the judgment. For example, the appeal to the 1969 Vienna Convention whenever requesting a controversial interpretation involves a realist motivation. In *LaGrand*, the ICJ relies entirely on Article 31 and 33(4) of the VCLT in order to ascertain the obligatory character of provisional measures.[21]

The way in which reality is presented affects the outcome of the argumentation. The importance of the historical background in the rhetorical structure of the judgment is exemplary in the distinction between preliminary objections and merits. In the 1996 preliminary judgment on the *Genocide* case (*Bosnia v. Yugoslavia*) the Court spends few paragraphs in recalling the facts that will be extensively analysed in the merits.[22] In comparison, in the 2011 preliminary judgment on the *Application of the International Convention on the Elimination of all Forms of Racial Discrimination* (*Georgia v. Russia*) the Court engages extensively in the description of facts that it will not analyse in declining its jurisdiction.[23] Judges use realist motivations to adapt the theme to the expectations of the audience in order to create semantic authority. On the one hand, in *Georgia v. Russia* judges speak to the clients of the Court, reassuring that jurisdiction is only

19 *Legal Consequences of the Construction of a Wall in the Occupied Palestinian Territory*, Advisory Opinion, ICJ Reports 2004, 136, 145, para. 17.

20 *Whaling in the Antarctic (Australia v. Japan: New Zealand intervening)*, Judgment, ICJ Reports 2014, 226, 257, para. 83.

21 *LaGrand (Germany v. United States of America)*, Judgment ICJ Reports 2001, 466.

22 *Application of the Convention on the Prevention and Punishment of the Crime of Genocide*, Preliminary Objections, Judgment, ICJ Reports 1996, 595.

23 *Application of the International Convention on the Elimination of All Forms of Racial Discrimination (Georgia v. Russian Federation)*, Preliminary Objections, Judgment, ICJ Reports 2011, 70.

based on consent; on the other hand, they speak to the international community using realism, describing the facts of the conflict.

Lastly, the aesthetic motivation reflects the characteristics of the literary genre creating a system of conventions between the writer and the reader. Every genre creates its inventory of motifs necessary to achieve authority. For example, in cases concerning maritime delimitations, the judgment creates its authority, developing a three-step procedure reproduced from case to case.[24]

Legal precedents are "argumentative burdens" with an aesthetic motivation that refers to the existence of a genre, creating the sense of membership to a community.[25] The authority of the Court develops through its "symbiotic relationship" with the legal community.[26] In literature, the phenomenon relates to the development of a genre, which reproduces formal conventions until something new appears to destroy them, imposing a new authoritative force. As the Court has repeatedly stated, there must be a compelling reason not to follow a precedent.[27] The judgment possesses a literary form in the context of its tradition and the development of a tradition shapes the attitude of a social group towards authority. The famous dialogue between the International Court of Justice and the International Criminal Tribunal for the former Yugoslavia on the rule of attribution under the law of state responsibility is a battle between two literary genres, public and criminal international law.[28]

---

24 *Territorial and Maritime Dispute (Nicaragua v. Colombia)*, Judgment, ICJ Reports 2012, 624, 695, para. 190.

25 Ridi, N. (2019), "The Shape and Structure of the 'Usable Past': An Empirical Analysis of the Use of Precedent in International Adjudication", *Journal of International Dispute Settlement* 10(2), 200–247; Von Bogdandy, A. and Venzke, I. (2014), *In Whose Name?: A Public Law Theory of International Adjudication*. Oxford: Oxford University Press, 36; Cohen, H.G. (2015), "Theorizing Precedent in International Law" In: Bianchi *et al.*, *supra* note 10, 268–289.

26 Vauchez, A. (2014), "Communities of International Litigators" In: C. Romano *et al.* (eds), *The Oxford Handbook of International Adjudication*. Oxford: Oxford University Press, 655–668.

27 *Application of the Convention on the Prevention and Punishment of the Crime of Genocide (Croatia v. Serbia)*, Preliminary Objections, Judgment, ICJ Reports 2008, 412, 428, para. 53.

28 *Application of the Convention on the Prevention and Punishment of the Crime of Genocide (Bosnia and Herzegovina v. Serbia and Montenegro)*, Judgment, ICJ Reports 2007, 43, 209, para. 403.

III. The Fabula *and the* Syuzhet

The second literary element that creates the rhetorical structure of the judgment concerns the sequence in which the motifs are presented. This technique reflects the judicial power to determine the order of the arguments. The Russian formalists discovered this formal element of the literary text distinguishing between the *fabula* and the *syuzhet*.[29]

The chronological order of the motifs creates the *fabula*, which is an abstract deconstruction of the literary work. The distribution of the motifs in the text is the *syuzhet*, which is the literary construction that the reader finds in the work. The tension that captivates the interest of the audience comes from the order in which the motifs are presented: "l'ordre de présentation des arguments modifie les conditions d'acceptation de ceux-ci"[30]. The author, who has the power to combine the motifs in an order that overturn chronology, creates the *syuzhet* by deliberate choice.

It is possible to differentiate between the *fabula* and the *syuzhet* even in judgments.[31] If the judgment is a chain of arguments that goes from A to D, judges can write following a linear path (A-B-C-D), or they can invert the order, for instance following an argumentative pattern ACBD. The *syuzhet* is what the reader finds in the text (A-C-B-D), while the *fabula* is the abstract reconstruction of an abstract order (A-B-C-D). The absence of a chronological dimension does not prevent the possibility to determine an order that links the arguments of a judgment. This order is based on the judicial genre and often creates a proceeding "by step", where the first element calls the second, the second the third, and so on.[32] The dynamic "step by step" is a typical movement of the judgment. The plain order of the arguments is the *fabula* of the judgment; its construction in the text is the *syuzhet*.

For example, in the *Arrest Warrant* case, the International Court of Justice overturned the order of the *fabula*, discussing immunity before universal jurisdiction.[33] Again, in the *Jurisdictional Immunities*, the Court over-

---

29 Tomaševski, *supra* note 11.

30 Perelman, *supra* note 4, 182.

31 Leubsdorf, J. (2001), "The Structure of Judicial Opinions", *Minnesota Law Review* 86(2), 447–495.

32 Sklovskij, V (1990), *Theory of Prose*. London: Dalkey Archive Press.

33 *Case Concerning the Arrest Warrant of 11 April 2000 (Democratic Republic of the Congo v. Belgium)*, Judgment, ICJ reports 2002, 3, para 46: "As a matter of logic, the second ground [immunity] should be addressed only once there has been a determination in respect of the first [universal jurisdiction], since it is only where

comes a "logical problem" discussing the facts of the case despite the fact that immunity could prevent a case from reaching the merits.[34]

The *fabula* is a sequence of conflicts. The typical movement of the judgment has a parallel in the tales of adventure where the hero has to fight difficult labours in order to complete his quest. The conflicts are represented in the singular motifs that create the *fabula*. International Courts usually present the *syuzhet* as if it imposes itself by logical necessity. They tend to motivate the structure, comparing it with a syllogism, under which the chain of reasoning derives from logical necessity. For example, in *Military and Paramilitary Activities*, the Court describes the structure of its work as deriving from inevitable necessity.[35]

---

a State has jurisdiction under international law in relation to a particular matter that there can be any question of immunities in regard to the exercise of that jurisdiction. However, in the present case, and in view of the final form of the Congo's submissions, the Court will address first the question whether, assuming that it had jurisdiction under international law to issue and circulate the arrest warrant of 11 April 2000, Belgium in so doing violated the immunities of the then Minister for Foreign Affairs of the Congo."

34 *Jurisdictional Immunities of the State (Germany v. Italy: Greece intervening)*, Judgment, ICJ Reports 2012, 99, paras. 82, 83: "At the outset, however, the Court must observe that the proposition that the availability of immunity will be to some extent dependent upon the gravity of the unlawful act presents a logical problem… If immunity were to be dependent upon the State actually having committed a serious violation of international human rights law or the law of armed conflict, then it would become necessary for the national court to hold an enquiry into the merits in order to determine whether it had jurisdiction. If, on the other hand, the mere allegation that the State had committed such wrongful acts were to be sufficient to deprive the State of its entitlement to immunity, immunity could, in effect be negated simply by skilful construction of the claim. That said, the Court must nevertheless inquire whether customary international law has developed to the point where a State is not entitled to immunity in the case of serious violations of human rights law or the law of armed conflict."

35 *Military and Paramilitary Activities in and against Nicaragua (Nicaragua v. United States of America)*, Merits, Judgment, ICJ Reports 1986, 14, para. 226: "(…) having outlined both the facts of the case as proved by the evidence before it, and the general rules of international law which appear to it to be in issue as a result of these facts and the applicable treaty-law, has now to appraise the facts in relation to the legal rules applicable. In so far as acts of the Respondent may appear to constitute violations of the relevant rules of law, the Court will then have to determine whether there are present any circumstances excluding unlawfulness or whether such acts may be justified upon any other ground."

The International Court of Justice is free to organize the structure of the judgment independently from the order represented in the *fabula*. The Court has the freedom to discuss in the middle of the judgment the facts,[36] the applicable law,[37] or even stating that it will first address the issue over which the respondent focused "as the proceeding progressed"[38]. The motifs are "linked" if they are indispensable to the *fabula*, otherwise they are "free". A free motif is only part of the *syuzhet* and it is an *obiter dictum*. The motif can be "dynamic" or "static" depending on if it moves the *fabula* further, or if it is a descriptive pause.

In order to get to the core of the theme, the Court usually adopts a *syuzhet* made of concentric circles. For example, the historical background of the case concerning immunity is divided into three concentric circles, describing first the 1947 peace treaty, then the compensation for all the victims, and lastly the individual case of Mr Ferrini (paras. 20–36). The following section of the judgment starts with the individual case of Mr Ferrini, continues with the subject matter of the case and ends with jurisdiction (paras. 37–51). The judgment is a chain. What was at the centre of the circle in one section became the first circumference in the following section.

IV. The Hero

The hero is the third element of the literary work that applies to judgments.[39] Other attempts to identify the structure of judicial reasoning considered that the characters are the individuals involved in the proceeding.[40] Conversely, I submit that the heroes are the legal arguments. For example, in the case concerning jurisdictional immunities of the state, one of the heroes of the judgment is the legal reasoning under which "the denial of immunity was justified on account of the particular nature of the acts forming the subject-matter of the claims before the Italian courts and the

---

36 *Application of the Convention on the Prevention and Punishment of the Crime of Genocide (Croatia v. Serbia)*, Preliminary Objections, Judgment, ICJ Reports 2008, 412.

37 *Sovereignty over Pedra Branca/Pulau Batu Puteh, Middle Rocks and South Ledge (Malaysia v. Singapore)*, Judgment, ICJ Reports 2008, 12.

38 *Application of the Interim Accord of 13 September 1995 (The former Yugoslav Republic of Macedonia v. Greece)*, Judgment, ICJ Reports 2011, 644, 656, para. 27.

39 Tomaševskij, *supra* note 11, 297.

40 Leubsdorf, *supra* note 31, 447.

circumstances in which those claims were made"[41]. It is divided into four motifs: the gravity of the violations; the relation between *jus cogens* and immunity; the "last resort" argument; and the combined effect.

The heroes are devices in the hands of judges without a hierarchical superiority in the mechanism of the work. The hero is the living form of the motifs, helping the reader to follow the theme. Judges create the emotional involvement of the reader between the two primitive forms of good and evil. These are fictitious element of the work created by the author. The heroes are the argumentative tools that move the cogwheels of the rhetoric of justice.[42]

In the aesthetic dimension of the judicial genre, the heroes are reproduced as fixed characters in different works. Judges used the same legal reasoning in different judgments, creating a sort of mythology. Judgments are written relying on a pantheon of legal arguments enshrined in the legal culture. We have *jus cogens* norms, *erga omnes* obligations, responsibility to protect, the equidistant line…; each with their own emotional connotation. The use of fixed characters in different works is not a novelty in the history of literature. For example, masks are the characters of the Italian comedy of art of the 16th and 17th Centuries, with their fixed characteristics reproduced from play to play.[43] Like characters are conventional elements in the tradition of a genre, judges use legal arguments to obtain similar effects in different contexts.

Heroes are created on the basis of the submissions of the parties. Orakhelashvili examined the freedom of the International Court of Justice in treating the submissions of the parties, and how it affects the settlement of the dispute.[44] He recognizes that on the one hand the Court declares its "freedom to select the ground upon which it will base its judgment, and is under no obligation to examine all the considerations advanced by the parties if other considerations appear to it to be sufficient for this purpose"[45]; while, on the other hand, the Court considers that it could not "substitute

41 *Jurisdictional Immunities of the State (Germany v. Italy: Greece Intervening)*, Judgment, ICJ Reports 2012, 99, para. 80.

42 Venzke, I. (2012), *How Interpretation Makes International Law*. Oxford: Oxford University Press, 198.

43 Molinari, C. (2008), *Storia del Teatro*. Rome: Editiori Laterza.

44 Orakhelashvili, A. (2007), "The International Court and Its Freedom to Select the Ground upon Which It Will Base Its Judgment", *International and Comparative Law Quarterly* 56(1), 171.

45 *Case concerning the Application of the Convention of 1902 Governing the Guardianship of Infants (Netherlands v. Sweden)*, Judgment, ICJ Reports 1958, 55, 61.

itself for them [the parties] and formulate new submissions simply on the basis of arguments and facts advanced"[46]. He finally recognizes that using the "freedom to select" in different circumstances has achieved different results.

The acceptance of the winning hero is the outcome of semantic struggles. Judgments can enhance the authority of the court depending on how the audience acclaims the heroes. For example, the authority of international judges as "beacons of humanity", speaking in the name of the international community, is pursued with the creation of the so-called universal audience.[47] Perelman considers that the universal audience is a construction of the speaker. It is not an objective reality and it varies in time and space. It is an argumentative tool itself.

The use of different heroes in different contexts shows that rhetorical instruments reflect contextual sources of authority. The legal arguments employed by judges do not come from a reason of necessity, but from the will to purse a specific goal. For instance, the community-oriented audience is created developing new heroes like *erga omnes* obligations. The famous *obiter dictum* in *Barcelona Traction* came after a crisis of legitimacy of the ICJ, mainly due to the criticism expressed against the Court after the decisions concerning Namibia.[48] The Court did not act in a vacuum, but it relied on existing provisions to pursue the legal discourse in a specific direction.[49]

The way in which legal arguments are written as heroes of the judgement represents the law-making function of international adjudicatory bodies. The authority to perform this function is gained through interpretative and argumentative practice embodying the interests enshrined in the community.[50] Theories of interpretation explain how to squeeze the mean-

---

46 *German interests in Polish Upper Silesia (Germany v. Poland)*, Judgment, PCIJ Ser. A, No 7, 35.

47 Perelman, C. and Olbrechts-Tyteca, L. (1971), *Traité de l'argumentation. La Nouvelle rhétorique* (2nd ed.). Brussels: Editions de l'Université de Bruxelles.

48 *Barcelona Traction, Light and Power Company, Limited* (*Belgium* v. *Spain*), Judgment, ICJ Reports 1970, 45–46, para. 85; *South West Africa Cases (Ethiopia v. South Africa; Liberia v. South Africa)*, Second Phase, Judgment, ICJ Reports 1966, 6; *South West Africa Cases (Ethiopia v. South Africa; Liberia v. South Africa)*, First Phase, ICJ Reports 1962, 387.

49 Petersen, N. (2012), "Lawmaking by the International Court of Justice – Factors of Success" in: A. von Bogdandy and I. Venzke (eds), *International Judicial Lawmaking: On Public Authority and Democratic Legitimation in Global Governance*. Berlin/Heidelberg: Springer, 411–437, 426.

50 Venzke, *supra* note 42, 34.

ing from a text and concern the collection of knowledge, while argumentation is the use of the acquired knowledge to convince an audience.

While interpretation is the creative result of the dialectical tension between text and context, argumentation represents the persuasive power of legal language. A theory of interpretation based on the role of the interpretative community has the effect of focusing on the technical tools able to influence the meanings within a community.[51] The study of how interpretation functions inside a community can be used to impose a particular meaning. Thus, interpretation becomes argumentation. The "semantic struggles" for the law are performed in the dialectic between interpretation and argumentation.

V. The Voice

The voice is the element of the text that represents the point of view from which a story is narrated. Using this tool, the empirical author of the work can play with who is speaking, hiding or showing her presence. There is always a difference between the empirical author and the voice. Even in autobiographical works, there is never a coincidence between who is writing (empirically) and who is telling the story within the text (in the fiction). Also in the judgment there is a difference between the judges as empirical authors and the fictitious narrator within the text. While judges are the empirical authors of the judgment, they rarely show themselves in the text, and interposed subjects present motifs, be it the court, the parties or the interveners. For instance, when judges need to present objective truths, they do not indicate who is speaking, and present facts as "largely uncontested between the parties". In other cases, the voice of the parties presents the fundamental arguments. For example, in *Nottebohm* "Guatemala [...] referred to a well-established principle of international law" concerning the bond of nationality between a state and an individual, but we do not know who said that the principle is well-established, Guatemala or the judges.[52]

51 Fish, S.E. (1980), *Is There a Text in This Class?: The Authority of Interpretive Communities*. Cambridge: Harvard University Press.

52 *Nottebohm case (Liechtenstein v. Guatemala)*, Preliminary Objection, Judgment, ICJ Reports 1953, 111, 120.

Literary theory distinguishes between four models of voice, deriving from the combination of two elements.[53] The first one concerns the narrative level and reflects the capacity of the narrator to be outside (extradiegetic) or inside (intradiegetic) the narration. Extradiegetic is a first level narration while intradiegetic is a second level narration, in which a second story is narrated within a first story. The second element concerns the relation that the narrator has with the story, and it reflects her capacity to be a voice within the story (omodiegetic) or not to be a voice within the story (eterodiegetic).

First, an extra and omodiegetic voice is used for first level stories narrated in first person, where the narrator speaks as if they were the empirical author, while being part of the story. For instance, this is the voice used by Salinger in "The Catcher in the Rye". This model of voice limits the point of view and creates subjectivism. It undermines the authority of the voice and judgments do not employ it. However, this is the voice employed in individual opinions, where judges use the first person ("I" or "we").

Second, an extra and eterodiegetic voice is used for first level stories narrated in third person, where the narrator speaks as if they were the empirical author while not being part of the story. For instance, Dostoyevsky uses this voice in "Crime and Punishment". It creates the illusion that the narrator and the empirical author coincide, showing omniscient knowledge on the facts of the story. Judges frequently use this voice, especially when they describe the facts of the case without mentioning who is speaking. Motifs became uncontested when the point of view is absent from the narration. This point of view is used when the empirical author writes "the Court says", recalling all of its authority for a particular section of the text.

Third, an intra and omodiegetic voice is used when a first person introduces a second level story. For instance, Conrad employs it in "Heart of Darkness" when the character Marlow introduces in first person a second level story. Again, judgments do not use it, but judges may employ this voice in individual opinions when they recall the submissions of the parties in a second level narration. For instance, Judge Trindade provides an example of this, when he shifts from the first person "I" to the third person of the point of view of a party to the proceeding in order to tell a second level story.[54]

---

53 Genette, G. (1972), *Figures III*. Paris: Seuil.

54 See, for instance, *Obligations concerning Negotiations relating to Cessation of the Nuclear Arms Race and to Nuclear Disarmament (Marshall Islands v. United Kingdom)*, Preliminary objection, Judgment, ICJ Reports 2016, para. 26.

Fourth, an intra and eterodiegetic voice is used for a second level story narrated by a third person. For instance, this is the voice used in "One Thousand and One Nights" when Scheherazade tells her stories. Judgments use this point of view when introducing a motif with the voice of a party to the proceeding. It is extremely frequent that the empirical author lets a third subject to tell a second level story. For instance, the former President of the United States Grover Cleveland and General Alexander were cited in the 2015 judgment *Costa Rica v. Nicaragua*, in order to describe the arbitral awards they issued on the subject matter of the case.[55]

VI. The Theme

Legal formalism contends that the requests submitted by the parties identify the theme of a judgment. The idea that judges cannot engage in off-road adventures is an argumentative tool itself, used to strengthen the reasoning. The artificial construction of the theme is evident in those judgments in which judges reshape the meaning of the question in order to provide a feasible answer. In its case law, the International Court of Justice has some freedom in interpreting and clarifying questions,[56] and it even reformulates them in order to discuss what they consider the legal dispute really at issue.[57] In the Kosovo Advisory Opinion, for example, the Court first recognized that the question was "narrow and specific"[58]. but then it challenged its wording in relation to the identity of the authors of the declaration of independence and with the meaning of "in accordance with international law"[59].

The freedom of identifying the theme is a fundamental liberty of international courts. Often, the narrow jurisdiction based on States' consent hides the dispute really at issue. For example, Greece brought before the

---

55 *Certain Activities Carried Out by Nicaragua in the Border Area (Costa Rica v. Nicaragua)* and *Construction of a Road in Costa Rica along the San Juan River (Nicaragua v. Costa Rica)*, Judgment, ICJ Reports 2015, 665, para. 72 ss.

56 *Legal Consequences of the Construction of a Wall in the Occupied Palestinian Territory*, Advisory Opinion, ICJ Reports 2004, 136, 153–154, para. 38.

57 *Application for Review of Judgment No. 273 of the United Nations Administrative Tribunal*, Advisory Opinion, ICJ Reports 1982, 325, 349, para. 47.

58 *Accordance with international law of the unilateral declaration of independence in respect of Kosovo*, Advisory Opinion, ICJ Reports 2010, 403, 423, para. 51.

59 Müller, D. (2015), "The Question Question" In: M. Milanović and M. Wood (eds), *The Law and Politics of the Kosovo Advisory Opinion*. Oxford: Oxford University Press, 118–132.

Court a dispute on the use of the name "Republic of Macedonia" or "Former Federal Republic of Macedonia".[60] Even more evidently, Georgia's attempt to find jurisdiction against Russia was limited to the International Convention on the Elimination of all Forms of Racial Discrimination, while the theme presented by the Court included an accurate description of facts that widen the dispute.[61]

The Court itself recognizes the distinction between the formal object of the dispute and the theme of the judgment, considering that "the subject of the dispute was not to be determined exclusively by reference to matters set out under the relevant section heading of the Application"[62], and stressing that "it is for the Court itself to determine the subject-matter of the dispute before it, taking account of the submissions of the Parties"[63].

The Court creates its authority by modelling the theme of the judgment around the expectations of its audience. As Koskenniemi considered, legitimacy is useful "to ensure warm feeling in the audience"[64]. The theme is not the mere object of the dispute and it is shaped reproducing the expectations of the readers. In the *Kosovo* Advisory Opinion, the will to avoid questions as to the scope of the principle of self-determination and the right of secession is constructed around the expectations and the exigencies of the Court's clients.[65]

In *LaGrand* the power to issue provisional measures was interpreted by shaping the theme between the contractual power of States that creates the statutes of international courts and the role of courts as independent entities.[66] The theme reflects the importance of the audience and the need to attract the interest of the reader through emotional participation. The values underneath the judgment are of the outmost importance, concerning the right to life and death penalty. The theme is not always built around the legal dispute, which in that case concerned a breach of the 1963 Vienna

---

60 *Application of the Interim Accord of 13 September 1995 (the former Yugoslav Republic of Macedonia v. Greece)*, Judgment, ICJ Reports 2011, 644.

61 *Application of the International Convention on the Elimination of All Forms of Racial Discrimination (Georgia v. Russian Federation)*, Preliminary Objections, Judgment, ICJ Reports 2011, 70.

62 *Certain Questions of Mutual Assistance in Criminal Matters (Djibouti v. France)*, Judgment, ICJ Reports 2008, 177, 207, para. 70.

63 *Territorial and Maritime Dispute (Nicaragua v. Colombia)*, Preliminary Objections, Judgment, ICJ Reports 2007, 832, 848, para. 38.

64 Koskenniemi, M. (2007), "Formalism, Fragmentation, Freedom: Kantian Themes", *No foundations: journal of extreme legal positivism* (4), 7–28, 16.

65 Müller, *supra* note 59.

66 *LaGrand Case* (*Germany v. USA*), Judgment, ICJ Reports 2001, 466.

convention on consular relations, but judges deliberately construct it as the unity of the elements that create the text. The dispute is only one element among others. The audience is the fundamental element around which the theme is created.[67] The judgment is written around its reading community. The readers are, in case of a judgment, the clients of the Court, other States, NGOs, the community of legal scholars and the broader public.[68]

Perelman and Olbrechts-Tyteca fostered the study of the audience as the preeminent element around which argumentation is created. They define it as the group of people over which the desired influence of the speaker is directed.[69] The Russian formalists had the same intuition, in literature, looking at how the reader will react determines the choice of the theme.[70] The argumentative exercise performed by judges is thus to determine the relevant audience. When judges direct their efforts toward the parties of the proceeding, they develop the authority of the Court as an instrument of dispute settlement.[71] Conversely, they gain authority from the international community when they focus on what Perelman calls universal audience. As an intermediate position, judges could focus on the legal regime that the court serves. The distinction between audiences is also applied by studies that distinguish between narrow, extensive and popular authority.[72]

In sum, the audience in argumentation resembles the distinction between interpretative communities.[73] For example, it has already been noted how there are different degrees of judicial innovation between the *Kosovo* opinion and the *Wall* opinion.[74] In the first case, the audience are the clients of the court; in the second, the audience is the international

67 Tomaševskij, *supra* note 11, 267.

68 Bianchi, A. (2013), "Gazing at the Crystal Ball (again): State Immunity and *Jus Cogens* beyond *Germany v Italy*", *Journal of International Dispute Settlement* 4(3), 457–475.

69 Perelman and Olbrechts-Tyteca, *supra* note 47.

70 Tomaševskij, *supra* note 11, 268.

71 Von Bogdandy and Venzke, *supra* note 25, 29.

72 Alter *et al.*, *supra* note 2.

73 Waibel, M. (2015), "Interpretive Communities in International Law" In: Bianchi *et al.*, *supra* note 10, 147–165; Johnstone, I. (2011), *The Power of Deliberation: International Law, Politics and Organizations*. Oxford: Oxford University Press; Johnstone, I. (1990), "Treaty Interpretation: The Authority of Interpretive Communities", *Michigan Journal of International Law* 12(2), 371–419.

74 Von Bogdandy, A. and Venzke, I. (2012), "Beyond Dispute: International Judicial Institutions as lawmakers" In: von Bogdandy and Venzke, *supra* note 49, 3–33, 7.

community. The different audience reflect the apologetic or utopian character of legal argumentation.[75]

There are other interesting analogies between the Russian formalists, Perelman's studies on rhetoric, and the practice of authority through legal argumentation. The Russian formalists considered that the importance of relying on abstract readers is expressed through the concept of "interest".[76] The interest for the theme is conquered by maintaining a high level of attention. It is gained by not only relying on the external functions of the judgment materialized in its legal consequences, but also through the participation of the theme, through values. The reader must feel part of the work. He must feel indignation, joy, perturbation.[77]

In *Nouvelle rhétorique*, Perelman focuses on *les valeurs* as the common background over which argumentation plays its role. Justice, one of the most powerful human feelings, shapes the theme of the judgment. It is the "rhetoric of justice" under which acceptance of interpretation is obtained, through the appeal to common values: "They appeal to a sense of justice and seek to find acceptance for interpretations by inducing a belief in the rightness of their interpretations"[78].

Judges guide the reader toward the success of the legal reasoning, sharing with their clients a common background of values. For example, in the *Diplomatic and Consular Staff in Tehran*, the Court develops the relation with its audience, noting that "the principle of the inviolability of the persons of diplomatic agents and the premises of diplomatic missions is one of the very foundations of this long-established regime, to the evolution of which the traditions of Islam made a substantial contribution"[79].

The theme has its own emotional connotation since the beginning of the work, and the reader discovers it piece by piece. The theme in a judgment is, at least, two-folded, representing the different ideas of justice claimed by the parties to the proceedings. In *Jurisdictional Immunities of the State*, the idea of justice that guides the reader is divided between the respect of sovereign equality and the interest of individuals in the repara-

75 Koskenniemi, M. (2006), *From Apology to Utopia: The Structure of International Legal Argument*. Cambridge: Cambridge University Press.

76 Tomaševskij, *supra* note 11, 268.

77 *Ibid.*, 270.

78 Venzke, *supra* note 42, 198.

79 *United States Diplomatic and Consular Staff in Tehran (United States of America v. Iran)*, Judgment, ICJ Reports 1980, 3, para. 86.

tion for violation of fundamental norms of international law.[80] The argumentative path taken in the case concerning immunities reflects the state-centric concept of international law at its apex.

VII. Conclusion

Armin von Bogdandy and Ingo Venzke affirmed that "The 'community' must not be closed and the 'college' must not be invisible" to contrast an autocratic rule of courts.[81] They propose to focus the process of democratization on three actions: first, independence, impartiality and legal expertise of international judges; second, publicness and transparency of the judicial process; third, the study of the forms of argumentation that constitute good judicial reasoning.[82] This paper ascribes to the last category, following the idea that "International law and its doctrine should be tested against the question of how they contribute to the legitimation of international actors' semantic authority"[83].

"Courtspeak" gives a name to the language employed by international tribunals and it assumes that the traditional bias for rhetoric is misplaced. As judges do, "[p]our communiquer avec son auditoire, l'orateur considérera le langage comme un vaste arsenal dans lequel il choisira les moyens qui lui semblent les plus favorables à sa thèse"[84]. This quote is more complex that it seems at first glance, implying that legal argumentation is not a form of rhetoric that attempts to hide the objective application of the law. Indeed, there is not such a thing as the objective application of the law and legal reasoning is argumentative and dialectic. Thus conceived, law is not separable from rhetoric. In law, interpretation is argumentation. The motivation, the *fabula* and the *syuzhet*, the heroes, the voice and the theme have been presented as five formal elements of the text that reflect *de facto* authority and create the rhetorical structure of the judgment.

80 *Jurisdictional Immunities of the State (Germany v. Italy: Greece Intervening)*, Judgment, ICJ Reports 2012, 99.
81 Von Bogdandy, A. and Venzke, I. (2012), "In Whose Name? An Investigation of International Courts' Public Authority and Its Democratic Justification", *European Journal of International Law* 23(1), 7–41, 38.
82 Von Bogdandy and Venzke, *supra* note 25.
83 Venzke, *supra* note 42, 224.
84 Perelman, C. (1981), *Logique juridique. Nouvelle rhétorique* (2nd ed.). Paris: Dalloz, para 60.

International Public Authority in Perspective: Comparing the Roles of Courts and International Organizations in Democratizing International Law

*André Nunes Chaib**

I. Introduction

It is an undeniable fact that international institutions of all sorts nowadays exercise some sort of authority over States, local populations, and individuals.[1] This topic has become central to modern international legal scholarship — as well as that of international relations — and comprises an assessment of not only the work of international organizations,[2] but also of international courts.[3] After analysing the process by which international organizations have increasingly centralized aspects of the management and administration of world economy, a question remains as to whom these organizations should answer in the exercise of their functions. From a social perspective, one may assume that they are accountable to their constitutive members — in this case, the States. Nevertheless, once the activi-

---

* Assistant Professor in Globalization and Law, Faculty of Law, Maastricht University.

1 Zürn, M. (2018), *A Theory of Global Governance. Authority, Legitimacy and Contestation.* Oxford: Oxford University Press, 107–111.

2 Both in international law and in international relations, this has been a topical subject. For an international legal perspective, see, e.g., von Bogdandy, A. *et al.* (eds) (2010), *The Exercise of Public Authority by International Institutions*. Heidelberg: Springer. For a conceptual discussion, see Goldmann, M. (2014), *Internationale Öffentliche Gewalt*. Heidelberg: Springer. In international relations, see, e.g., Zürn *supra* note 1; Hurd, I. (2013), *International Organizations. Politics, Law, Practice*. Cambridge: Cambridge University Press; Sending, O.J. *et al.* (eds) (2015), *Diplomacy and the Making of World Politics*. Cambridge: Cambridge University Press; Pouliot, V. (2016), *International Pecking Orders. The Politics and Practice of Multilateral Diplomacy*. Cambridge: Cambridge University Press.

3 In this respect, see, for instance, Alter, K. (2014), *The New Terrain of International Law: Courts, Politics and Rights*. Princeton: Princeton University Press; also, von Bogdandy, A. and Venzke, I. (2014), *In Whose Name? A Public Law Theory of International Adjudication*. Oxford: Oxford University Press; and more recently, see also Grossman, N *et al.* (eds) (2018), *Legitimacy and International Courts*. Cambridge: Cambridge University Press.

ties of these organizations end up effecting changes in the legal, political or social condition of other entities that do not form the organizations' constituencies, one needs to find appropriate means to justify or at least to create the conditions for making them more broadly accountable or responsible. One method — used continuously in legal scholarship — is to look for the *principles* that should guide an organization's actions.

In the search for such a principle, or principles, two fundamental elements have to be investigated: 1) are the organizations in question recognized as exercising authority over agents in the international social order other than their constitutive members? 2) Is this authority characteristic of public power? These are precisely some of the points this section addresses. It argues that international organizations need to be bound necessarily by certain principles that typically govern the work of public authorities and powers in domestic settings. Differently from international courts — which in analogy with domestic courts (in particular Constitutional and Supreme Courts) —play an essential counter-majoritarian role in international politics, international organizations must have their actions always guided by certain norms to guarantee the appropriateness of their actions in respect of those affected by them. Precisely because in many cases, IOs have developed a "law-making" function,[4] attempts to verify the principles upon which they work are of fundamental importance.[5] In the particular case of IOs, if one considers that these organizations have been legally and political modelled on domestic ideals of administration, it is only reasonable that one makes an attempt at applying the principle of democracy to understanding their function, but also to provide them with normative guidance. Ultimately, it can be argued that a democratic principle applied to international organizations might create better chances to develop a democratic generality and allow for the democratization of international law.

One needs to recognise the fact that certain international courts, such as the ICJ, the WTO Dispute Settlement Mechanism, or even ICSID, within the World Bank Group, are considered in one way or another as integral parts of international organizations. This is true of their organizational and structural origins, and it is undeniable that their work remains in large part attached to the principles that govern the whole of the organization. Yet the authority they have acquired to perform their functions that they

4 See, generally, Alvarez, J. (2006), *International Organizations as Law-Makers.* Oxford: Oxford University Press.

5 *Ibid.*, 67–75.

have come to exercise over time has become detached from the organization that created them. For instance, one can argue that despite having been created by Security Council resolutions, the International Criminal Tribunal for Rwanda (ICTR), and the International Criminal Tribunal for the ex-Yugoslavia (ICTY) developed their authority, created their spaces for contestation, and elaborated on their *public* well beyond of the confines initially established by the UN instrument. Although organs of international organizations, these courts became beings in their own right and therefore can have their relation characterization as *public authorities* well-distinguished, and also compared to those of international organizations exercising mostly an *executive* function at the international level.

This chapter briefly compares how the democratic principle effect changes in different international institutions. In this respect, it will compare the exercise of public authority by courts and international organizations and assess to which extent the various public law theories may be used to create a democratically oriented framework that seeks to legitimize these organizations' activities. The first step is to establish the conditions under which the actions of an international organization can be said to constitute those of a public authority — similar to those in domestic public administrations. One can also raise the question as to whether the general fragmentation of international law and politics poses a problem to the creation of a proper public and a democratic generality to these international organizations.

II. *Conceptualizing Authority for International Institutions*

As part of the investigation into the nature of the power or authority that is exercised by international institutions, more specifically international organizations — with a view to compare them with international courts —, a few conceptual clarifications ought to be made. The previous paragraphs have referred to the potential of international courts and IOs for exercising public authority.[6] Before delving into the nature of the authority international organizations exercise, one needs first to define what is to be understood by this authority. It matters to know how and why they can exercise any authority towards other entities participating in the international political life. In this context, authority needs to be distinguished from other means of conditioning others' actions, such as, for instance, power,

6 Zürn, *supra* note 1, 38–40.

coercion, and violence.[7] A brief survey of these usages will clear the ground for our understanding of authority and provide a stronger justification for why it seems necessary to couple it with the principle of democracy.

Although international organizations exercise functions similar to public administrations and governments, differently from the "State", they do not possess the monopoly of violence, or the conditions to exercise any physical threat proper to make effective their decisions.[8] The exercise of power by international organizations is, therefore, hindered. In short, the lack of power of international organizations can be summarized by their incapacity to directly impose direct sanctions on those outside their organizational ambit, such as States or private entities, in the cases where they violate a norm established by the organization or one that the organization holds as being a necessary conditioner of behaviour for those actors. Therefore, IOs rely, to make their decisions effective, either on the will of States to bring them to consecution or on the authority they exercise over them. This is why the concept of authority becomes so instrumental in understanding the role they have in shaping international politics and international law. More specifically concerning international law, precisely because IOs lack those necessary elements to exercise proper power, but do exercise authority and effect changes in the law, it becomes essential to understand the conditions under which the exercise of such authority is made legitimate. Thus to guarantee that the authority of the organizations is adequate, there should be a certain number of principles to which this exercise should attend to. In turn, the application of (legal) principles to the activity of international organizations should also prompt an immediate change in the way the activities are exercised. Here lies the fundamental importance of grasping the meaning of authority for these organizations. This is, for instance, the point of departure the ILA took in its final report on the accountability of IOs, for attempting to precisely understand what rules and principles apply to IOs to determine their "accountability": "The starting point for the rules and recommended practices is that, as a matter

7 Arendt, H. (2006) [1954], *Between Past and Future*. New York: Penguin, 92.
8 Weber, M. (1992), "*Politik als Beruf*" In: H. Baier *et al.* (eds), *Max Weber Gesamtausgabe*. *Abteilung 1: Schriften und Reden. Band 17.* Tubingen: Mohr Siebeck, 158–159.

of principle, accountability is linked to the authority and power of an IO. Power entails accountability, that is, the duty to account for its exercise."[9]

In this context, one does well to go back to Max Weber's definition of authority. Weber's definition, although simple, is rather useful: authority is the case where a command attributed to a specific person will be obeyed.[10] Similar to that definition put forward by Hannah Arendt, authority here is also defined in opposition to power.[11] For Weber, power exists when within the framework of social relations; one is capable of imposing her will on another even against the latter's resistance.[12] Authority is therefore exercised wherever, from both the commanding and the recipient's position, there is a clear recognition that the command is to be obeyed without the further exercise of force. This relationship is further clarified by Chapter 3 of Weber's oeuvre *Economy and Society*, when he includes the *interest* of the addressee of a command as a fundamental element of obedience to authority.[13] Whether there is a moral obligation or not to follow commands from authorities, especially when authority and power are somewhat exercised concomitantly, is not a question that needs to be necessarily tackled here.[14] This definition of authority remains central in the principal doctrines of international relations and law. It informs much of the understanding of what public administrations in both domestic and international settings can and should do. In international politics, in particular, where most international organizations are not endowed with means to exercise proper power,[15] authority remains their main way to guarantee the effectiveness of decisions. Authority relationships are broadly more prevalent in global governance, especially because one can identify

---

9 ILA Committee on Accountability of International Organisations, "Report of the Seventy first Conference, Berlin 2004. Accountability of International Organisations: Final Report", 5, available at <https://www.ila-hq.org/index.php/committees>, accessed 6 December 2019.

10 Weber, M. (1980) [1921], *Wirtschaft und Gesellschaft* (5th ed.). Tubingen: Mohr Siebeck, 28.

11 *Ibid.*, 28–29.

12 *Ibid.*, 28.

13 *Ibid.*, 122.

14 Particular reference is made to a question raised by H.L.A. Hart in his *Concept of Law*. In chapter IX, Hart is attempting to differentiate the reasons why one follows legal rules. He recognizes the exercise of power – of the coercive element – by legal rules, but also that one follows legal rules because its authority is recognized. The fundamental issue he raises is whether this recognition of the authority cannot somewhat be mistaken by a moral obligation to follow the legal rule. Hart, H.L.A. (2012), *The Concept of Law*. Oxford: Oxford University Press, 203.

15 Zürn, *supra* note 1.

various situations where States and other social actors follow obligations created by international institutions that go against their "stated interests".[16] International authority, therefore, is founded on the fact that these are obligations that are followed without the exercise of coercion or persuasion,[17] and are fundamentally based on an idea and presumption that their execution is done in favour of a common good.[18] More importantly, in this context, is the recognition of authority's normative impact and the fact that when exercised it may create obligations, duties — and eventually rights — for those under it.[19] Yet the concept of authority has to be further refined to allow one to grasp in fuller detail its content and how it occurs when exercised by international organizations.

In Max Weber's conceptualization, it is also necessary to assume that the actors act in accordance with authorities' commands based on reasons.[20] As we have previously indicated, it matters to know the quality and type of authority being exercised by international economic organizations. For this reason, Michael Zürn's understanding of both reflexive and public authority is instrumental for gauging how IOs exercise their authority. An initial question that drives the search for an appropriate conception of public authority at the international level is the following question: if at the basis of an authority relationship there has to be an *interest* or *reason* for the addressee of a command to follow it, how is that transposed to the international? In other words, why would a State follow the authority of an international organization, especially considering that States themselves may have all sorts of different means to contest such authority?[21] This is the question that leads Zürn to develop the concept of a reflexive public authority. Such a concept builds on two different approaches of authority: the contracted and the inscribed authority. The former is "reason-based" and sees authority as based on different forms of contract.[22] Authority exists when one party sees the command of another as "legitimate" and from it derives "an obligation to obey".[23] The latter approach regards

16 *Ibid.*, 37.

17 Zürn, M. (2007), "From Constitutional Authority to Loosely Coupled Spheres of Liquid Authority: A Reflexive Approach", *International Theory*, 9(2), 261–285, 263–264.

18 Zürn, *supra* note 1, 37.

19 Roughan, N. (2013), *Authorities. Conflicts, Cooperation and Transnational Legal Theory*. Oxford: Oxford University Press, 20–21.

20 *Ibid.*, 263.

21 Zürn, *supra* note 1, 39.

22 *Ibid.*, 41.

23 *Ibid.*

authority as being formed through processes of socialization of agents and identifies authority as a "relationship in which habits are activated and reproduced by actors"[24]. Authority is, therefore, the capacity to, through discourse and practice, induce certain behaviours on others.[25] Reflexive authority comprises elements of these two approaches to conclude that authority is founded on a "logic of action other than the logic of appropriateness or the logic of consequentiality"[26].

Ultimately, according to Zürn, reflexive authority is materialized in two different forms: epistemic authority and political authority.[27] The former corresponds to the authority to make interpretations and the latter to make decisions.[28] Political authority means the identification of a specific institution capable of making "enforceable" decisions in respect of a "collective".[29] Generally, international institutions make their way through asserting their political authority through the establishment of mechanisms of majority voting or by the consistent "exercise of dominance by a hegemonic power"[30]. By exercising political authority, international institutions exert direct or indirect influence over the domestic politics of its members.[31] On the other hand, epistemic authority is the capacity through interpretation to condition others' behaviours.[32] It relies on the assumption that knowledge is unequally distributed and that those exercising it have not only expert knowledge in a certain field but also some degree of moral integrity.[33] As Zürn argues, the epistemic authority has become very much institutionalized with global governance, with many international organizations exercising it.[34] These two forms of authority are instrumental in understanding how international organizations, for instance, condition the behaviour of States and peoples. It also points to the potential means they may use to create new obligations for them informally.

From their creation until today, international organizations' constant impact on policy-making, economic design, and law-making in various countries has only increased. This practice alone would justify speaking of

---

24 *Ibid.*, 43.
25 *Ibid.*
26 *Ibid.*, 45.
27 *Ibid.*
28 *Ibid.*, 50–51.
29 *Ibid.*, 51.
30 *Ibid.*
31 *Ibid.*
32 *Ibid.*, 52.
33 *Ibid.*
34 *Ibid.*, 52–53.

the *public* character of the authority they exercise. Yet there remain theoretical challenges as to why their authority would be considered of a public nature, whereas other private organizations having the same kind of impact on domestic affairs will not be considered to exercise public authority. This has formed the object of inquiry of authors in both law and political sciences and has been central to the development of many contemporary theories seeking to restrain the activity of these organizations based on public law principles.

III. Democracy as Public Value for International Institutions

Before delving into whether IOs, in comparison to international courts, are capable of provoking such transformations, one needs to ask the question of whether democratic generalities are indeed necessary for contemporary international law to function correctly. This brings back the question about what role democracy plays or should play in international law and politics. If one argues that IOs exercise public authority in the sense that their decisions and activities have far-reaching consequences, then it becomes again important to discuss the conditions under which there can be a reconcilement between individual and democratic self-determination in the international context. Amongst the many principles of public law that attempt to solve such tension is the principle of democracy itself. The concept of democracy is one that is hard to define, and which has throughout history, found a variety of expressions.[35] Some of these have adapted to a modern context where international standards are taken into account, and which allows for a more significant consideration of "social, political and cultural diversity", such as the idea of a consociational democracy.[36] Yet all of these theories will lack, in one way or another, elements for a general holistic explanation of the scheme wherein international institutions and individual entities intent to assert their legal and political positions. In this respect, a question remains as to whether "the democratic legitimacy of international institutions must be built upon the democratic mechanisms of their members"[37].

35 For a general overview of such expressions, see Schmidt, M.G. (2006), *Demokratietheorien. Eine Einführung* (3rd ed.). Wiesbaden: VS Verlag für Sozialwissenschaften. Also, Cartledge, P. (2016), *Democracy. A Life.* Oxford: Oxford University Press.

36 Von Bogdandy and Venzke, *supra* note 3, 146.

37 *Ibid.*

In light of the fact that IOs exercise in no small degree some executive or almost government functions, it does not seem unsurprising that the concept of democracy appears as a decisive element. By and large, governments act in the international sphere based on a legitimate mandate given to them by their people.[38] This does not mean, however, that there does not remain a sizeable democratic deficit in international law — in particular considering democracy is not the main objective of international law itself —, especially within a context of globalization and fragmentation.[39] To the extent that governments have the freedom to act internationally, they manage many times to create circumstances that ignore the very will of their constituencies. Parliamentary control sometimes is not enough to constrain the actions of governments, given many of the current international legal instruments used nowadays are either informal[40] or do not constitute proper hard law.[41] Parliaments are left aside in many critical decision-making processes. Reliance on domestic mechanisms to guarantee the democratic character of international law does not appear as of yet an outstanding option.[42]

---

38 As Thomas Franck has pointed out, in fact, most States see that only democratic countries are able to properly validate their actions in global governance, which prompts the thinking about the emergence of an international right to democratic governance. Franck, T. (1992), "The Emerging Right to Democratic Governance", *American Journal of International Law* 86(1), 46–91, 47.

39 Wheatley, S. (2011), "A Democratic Rule of International Law", *European Journal of International Law* 22(2), 525–548, 528; Also, Bast, J. (2009), "Das Demokratiedefizit fragmentierter internationalisierung" In: H. Brunkhorst (ed.), *Demokratie in der Weltgesellschaft*. Baden-Baden: Nomos, 185–193, 190–191.

40 See Pawlyn, J. *et al.* (eds) (2012), *Informal International Law-making*. Oxford: Oxford University Press.

41 On the problem of how the "relative" normativity of many legal instruments impact the relations between international actors and how it fundamentally defines the structure of international law, see, the still classic, Weil, P. (1983), "Towards Relative Normativity in International Law?", *American Journal of International Law* 77(3), 413–442.

42 Although Franck pointed out to the constant (and consistent) move towards requiring that governments be democratic in order to have their will properly validated at the international level, there remains effective mechanisms to guarantee that such a requirement becomes a method to asserting the formation of a proper democratic space in international law, especially when considering the modes of governance of many international organizations, such as the UN, the WB or the IMF. Also, as James Crawford has pointed out, from its beginning, international law never made of democracy a central value: Crawford, J. (2013), "Chance, Order and Change: The Course of International Law", *Collected Courses of the Hague Academy of International Law* 365, 279–283. This is also the opinion of Hillary

IV. The Role of International Institutions in Democratizing the International Public

A. The Potential for International Institutions to Create Public and Democratic Generalities

It is difficult to compare ICs and IOs, especially considering their variety in terms of structure and subjects with which they deal. Nevertheless, in terms of how much they can accomplish considering their roles within the legal order, there is room to assess under which conditions they can, in the lack of proper "powers" at the international plane, create democratic conditions for the exercise of their own activities; And consequently how much can they contribute to the development of a global public sphere and a proper international democratic generality. This chapter argues that international courts have less of a potential to create democratic generalities when compared to IOs. It will be argued that it is not the ICs function to act as catalysers of democratic publics in international law. However, this does not mean that they should not act, to the extent possible, in such a way as to promote such values.

Nevertheless, the very nature of their functions requires them to take on a more restrictive approach when acting, even if by exercising their typical activities ICs end up creating law – a function typically outside the scope of their actions. On the other hand, IOs are much better placed to create the conditions for a democratic generality at the international level. Their forum-like structure and their proneness to politicization make them an adequate place to attempt such a transformation. Therefore, a theory of democracy and public authority that is applied to these institutions appears to have a larger chance of success.[43] Moreover, the single fact that IOs are organizations focused on specific issues with a broad range of members grants them a much wider reach than international courts. In this sense, even though there may be suggestions that procedural transformations may place courts in a more "democratic" position, they are not as well placed as IOs to perform some fundamental changes in the international social order. This should not, however, ignore the fact that international courts play a crucial role in stabilizing institutions within such

---

Charlesworth: Charlesworth, H. (2015), "Democracy and International Law", *Collected Courses of the Hague Academy of International Law* 371, 70–74.

43 See von Bogdandy, A. *et al.* (eds) (2010), *The Exercise of International Public Authority by International Institutions: advancing international institutional law*. Heidelberg: Springer.

social order. As previously mentioned, decisions by courts have the power to reinforce the position of individual institutions within society. In doing so, they also have an essential role in determining the axiological spectrum of social order. It is precisely within this context that one ought to assess the conditions in which these different institutions — courts and international organizations — can generate democracy in international law.

B. *The Potential of International Courts*

The question of how to provide elements sufficient to develop or justify the democratic character of international law has for a long time had a central place in theoretical and doctrinal discussions within the field of international law.[44] One issue is central to the question as to whether international courts can effect changes in the international public is the effect of the fragmentation of international law and politics as a challenge to democratic generality they would hope to create.

International courts do, however, have a strong potential for institutionalizing a field of international law, as it has already been largely demonstrated in international economic law. This can be seen already in some work of the PCIJ. Interestingly, the PCIJ saw that international law offered good instruments to tackle issues concerning economic questions of States, but that its effect, again, ought to be restricted to the parties.

> “But it would be scarcely accurate to say that only questions of international law may form the subject of a decision of the Court. It should be recalled in this respect that paragraph 2 of Article 36 of the Statute provides that States may recognize as compulsory the jurisdiction of the Court in legal disputes concerning "the existence of any fact which, if established, would constitute a breach of an international obligation". And Article 13 of the Covenant includes disputes of the sort above mentioned — "among those which are generally suitable for submission to arbitration or judicial settlement". Clearly, amongst others, disputes concerning pure matters of fact are contemplated, for the States concerned may agree that the fact to be established would

44 See, for instance, Lauterpacht, H. (1937), “Règles générales du droit de la paix”, *Collected Courses of the Hague Academy of International Law* 62; Alter, K. (2014), *The New Terrain of International Law. Courts, Politics and Rights*. Princeton: Princeton University Press; Grossmann *et al.*, *supra* note 3; and also von Bogdandy and Venzke, *supra* note 3.

> constitute a breach of an international obligation; it is unnecessary to add that the facts the existence of which the Court has to establish may be of any kind".[45]

In any case, the elements derived from such a public law theory must still be translated into mechanisms allowing for greater inclusion of other interested parties in the proceedings leading to the court's decision.[46] These mechanisms, however, do not merely include measures to allow for third-party participation in the proceedings, such as *amicus curiae*, or interventions. They also include the need to provide *reasons* for a decision as a fundamental element to guarantee democratic legitimacy.[47] For instance, an argument runs in the sense that there is the necessity of revising how international courts' judges are selected, with a view of making such a selection more open and transparent.[48] One can see that these mechanisms bear importance for moments not necessarily related to the judicial process itself, but also for the whole process of constructing the court's very identity within the international legal order. Many of the criteria — transparency, political inclusion, etc. — devised by these theories,[49] are mostly translated into procedural mechanisms which would ultimately grant a reasonable level of democratic legitimacy to the courts' decisions bear strong similarities to those set up, for instance, by the Global Administrative Law to determine the legitimacy of IOs' decisions.[50] However, it remains an undeniable fact that in international law, international courts derive their legitimacy primarily from their constituent treaties and the normative instruments they base their decisions on. After all, it is mostly by the type and quality of their work that international courts establish themselves socially. This is also the case, for international courts in many aspects perform a counter-majoritarian function similar to constitutional

45 *Payment of Various Serbian Loans Issued in France (Fr. v. Yugo.)*, Judgement of 12 July 1929, P.C.I.J. (ser. A) No. 20, 19.

46 Grossmann *et al.*, *supra* note 3, 18–19.

47 This brings back the discussion about the exercise of authority by international courts. As it has been shown above reasons are a crucial element in determining whether an entity exercises authority over another. This is and should be no different with international courts. For an informative discussion of this within courts, see von Bogdandy and Venzke, *supra* note 3, 109–110.

48 *Ibid.*, 158–161.

49 *Ibid.*, 136–137.

50 This is based largely on the criteria of transparency and participation.

courts or supreme courts, at the international level.[51] That means that international courts need not necessarily respond to the same demands as legislatures or even executive bodies, but rather should remain attached to the law and find the grounds for justifying the legitimacy of its decisions. It remains mostly unconvincing that by providing procedural conditions for a broader public to either influence the selection of judges or participate in the proceedings would guarantee the democratic legitimacy of these courts.

It could be the fact that creating the conditions for more political inclusion and deliberation would not be sufficient to justify the exercise of public authority by international courts democratically. In addition, fragmentation of international law poses a further challenge to the creation of a democratic generality. After all, democratic legitimacy may not be the necessary condition to guarantee that courts' decisions are seen as legitimate in themselves. Instead, some form of justified "self-determination"[52] might be how ICs confirm their authority to a wider public, especially a public that is directly affected by its decisions. Even if a concept of legitimacy based on the idea of "self-determination" may also be translated into procedural measures,[53] it still cannot be said to provide a general democratic legitimacy. In this respect, even if considered as a means to justify the court's authority, participation in the proceedings or in the instances defining its structure, procedural mechanisms meant to reinforce the democratic legitimacy of an international court can only be said to be so insofar as they allow for interested parties to more effectively affect the court's work. It does not create a democratic generality, but slightly smaller social pockets, which themselves can be democratic and are composed of those somehow affected by the court's activities. Thus, the hope of constructing a social order corresponding to a democratic space based on the work of an international court is somewhat limited.

---

51 In general, Constitutional and Supreme Courts exercise an important counter-majoritarian function, in that they are bound to interpret the constitution, regardless of whatever may be stated in public opinion or in the other powers.

52 Möllers, C. (2015), *Die drei Gewalten. Legitimation der Gewaltengliederung in Verfassungsstaat, europäischer Integration und Internationalisierung*. Weilerwist: Velbrück Wissenschaft, 51. And Möllers, C. (2005), *Gewaltengliederung. Legitimation und Dogmatik im nationalen und internationalen Rechtsvergleich*. Tübingen: Mohr Siebeck.

53 Möllers (2015), *supra* note 52, 52.

This limited political space created by each international court risks deepening a long-occurring process of fragmentation, instead of hindering it. In fact, not only this would reinforce processes of fragmentation, but would also enhance a potential asymmetry between the work done by the courts and the outcomes produced by it. A solution has been offered to tackle this issue and that of the construction of a broader democratic public. It comes from an interpretation of Article 31 (3) c of the Vienna Convention on the Law of Treaties (VCLT).[54] In this context, a systemic interpretation, along the lines of the cited article of the VCLT could serve as a way to counter this lack of unity. This would also allow for the cognition of a potentially democratic public. However, this recourse to the interpretation technique suggested in the Vienna convention seems unlikely to solve the problem of democratic generality; especially if one considers that the public made explicit by this interpretative exercise would be one made after the decision-making takes place, *a posteriori*. Furthermore, attempting to reconcile principles of democracy with the exercise of public authority by international courts, actually risks their excessive politicization within their fields and might end up deepening the distance between different international courts, and between the courts and their addressees.

In other words, if courts do open themselves up for more involvement of actors, the degree of participation not only not change the condition of those affected, but it may end up revealing a more profound problem of democratic representation in the international plane. The level of participation will never equal the effects of the decision. For as much as there may be more participation in the various instances leading to decision-making, it will never be as far-reaching as the effects of such decision-makings may be. Given there is no means of justifying or deciding on proper representation by actors at the international level, one can say that the outcomes may even be "good", but they surely cannot be said to be "democratic". That is to say that even if, for example, non-governmental organizations were allowed to intervene in proceedings in the form of *amicus curiae*, the effects of the judicial decision cannot be said to have been more legitimate just because there was more representation of "civil society". In this particular case, no one knows "who" these civil society representatives represent.

54 Bogdandy and Venzke, *supra* note 3, 189–192.

C. The Potential of International Organizations

A public law approach may be more useful as a normative argument for international institutions other than international courts, in particular to international organizations — and potentially even more for those concerned with the world economy. The democratic principle —applied to international organizations takes on a different dimension, and the procedural adaptations made would be undoubtedly different.[55] In this context, a public law theory applied to the activities of international organizations has the potential to effectively create the conditions for the development of a democratic generality affecting decision-making. It seems more reasonable to require a democratic legitimation of their activities, especially within a context where, given the functions of international organizations — especially those of supervision and administration.[56] Public participation, transparency, amongst other principles, could indeed reinforce the process of "politicization" these organizations are going through.[57] Even though international courts may create law, the question remains about whether their acts need to be "democratically" justified. As opposed to other international institutions, international courts may be the institutions that at this point, need the least to seek democratic legitimacy. They should rather focus on guaranteeing their functional and normative legitimacy instead.

As mentioned above, comparing different types of international institutions may be very difficult. Nevertheless, there is great value in attempting to see how in their various roles, they may aid in the development of democratic publics that support in legitimizing the decision making processes. In this context, this sub-section argues that IOs dispose of much more autonomy in the execution of their activities and therefore not only should constitute more the object of a democratic legitimation analysis but also have the potential, thus, of creating a more substantial democratic generality.[58] Moreover, IOs present a much better space for politicization, which also creates better conditions for the creation of a democratic generality.[59] These are two main points that will be raised to argue that IOs have

55 Charlesworth, *supra* note 42, 107.

56 This is very well shown in von Bogdandy *et al.*, *supra* note 2.

57 Zürn, M. and Ecker-Ehrhardt, M. (eds) (2013), *Die Politisierung der Weltpolitik*. Frankfurt am Main: Suhrkamp. In particular, the chapter written by the authors "Die Politisierung der Weltpolitik".

58 *Ibid.*, 347–348.

59 *Ibid.*, 365.

a better chance of creating an international democratic space than international courts.

Even if within the constraints of the internal rules of such organizations — constitutive agreement, internal regulations, etc. — the degree of autonomy of IOs remains relatively high. Whether this can be said to represent an institutional position or a mere transposition of collective wills remains the object of much debate in scholarship.[60] Nonetheless, the fact that IOs are capable of acting with a considerable amount of autonomy in the international political space is beyond doubt. Against this backdrop, it is far more plausible to argue that IOs exercise international public authority and that this has to come with some legitimation that goes beyond mere rules of international law.[61] This is especially true once one recognizes that the significant interlocutors of IOs nowadays are not necessarily the States, even though we are not yet capable of speaking of an international *demos* or international political citizenry.[62]

There is another side to this story, and many still see IOs as the vehicles of great powers. Nancy Fraser, for example, recognizes that the construction of a transnational public sphere is rendered rather difficult given IOs still are the place of institutionalized forms of hegemony.[63] This is a hegemony, however, that in the present context, "operates through a post-Westphalian model of disaggregated sovereignty"[64]. Other authors have conducted empirical work to show how great powers (in particular the United

60 On this, see Lagrange, E. (2002), *La Représentation Institutionnelle dans l'Ordre International. Une contribution à la théorie de la personnalité morale des organisations internationales*. Alphen aan den Rijn: Kluwer Law International. Also, somehow showing how international organizations in general are still somehow limited in their actions by internal rules: Klabbers, J. (2015), *An Introduction to International Organizations Law*. Cambridge: Cambridge University Press. From a political science perspective, see Hawkings, D.G. *et al.* (2006), *Delegation and Agency in International Organizations*. Cambridge: Cambridge University Press; Johnson, T. (2014), *Organizational Progeny. Why Governments are Losing Control over the Proliferating Structures of Global Governance*. Oxford: Oxford University Press; Abbott, K.W. *et al.* (2015), *International Organizations as Orchestrators*. Cambridge: Cambridge University Press.

61 From a discourse theory perspective on this topic, see Goldmann, M. (2015), *Internationale öffentliche Gewalt*. Heidelberg: Springer. A more traditional take on the matter is Brölmann, C. (2007), *The Institutional Veil in Public International Law*. London: Hart.

62 Fraser, N. (2010), *Scales of Justice. Reimagining Political Space in a Globalizing World*. New York: Columbia University Press, 85.

63 *Ibid.*, 86.

64 *Ibid.*, 87.

States) have been very successful in guiding international institutions to attain their interests.[65]

Nevertheless, the fact that, historically, IOs have opened themselves up for the participation of actors other than States cannot be denied, with some becoming participants of the IO's central activities. The ILO is such an example, where not only States, but also employers' associations and trade unions participate in the law-making processes.[66] Moreover, despite being given a looser or weaker status, civil society representatives can, for instance, effectively affect how specific procedures are transformed within the World Bank.[67] This goes to show that IOs have already been continuously integrating different actors into their decision-making process, thus rendering such processes wider in scope in terms of participation.

With such opening of participation, there also come the demands of these new actors which include, for example, that such processes be conducted transparently. These new claims have an impact in the structure of the organization and the way the organization behaves. Yet, what does this say about the potential of IOs to create democratic generalities? One very interesting aspect is that participation of different actors in IOs is not forcefully guided by the interest they have in one case with which the IO is dealing. IOs are generally oriented in their behaviour by their constitutive object, which is contained in their constitutive agreement. It is an interest in this "object" that drives other actors to demand participation in decision-making in IOs. Also, the reach of IOs actions is far more comprehensive than those of international courts. They are bound to their legal mandate and accountable — in simple terms — to their constituents. This means that, as previously stated, their mandates have to be continuously interpreted to reflect their current social position within the international sphere and to "justify" their actions before their members and those upon whom their actions will have some effect. This alone should be enough reason to argue that, considering democracy as a good value, these organizations should be made more democratic. Besides, once the democratic principle is materialised in these IOs, given their more extensive reach, the chances they might create a larger democratic public are greater than those of ICs. This "virtuous" circle depends, however, mainly on the will of State

65 A good example of this sort is Lavelle, K.C. (2011), *Legislating International Organizations: The US Congress, the IMF and the World Bank*. Oxford: Oxford University Press.

66 ILO Constitution, Article 3(1).

67 For this, see http://consultations.worldbank.org/consultation/review-and-update-world-bank-safeguard-policies, accessed 29 January 2020.

members to conduct the necessary structural changes in these IOs, allowing for this transformation to happen. This dependency, however, shows how IOs are also still very much at the will of States, despite being better placed than international courts to create democratic publics. Arguing that they have a better chance of creating democratic generalities does not necessarily mean they will do so.

In this respect, it is important to have a historical glimpse at what was understood as being the powers of international organizations, at the beginning of the 20th century. The PCIJ, for example, had already provided some thoughts on what could be the powers of IOs, in assessing the commission for the Danube. It recognized that if it cannot reach "central economic centres" its work loses its object —, which also shows that the court already identified a broader potential for the IO in the international social order. The organization was "economic" in its essence also.

> "It is also certain, as has been shown above, that the European Commission of the Danube possesses and has possessed since 1865, at all events some powers upon the Galatz-Braila sector, that is to say powers exercised in favour of sea-going shipping. Indeed, commercial shipping loses its whole object if it cannot reach economic centres; so that sea-going shipping on the Danube must be able to reach the terminal port of such shipping. This view is especially indicated because, before 1921, the fluvial Danube was not effectively internationalized, so that the régime of freedom of navigation, as far as the (*jusque dans le*) port of Braila, could before the war only be assumed by the European Commission of the Danube, in so far as that duty rested with an international organization".[68]

The second point to be raised is that of the potential of IOs to become ever more politicized. In short, by dealing with matters interesting to a variety of populations, IOs have become not only the vehicles of States for the construction of international public policies but also the object of peoples in their political discourses. IOs have increasingly positioned themselves politically not only at the international level but also in domestic settings. As opposed to being mere "functional" structures, IOs take political positions when deciding on particular public policies, regardless of the position of their Member States. IOs decisions nowadays have remarkable dis-

68 *Jurisdiction of European Commission of Danube Between Galatz and Braila*, Advisory Opinion of 8 December 1927, P.C.I.J. (ser. B) No. 14, 57.

tributive effects, even when they deal with very technical issues.[69] Therefore, a variety of actors, either in the forms of activism, organized civil society groups, or even individuals, claim a larger space in IOs structure.

Michael Zürn and Matthias Ecker-Ehrhardt have come up with two different conditions for politicization: 1) a legitimation deficit (*Legitimationsdefizits*) and 2) a regulation deficit (*Regelungsdefizit*).[70] These two types of the problem appear as the main requirements for the processes of politicization of IOs and significantly contribute to the claim of actors other than States to take part in the IOs activities.[71] Once one looks at the wide-range effects of IOs activities and the problems posed by these types of deficit that they generate when acting, it is possible to see how IOs have a better chance at creating democratic generalities. After all, the public willing to subject itself to a more democratic structure within IOs is already there. What needs to be done is the construction of the proper institutional mechanisms for this public to take effective part in the decision-making processes. Therefore, we can see that certain conditions, such as the existence of a proper democratic public, are already given in respect of IOs.

Conclusion

The present chapter looked at how the authority of modern IOs has, together with that of ICs, raised the fundamental question as to how and whether democracy ought to be considered a decisive factor in their structuration. It compared the capacity of both international organizations and international courts to generate democratic generalities and to guide their activities on the basis of such generalities. In doing so, it showcased the difficulties these institutions have in articulating their relationship with international law with a general principle of democracy. It did, however, point to the fact that courts may have less to do or say about democracy at the international level than expected. Of all these international institutions known today, perhaps international organizations remain the most apt to induce the creation of democratic generalities — irrespective of the fact that one sees them as being *good* or *bad* institutions — or potentially more prone to the application of such a principle of democracy as an analytical

69 Zürn and Ecker-Ehrhardt, *supra* note 57, 335.
70 *Ibid.*, 346.
71 *Ibid.*

tool to assess their activities. Nevertheless, it so remains the fact that IOs reconstruct — sometimes by taking a "positivist" stance concerning their constitutive agreements — the normative spaces they inhabit and how international law, both general and specific domains, affect the way they behave in relation to their members and those affected by their actions. International courts seem to have less of an alternative or control in that respect. If democracy can be used as a lens through which one can look at the work of international organizations, it is less though the case to assess international courts' activities.

The Dispute Settlement Function of the International Court of Justice in *Croatia v. Serbia*

Cecily Rose[*]

1. *Introduction*

This chapter revisits a central premise of the public law theory of adjudication, namely, the view that the traditional understanding of courts as dispute settlers is inadequate. Admittedly, the function of international courts is larger than the settlement of disputes, and in this sense the traditional understanding is incomplete. International courts are undoubtedly more than "mere instruments of dispute settlement whose activities are justified by the consent of the states that created them and in whose name they decide"[1]. International courts can also act as law-makers, as promoters of global interests, as institutions within larger legal regimes, and also as institutions that exercise public authority. To an extent, the function of an international court is in the eye of the beholder, whether a judge, a scholar, a diplomat, or a member of the public. Each of these actors may perceive a given judgment or award through a particular lens. A judgment may strike a judge as an opportunity for the court to promote global interests, while an academic, observing from the outside, may primarily understand the same judgment as an instance of law-making. In light of the many ways in which international courts may be perceived, the dispute settlement account does indeed paint only part of the picture.

This contribution argues, however, that the dispute settlement function of international courts merits a more nuanced account. Before we set aside the conception of courts as instruments of dispute settlement, in search of a more satisfactory explanation of the role that international courts are playing today, some of the finer aspects of their dispute settlement function ought to be detailed. This chapter therefore offers a critique of the

---

* Assistant Professor of Public International Law, Grotius Centre for International Legal Studies, Leiden Law School. The author is grateful to Fernando Lusa Bordin for his comments on an earlier version of this piece.

1 Von Bogdandy, A. and Venzke, I. (2014), *In Whose Name? A Public Law Theory of Adjudication*. Oxford: Oxford University Press, 1.

premises of the public law theory of adjudication, by sketching a more complex picture of the dispute settlement function. The focus of this discussion will be on the International Court of Justice (Court or ICJ), the longest-standing international judicial institution, which can be fairly described as generally embracing a "state-centric" conception of courts as instruments of dispute settlement.[2] The Court's contentious jurisdiction is, after all, limited to inter-state disputes, and depends on states explicitly consenting to the Court's settlement of their disputes. Despite the importance of non-state actors in contemporary international relations, the Court, of course, has no jurisdiction over such entities. Moreover, the Court is best positioned for the settlement of bilateral rather than multilateral inter-state disputes. At times the Court has taken a strict approach to interventions by third states, and to the *Monetary Gold* principle, which precludes it from ruling on the rights or obligations of a third party that has not consented to its jurisdiction.

However, such an account of the ICJ as an instrument of dispute settlement does a disservice to this institution by focusing on what the Court is not. The Court is not open to non-state actors or to *amicus curiae*. It is relatively closed to third-party interventions and it is ill-suited to the settlement of multilateral disputes. Highlighting the Court's fundamental limitations as a judicial institution does little to advance our understanding of how the Court actually contributes to the settlement of disputes in the inter-state, mostly bilateral, cases that come before it. How does the Court carry out its role as an instrument of dispute settlement and what does this tell us about its judicial function?

A closer look at the practice of the Court shows us, for example, that its role in dispute settlement is not necessarily limited to the issuance of judgments that resolve legal disputes between states. In fact, in some cases, the manner in which the Court exercises its functions causes it to resemble other forms of dispute settlement listed in Article 33 of the UN Charter, such as inquiry or conciliation. In the *North Sea Continental Shelf* cases, for example, the Court's approach to the dispute arguably resembled the approach of a conciliation commission. At the behest of the parties, the Court did not actually decide the underlying dispute between the Netherlands, Germany, and Denmark about the course of their maritime boundaries, but instead laid out the factors to be taken into account by the parties in their subsequent negotiations, much as a conciliation commission

2 *Ibid.*, 29, 36–43.

would make recommendations.[3] The Court can also play an important role in encouraging other forms of dispute settlement, such as negotiations. The prospect of imminent oral proceedings before the bench, for example, has helped to bring about the resolution of disputes through negotiations. Without even issuing a judgment, the Court can help to catalyze stalled negotiations by simply representing a less desirable dispute settlement method, over which the disputing parties exercise relatively little control.[4]

The remainder of this chapter pursues the argument that the Court, in its February 2015 judgment in *Application of the Convention on the Prevention and Punishment of the Crime of Genocide (Croatia v Serbia)*, played a role similar to that of a fact-finding body.[5] A controversial jurisdictional maneuver by the Court in its judgment on the merits allowed it to engage with the parties' factual allegations about the commission of genocide during the conflict between Croatia and Serbia in the early to mid-1990s. Without ruling on what it ought to have characterized as a jurisdictional question, the Court went on to issue a lengthy judgment that covered disputed facts at great length, in a manner arguably reminiscent of a commission of inquiry. In doing so, the Court gave less weight to the issue of consent than one might expect based on the standard, state-oriented account of the Court as an instrument of dispute settlement. The Court's approach was perhaps motivated by its awareness of the sensitivity and importance of the case to the governments and the populations of the two disputing parties, and the relatively great length of time that the case had been on its docket. These considerations fit uneasily with the state-centered understanding of the Court's function as an instrument of dispute settlement, and should perhaps cause us to revisit this account. The following case study is thus geared towards painting a fuller, more detailed picture of the Court as an instrument of dispute settlement—an account that recognizes the Court's sometimes flexible approach towards consent, as well as the varied roles that it can play in dispute settlement.

This chapter begins with a description of the Court's jurisdictional rulings in *Croatia v Serbia* (Part 2), followed by a critique of the Court's jurisdictional maneuver (Part 3). The Chapter concludes by considering the

3 *North Sea Continental Shelf (Federal Republic of Germany v. Denmark; Federal Republic of Germany v. Netherlands)*, Judgment, ICJ Reports 1969, 3.

4 See, e.g., *Aerial Herbicide Spraying (Ecuador v Colombia)*.

5 *Application of the Convention on the Prevention and Punishment of the Crime of Genocide (Croatia v Serbia)*, Preliminary Objections, Judgment, ICJ Reports 2015, 3.

fact-intensive character of this judgment, and its broader implications for the ICJ as an institution of dispute settlement (Part 4).

2. *The Court's Jurisdictional Rulings in* Croatia v Serbia

The Court's 2015 judgment on the merits in *Croatia v Serbia* was the culmination of sixteen years of litigation involving multiple challenges by Serbia to the Court's jurisdiction. In its Application instituting proceedings in July 1999, Croatia alleged that Serbia was responsible for breaching the Genocide Convention in Croatia between 1991 and 1995.[6] Serbia responded with counter-claims likewise alleging that Croatia was responsible for breaches of the Genocide Convention in the Republic of Serbian Krajina in 1995.[7]

In 2002, however, Serbia also raised three preliminary objections to the jurisdiction of the Court and the admissibility of Croatia's claims. In its 2008 judgment on preliminary objections, the Court rejected Serbia's first and third preliminary objections, leaving only the second preliminary objection for the merits.[8] Serbia's second objection concerned the Court's jurisdiction *ratione temporis*, or temporal jurisdiction—an unusually complex issue in this case due to the dissolution of the former Yugoslavia and the changing status of Serbia as a state in the 1990s. Serbia asked the Court to declare inadmissible and outside of the Court's jurisdiction the claims by Croatia that were based on acts or omissions that took place before the Federal Republic of Yugoslavia (FRY) came into existence on 27 April 1992. Serbia argued that because any acts or omissions occurred before the FRY became a State and also a party to the Genocide Convention, they fell

6 *Application Instituting Proceedings, Application of the Convention on the Prevention and Punishment of the Crime of Genocide (Croatia v. Yugoslavia)* 2 July 1999.

7 Counter-Memorial Submitted by the Republic of Serbia, December 2009, Chapter XIV.

8 *Application of the Convention on the Prevention and Punishment of the Crime of Genocide (Croatia v Serbia), Preliminary Objections, Judgment, ICJ Reports 2008*, 412. In its first preliminary objection, Serbia claimed that the Court lacked jurisdiction. Serbia's second and third preliminary objections were in the alternative. In its second preliminary objection Serbia claimed that the acts or omissions that took place before 27 April 1992 were outside of the Court's jurisdiction and inadmissible. In its third preliminary objection, Serbia argued that claims referring to the trial of certain persons within Serbia's jurisdiction, the provision of regarding the whereabouts of missing Croatian citizens, and the return of cultural property were outside of the Court's jurisdiction and inadmissible.

outside the scope of the Genocide Convention, and therefore outside the Court's jurisdiction. The Court not only declined to rule on this issue at the preliminary objections stage, but it also avoided the issue at the merits stage.

Serbia based its challenge to the Court's temporal jurisdiction on a declaration by the FRY on 27 April 1992. In its declaration, the FRY proclaimed its status as the continuator of the Socialist Federal Republic of Yugoslavia (SFRY) and declared that it would fulfill all of the international legal obligations assumed by the SFRY.[9] In its judgment on preliminary objections, the Court determined that this declaration served as a notification of the FRY's succession to treaties to which the SFRY was a party, including the Genocide Convention.[10] However, the Court's 2008 judgment went no further than this. The Court decided that it would "need to have more elements before it" in order to determine whether the Genocide Convention applied to the FRY before 27 April 1992, and what the consequences would be for the FRY under the rules of state responsibility.[11] The Court therefore reserved Serbia's second preliminary objection for the merits because it did not possess "an exclusively preliminary character".[12]

At the merits stage, the Court emphasized that the Genocide Convention's compromissory clause, contained in Article IX, provided the only basis for jurisdiction in this case.[13] In the Court's determination, this had two consequences.[14] First, the dispute had to concern the interpretation, application or fulfillment of the Genocide Convention, as required by Article IX.[15] Second, the dispute had to concern obligations under the Convention itself, rather than obligations under customary international law on genocide.[16] The Court noted that the dispute "would appear to fall squarely within the terms of Article IX" because the dispute's "essential subject-matter" is whether Serbia is responsible for violations of the Con-

---

9 2015 Judgment para 76.

10 2008 Judgment para 111.

11 2008 Judgment para 129.

12 2008 Judgment para 146, point 4.

13 2015 Judgment para 84. Article IX of the Genocide Convention provides that: 'Disputes between the Contracting Parties relating to the interpretation, application or fulfillment of the present Convention, including those relating to the responsibility of a State for genocide or for any of the other acts enumerated in article III, shall be submitted to the International Court of Justice at the request of any of the parties to the dispute.'

14 2015 Judgment para 85.

15 *Ibid.*, paras 85, 89.

16 *Ibid.*, paras 87–89.

vention.[17] But it also determined that the compromissory clause does not serve as "a general provision for the settlement of disputes" with no temporal limitation.[18] The Court found that the temporal scope of Article IX is linked to the temporal scope of the Convention's provisions, which do not apply retroactively to acts that occurred before a State became bound by the Convention.[19]

The Court then addressed Croatia's claims that acts or omissions that occurred before 27 April 1992 may still fall within the scope of Article IX. Croatia based this argument on Article 10(2) of the International Law Commission's Articles on State Responsibility, which concerns the attribution of the conduct of a movement that succeeds in establishing a new State.[20] Article 10(2) provides that "[t]he conduct of a movement, insurrectional or other, which succeeds in establishing a new State in part of the territory of a pre-existing State or in a territory under its administration shall be considered an act of the new State under international law". According to Croatia, the "Greater Serbia" movement, which took control of the Yugoslav's People's Army (JNA) and the SFRY, eventually succeeded in creating the FRY, which bears State responsibility for acts or omissions attributable to the movement.[21] The Court, however, rejected Croatia's argument due to its finding that Article 10(2) concerns only the attribution of conduct, not the creation of obligations binding on the movement or the new State.[22] Conduct attributable to the "Greater Serbia" movement could have only involved violations of the customary international law prohibition on genocide, and not the Genocide Convention, to which the movement was not a party.[23] On account of this conclusion, the Court did not address the question of whether Article 10(2) formed part of customary international law in 1991–1992 or thereafter.[24]

The Court then turned to Croatia's alternative argument that the FRY succeeded to the responsibility of the SFRY for acts or omissions prior to 27 April 1992 that were attributable to the SFRY and in breach of the SFRY's obligations under the Genocide Convention.[25] At this point, the

17 *Ibid.*, para 90.
18 *Ibid.*, para 93.
19 *Ibid.*, paras 93, 100.
20 *Ibid.*, paras 102–105.
21 *Ibid.*, para 102.
22 *Ibid.*, para 104.
23 *Ibid.*, para 105.
24 *Ibid.*, para 105.
25 *Ibid.*, para 106.

Court explained that it was in possession of the "additional elements" needed to distinguish between issues of jurisdiction and the merits, and to make findings on these issues.[26] These additional elements were missing during the preliminary objections phase in 2008, but after further written pleadings and oral arguments on the merits, the Court was apparently satisfied with the "elements" before it, though it did not elaborate.[27]

The Court decided that the jurisdictional question must be confined to whether the dispute between the Parties falls within Article IX of the Genocide Convention, which covers disputes about the treaty's interpretation, application, and fulfillment. The Court boiled down this dispute to three contested points:

(1) whether the acts relied on by Croatia took place; and if they did, whether they were contrary to the Convention;
(2) if so, whether those acts were attributable to the SFRY at the same time that they occurred and engaged its responsibility; and
(3) if the responsibility of the SFRY had been engaged, whether the FRY succeeded to that responsibility.[28]

The Court then determined that these three issues fall "squarely" within the Court's jurisdiction *ratione materiae* under Article IX, as they involve matters of breach, attribution, and the responsibility of the SFRY.[29] The Court further explained that the third issue, concerning succession to responsibility, raises serious questions of law and fact that form part of the merits of the dispute and require a decision only after the first two issues concerning breach and attribution have been decided.[30] Moreover, the Court determined that this dispute concerning succession to responsibility falls within the scope of Article IX even though it is governed not by the Convention's provisions, but by rules of general international law, like the rules on treaty interpretation and State responsibility.[31] Because the Convention itself does not specify when State responsibility arises, the Court decided that it must look to general international law in order to resolve this issue.

---

26 *Ibid.*, para 110.
27 *Ibid.*, para 110; see also Separate Opinion of President Tomka, paras 3–4.
28 2015 Judgment para 112.
29 *Ibid.*, para 113.
30 *Ibid.*, para 114.
31 *Ibid.*, para 115.

Finally, the Court rejected Serbia's contention that the *Monetary Gold* principle applied in this case. As the Court explained it, this principle means that the Court cannot adjudicate where doing so would be "contrary to the right of a State not party to the proceedings to not have the Court rule upon its conduct without its consent".[32] The Court dismissed the relevance of this principle because the SFRY no longer exists, and therefore no longer has any rights or the capacity to give or withhold consent to the Court's jurisdiction.[33] Furthermore, the Court considered that ruling on the "legal situation" of the other successor States to the SFRY was not a "prerequisite" in order to determine the present claim.[34]

The Court concluded its finding that it had jurisdiction over acts that occurred before 27 April 1992 by noting that questions about breach, attribution and succession to responsibility are all matters for the merits.[35] Six of the seventeen judges on the bench dissented from the Court's ruling that it had jurisdiction to entertain Croatia's claims concerning conduct that occurred prior to 27 April 1992, and their separate and dissenting opinions and declaration on this issue suggest that it was a matter of considerable controversy during deliberations.[36] On the merits of the dispute, the Court held that while Croatia and Serbia had both established the requisite *actus reus* for genocide, in support of their claim and counterclaim, respectively, they had not proven the requisite *mens rea*. The Court therefore rejected Croatia's claim and Serbia's counterclaim, and never reached the final issue in contention—succession to responsibility.

3. *A Critique of the Court's Treatment of the Issue of Succession to Responsibility*

The Court's approach to the issue of succession to responsibility may be questioned on at least two grounds.[37] First, the manner in which the Court ordered the issues in contention between the parties allowed it to shift a

32 *Ibid.*, para 116.
33 *Ibid.*, para 116.
34 *Ibid.*, para 116.
35 *Ibid.*, para 117.
36 President Tomka; Judges Owada, Skotnikov, Xue, Sebutinde; Judge *ad hoc* Kreca.
37 For a broader discussion of other jurisdictional and procedural aspects of this case, see Bordin, F.L. (2015), "Procedural Developments at the International Court of Justice", *The Law and Practice of International Courts and Tribunals* 14(2), 340.

preliminary, jurisdictional issue to the end of its inquiry, and ultimately beyond the scope of the judgment. Second, the *Monetary Gold* principle may have had more relevance in this case than the Court allowed.

a. The Court's Sequencing of the Issues in Contention

Reordering the issues in contention is, in fact, a judicial technique that the Court has employed on numerous occasions to achieve various ends. By altering the sequence in which it considers the issues before it, the Court can ensure that it avoids undesirable issues, or that it reaches issues that would not otherwise come under consideration. The *Oil Platforms* case is an apt illustration of the latter possibility.[38]

The dispute in *Oil Platforms* concerned Article X, paragraph 1 of the 1955 Treaty of Amity, Economic Relations and Consular Rights between the United States and Iran, which provides that "[b]etween the territories of the two High Contracting Parties there shall be freedom of commerce and navigation"[39]. Iran alleged that the United States had breached this provision by attacking and destroying Iranian oil platforms in 1987 and 1988. The United States, however, claimed that these were justified acts of self-defence in response to armed attacks by Iran.[40] The basis for this argument by the United States was paragraph 1(d) of Article XX, which could be characterized as an exception to Article X, paragraph 1. Article XX, paragraph 1(d) provides that "[t]he present Treaty shall not preclude the application of measures… necessary to fulfill the obligations of a High Contracting Party for the maintenance or restoration of international peace and security, or necessary to protect its essential security interests".

Ordinarily, the Court might be expected to determine the existence of a breach before examining whether the breach may be justified on grounds of self-defence.[41] In this case, however, the Court decided that "particular considerations" militated in favour of examining the issue of self-defence

38 *Oil Platforms (Islamic Republic of Iran v United States of America)*, Judgment, ICJ Reports 2003, 161.

39 *Ibid.*, para 31.

40 *Ibid.*, para 37.

41 See, e.g., the Court's treatment of substantially identical provisions in the 1956 Treaty of Friendship, Commerce and Navigation between the United States and Nicaragua. *Military and Paramilitary Activities in and against Nicaragua (Nicaragua v. United States of America), ICJ Reports 1986*, 117, para 225.

before examining the issue of breach.[42] The Court took into consideration the fact that the original dispute between the parties related not to the 1955 Treaty of Amity, but to the legality of the use of force by the United States.[43] The Court further emphasized that the issues of self-defence presented in this case "raise matters of the highest importance to all members of the international community" and had important implications for the field concerning the use of force.[44] Perhaps in light of the fact that the March 2003 US invasion of Iraq took place just days after the oral proceedings in this case ended and its deliberations began, the Court appears to have attached special importance to addressing issues relating to the use of force—even if doing so required it to consider the parties' claims out of their logical sequence.[45]

The Court ultimately determined that it could uphold neither the claims made by the United States on grounds of self-defence, nor Iran's assertions that those actions breached the obligation of freedom of commerce under the 1955 Treaty.[46] Had the Court dealt with the issue of breach first, then there would have been no need for it to proceed to the question of whether the actions of the United States could be justified. As a matter of judicial economy, this ordering of the issues would have been more efficient. But the Court noted that it has freedom to select the ground on which it will base its judgment.[47] In this case, the Court opted to base its judgment on two grounds, seemingly for the sake of ensuring that it reached issues of use of force, due to their importance in the particular case, and also at this moment in history. The Court's unusual approach prompted a third of the bench to discuss their concerns about the Court's ordering of the issues in separate opinions, and it also gave rise to scholarly criticism.[48]

42 *Oil Platforms, supra* note 38, para 37.
43 *Ibid.*
44 *Ibid.*, para 38.
45 See, e.g., Separate Opinion of Judge Simma, para 6.
46 *Oil Platforms, supra* note 38, para 125(1).
47 *Ibid.*, para 37, quoting *Application of the Convention of 1902 Governing the Guardianship of Infants*, Judgment, ICJ Reports 1958, 62.
48 Separate opinions of Judges Buergenthal, Higgins, Kooimans, Owada, and Parra-Aranguren; see also Small, D.H. (2004), "The *Oil Platforms* Case: Jurisdiction Through the – Closed – Eye of the Needle", *The Law and Practice of International Courts and Tribunals* 3(1), 113; Taft, W.H., IV (2004), "Self Defense and the *Oil Platforms* Decision", *Yale Journal of International Law* 29(2), 295; but see Separation Opinion of Judge Simma.

In *Croatia v Serbia*, the same judicial technique allowed the Court not only to reach the parties' substantive claims about the commission of genocide, but also to avoid the issue of temporal jurisdiction. The Court ordered the issues in contention so that the first two issues requiring examination were breach and attribution, while the question of state succession to responsibility followed in third place. The Court's sequencing is both surprising and counter-intuitive. The issue of state succession to responsibility amounts to a question concerning the Court's temporal jurisdiction. The question whether Serbia could succeed to the responsibility of the FRY for acts that occurred pre-April 1992 had direct bearing on the scope of the Court's temporal jurisdiction over Serbia. The extent of the Court's temporal jurisdiction was especially important in this case because the bulk of the acts alleged by Croatia took place before 27 April 1992.

The Court's sequencing is surprising because the Court had previously treated the issue of state succession to responsibility as a jurisdictional question, albeit a jurisdictional question that did not possess an exclusively preliminary character. The Court's 2008 judgment implied that this question was appropriate for consideration at the merits stage because it was closely linked with the merits of the case and the Court required more information in order to rule on the issue. Having apparently acquired additional information at the merits stage, one would still expect to see the Court take up this question as a threshold issue, before examining breach and attribution. Questions concerning the Court's temporal jurisdiction should logically be considered prior to questions of breach and attribution, as the Court cannot otherwise be assured that it has jurisdictional competence to determine whether an internationally wrongful act has occurred. The Court's sequencing is also counter-intuitive because jurisdictional issues are always threshold issues, even when they do not have an exclusively preliminary character and thus require additional information linked to the merits.

The Court justified its sequencing with some questionable, and also quite limited, legal reasoning. In essence, the Court excised the issue of state succession to responsibility from the jurisdictional questions before it, and merged the issue with the merits. In the Court's view, the jurisdictional question before it at the merits stage was confined to whether the issues in contention concerned the interpretation, application or fulfillment of the Genocide Convention, as required by Article IX. The sole jurisdictional question before the Court was therefore limited to its subject matter jurisdiction, or jurisdiction *ratione materiae*. By identifying succession to responsibility as an issue falling within the scope of its subject matter jurisdiction, along with breach and attribution, the Court re-characterized it as a question for the merits. Along the way, the Court dropped the term jurisdiction *ratione temporis*, and instead referred to this issue as one concerning state succession to responsibility.

The Court's jurisdictional maneuver ensured that it never reached the issue of state succession to responsibility, as its inquiry began and ended with an examination of the first issue in contention—whether the two states breached the Genocide Convention. After determining that the *mens rea* necessary for breach had not been proven by either party, there was no need for the Court to proceed to the second and third issues in contention. The judgment therefore leaves open the possibility that its rulings on incidents that took place prior to April 1992 may have actually exceeded its temporal jurisdiction. Given the lack of certainty among the judges of the Court and in academic circles about the existence of a rule on state succession to responsibility, this is a very real possibility.[49] Without delving into this legal debate, this chapter proceeds under the assumption that the existence of such a rule is uncertain.

The ramifications of the Court's approach would have become clearer had the Court actually attributed wrongful conduct to the SFRY, but then determined that Serbia could not be held responsible for the wrongful acts of the SFRY on account of the absence of a rule of state succession to responsibility. In these circumstances, the Court's ruling on the responsibility of a third party not before the Court—the SRFY—might have had direct consequences for all of the successor states of the SFRY.[50] This brings us to the second part of this critique, concerning the *Monetary Gold* principle, which the Court dismissed partly on account of the fact that the SFRY no longer exists.

b. *The Court's Treatment of the* Monetary Gold *Principle*

While the *Monetary Gold* principle may not have applied to the circumstances of this case, this was not on account of the SFRY's disappearance. Given the existence of five successor States to the SFRY, all of which may potentially be allocated responsibility for claims against the SFRY, the SFRY has not actually disappeared for legal purposes. In the *Monetary Gold*

49 Separate Opinion of Judge Skotnikov, para 4; Paddeu, F. (2015), "Ghosts of Genocides Past? State Responsibility for Genocide in the Former Yugoslavia", *Cambridge Law Journal* 74(2), 198, 200–201.

50 Separate Opinion of President Tomka, para 32.

case the Court held that adjudicating on the international responsibility of a third party "without her consent would run counter to a well-established principle of international law embodied in the Court's Statute, namely, that the Court can only exercise jurisdiction over a State with its consent"[51]. In this case, the legal interests of the third party, Albania, would not only have been affected by the Court's decision, but would have been "the very subject-matter of the decision"[52]. Since the *Monetary Gold* case, the Court has applied this principle in a rather case-by-case, nuanced manner.[53]

In *Croatia v Serbia*, the Court determined that the *Monetary Gold* principle was inapplicable in part because the SFRY no longer exists, and therefore does not have any rights, and cannot consent to the Court's jurisdiction. Undoubtedly, a state that no longer exists cannot consent to jurisdiction. But the rights and obligations of a former state do not necessarily disappear when the state ceases to exist.[54] To the extent that former states have outstanding assets and liabilities, archives, and former employees with pensions, for example, former states can and do live on from a legal perspective. Most significantly, for the purposes of the dispute between Croatia and Serbia, former states can have outstanding obligations—a fact that went unmentioned in the Court's judgment. An obligation to make reparations could, for example, arise out of a determination that the SFRY committed internationally wrongful acts prior to April 1992. Had the Court held the SFRY responsible for acts of genocide, then such a ruling potentially could have implicated all successor states. In particular, the successor states might have been implicated had a ruling by the Court on the SFRY's responsibility been coupled with a ruling that Serbia did not succeed to the SFRY's responsibility.

---

51 *Monetary Gold Removed from Rome in 1943, Preliminary Question,* Judgment, ICJ Reports 1954, 19, 22.

52 *Ibid.*

53 See, e.g., *Certain Phosphate Lands in Nauru (Nauru v. Australia), Preliminary Objections*, Judgment, ICJ Reports 1992, 240; *East Timor (Portugal v. Australia)*, Judgment, ICJ Reports 1995, p. 90; Thienel, T. (2014), "Third States and the Jurisdiction of the International Court of Justice: The *Monetary Gold* Principle", *German Yearbook of International Law* 57, 321; Orakhelashvili, A (2011), "The Competence of the International Court of Justice and the Doctrine of the Indispensable Party: from *Monetary Gold* to *East Timor* and Beyond", *Journal of International Dispute Settlement* 2(2), 373.

54 Declaration of Judge Xue, paras 24–25.

Moreover, the existing succession agreement between the five successor states to the SFRY likely would not cover such legal obligations. In 2001, the successor states (Bosnia and Herzegovina, Croatia, Macedonia, Slovenia, and the FRY) concluded an Agreement on Succession Issues. While this agreement covers a range of issues, including financial assets and liabilities, an obligation to provide compensation or some other form of reparation for acts of genocide committed by the SFRY would likely fall outside of the scope of the Agreement. The Agreement, however, provides that claims against the SFRY, which are not otherwise covered, shall be considered by a Standing Joint Committee established in accordance with the Agreement.[55] The practical consequences of a finding of responsibility against the SFRY would therefore be quite uncertain. While a claim against the SFRY would be a claim against all successor states, the Standing Joint Committee would, of course, have to grapple with the complicating fact that both parties are themselves successor states (Croatia and Serbia, respectively).

If the Court had attributed wrongful conduct to the SFRY, then the rights and obligations of all of the successor States would potentially have been impacted by the Court's ruling. But whether such a ruling would have actually conflicted with the *Monetary Gold* principle, thereby rendering the claims inadmissible, is debatable in light of the Court's varied jurisprudence concerning this rule. While the attribution of responsibility to the SFRY would have had implications for the legal situation of the successor states, the rights and obligations of all five successor states would not necessarily have been the "very subject matter" of the Court's ruling.[56] In other words, a ruling by the Court on the SFRY's responsibility would not have been based on a determination regarding the legal situation of the five successor states, though it might have had implications for them. The Court thus upheld a distinction between rulings that are based on determinations regarding the legal situations of third parties, and rulings that merely have implications for the legal situation of third parties. One may question, however, whether such a distinction is really sustainable in cases involving succession from a federal entity. The SFRY lives on, from a legal perspective, in the form of its five successor states, such that rulings about reparations owed by the SFRY arguably amount to rulings about reparations owed by its successor states. Regardless, the point to be emphasized

55 Agreement on Succession Issues, Annex F, art 2.

56 Such a ruling would have arguably been in keeping with *Certain Phosphate Lands in Nauru*, para 55.

here is that the *Monetary Gold* principle did not lose its relevance simply because the SFRY no longer exists. The applicability of the *Monetary Gold* principle is indeed debatable in this instance, but not on account of the SFRY's non-existence. Both the brevity and the substance of the Court's reasoning on this issue may be taken as another example of its willingness to skirt jurisdictional issues, and in particular succession to responsibility, in this judgment. Moreover, had the Court considered the issue of succession to responsibility, and found that such a rule exists, then its discussion of the *Monetary Gold* principle might have been more nuanced.

4. *The Court as Fact-Finder*

If the Court had addressed the issue of state succession to responsibility in the section on jurisdiction and admissibility, before reaching the merits of the case, its judgment might have come to an early end. To the disappointment of many, sixteen years of litigation, concerning events of great importance for the states concerned, might have ended with a finding by the Court that it lacked temporal jurisdiction over most of the alleged acts of genocide. In deciding to order the issues as it did, the Court, of course, knew what its rulings would be on the three issues in contention. The judges would have already determined that the parties had failed to prove the requisite *mens rea* for genocide, thus foreclosing the need for it to proceed further, to the issue of state succession to responsibility. By examining the issue of breach first rather than second (after the issue of temporal jurisdiction), the Court greatly extended the length of the judgment, and delved into the merits of the case. The Court's jurisdictional maneuver effectively allowed it to reach the substance of the parties' claims about the commission of genocide.[57]

From the perspective of the Court's role as a dispute settlement body, its approach to the case demonstrates that in certain circumstances, its insistence on the need for consent may waver. The thoroughness or coherency of its findings on jurisdiction may bear some connection to the significance of the parties' substantive claims. The Court's various and inconsistent rulings on jurisdiction in another case involving allegations of acts of

---

57 See also Van den Herik, L. (2015), "Introductory Note to *Application of the Convention on the Prevention and Punishment of the Crime of Genocide (Croatia v Serbia)* (ICJ)", *International Legal Materials* 54(5), 787, 789.

genocide—the *Bosnia Genocide* case—have also raised eyebrows.[58] In *Croatia v Serbia*, the Court's willingness to sidestep a potentially significant jurisdictional obstacle allowed it to examine the parties' factual allegations, which it did in relatively great depth, over the course of approximately 70 pages.

The judgment's main contribution to the settlement of the dispute between the parties therefore consists primarily in establishing an authoritative record of what occurred during the conflict between Croatia and Serbia. The Court methodically considered, region by region, whether specific acts met the *actus reus* for genocide under Article II of the Genocide Convention, before determining that the requisite genocidal intent (*dolus specialis*) was missing. As a document that primarily serves as a record of the atrocities that took place in the early to mid-1990s in Croatia and in the Republic of Serbian Krajina, the judgment arguably resembles the reports of commissions or panels of inquiry. This is not to say that the Court merely establishes a factual record without providing legal rulings. Indeed, the Court does make legal assessments (as do many commissions of inquiry, for that matter). But the judgment's primary contribution is arguably factual rather than legal in part because the Court had already worked through many of the relevant legal issues in the 2007 *Bosnia Genocide* judgment. The Court's judgment in *Croatia v Serbia* does not significantly advance our understanding of the legal aspects of state responsibility for genocide beyond the *Bosnia Genocide* case. It does, however, provide an authoritative account of certain aspects of the conflict in Croatia and the Republic of Serbian Krajina, by drawing together witness statements, findings of the International Criminal Tribunal for the former Yugoslavia, etc. But the Court's apparent willingness in this case to engage with a relatively vast and complex evidentiary record should be distinguished from the manner in which the Court went about assessing the evidence, which has been the subject of some criticism (and which lies beyond the scope of this chapter).[59]

---

58 Separate Opinion of Judge Skotnikov, paras 8–9; Bordin, F.L. (2011), "Continuation of Membership in the United Nations Revisited: Lessons from Fifteen Years of Inconsistency in the Jurisprudence of the ICJ", *The Law and Practice of International Courts and Tribunals* 10(2), 315.

59 Gattini, A. and Cortesi, G. (2015), "Some New Evidence on the ICJ's Treatment of Evidence: The Second Genocide Case", *Leiden Journal of International Law* 28(4), 899.

In light of the Court's prior judgment in the *Bosnia Genocide* case, the parties in *Croatia v Serbia* must have suspected that their claims would fall short of what the Court requires for a showing of genocidal intent. The Court set a high bar for proving *mens rea* in the *Bosnia Genocide* case, and Croatia and Serbia could not have reasonably expected the Court to depart from this jurisprudence. Given that the parties could have foreseen the Court's rulings on the issue of breach, one might have expected the parties to discontinue their litigation after the Court's 2007 *Bosnia Genocide* judgment, by agreeing to an out-of-court settlement.[60] Perhaps an authoritative account of the atrocities committed during the conflict was, in good part, what the parties sought through litigation at the ICJ.

The argument here is not that the Court refashioned itself as a commission of inquiry. This would be an unsustainable position in part because commissions of inquiry generally refrain from making rulings on state responsibility. Instead, this chapter pursues the possibility that the judgment's most significant contribution to dispute settlement was factual rather than legal, in much the same way that commissions of inquiry contribute to dispute settlement by providing an authoritative account of disputed facts.

5. *Conclusion*

The case of *Croatia v Serbia* fits somewhat uneasily with the conception of the ICJ as an institution that is highly deferential to state sovereignty and whose activities are justified by state consent. In this case, a plausible, if not strong argument could be made that the Court lacked temporal jurisdiction over many of the claims made by Croatia. The Court, however, employed a jurisdictional maneuver that allowed it to bypass this jurisdictional obstacle and to reach some aspects of the merits of the parties' claims. In doing so, the Court displayed a weaker attachment to the importance of consent than one might expect, and its judgment took on a distinctly fact-heavy character, not unlike reports of commissions of inquiry.

---

60 For one explanation of why the parties failed to agree to an out-of-court settlement, see Simons, M. (2015), "Croatia and Serbia Cleared of Genocide by Hague Court", *The New York Times*, 3 February ("Serbia has long been trying to work on an out-of-court settlement rather than continue the costly legal proceedings. Some political leaders in Croatia have said privately they agreed, but they could not be seen dropping the genocide case for fear of ridicule as weaklings and traitors by the opposition").

All of this suggests that the standard account of international courts as dispute settlers may benefit from greater nuance. In issuing an authoritative account of the events in dispute, the Court may have also signaled an awareness of the import of the allegations made by the parties. However, the Court also displayed an awareness of the fact that it might have been untenable, from a public relations perspective, to decline to rule at such a late stage on the bulk of Croatia's allegations due to a lack of jurisdiction. In this case, the Court appears to have ruled in the name of the states whose governments could not manage to settle this case throughout many years of litigation, and also in the name of their newspaper-reading citizens, for whom a decision not to rule on the merits would have been difficult, if not impossible to explain.

The Public Authority of the International Tribunal for the Law of the Sea

*Lan Ngoc Nguyen**

I. Introdruction

The 1982 United Nations Convention on the Law of the Sea ("UNCLOS" or "the Convention") establishes a system for dispute settlement which constitutes an integral part of the Convention.[1] As part of this system, States decided to establish a new, permanent tribunal specializing in law of the sea disputes, called the International Tribunal for the Law of the Sea ("ITLOS" or "the Tribunal"). The reason behind the creation of this new tribunal, alongside the International Court of Justice (ICJ) which had been the main forum for law of the sea disputes until then, was the high level of dissatisfaction on the part of many developing States with the ICJ following some of its controversial judgments.[2] In other words, ITLOS came about as a demonstration of developing countries' rejection of the ICJ's authority. ITLOS was expected to be less conservative than the ICJ, more representative of various legal systems and the different regions of the world, as well as more accessible to non-State actors.[3] As such, ITLOS was a timely response to the transformation of international society through globalization.[4] The rationale behind the establishment of ITLOS and the fact that it is a permanent and specialized tribunal thus suggest that the Tribunal would become the judicial authority in the field of the law of the sea.

---

* Assistant Professor of Public International Law, Faculty of Law, Economics and Governance, Utrecht University.

1 United Nations Convention on the Law of the Sea, Dec. 10, 1982, 1833 UNTS 396.

2 See, e.g., *South West Africa (Ethiopia and Liberia v. South Africa)*, Second Phase, Judgment, ICJ Reports 1966, 6.

3 See, e.g., the statements of El Salvador, Cyprus, Peru, Zaire, Tunisia, Fiji in the Plenary during the fourth session (1976). Virginia Commentary, Volume V, 42.

4 Caminos, H. (2009), "The Creation of the International Tribunal for the Law of the Sea as a Specialized Court" In: A. Constantinides and N. Zaikos (eds), *The Diversity of International Law: Essays in Honour of Professor Kalliopi K. Koufa.* Leiden/Boston: Martinus Nijhoff, 97–108.

However, after ITLOS was established, it immediately met with considerable scepticism, notably regarding the redundancy and contribution to the problem of international law.[5] While these criticisms were certainly not endorsed by all,[6] they signalled that from the very beginning, not only the existence of ITLOS but also its potential to exert any authority was cast into doubt. Moreover, after more than twenty years existence, the fact that ITLOS docket comprises only 24 cases and two advisory opinion requests has spurred criticism that ITLOS is heavily underutilized. In fact, ITLOS is constantly in competition with the ICJ and *ad hoc* arbitral tribunals for cases. Despite being the specialized court for the law of the sea, many States still refer their cases to the latter two. This could partly be explained by the fact that Annex VII arbitration, not ITLOS, is the default forum under UNCLOS.[7] However, as the new standing court for the law of the sea, ITLOS's lack of activity may be an indication of a sense of mistrust on the part of the State parties of the Tribunal's competence and calls into question the Tribunal's authority in resolving disputes and developing the law of the sea in general.

Against this background, this paper seeks to examine ITLOS' exercise of public authority in the field of the law of the sea, by exploring whether ITLOS has been able to exercise public authority and if so, in what ways. In order to do so, the paper will use the conceptual framework developed by von Bogdandy and Venzke in their book *In Whose Name? A Public Law Theory of International Adjudication*. The departure point for analysis is the conception of public authority described by the authors as "the capacity, based on legal acts, to impact other actors in their exercise of freedom, be it legally or simply de facto"[8]. In particular, von Bogdandy and Venzke contend that there are two ways in which international courts and tribunals

5 See, e.g., Oda, S. (1995), "Dispute settlement prospects in the Law of the Sea", *International and Comparative Law Quarterly* 44(4), 863–872.

6 See, e.g., Treves, T. (2000), "New Trends in the Settlement of Disputes and the Law of the Sea Convention" In: H.N. Scheiber (ed.), *Law of the Sea: The Common Heritage and Emerging Challenges*. The Hague/Boston: Kluwer, 61–86; Charney, J. (1998), "Is international law threatened by multiple international tribunals?", *Collected Courses of the Hague Academy of International Law* 271, available at https://referenceworks.brillonline.com/entries/the-hague-academy-collected-courses/*A9789041112101_03, accessed 27 December 2017.

7 Annex VII arbitration is deemed to have been accepted either when States have not declared their preferred choice or forum (Article 287(3)) or when they have not accepted the same forum (Article 287(5)).

8 Von Bogdandy, A. and Venzke, I. (2014), *In Whose Name? A Public Law Theory of International Adjudication*. Oxford: Oxford University Press.

exercise public authority: one in the decision vis-à-vis the state at the losing end of a case[9] and two, in the ability to establish interpretation as points of reference for the legal discourse beyond legal bindingness in a single case. The latter is determined by looking at the power of precedents, specifically the legitimizing effect of precedents. As von Bogdandy and Venzke further argue, the exercise of public authority by international courts and tribunals transpires through judicial law-making, but in that process, "courts depend on a suitable case being brought to them"[10]. Accordingly, based on the analysis of the cases that have been decided by ITLOS to date, this paper will examine the two abovementioned elements of public authority in the particular context of ITLOS in order to understand whether and to what extent they manifest themselves in the Tribunal's operation. As space does not allow for a detailed examination of each and every case, the paper will proceed to analyse ITLOS' decisions according to the types of proceeding which fall under the Tribunal's jurisdiction, namely prompt release proceedings, provisional measures, contentious cases and advisory opinions.

II. ITLOS' *Exercise Of Public Authority*

1. Prompt release proceedings

Coastal States have the right to arrest a vessel alleged to have violated their laws and regulations on the exploitation and conservation of living resources under Article 73(1) UNCLOS. However, after the flag State of the detained vessel has posted a reasonable bond or other security, the coastal State has the obligation to release the vessel and the crew under Article 73(2). Should the coastal State fail to do so, the flag State may initiate a prompt release proceedings pursuant to Article 292 UNCLOS. Prompt release proceedings thus essentially revolve around whether the bond that has been posted is "reasonable". The Convention, however, provides no guidance for the interpretation of "reasonable bond".

In *M/V Saiga*, the first case in which ITLOS assessed the reasonableness of a bond, it only stated in a general manner that "the criterion of reasonableness encompasses the amount, the nature and the form of the bond or financial security. The overall balance of the amount, form and nature of

9 *Ibid.*, 114.
10 *Ibid.*, 109.

bond or financial security must be reasonable."[11] Then in *Camouco*, ITLOS for the first time provided a list of factors relevant in an assessment of the reasonableness of bonds or other financial security,[12] which included the gravity of the alleged offences, the penalties imposed or imposable under the laws of the detaining State, the value of the detained vessel and of the cargo seized, the amount of the bond imposed by the detaining State and its form.[13] The list of factors relevant for the determination of reasonable bond in *Camouco* was later adopted in *Monte Confurco*.[14] In determining the reasonable bond, it is evident that ITLOS was only occupied with the gravity of the offence committed by the vessel, by reference to the penalties imposed or imposable under the law of the detaining State.[15] It was not until the *Hoshinmaru* case that ITLOS took note of conservation concerns in the wider context of widespread illegal fishing in order to properly assess the gravity of the offence.

In conclusion, even though the term "reasonable bond" was deliberately left open by UNCLOS drafters, the consolidated factors emerging from ITLOS prompt release judgments have filled this void and provided some guidance as to how reasonableness is to be determined. ITLOS progressed from setting out general criteria in the first case to elaborating on more specific criteria for determining the reasonableness of the bond, while endeavouring to balance predictability and flexibility in its assessment of reasonableness.[16] As a consequence, ITLOS provided much-needed clarity to the term reasonable bond – a key term in prompt release proceedings. The criteria that ITLOS developed to assess what constitutes "reasonable bond" are perhaps the most visible contribution that ITLOS has made to developing UNCLOS, thus providing important guidance to States in exercising their rights and obligations under the Convention.

It can also be seen that ITLOS strived to build on its own case law. Even when ITLOS gradually incorporated non-quantitative elements in the assessment of reasonable bond, it still endeavoured to ground its analysis

11 *M/V Saiga* M/V "SAIGA" (*Saint Vincent and the Grenadines v. Guinea*) (Prompt Release, Judgment) ITLOS Reports 1997, 6 para. 82.

12 *Camouco (Panama v. France)* (Prompt Release, Judgment) ITLOS Reports 2000, para. 10.

13 *Ibid.*, para. 67.

14 *Monte Confurco (Seychelles v. France)* (Prompt Release, Judgment) ITLOS Reports 2000, para. 86.

15 *Ibid.*, para. 89.

16 Türk, H. (2012), "The Work of the International Tribunal for the Law of the Sea", *Ocean Yearbook Online* 26(1), 181–208.

on the list of factors drawn up in the first cases. In doing so, ITLOS has developed a coherent body of case law which becomes the reference point for prompt release proceedings under UNCLOS. It is interesting to note that since 2007, ITLOS has not received any requests for prompt release. This is a great contrast to the first ten years of its existence when the majority of cases in its docket were prompt release cases. It is not exactly certain why this is the case, but one can speculate that the consolidated criteria for determining the bond as established in ITLOS case law have provided useful guidance for both the coastal State and flag State to deal with prompt release cases out of court. This, in turn, confirms that ITLOS' authority transcends the courtroom, and in the context of prompt release procedures, ITLOS' judgments arguably have a legitimising impact on the behaviour of States.

2. *Provisional measures*

Similar to several other courts and tribunals, ITLOS has the power to order provisional measures under Article 290 UNCLOS. Admittedly, due to the nature of provisional measures proceedings, the extent to which ITLOS could engage in a detailed exposition of substantive legal issues is limited. However, it is argued that ITLOS' provisional measures cases still provide useful material to examine ITLOS' public authority vis-à-vis the parties to the case. This is due to the unique competence conferred upon ITLOS with regard to provisional measures. First, Article 290(5) allows the parties which initiated a case before an Annex VII arbitral tribunal to, pending the institution of the arbitral tribunal, request ITLOS to prescribe provisional measures. In other words, ITLOS has the competence to prescribe provisional measures in a case whose merits will be heard in another forum. This means that the measures it prescribes will be addressed to parties which have not accepted its jurisdiction in respect of the dispute.[17] The arbitral tribunal, in turn, has the power to revoke the provisional measures prescribed by ITLOS. Second, under Article 89(5) of the Rules of the Tribunal, ITLOS has power to prescribe provisional measures that differ from those requested by the parties. Taken together, this means that there is no guarantee that ITLOS' provisional measures will be accepted by States,

17 Mensah, T.A. (2002), "Provisional Measures in the International Tribunal for the Law of the Sea (ITLOS)", *Zeitschrift für ausländisches öffentliches Recht und Völkerrecht* 62, 43–54, 46.

unless the parties acknowledge the Tribunal's authority and act accordingly. The remainder of this part will thus be devoted to exploring whether ITLOS' provisional measures had any impact on the parties to the case.

ITLOS has to date issued six provisional measures orders, all with different natures from the restriction of fish catch in *Southern Bluefin Tuna*, the cooperation and consultation in *MOX Plant*, the establishment of expert groups in *Land Reclamation*, to the release of vessel and crew in *ARA Libertad* and *Arctic Sunrise*, and the suspension of domestic judicial proceedings in *Enrica Lexie*. In all but one of these orders, the parties complied with and gave effect to the measures prescribed by the Tribunal.

In fact, for four of them, namely *Southern Bluefin Tuna, MOX Plant, Land Reclamation* and *ARA Libertad*, ITLOS' provisional measure played a significant role in resolving the disputes, as the respective arbitral tribunals that were established did not, for various reasons, render an award in the merits phase in the end. For example, in *MOX Plant*, the fact that ITLOS' provisional measure was directed at both parties, instead of only at the Respondent as requested by the Applicant, proved instrumental in pushing the parties to reach a subsequent agreement on a wide range of measures, and improve bilateral co-operation on civil nuclear matters by the time the case was withdrawn by Ireland.[18] In *Land Reclamation*, ITLOS ordered the establishment of a group of independent experts with the mandate to conduct a study on the effects of Singapore's land reclamation and to propose measures to deal with any adverse effects of such land reclamation.[19] While this was not the measure that it requested, Malaysia still proceeded to set up a group of experts with Singapore as instructed. The parties were able to subsequently reach an agreement based on the work of the Group of Experts and did not proceed with arbitration.[20] The provisional measure ordered by ITLOS was thus key in the settlement of the dispute between the two parties.[21] Even when the provisional measure is subsequently revoked as in the case of *Southern Bluefin Tuna* because the Annex VII arbi-

18 Remarks by Ms Jill Barrett at Workshop "ITLOS At 20: Impacts of the International Tribunal for the Law of the Sea" (London, 23 May 2016), available at https://www.lcilp.org/wp-content/uploads/2017/06/ITLOS-at-20-Event-Report.pdf, accessed 27 December 2017.

19 *Land Reclamation in and around the Straits of Johor (Malaysia v. Singapore)* (Provisional Measures, Order of 8 October 2003) ITLOS Reports 2003, 10 para. 106.

20 *Case Concerning Land Reclamation by Singapore in and around the Straits of Johor (Malaysia v. Singapore)* Award on Agreed Terms, para. 19, available at http://www.pca-cpa.org/MASI%20Awardb1ca.pdf?fil_id=364.

21 *Ibid.*, para. 21.

tral tribunal found that it did not have jurisdiction to hear the case, both the arbitral tribunal and the parties were highly appreciative of ITLOS' provisional measures. Australia, for example, acknowledged that "the ITLOS Order already had played a significant role in encouraging the Parties to make progress on the issue of third-party fishing"[22].

The only provisional measure which was rejected by one of the parties is the *Arctic Sunrise* case. Russia refused to appear before ITLOS and also refused to comply with the request of ITLOS to immediately release the Arctic Sunrise and allow the non-Russian crew members to leave the country. What is noteworthy, however, is that despite the rhetoric of rejecting ITLOS' authority, Russia eventually implemented the measures prescribed by ITLOS. Even though the authorities released the vessel and the crew pursuant to domestic legislation and no mention was made to ITLOS' order,[23] the ultimate effect was the same.

In conclusion, the abovementioned provisional measures orders illustrate ITLOS' capacity to impact other actors, in this case, the parties to the case in their exercise of freedom. Even when the measures prescribed were not requested by either party or revoked, States were still willing to accept them and respect the authority of ITLOS. In this sense, as defined by Bogdandy and Venzke, ITLOS has managed to build its authority vis-à-vis the parties to the case. Some authors have criticized the fact that ITLOS' authority is only limited to provisional measures proceedings – and prompt release proceedings for that matter – making it more of a first instance court rather than a specialized body for law of the sea disputes.[24] Such critiques are to a certain extent true. However, that does not mean that within these types of proceedings, ITLOS does not exercise authority. ITLOS, when dealing with provisional measures proceedings, has proven that it can have a significant impact on the conduct of the parties, and thus exercises its public authority over these States.

---

22 *Southern Bluefin Tuna Case (Australia and New Zealand v. Japan),* Award on Jurisdiction and Admissibility (4 August 2000) 39 ILM 1359, para. 69.

23 "Russia Releases Greenpeace's Arctic Sunrise Ship", *The Moscow Times*, 6 June 2014, available at https://www.themoscowtimes.com/2014/06/06/russia-releases-greenpeaces-arctic-sunrise-ship-a36246?, accessed 27 December 2017.

24 Rah, S. and Wallrabenstein, T. (2006), "Sustainability Needs Judicial Support: What Does ITLOS Offer in This Respect" In: P. Ehlers and R. Lagoni (eds), *International Maritime Organisations and Their Contribution Towards a Sustainable Marine Development*. Hamburg: LIT Verlag, 285–315.

3. Contentious cases

ITLOS has only decided five contentious cases to date.[25] Quantitatively speaking, five cases in twenty years of its existence is rather low and the criticism usually heard during the Tribunal's early days regarding its redundancy may thus seem to have some merits. The low number of cases also suggests that the extent to which ITLOS could exercise public authority is limited. After all, if there is no precedent generated in the first place, how can one speak of the power or impact of precedents? However, assessing the extent of public authority based solely on the number of judgments rendered would arguably be mistaken. First, it should be noted that the compliance rate for the judgments rendered by ITLOS is relatively high. A recent study shows that an overwhelming majority of the decisions by UNCLOS dispute settlement bodies have been implemented by parties to the case, including those that are considered super powers at the losing end of the cases. It follows, therefore, ITLOS has authority of the States.[26] Second, in terms of authority in providing legal guidance, the important question to be asked is whether ITLOS has been able to provide authoritative interpretation in the limited number of cases that it has heard, and whether the Tribunal's decisions have become or have the potential to become points of reference for the legal discourse. In other words, the focus should be on the quality of the decision, particularly on whether ITLOS has made an impact beyond the cases decided and on whether the Tribunal's reasoning and decisions may "create legitimate expectations and must therefore be taken into account in future decisions"[27].

---

25 *M/V "SAIGA" (No. 2) (Saint Vincent and the Grenadines v. Guinea)*, Judgment, ITLOS Reports 1999, para. 10; *Delimitation of the maritime boundary in the Bay of Bengal (Bangladesh/Myanmar)*, Judgment, ITLOS Reports 2012, para. 4; *M/V "Virginia G" (Panama/Guinea-Bissau)*, Judgment, ITLOS Reports 2014, para. 4; *Dispute Concerning Delimitation of the Maritime Boundary between Ghana and Côte d'Ivoire in the Atlantic Ocean (Ghana/Côte d'Ivoire)*, Judgment, 23 September 2017; *M/V "Norstar" (Panama v. Italy)*, Judgment, 10 April 2019. The *M/V "Louisa"* case was also brought before ITLOS as a contentious case. However, the Tribunal found that it lacked jurisdiction and thus did not hear the merits of the case. See *M/V "Louisa" (Saint Vincent and the Grenadines v. Kingdom of Spain)*, Judgment, ITLOS Reports 2013, para. 4.

26 Duy Phan, H. (2019), "International Courts and State Compliance: An Investigation of the Law of the Sea Cases", *Ocean Development & International Law* 50(1), 70–90.

27 Van Bogdandy and Venzke, *supra* note 8, 116.

The role of international courts in the development of the law is "interstitial", meaning that the court "stands between the past and the future"[28]. Thus it is difficult, even impossible, to fully appreciate the impact of a court or tribunal's decision without the benefit of hindsight in light of later developments. In other words, a certain amount of time ought to elapse before any definitive conclusion could be drawn with respect to the impact of a judicial decision on the legal discourse or on States' behaviour.[29] For a relatively young tribunal such as ITLOS and given the relatively low number of cases, this may prove difficult. However, it is argued that an assessment of the impact of a judicial decision, albeit only preliminarily, could still be made based on the quality of the judicial decisions, in which due attention should be paid to the legal reasoning as much as the result. This paper thus agrees with the analysis on the important role that judicial reasoning plays in assessing the authority of international courts and tribunals, particularly in their judicial law-making role, as elaborated in Bogdandy and Venzke's book. The persuasiveness of the legal reasoning provides a useful, even if inconclusive, indicator of the potential impact of judicial decisions in the longer term. Accordingly, the remainder of this section will examine two cases in which ITLOS's judgments are considered to be of particular importance in developing the law of the sea. As explained, it will not only examine the decisions that ITLOS reached, but also the cogency of legal reasoning.

a. *Virginia G*

ITLOS in *Virginia G* engaged in a detailed examination of coastal States' regulatory and enforcement power in the exclusive economic zone (EEZ).[30] In this case, ITLOS was faced with the question of whether a coastal State may regulate the bunkering of fishing vessels in the EEZ

---

28 Venzke, I. (2011), "The Role of International Courts as Interpreters and Developers of the Law: Working out the Jurisgenerative Practice of Interpretation", *Loyola Los Angeles International and Comparative Law Journal* 34(1), 99–131,121.

29 Most of the assessment of the contributions of the PCIJ and the ICJ, for instance, is based on decades-old decisions, which allows the authors to track whether the Court's pronouncements have been accepted by States and other actors, and subsequently incorporated into formal sources of law. See Tams, C.J. and Sloan, J. (2013), *The Development of International law by the International Court of Justice*. Oxford: Oxford University Press.

30 *M/V "Virginia G" (Panama/Guinea-Bissau)*, Judgment, ITLOS Reports 2014, para. 4.

under its fisheries laws and regulations. This activity is not explicitly listed under Article 62(4) as one which the coastal State may regulate. Given the prevalence of offshore bunkering activities and their economic benefits,[31] a definitive answer to legal nature of the activity was highly needed. In *Virginia G*, ITLOS established a connection between Article 56(1) and 62(4) and further noted that the wording of Article 62(4) of the Convention, in particular, the use of "inter alia", indicated that this list is not exhaustive.[32] In order for an activity to fall under Article 62(4), ITLOS determined that there must be a direct connection to fishing. ITLOS then observed that such a connection to fishing existed for the bunkering of foreign vessels fishing in the EEZ, since this enables fishing vessels to continue their activities without interruption at sea.[33] For the above reasons, ITLOS concluded that coastal States may regulate the bunkering of foreign vessels fishing in its EEZ to conserve and manage its living resources under Article 56 of the Convention read together with Article 62(4) of the Convention. [34]

Turning to coastal States' enforcement power, in order for coastal States to ensure compliance with their laws and regulations on fisheries, Article 73(1) lists several measures permitting them to deal with foreign vessels illegally fishing in the EEZ, such as boarding, inspection, arrest and judicial proceedings. On the other hand, Article 73(3) prohibits imprisonment or any other form of corporal punishment as penalties for violations of fisheries laws and regulations. This leaves open the question as to whether a coastal State is allowed to take a measure which is not specified in Article 73(1) but also not prohibited under Article 73(3). Confiscation was one prominent example in ITLOS' cases, however, it was, again, only in *Virginia G* that the ITLOS was able to substantively deal with the legality or otherwise of this measure.[35]

---

31 See Lagoni, R. (2007), "Offshore bunkering in the Exclusive Economic Zone" In: T.M. Ndiaye and R. Wolfrum (eds), *Law of the Sea, Environmental Law and Settlement of Disputes: Liber amicorum Judge Thomas A. Mensah*. Leiden: Brill/Nijhoff, 613–627, 614; *M/V "SAIGA" (No. 2) (Saint Vincent and the Grenadines v. Guinea)*, Separate Opinion of Judge Anderson, para. 137; *M/V "Virginia G" (Panama/Guinea-Bissau)*, Dissenting Opinion of Judge Ndiaye, paras 258–270.

32 *Ibid.*, para. 213.

33 *Ibid.*, para. 215.

34 *Ibid.*, para. 217.

35 The issue of whether coastal State could legitimately confiscate foreign fishing vessels to ensure compliance with its fisheries law came up in three cases, namely in *Grand Prince*, *Tomimaru* and *Virginia G*. The first two were prompt release cases, thus ITLOS did not deal with the question in much detail.

ITLOS first established whether (i) the legislation promulgated by Guinea-Bissau for the EEZ was in conformity with the Convention and (ii) whether the measures taken in implementing this legislation were necessary to ensure the compliance with the law and regulations adopted by the Coastal State.[36] In answering the first question, ITLOS held that a law providing for the confiscation of a vessel offering bunkering services to foreign vessels fishing in the EEZ of Guinea-Bissau was not *per se* in violation of Article 73(1) of the Convention. Whether or not confiscation was justified in a given case depended on the facts and circumstances.[37] For the second question, ITLOS determined that "the breach of the obligation to obtain written authorization for bunkering and to pay the prescribed fee was a serious violation" but that it was the result of "a misinterpretation of the correspondence" between the fishing vessels and the authorities of Guinea-Bissau.[38] Therefore, ITLOS found that the confiscation of the vessel and the gas oil on board "was not necessary either to sanction the violation committed or to deter the vessels or their operators from repeating this violation"[39].

Virginia G was the first case in which ITLOS engaged in the interpretation of Article 73(1) which determines the scope of coastal States' enforcement power in the EEZ. What ITLOS managed to make clear was that confiscation is not a measure that is per inconsistent with Article 73, and that coastal States are permitted to take measures which are not explicitly mentioned in Article 73(1). However, the most crucial term in Article 73(1) was arguably "necessary" as this would determine whether the measure was consistent with UNCLOS. ITLOS, however, did not explain what was meant by "necessary"; instead, it only determined the gravity of the offence in question then compared it with the penalty imposed by the coastal State. Compared with how the term "necessary" has been interpreted by other international courts,[40] ITLOS' necessity test was overly simplistic and rather arbitrary as it lacked an objective, guiding principle concerning the

36 *Virginia G*, *supra* note 30, para. 256.
37 *Ibid.*, para. 257.
38 *Ibid.*, para. 269.
39 *Ibid.*
40 See, for example, WTO Appellate Body's necessity test under Article XX(b) GATT or Article XIV(a) GATS in Appellate Body Report, *Korea-Measures Affecting Imports of Fresh, Chilled and Frozen Beef*, WT/DS161,169/AB/R (Dec. 11, 2000); Appellate Body Report, *European Communities-Measures Affecting Asbestos and Asbestos-Containing Products*, WT/DS135/R (Mar. 12, 2001); Appellate Body Report, *United States – Measures Affecting Cross-Border Supply of Gambling and Betting Services* WT/DS285/AB/R (Apr. 7, 2005).

interpretation of the term "necessary". A case-specific answer, unaccompanied by sound reasoning and clear guidance would make it difficult for coastal States to grasp the exact extent of the enforcement power granted to them in conserving fisheries resources, thus restricting the broader impact of ITLOS' decision, and thus ITLOS' authority in this regard.

b. Bangladesh/Myanmar

Bangladesh/Myanmar was the first case in which an international tribunal proceeded to delimit the continental shelf beyond 200nm, also known as the outer continental shelf.[41] In doing so, the Tribunal was also the first to spell out the relationship between an international court and tribunal and the Commission on the Limits of the Continental Shelf (CLCS) – a technical body established under UNCLOS which deals with the establishment of the outer limits of the continental shelf. As the first international tribunal to venture into examining these important but hitherto unexplored issues, some scholars have predicted that "the ITLOS decision may prove to be influential in the context of future dispute resolution, whether through third party adjudication or not"[42]. The *Bangladesh/Myanmar* case therefore presents a unique opportunity to see whether ITLOS indeed managed to seize the opportunity and exert its public authority.[43]

41 *Delimitation of the maritime boundary in the Bay of Bengal (Bangladesh/Myanmar)*, Judgment, ITLOS Reports 2012, para. 4.

42 Lin, S. and Schofield, C. (2014), "Lessons from the Bay of Bengal ITLOS case: Stepping Offshore for a "Deeper" Maritime Political Geography", *The Geographical Journal* 180(3), 260–264, 263.

43 *Ghana/Cote d'Ivoire* essentially follows the approach of *Bangladesh/Myanmar*. Thus, for the sake of simplicity, only Bangladesh/Myanmar will be mentioned in the analysis.

While there had been some confusion relating to the use of the terms "delimitation" and "delineation",[44] ITLOS made clear in *Bangladesh/Myanmar* that delineation and delimitation are two distinct concepts,[45] and that delimitation would not depend on delineation.[46] On the basis of this distinction, ITLOS clarified the much debated relationship between the UNCLOS tribunals and the CLCS.[47] More specifically, ITLOS stated that, as a dispute settlement body, it has the legal expertise to interpret and apply the provisions of the Convention; while the CLCS deals with scientific and technical issues.[48] ITLOS noted that there was nothing in the Convention, the Rules of Procedure of the Commission or in its practice to indicate that delimitation of the continental shelf constituted an impediment to the performance by the Commission of its functions.[49] Similarly, the CLCS should exercise its technical function "without prejudice to questions of delimitation" as required under Article 76(10). ITLOS thus adopted the view that the absence of a CLCS recommendation relating to the limits of the continental shelf beyond 200 nm could not prevent it from determining the existence of entitlement to the continental shelf and delimiting the continental shelf between the parties concerned.

The clarification of the interrelated but independent relationship between the two institutions has a significant bearing on the temporal order in which delimitation and delineation are to be carried out. This approach stood in contrast with earlier decisions by other international

---

44 In the context of the outer continental shelf, "delimitation" refers to the establishment of a boundary that divides overlapping entitlements lying beyond 200 nm from the baselines of one or more States, whereas delineation refers to the establishment of the limits of the continental shelf. See, e.g., Macnab, R. (2004), "The Case for Transparency in the Delimitation of the Outer Continental Shelf in Accordance with UNCLOS Article 76", *Ocean Development and International Law* 35, 1–17; Rangel, V.M. (2006), "Settlement of Disputes Relating to the Delimitation of the Outer Continental Shelf: The Role of International Courts and Arbitral Tribunals", *The International Journal of Marine and Coastal Law* 21(3), 347–362.

45 *Bangladesh/Myanmar, supra* note 41, para. 376.

46 *Ibid.*, paras 397–399.

47 See Kunoy, B. (2012), "The Terms of Reference of the Commission on the Limits of the Continental Shelf: A Creeping Legal Mandate", *Leiden Journal of International Law* 25(1), 109–130; Oude Elferink, A.G. (2004), "The Continental Shelf beyond 200 Nautical Miles: The Relationship between the CLCS and Third Party Dispute Settlement" In: A.G. Oude Elferink and D. Rothwell (eds), *Oceans Management in the 21st Century: Institutional Frameworks and Responses*. Leiden: Martinus Nijhoff, 107–124, 118.

48 *Bangladesh/Myanmar, supra* note 41, para. 411.

49 *Ibid.*, para. 377.

courts and tribunals, such as *Canada/France* arbitration in 1992, in which the arbitral tribunal declined to recognize any rights of the parties over the outer continental shelf in the absence of a determination as to where their entitlements ended;[50] or *Nicaragua v. Honduras* in 2007, in which the ICJ held that "any claim of continental shelf rights beyond 200 miles must be in accordance with Article 76 of UNCLOS and reviewed by the Commission on the Limits of the Continental Shelf established thereunder"[51]. After ITLOS rendered its judgment in *Bangladesh/Myanmar*, the annex VII arbitral tribunal in Bangladesh/India essentially the same approach and in fact, frequently referred to the ITLOS judgment.[52] It is also interesting to note that the ICJ seems to have adopted the view of ITLOS in *Bangladesh/Myanmar* regarding the relationship between delineation and delimitation and that between the CLCS and international tribunals.[53] The 2016 *Nicaragua v. Colombia* judgment thus presented an important shift in the approach of the ICJ to the relationship between itself and the CLCS. Moreover, both Nicaragua and Colombia relied extensively on the two Bay of Bengal cases in their pleadings to advance their arguments.[54] Even when Colombia urged the ICJ not to confirm jurisdiction to delimit the outer continental shelf beyond 200 nm, it did not argue that the conclusions reached by ITLOS were wrong or unreasonable. It merely contended that the factual circumstances of the case before the Court differed substantially from those of the Bay of Bengal case, so that ITLOS' conclusions were not applicable to the case.[55] This illustrates that the significance of ITLOS' decision transcended the case in which it were delivered. With the 2016 *Nicaragua v. Colombia* judgment, the approach of international courts and tribunals regarding the relationship between a dispute settlement body

---

50 *Delimitation of Maritime Areas between Canada and France* (10 June 1992) RIAA Volume XXI 265–341, [81].

51 *Territorial and Maritime Dispute between Nicaragua and Honduras in the Caribbean Sea (Nicaragua v. Honduras)* (2007) ICJ Rep 659, para. 319.

52 *Bay of Bengal Maritime Boundary Arbitration (Bangladesh/India)* (7 July 2014), paras 75, 80, available at http://www.pcacases.com/web/sendAttach/383, accessed 27 December 2017.

53 *Ibid.*, para. 112.

54 *Nicaragua v. Colombia*, Written Statement of the Republic of Nicaragua to the Preliminary Objections of the Republic of Colombia (19 January 2015) paras 2.25, 2.27, 2.29, 2.31, available at http://www.icj-cij.org/docket/files/154/18780.pdf, accessed 27 December 2017.

55 *Nicaragua v. Colombia*, Preliminary Objections of the Republic of Colombia, Volume I (14 August 2014) paras 5.68, 7.16, available at http://www.icj-cij.org/docket/files/154/18778.pdf, accessed 27 December 2017.

and the CLCS, along with its implications on the former's jurisdiction to delimit the outer continental shelf seems to have converged.

However, the broader impact of the case should be assessed with caution. The Bay of Bengal is highly unique, in that the entire bay is covered under a thick layer of sediment, and Bangladesh and Myanmar had made their submissions to the CLCS indicating their entitlement to the continental margin extending beyond 200 nm based on the thickness of sedimentary rocks pursuant to the formula contained in Article 76(4)(a)(i) of the Convention.[56] Therefore, it was beyond any doubt that the parties had entitlement to an outer continental shelf based on the thickness of the sediment on its floor. This enabled ITLOS to reach the conclusion that it could proceed to delimitation even when the CLCS had not issued its recommendations which might not be feasible in other cases due to different geographical and geomorphological characteristics of the area in question.

In conclusion, the limited number of cases brought before ITLOS means its decisions may not be far-reaching in terms of the number of legal issues elucidated. However, ITLOS managed to make good use of the opportunity afforded to it and made some important contributions to clarifying the law in two areas: coastal States' power in the EEZ and the regime of the outer continental shelf. Bunkering and confiscation of fishing vessels are common practice around the world but their legitimacy had always been controversial. Thus, ITLOS' answers had an impact that was not confined to the specific case of Virginia G, but rather had a legitimizing effect and provided important guidance for States when conducting their activities at sea. As no other international courts or tribunals have dealt with these issues, ITLOS' decision remains the authority in this regard. Moreover, ITLOS was also the pioneer in examining issues concerning the legal regime of the outer continental shelf – an issue which had been avoided, or only superficially examined, by other international courts or tribunals. The fact that the ICJ in the 2016 *Nicaragua v. Colombia* case adopted a simi-

56 Continental Shelf Submission of the Union of Myanmar, 3, available at http://www.un.org/Depts/los/clcs_new/submissions_files/mmr08/mmr_es.pdf, accessed 27 December 2017; Submission by the People's Republic of Bangladesh to the Commission on the Limits of the Continental Shelf, para 6.5, available at http://www.un.org/Depts/los/clcs_new/submissions_files/bgd55_11/Executive%20summary%20final.pdf, accessed 27 December 2017; The Indian Continental Shelf, Partial Submission to the Commission on the Limits of the Continental Shelf, Pursuant to Article 76, paragraph 8 of the United Nations Convention on the Law of the Sea, Appendix 1, available at http://www.un.org/Depts/los/clcs_new/submissions_files/ind48_09/ind2009executive_summary.pdf, accessed 27 December 2017.

lar approach to that of ITLOS, despite having refused to do so in 2012 and the lack of any reference to ITLOS' decision, provides evidence of the latter's authority.

4. Advisory opinion

Similar to the ICJ, ITLOS as a standing tribunal also has the jurisdiction to give advisory opinions. However, unlike the ICJ, the advisory function is only explicitly conferred on the Seabed Disputes Chamber (SDC) under Article 191 UNCLOS, not upon ITLOS as a whole.[57] The SDC has exclusive jurisdiction to render advisory opinions concerning activities in the Area under Article 190 UNCLOS. The SDC exercised its advisory power in the *Advisory Opinion on Activities in the Area* and clarified the nature and content of sponsoring States' "obligation to ensure" over activities in the Area as found in Article 139. *The Advisory Opinion on Activities in the Area* will likely have an important role in the development of the Mining Code by the International Seabed Authority. The SDC's exclusive advisory jurisdiction and the significance of the Advisory Opinion on Activities in the Area mean that the authority of ITLOS in the development of the rules regulating deep seabed activities is hardly questionable.

However, as mentioned, UNCLOS only confers advisory jurisdiction to the SDC, not the full ITLOS. This has prompted the long-debated question of whether ITLOS as a full tribunal also has jurisdiction to give advisory opinions.[58] ITLOS finally answered this question in the positive in the

57 Under Article 191 UNCLOS, the SDC is mandated to "give advisory opinions at the request of the Assembly or the Council on legal questions arising within the scope of their activities".

58 See, e.g., Kim, D. (2010), "Advisory Proceedings before the International Tribunal for the Law of the Sea as an Alternative Procedure to Supplement the Dispute-Settlement Mechanism under Part XV of the United Nations Convention on the Law of the Sea", *Issues in Legal Scholarship* 11, 1; Jesus, J.L. (2006), "Commentary on Article 138 of the Rules of the Tribunal" In: P. Chandrasekhara Rao and Ph. Gautier (eds), *The Rules of the International Tribunal for the Law of the Sea: A Commentary*. Leiden: Martinus Nijhoff, 39; Rosenne, S. (1998), "International Tribunal for the Law of the Sea: 1996–97 Survey", *The International Journal of Marine and Coastal Law* 13(4) 487–514; You, K.J. (2008), "Advisory Opinions of the International Tribunal for the Law of the Sea: Article 138 of the Rules of the Tribunal, Revisited", *Ocean Development & International Law* 39(4), 360–371; Ndiaye, T.M. (2010), "The Advisory Function of the International Tribunal for the Law of the Sea", *Chinese Journal of International Law* 9(3), 565–587.

Advisory Opinion on IUU *Fishing* in 2015. ITLOS founded its advisory jurisdiction on the basis of a combined reading of Article 288(1) of UNCLOS, Article 21 of that ITLOS Statute and Article 138 of the Rules of Procedure of ITLOS. More specifically, ITLOS held that Article 21 of ITLOS Statute, existing independently of Article 288 of the Convention,[59] allows the tribunals to exercise jurisdiction over not only "disputes" and "applications" but also "all matters provided for in any other agreement which confers jurisdiction on the Tribunal"[60]. The words "all maters" in ITLOS's view, "must mean something more than only 'disputes'" and "that something more must include advisory opinions if specifically provided for in any other agreement"[61]. ITLOS also found that "the prerequisites that need to be satisfied before the Tribunal can exercise its advisory jurisdiction" under Article 138 of the Rules were further met in that instance.[62]

Thus, the fact that the full ITLOS was determined to establish advisory jurisdiction arguably denotes an underlying desire on the part of the Tribunal to expand its competence and thus to increase its authority in the field of the law of the sea, despite the lack of an explicit legal basis under UNCLOS and the ITLOS Statute. ITLOS saw the advisory jurisdiction as an important opportunity for it to expand its authority beyond contentious cases, which, as mentioned, have been few and far between. The determination to assert jurisdiction despite the fierce objection from State parties to UNCLOS as demonstrated in their oral pleadings, as well as from the scholarly community,[63] seems to bear out Bogdandy and Venzke's observation that international courts "are by no means interested solely in making an interesting contribution to a general discussion; rather, many decisions seem tailored toward laying authoritative premises for the future"[64].

59 *Request for Advisory Opinion submitted by the Sub-Regional Fisheries Commission* (Advisory Opinion, 2 April 2015) ITLOS Reports 2015, paras 4, 52.

60 *Ibid*., para. 4.

61 *Ibid*., para. 56.

62 *Ibid*., para. 59.

63 Ruys, T. and Soete, A. (2016), "'Creeping' Advisory Jurisdiction of International Courts and Tribunals? The Case of the International Tribunal for the Law of the Sea", *Leiden Journal of International Law* 29(1), 155–176; Lando, M. (2016), "The Advisory Jurisdiction of the International Tribunal for the Law of the Sea: Comments on the Request for an Advisory Opinion Submitted by the Sub-Regional Fisheries Commission", *Leiden Journal of International Law* 29(2), 441–461.

64 Von Bogdandy and Venzke, supra note 8. 106.

In terms of the substance, the questions asked of ITLOS was that relating to flag States' Similar to the Advisory Opinion on Activities in the Area, ITLOS managed to shed light on the nature of flag States' obligations over fishing vessels operating in another State's EEZ, on which UNCLOS is silent. ITLOS made an important contribution to the law on fisheries and protection of the marine environment by imposing on flag States an "obligation to".[65] While ITLOS stated that the SDC's exposition of the "responsibility to ensure" in the context of recalling that sponsoring States' activities in the Area was "fully applicable in the present case", it still elaborated on the meaning of "due diligence obligation", and specified the content of this obligation and identified concrete obligations to be taken with in dealing with IUU fishing.[66]

Even though the obligations and measures that ITLOS spelled out may still seem general, they at least provide a minimum standard and a yardstick to assess whether the due diligence obligation has been met. The authoritative weight of ITLOS' opinion is further highlighted in light of the fact that, in contrast to other areas such as marine pollution and sea safety, there are no globally agreed minimum standards of flag State responsibilities in the fishing sector.[67] In other words, even when the Advisory Opinion has no legal binding force, it "create[s] legitimate expectations and must therefore be taken in account in future decisions"[68]. In fact, in the *South China Sea* arbitration, which was decided by an arbitral tribunal established under Annex VII of UNCLOS, the arbitral tribunal recalled ITLOS' findings and applied the standard of due diligence as elaborated by ITLOS to the facts of the case in question in dealing with Chinese fishing vessels' alleged violations of various obligations under the Convention.[69] This illustrates the impact of ITLOS' interpretation of the law, demonstrating that its exercise of public authority has reached beyond the confine of the Advisory Opinion and has become a point of reference in the legal discourse.

65 *Advisory Opinion on IUU Fishing*, *supra* note 59, para. 124.
66 *Ibid.*, para. 125.
67 Zwinge, T. (2011), "Duties of Flag States to Implement and Enforce International Standards and Regulations – And Measures to Counter Their Failure to Do So", *Journal of International Business and Law* 10(2), 297–323.
68 Von Bogdandy and Venzke, *supra* note 8, 116.
69 *South China Sea (Philippines v. China)*, Arbitral Award on the Merits, para. 744, available at https://www.pcacases.com/web/sendAttach/2086, accessed 27 December 2017.

In short, by establishing advisory jurisdiction for the full tribunal, ITLOS expanded its power beyond what is explicitly provided for under the Convention. Some commentators have argued that advisory proceedings give international courts and tribunals more leeway to develop the law.[70] If this is the case, ITLOS has opened a door for itself to increase its authority, albeit amidst considerable controversy. The substance of the two Advisory Opinions that ITLOS has issued have proved to be less controversial and are significant contributions to the law of the sea.

III. Conclusion

ITLOS was established to deal specifically with law of the sea disputes arising from UNCLOS, and was the product of a large number of developing States' dissatisfaction with and mistrust in the ICJ. The fact that ITLOS is a permanent tribunal, set up specifically to deal with the law of the sea disputes anticipates a special place for the Tribunal in the law of the sea dispute settlement scene. However, from its inception, ITLOS faced considerable scepticism regarding its capacity to act as a specialized court and its utility when operating alongside the existing ICJ. Indeed, critiques to date remain critical, pointing to the small docket of cases and the fact that the cases that make up the bulk of the Tribunal's docket have been those concerning prompt release and provisional measures. As a result, ITLOS has always struggled to prove the usefulness of its existence and its capacity. All these factors cast a negative shadow over the discussion regarding the exercise of its public authority as an international tribunal.

This paper sought to examine ITLOS' exercise of public authority using the definition of "public authority" developed by Bogdandy and Venzke. While not claiming to be completely comprehensive, it finds that ITLOS has indeed exercised different elements of public authority as defined by these authors. The Tribunal's authority over the parties to the case, ie the

70 Lachs, M. (1983), "Some Reflections on the Contribution of the International Court of Justice to the Development of International Law", *Syracuse Journal of International Law and Commerce* 10(2), 239–278, 249; Kateka, J.L. (2013), "Advisory Proceedings before the Seabed Disputes Chamber and before the ITLOS as a Full Court", *Max Planck Yearbook of United Nations Law* 17(1), 159–171, 161; Oellers-Frahm, K. (2012), "Lawmaking Through Advisory Opinions?" In: A. von Bogdandy and I. Venzke (eds), *International Judicial Lawmaking: On Public Authority and Democratic Legitimation in Global Governance*. Heidelberg: Springer, 69–98, 86.

capacity to impact their behaviour, could be most prominently observed in provisional measures cases. The parties concerned complied with and were appreciative of the measures that the Tribunal prescribed in all cases, even when the measures were not what they initially requested or were subsequently revoked.

The second element of public authority, i.e. the ability to establish interpretation as points of reference for legal discourse, can be observed in the three other types of proceedings. In particular, in prompt release proceedings, ITLOS' elaboration of what constitutes "reasonable bond" furnished this crucial but vague term with meaning. The specific criteria for assessment that ITLOS continuously developed and refined in the first ten years of its existence have arguably become an authoritative point of reference and made it possible for States to have a clear understanding of their obligations, enabling them to deal with similar situations out of court. As a result, ITLOS has not received any prompt release cases since 2007. In contentious proceedings, the number of legal issues it has dealt with is admittedly rather modest. However, it should also be acknowledged that some of these had been highly controversial issues, with which ITLOS was the first international tribunal to deal with. Whatever the debate was, it is now clear from *Virginia G* that coastal States can regulate bunkering of fishing vessels in their laws and confiscate foreign vessels fishing in their EEZ provided that such a measure is "necessary". In light of *Bangladesh/Myanmar*, the distinction between delimitation and delineation is evident, as is the relationship between a court or tribunal and the CLCS when it comes to delimiting the outer continental shelf. ITLOS' approach to the delimitation of the outer continental shelf was a clear departure from other courts and tribunals' previous cases, but has now seem to be taken up by other judicial bodies, including both arbitral tribunals and the ICJ. As a result, ITLOS' judgments were important in determining the direction in which the law should develop, putting an end to years of uncertainty. While ITLOS' semantic authority in the long-term ought to be assessed with caution due to the fact-dependent reasoning that the Tribunal provided, there is evidence to show that ITLOS also exercises authority over other courts and tribunals. Finally, ITLOS expanded its advisory jurisdiction beyond what is explicitly stipulated in the Convention. This decision certainly raises questions of legitimacy, but it cannot be denied that it paved the way, perhaps intentionally, for ITLOS to increase its authority in the field. In contrast, the substance of the two Advisory Opinions that ITLOS has so far rendered is much less controversial and in fact, highly welcome. The Advisory Opinions have proved to be powerful point of reference in the legal discourse, particularly with regard to the law on marine environment protection.

In sum, amidst the cynicism, ITLOS has shown that it can and does exercise elements of public authority in the field of the law of the sea. While limited in magnitude, ITLOS' judgments have the capacity to influence the behaviour of States and other judicial bodies, and serve as the reference point in the legal discourse, at least with regard to issues concerning coastal State's power in the EEZ and the outer continental shelf regime.

Not in My Name! Claudia Pechstein and the Post-Consensual Foundations of the Court of Arbitration for Sport

*Antoine Duval**

"In whose name?" do international courts adjudicate is the fundamental question posed by Armin von Bogdandy and Ingo Venzke.[1] In the present chapter, I aim to transpose some of their reflections to the context of the Court of Arbitration for Sport (CAS). To illustrate the suitability of this transposition, I will focus on the decisions rendered by the Landgericht (LG) and the Oberlandesgericht (OLG) München and by the Bundesgerichtshof (BGH) in a highly publicized dispute involving Claudia Pechstein, a famous German speed-skater and Olympic champion.[2] The case will now potentially move to the Bundesverfassungsgericht.

Von Bogdandy and Venzke's first fundamental claim is that international courts are multifunctional. By that they mean that international courts "transcend the one-dimensional fixation on dispute settlement"[3]. They argue that courts also stabilize normative expectations, are instruments of lawmaking, and a means to control and legitimize public authority.[4] Additionally, they suggest that international courts exercise international public authority. They define public authority as "the ability, grounded in law, to restrict the freedom of other actors, or to shape their use of freedom in a similar way"[5]. From a descriptive standpoint, I contend

* Senior Researcher, Asser Institute – Institute for International & European Law.

1 Von Bogdandy, A. and Venzke, I. (2014), *In Whose Name? A Public Law Theory of International Adjudication*. Oxford: Oxford University Press. See also the shorter version of their argument in: Von Bogdandy, A. and Venzke, I. (2012), "In Whose Name? An Investigation of International Courts' Public Authority and Its Democratic Justification", *European Journal of International Law* 23(1), 7–41.

2 BGH, Urteil v. 7. Juni 2016- KZR 6/15 http://juris.bundesgerichtshof.de/cgi-bin/rechtsprechung/document.py?Gericht=bgh&Art=en&nr=75021&pos=0&anz=1, accessed 21 February 2020.

3 Von Bogdandy and Venzke (2014), *supra* note 1, 5.

4 *Ibid.*, 10–16.

5 *Ibid.*, 17. On their understanding of authority, see also: Venzke, I. (2013), "Between Power and Persuasion: On International Institutions' Authority in Making Law", *Transnational Legal Theory* 4(3), 354–373; von Bogdandy and Venzke (2012), *supra* note 1.

that the CAS can also be qualified as a multifunctional Court exercising international public authority.[6] CAS awards are embedded in a wide network of decisions constituting a specific jurisprudence and contributing to the stabilization of normative expectations in the global sporting field.[7] The CAS also engages in judicial lawmaking via its recourse to general principles and has become an important institutional avenue to control and challenge the exercise of international public authority by the Sports Governing bodies (SGBs).[8] Finally, its decisions affect the life of thousands of athletes, clubs and fans around the world.[9] The question is then how to legitimize this exercise of international public authority. As pointed out by von Bogdandy and Venzke, the "traditional understanding"[10] is that it is the consensus of the (states or private) parties that justifies the exercise of public authority by international courts. But, in whose name does the CAS operate? The automatic answer from a private international law perspective must be: in the name of the parties. This chapter will show that this conventional wisdom is challenged in practice. In fact, Claudia Pechstein's loudly resonating (and convincing) answer to this same question is: Not in my name!

I aim to show in the first part of this article that she is right to consider that her free consent cannot be a credible foundation for CAS arbitration. Nonetheless, I will discuss in the second part other, more or less persuasive, names which can be (and have been) invoked to support the legitimacy of post-consensual CAS arbitration.

---

6 For a similar claim, see Casini, L. (2011), "The Making of a *Lex Sportiva* by the Court of Arbitration for Sport", *German Law Journal* 12(5), 1317–1340.

7 Discussing the emergence of a CAS jurisprudence, see: Kaufmann-Kohler, G. (2007), "Arbitral Precedent: Dream, Necessity or Excuse?", *Arbitration International* 23(1), 357–378; Maisonneuve, M. (2011), *L'arbitrage des litiges sportifs*. Paris: L.G.D.J, 443–477.

8 See Latty, F. (2007), *La Lex sportiva: recherche sur le droit transnational*. Leiden/Boston: Martinus Nijhoff; and Casini, *supra* note 6.

9 On the concept of *lex sportiva* and the role of the CAS, see Latty, *supra* note 8; and Duval, A. (2013), "Lex sportiva: a playground for transnational law", *European Law Journal* 19(6), 822–842.

10 Von Bogdandy & Venzke (2014), *supra* note 1, 18.

I. Not in my name! *Why* CAS *does not speak in the name of Claudia Pechstein*

Von Bogdandy and Venzke's overture to their book reformulated to match this case study would read as follows: *viewed in light of an important and still dominant understanding of private international law, international arbitration tribunals are mere instruments of dispute settlement whose activities are justified by the consent of the parties that created them and in whose name they decide.*[11] The post-consensual shift openly discussed in public international law[12] remains a taboo as far as international arbitration is concerned.[13] As one of the most prominent international (and CAS) arbitrators, Jan Paulsson, has put it: "The idea of arbitration is that of binding resolution of disputes accepted with serenity by those who bear its consequences because of their special trust in chosen decision-makers."[14]

It is a natural assumption: CAS jurisdiction must be grounded in the "serene" consent of the parties. As this chapter will show, this apparent truism does not hold in practice, as the LG and OLG München acknowledged in their respective rulings in the Pechstein case.

---

11 The original quote reads: "Viewed in light of an important and once even dominant understanding of international law, international courts are mere instruments of dispute settlement whose activities are justified by the consent of the states that created them and in whose name they decide". *Ibid.*,1.

12 On this shift, see Romano, C. (2007), "The Shift from the Consensual to the Compulsory Paradigm in International Adjudication: Elements for a Theory of Consent", *New York University Journal of International Law & Politics* 39(4), 791–872. See also the discussion in Von Bogdandy and Venzke (2014), *supra* note 1, 3.

13 A slowly cracking taboo as some recent PhD theses are tackling the issue, see Diallo, O. (2010), *Le consentement des parties à l'arbitrage international*. Paris: L.G.D.J.; Steingruber, A.-M. (2012), *Consent in International Arbitration*. Oxford: Oxford University Press.

14 The quote continues: "It is difficult for courts to achieve this kind of acceptance; public justice tends to be distant and impersonal. Arbitration is a private initiative. It does not ask that ordinary citizens struggle with Rousseau or Locke or other philosophers' abstractions of a general 'social contract', lacking any mooring in time and space, which might otherwise be enlisted to justify law's dominion. The ideal of arbitration is freedom reconciled with law". Paulsson, J. (2013), *The Idea of Arbitration*. Oxford: Oxford University Press, 1.

A. Free consent as foundation for the CAS

The CAS and the Swiss Federal Tribunal (SFT) attempt to keep alive the consensual myth that must, in principle, underlie CAS arbitration.

1. The roots of the consensual myth

In the eyes of a majority of arbitration scholars, consent is the sine qua non requirement, the "cornerstone"[15], delimiting the reach of the conceptual territory of the notion of arbitration.[16] Forced arbitration is at the "antipodes"[17] of the traditional understanding of arbitration. It is thus very understandable that the literature, the CAS and the SFT have had extreme difficulties in parting with this foundation. For many, the CAS is simply an "arbitration tribunal whose jurisdiction and authority are based on agreement of the parties"[18]. Indeed, "[s]ports arbitrations only exist because the athlete, the national governing body, and others in the sport world have agreed to be bound by arbitration and the outcome of the case"[19]. Hence, the jurisdiction of the CAS is perceived as "voluntary"[20] and the parties' consent as "paramount"[21]. It is just common sense, "[a]s with any arbitration [...]the disputing parties must consent to have their dispute resolved

15 Rigozzi, A. and Robert-Tissot, F. (2012), "La pertinence du 'consentement' dans l'arbitrage du Tribunal Arbitral du Sport", *Jusletter*, 16 July, 2.

16 Jarrosson, C. (2001), "Les frontières de l'arbitrage", *Revue de l'Arbitrage* (1), 5–41, 19–20.

17 "Le forçage est tellement aux antipodes de la conception communément admise de l'arbitrage, assis sur des bases conventionnelles, qu'il paraît impossible de parler d'arbitrage forcé." Pinna, A. (2008), "Réflexions sur l'arbitrage forcé", *Gazette du Palais* (351), 14–16 December, 6.

18 Mitten, M.J. and Opie, H. (2010), "Sports Law: Implications for the development of International Comparative and National law and Global Dispute Resolution", *Tulane Law Review* 85(2), 269–322, 285.

19 McLaren, R.H. (2001), "The Court of Arbitration for Sport: An Independent Arena for the World's Sports Disputes", *Valparaiso University Law Review* 35(2/3), 379–405, 382.

20 Ansley, C. (1995), "International Athletic Dispute Resolution: Tarnishing the Olympic Dream", *Arizona Journal of International and Comparative Law* 12(1), 277–302, 298.

21 Reilly, L. (2012), "An Introduction to the Court of Arbitration for Sport (CAS) & the Role of National Courts in International Sports Disputes", *Journal of Dispute Resolution* 5(1), 63–81, 66.

by an arbitration administered by the CAS"[22]. Even when this foundation is characterized as "highly unusual", it is nevertheless deemed as having "consensual origin".[23]

The CAS Code[24] has been feeding this consensual myth, as its Article R27 indicates that: "These Procedural Rules apply whenever the parties have agreed to refer a sports- related dispute to CAS. Such reference may arise out of an arbitration clause contained in a contract or regulations or by reason of a later arbitration agreement (ordinary arbitration proceedings) or may involve an appeal against a decision rendered by a federation, association or sports-related body where the statutes or regulations of such bodies, or a specific agreement provide for an appeal to CAS (appeal arbitration proceedings)."

The official commentary of the CAS Code indicates under this provision that "[t]he basic requirement for CAS arbitration is the parties' agreement to arbitrate, which includes an offer to arbitrate and an acceptance thereof"[25]. The agreement, or consent, of the parties is clearly seen as the trigger of the jurisdiction of the CAS. Furthermore, Article 178 of the Swiss Statute for Private International Law (PILA) provides the conditions of validity of an arbitration agreement in international arbitration seated in Switzerland Two main requirements need to be fulfilled:

1. The arbitration agreement must be made in writing, by telegram, telex, telecopier or any other means of communication which permits it to be evidenced by a text.
2. Furthermore, an arbitration agreement is valid if it conforms either to the law chosen by the parties, or to the law governing the subject-matter of the dispute, in particular the main contract, or to Swiss law.

It is important to keep in mind that the validity of the agreement needs to be recognized either by the law chosen by the parties, the law governing the subject matter of the dispute or Swiss law. The Swiss Federal tribunal has held that under Swiss law, "it is to be understood as an agreement by

---

22 Coccia, M. (2003), "International Sports Justice: The Court of Arbitration for Sport", *European Sports Law and Policy Bulletin* (1), 23–76, 34.

23 Paulsson, J. (1993), "Arbitration of International Sports Disputes", *Arbitration International* 9(4), 359–370, 369.

24 The latest version of the Code is available at http://www.tas-cas.org/fileadmin/user_upload/Code_2017_FINALen_.pdf, accessed 1 February 2017.

25 Mavromati, D. and Reeb, M. (2015), *The Code of the Court of Arbitration for Sport. Commentary, Cases and Materials*. Alphen aan den Rijn: Wolters Kluwer International, 33.

which two or more determined or determinable parties agree to submit one or several existing or future determined disputes bindingly to an arbitral tribunal and to the exclusion of the original state jurisdiction according to a legal order immediately or indirectly determined"[26]. This implies that "[b]eing a contract, the arbitration agreement is effective when the parties displayed their willingness to resort to arbitration reciprocally and in a concordant manner"[27]. Thus, "waiving the legal protection provided by the state is not done lightly, but is the result of a well-established desire to do so"[28].

In short, the prevalent state of mind as stated by a CAS panel discussing its jurisdiction is that: "Arts. R27 and R47 of the CAS Code state the obvious with respect to jurisdiction: A court of arbitration has jurisdiction only if the parties to a dispute have made an agreement to that effect."[29]

This has led the CAS and the SFT to develop specific legal strategies to circumvent the thinness of the consensual foundation of the agreement to arbitrate a sporting dispute at the CAS.[30]

2. *Keeping the consensual myth alive: The legal strategies of the CAS and the SFT*

The main legal strategy used by both the CAS and the SFT to uphold the validity of forced arbitration agreements in favour of the CAS, has been to deny any relevance of the free will of the athletes/clubs and to focus instead on the existence of a CAS arbitration agreement in a written document (the entry form to the Olympics for example) or in statutes and regulations

26 *A. v. Trabzonspor Kulübü Dernegi & Turkish Football Federation (TFF)*, SFT Case 4A_404/2010, Judgment of 19 April 2011, para. 4.2.2. Where not otherwise indicated we use the English translations of the SFT's judgments available at http://www.swissarbitrationdecisions.com/, accessed 1 February 2017.

27 *Egyptian Football Association v. Al-Masry Sporting Club*, SFT Case 4A_682/2012, Judgment of 20 June 2013, para. 4.4.1.

28 *Nagel v. Fédération Equestre Internationale*, SFT Case 4C_44/1996, Judgment of 31 October 1996, para. 2. The English translation used is the one provided in Reeb, M. (ed.) (1998), *Digest of CAS Awards 1986–1998*. Alphen aan den Rijn: Kluwer, 585–592.

29 *Telecom Egypt Club v. Egyptian Football Association (EFA)*, CAS case 2009/A/1910, award of 9 September 2010, para. 6.

30 This article focuses on arbitration between SGBs and athletes/clubs through the CAS appeal procedure. The CAS ordinary procedure features disputes usually grounded on a classical consensual agreement between two private parties.

to which a written document signed by an athlete refers.[31] The latter option, the so-called arbitration agreement by reference,[32] is the most popular as it requires only a global reference to the rules and regulations of an SGB to be deemed valid. The SFT has repeatedly condoned this legal construct, chiefly in the Nagel[33] and Roberts[34] cases.

The Nagel case involved a rider contesting an anti-doping sanction imposed by the Fédération Equestre Internationale (FEI) seated in Lausanne. The rider brought an action against the decision of the FEI in front of the Swiss courts, which accepted the objection of arbitration raised by the FEI. This led to an appeal by Nagel to the SFT challenging the validity of the arbitration clause. The court considered it "not admissible to hold that an arbitration agreement resulting from a global reference does not bind the person who, already knowing the existence of the arbitration clause when he signs the document referring to it and thereby satisfies the requirement of the written form, makes no objection to such a clause, and regards himself as bound by it"[35]. This behaviour "allows the author of the communication logically to deduce that the arbitration agreement corresponds to the actual wish of the person to whom it was addressed at the time when he accepted, in the specified form, the global reference"[36]. In this case, it was "established that the plaintiff already knew the arbitration clause inserted in the FEI regulations when he signed the model agreement, and he actually made use of it to have recourse to the CAS on the occasion of a previous dispute"[37]. Thus, "one is forced to conclude that the plaintiff agreed to submit to the arbitration agreement, validly giving his consent in formal terms by signing the model agreement, and confirming

---

31 For a comprehensive review of the jurisprudence of both the CAS and the SFT on the issue of consent to CAS jurisdiction, see Mavromati, D. (2015), "Arbitration clause in the contract or in the rules of the federation in disputes brought before the CAS", available at www.ssrn.com/abstract=2573612, accessed 1 February 2017.

32 For a first elaboration on this contractual structure, see Netzle, S. (1998), "Arbitration agreements by reference to regulations of sports organisations", *Arbitration of Sports-Related Disputes ASA Special Series* 11, 45–58. See more recently, Mavromati and Reeb, *supra* note 25, 35–37.

33 *Nagel v. Fédération Equestre Internationale*, *supra* note 28.

34 *Roberts v. International basket Federation (FIBA) & Court of Arbitration for Sport (CAS)*, SFT Case 4P.230/2000, Judgment of 7 February 2001. See also the original *R. v. International Basketball Federation (FIBA)*, CAS award CAS 2000/A/262, preliminary award of 28 July 2000.

35 *Nagel v. Fédération Equestre Internationale*, *supra* note 28, para. 3.c.

36 *Ibid.*

37 *Ibid.*

it by his unreserved acceptation of the arbitration clause contained expressis verbis in the documents sent to him when he entered for the competition in San Marino"[38]. The Court quickly brushed over the question of the free will of the athlete, it simply noted "[i]t does not emerge from the unappealable findings of the cantonal judges that the plaintiff would not have obtained his licence, and hence would not have been able to take part in the equestrian event such as the one in San Marino, if he had not accepted the arbitration agreement"[39]. This is definitely a rather formalistic way to deal with a thorny problem for CAS arbitration: athletes are in practice forced to accept the jurisdiction of the CAS or they will not get a license to compete. More importantly, the SFT added: "it is in all cases out of the question to treat as an excessive obligation, within the meaning of article 27 CC, adoption by reference of the arbitration clause contained in the defendant's regulations"[40]. In other words, the SFT held that even if the athlete's consent is forced, the validity of the clause would be upheld through a balance of interests.[41]

The permissive stance of the SFT with regard to the validity of CAS arbitration agreements was further reinforced by the Roberts decision in 2001. The decision involved a Basketball player challenging an arbitration clause in favour of the CAS included in the regulations of the International Basketball Federation (FIBA). The player was not a member of FIBA or of one of its affiliates. The SFT referred to the Swiss principle of trust (Vertrauensprinzip) to interpret whether the parties were bound by an arbitration clause by reference and concluded that an athlete is consenting to the general regulations of an SGB (and the CAS arbitration clause included therein) when he or she claims a license to participate in the competitions it organizes.[42] Furthermore, the Court considered that "by his recourse to the Appeals Commission under those Internal Regulations, without entering any reservation regarding the arbitration clause of which he was aware, [Roberts] signified his consent to that clause"[43]. Moreover, "by lodging the

---

38 *Ibid.*

39 *Ibid.*, para. 4. b).

40 *Ibid.*

41 In this context, the SFT evaluates whether the forced CAS arbitration is in the interest of the athlete. See Handschin, L. and Schütz, T.M. (2014). "Bemerkungen zum Fall Pechstein", *Sport und Recht* 21(5), 179–181.

42 *Roberts v. International basket Federation (FIBA) & Court of Arbitration for Sport (CAS)*, *supra* note 34, para. 2. a).

43 *Ibid.*, translation from Reeb, M. (ed.). (2002), *Digest of CAS Awards 1998–2000* (Vol. 2). The Hague: Kluwer Law International, 812.

appeal he was implicitly applying for a general permit to play and the respondent was therefore also entitled to assume from this that he would recognize its rules, with which he was familiar"[44]. In other words, Roberts had to assume that FIBA was inviting him to take part in a process that would eventually lead him to abide by an arbitration clause in favour of CAS. Nagel and Roberts became a reference point in the jurisprudence of both the CAS[45] and the SFT[46]. In both Roberts and Nagel, the SFT rightly insisted that the athletes did not object ex ante to the particular arbitration agreement, yet it fails to problematize the fact that if they had done so, they would not be allowed to compete. The imbalanced power constellation, as an SGB controls all the potential economic opportunities of an athlete or club in a particular sport, leaves no room for free choice from the side of the athlete or the club.

In its more recent jurisprudence, the SFT further entrenched its favourable assessment of arbitration by reference. In the Dodo case, a Brazilian football player was contesting the jurisdiction of the CAS to hear an appeal against an anti-doping decision adopted by a Brazilian anti-doping tribunal. The national federation did not include in its rules and regulations an arbitration clause referring this type of dispute to CAS. Nevertheless, the SFT held that the regulations of the Fédération Internationale

---

44 *Ibid.* The CAS had considered similarly that the "Appellant knew at the time he lodged the appeal and when he signed and accepted the Order of Procedure about the existence of the arbitration clause according to article 12.9 of the IR. Applying the principle of trust it was his obligation to decline the arbitration (and by that most probably also the right to appeal to the AC). Failing to do so, he had accepted the arbitration clause, which had been offered to him by Respondent." *Roberts v. International basket Federation (FIBA) & Court of Arbitration for Sport (CAS), supra* note 34, para. 11.

45 For the *Nagel* case see *Roberts v. International basket Federation (FIBA) & Court of Arbitration for Sport (CAS), supra* note 33, paras 39, 44. For the *Roberts* case see *Union Cycliste Internationale (UCI) v. R. & Fédération Française de Cyclisme (FFC)*, Arbitrage TAS Case 2002/A/431, award of 23 May 2003, para. 4.

46 See *A. v. B.*, SFT Case 4P.253/2003, Judgment of 23 March 2004, para. 5.3; *Cañas. v. ATP Tour*, SFT Case 4P.172/2006, Judgment of 22 March 2007, para. 4.3.2.3; *A. v. Fédération International de Football Association (FIFA) & World Anti-Doping Agency (WADA)*, SFT Case 4A_460/2008, Judgment of 9 January 2009, para. 6.2; *A. v. World Anti-Doping Agency (WADA)*, SFT Case 4A_358/2009, Judgment of 6 November 2009, para. 3.2.4; *X. v. Y. & Fédération Internationale de Football Association (FIFA)*, SFT Case 4A_548/2009, Judgement of 20 January 2010, paras 3.2.2 and 4.1; *A. v. World Anti-Doping Agency (WADA), Fédération International de Football Association (FIFA) & Cyprus Football Association (CFA)*, SFT Case 4A_640/2010, Judgment of 18 April 2011, para. 3.2.2.

de Football Association (FIFA) providing for an appeal to CAS in doping cases are binding on the player. It observed that "[a]s a professional football player playing at the international level, he is a member of the Brazilian Football Association CBF, which for its part is a member of FIFA"[47]. Thus, "the FIFA Rules, particularly the jurisdiction of the CAS according to Art. 61 of the FIFA Statutes, apply also to the Appellant"[48]. This follows mainly from Article 1 (2) of the CBF Statutes, as it "provides, among other things, that a player belonging to the CBF must follow the FIFA Rules"[49]. It concluded by finding that "[s]uch a general reference to the FIFA Rules and thus to the appeal rights of FIFA and WADA contained in the FIFA Statutes is sufficient to establish the jurisdiction of the CAS pursuant to R47 of the CAS-Code"[50]. In other words, a player forced to submit to the statutes of the Brazilian federation to exercise his profession, is bound to the jurisdiction of the CAS enshrined in the Statutes of a Swiss association of which he is not even a member. Distinguishing a consensual basis in this factual constellation is undoubtedly a masterpiece of legal fiction by the SFT. The validity of this type of consent to CAS arbitration, via a global reference made by the statutes of a national federation to the FIFA statutes, was later confirmed by the SFT[51] and the CAS[52].

The willingness of the SFT to recognize the validity of the consent to CAS arbitration is not solely embodied in its jurisprudence on arbitration clauses by reference, it is also vividly visible in other decisions. An example is a decision regarding the competence of the CAS to deal with a dispute resulting from a request made to the FIFA by a club and a player for an International Transfer Certificate (ITC).[53] Obtaining an ITC is a requirement for fielding a player coming from a different Football Association than the one the new club is affiliated to. In that case, the former association of the player refused to deliver the ITC due to an outstanding contractual dispute between the player and its former club. This dispute was

---

47 *A. v. Fédération International de Football Association (FIFA) & World Anti-Doping Agency (WADA)*, *supra* note 46, para. 6.2.

48 *Ibid.*

49 *Ibid.*

50 *Ibid.*

51 *A. v. World Anti-Doping Agency (WADA), Fédération International de Football Association (FIFA) & Cyprus Football Association (CFA)*, *supra* note 46, para. 3.2.2.

52 *Fédération Internationale de Football Association (FIFA) v. Malta Football Association (MFA) & M* and CAS 2008/A/1627 *World Anti Doping Agency (WADA) v. MFA & M.*, CAS Case 2008/A/1575, award of 9 February 2009, paras 1–7.

53 *X. v. Y. & Fédération Internationale de Football Association (FIFA)*, *supra* note 46, partial award on *lis pendens* and jurisdiction of 7 October 2009.

referred to the FIFA Dispute Resolution Chamber (DRC) and the player contested the jurisdiction of CAS to review the decision of the DRC. The SFT considered that the player could not invoke a lack of knowledge of the FIFA Regulations on the Status and Transfer of Players (RSTP), which foresees that the DRC's decisions are exclusively appealable to the CAS.[54] Instead, by requesting an ITC, the player "admitted the application of the specific regulation adopted by the Respondent federation and he submitted to the procedure foreseen by the regulations to decide the disputes in connection with the filing of a request for an ITC"[55]. Thus, the SFT held that "[i]t must be acknowledged with the CAS that the Appellant could not without violating the rules of good faith submit a request for an ITC to FIFA (or at least participate in such a request in his favour) and invoke the specific provision of the RSTP whilst refusing to participate in the procedure instituted by the same provision to resolve the disputes in connection with such a request, in other words by compelling the other party, allegedly victim of a breach of contract he committed, to sue him in front of an ordinary court to dispose of a dispute which was not within the exclusive jurisdiction of the ordinary courts"[56]. Moreover, the player "subsequently let himself be drawn in front of the DRC without the least objection"[57]. Hence he "conclusively showed by his behavior that he submitted to the regulations adopted by [FIFA] to decide disputes such as the one at hand"[58]. As in the Nagel and Roberts case, the SFT seems to reproach the player's lack of early objection to CAS arbitration and locates his consent in his appearance in front of the FIFA DRC. This is notwithstanding the fact that, if the player was to be able to play quickly for a new club, i.e. exercise his right to work, the club was in practice forced to obtain an ITC from FIFA.

Nonetheless, there is a limit to the liberalism of the SFT. The jurisdiction of the CAS is only recognized if there is a written reference to the statute or the rules and regulations of a SGB where one can find a CAS arbitration agreement. Thus, for example, the SFT has supported a CAS panel denying its jurisdiction in a case involving the FIFA RSTP, because at that point in time FIFA had not introduced any arbitration clause in favour of the CAS.[59] Similarly, if a national federation did not include a

---

54 *Ibid.*, para. 4.2.2.
55 *Ibid.*
56 *Ibid.*
57 *Ibid.*
58 *Ibid.*
59 *Ibid.*

clear arbitration clause in its statutes or regulations, the global reference to the FIFA rules is insufficient, as they do not provide for a CAS arbitration clause covering all types of football disputes. The SFT[60] and the CAS[61] have repeatedly found that the CAS has no jurisdiction to deal with this kind of dispute. Alternatively, the arbitration clause might refer to a precise characteristic of the dispute as its "international dimension". If this characteristic is absent then no recourse to CAS arbitration can be made.[62] Finally, the SFT held that a general jurisdiction of CAS could not derive, as the CAS panel had thought,[63] from an arbitration clause included in the entry form to a specific international competition, as the dispute en cause was not directly connected to that competition.[64] These cases point at the need for the existence of a rule referring a specific dispute to the jurisdiction of the CAS, they embody the well-known principles of legality and publicity. However, they do not imply free consent as a prerequisite.

As pointed out by a seasoned observer of the CAS and the SFT, an "appeal on the grounds that the athlete had no alternative but to submit to the arbitration agreement in favour of the CAS and that therefore there was a lack of free will on the part of the athlete when he entered into the corresponding agreement making the arbitration agreement void will [...] probably have little prospect of succeeding"[65]. The SFT is careful not to take into account whether the athletes have any free choice in subjecting themselves to the SGBs' regulations and the CAS arbitration clauses they include. Yet, if athletes wish to take part in the Olympics, the world speedskating championships, or just the Brazilian football league they must accept the rules imposed by the SGBs. In any event, there is very little value, in the course of a short professional career, in starting multi-year litigation to obtain in front of a national court the right to compete in sport-

60 *X v. Y*, SFT Case 4A_160/2007, Judgment of 28 August 2007.

61 The CAS has had to deal with this particular question in numerous instances. For a good summary of its view on the matter, see *Al-Wehda Club v. Saudi Arabian Football Federation (SAFF)*, CAS Case 2011/A/2472, award of 12 August 2011, para. 20.

62 *A. v. Trabzonspor Kulübü Dernegi & Turkish Football Federation (TFF)*, *supra* note 26, confirming *Omer Riza v. Trabzonspor Kulübü Dernegi & Turkish Football Federation*, CAS case 2010/A/1996, award of 10 June 2010.

63 *World Anti-doping Agency (WADA) v. International Ice Hockey Federation (IIHF) & Florian Busch*, CAS case 2008/A/1564, award of 23 June 2009, paras 1–26.

64 *A. v. World Anti-Doping Agency (WADA)*, *supra* note 46, paras 3.2.3 and 3.2.4.

65 Netzle, S. (2011), "Appeals against Arbitral Awards by the CAS", *Bulletin TAS/CAS* (2), 19–26, 23.

ing competitions.[66] Hence, in practice, there is not much an athlete can do, but to defend his case in front of the federations' disciplinary bodies and by doing so he will most likely be deemed as having accepted a CAS arbitration clause. This état de fait has been recognized in the literature, and acknowledged by the SFT itself, before the German courts decided to tackle it in the Pechstein case.

B. *The* Pechstein *case: Endpoint for the consensual myth?*

The weakness of the consensual myth as support for the validity of CAS arbitration agreements imposed on athletes and clubs by the SGBs has long been acknowledged.[67] However, it is only with the two Pechstein rulings of the LG and OLG München that it has finally been openly confronted.

66 A point well illustrated by the judicial "ordeal" suffered by German athlete Katrin Krabbe in the 1990s, recalled in Faylor, J.A. (2001), "The Dismantling of a German Champion: Katrin Krabbe and her Ordeal with the German Track and Field Association and the International Amateur Athletic Federation (IAAF)", *Arbitration International* 17(2), 163–172.

67 See Netzle, *supra* note 32, 53.

1. *The mounting realist critique: This is not a consensual arbitration*

a. The realism of the *doctrine*

The problematic role of free consent as a foundation to arbitration is not exclusive to sports arbitration.[68] It has been abundantly debated in the framework of consumer and employment arbitration in the US.[69] However, the key difference is that both consumers and employees have a (limited) choice regarding their contractual partners and the conditions offered. This choice is relative as few are capable of deciphering the legal fine print of a consumer contract or in a position to refuse a specific job, but it is potentially there. In sports the situation is structurally different: there is not even a potential choice. The monopoly of the SGBs over their competitions is such that an international-level athlete wanting to compete is left with no real alternative: accept a CAS arbitration clause or play alone in your garden.[70] The consensual myth has been convincingly exposed as a "dogma"[71] by numerous authors.[72] Some refer in euphemistic terms to

68 Forced arbitration in the US recently came under intense scrutiny by the *New York Times*. See Silver-Greenberg, J. and Gebeloff, R. (2015), "Arbitration Everywhere, Stacking the Deck of Justice", *New York Times*, 31 October, available at http://www.nytimes.com/2015/11/01/business/dealbook/arbitration-everywhere-stacking-the-deck-of-justice.html, accessed 1 February 2017; Silver-Greenberg, J. and Gebeloff, R. (2015), "In Arbitration, a Privatization of the Justice System", *New York Times*, 1 November, available at http://www.nytimes.com/2015/11/02/business/dealbook/in-arbitration-a-privatization-of-the-justice-system.html, accessed 1 February 2017.

69 See, for example, Demaine, L.J. and Hensler, D.R. (2004), "'Volunteering' to Arbitrate Through Predispute Arbitration Clauses: The Average Consumer's Experience", *Law and Contemporary Problems* 67(1–2), 55–74; Roma, E. (2011), "Mandatory Arbitration Clauses in Employment Contracts and the Need for Meaningful Judicial Review", *Journal of Gender, Social Policy & Law* 12(3), 519–544; Moses, M.L. (2014), "Challenges for the Future: the Diminishing Role of Consent in Arbitration", *Transnational Dispute Management* 11(4), 1–10.

70 This is a famous alternative referred to by the SFT in its *Cañas* case. See *Cañas. v. ATP Tour*, *supra* note 46, para. 4.3.2.2.

71 "L'auteur prend notamment le pari de se départir du dogme du caractère consensuel de l'arbitrage pour affirmer sans détours que l'arbitrage sportif n'est pas consensuel." The words are from Gabrielle Kaufmann-Kohler in her preface to Rigozzi, A. (2005), *L'arbitrage international en matière de sport.* Basel: Helbing & Lichtenhahn, XV.

72 See *Ibid.*, 421–433; Rigozzi, A. and Robert-Tissot, F. (2015), "Consent in Sports Arbitration: Its Multiple Aspects" In: E. Geisinger and E. Trabaldo de Mestral (eds), *Sports Arbitration: A Coach for other players?*. New York: Jurisnet LLC, 59–94; Maisonneuve, *supra* note 7, 191–225; Steingruber, *supra* note 13; Pinna, *supra* note

"inherent particularities"[73], and acknowledge "that the formal requirements of Article 178 PILA as well as the consent to arbitrate are not always clearly established"[74]. In short, "sports arbitration is far from the traditional idea of arbitration being the consensual alternative dispute adjudication process that we read about in every textbook on arbitration"[75]. Rather, "it is clear that sports arbitration is fundamentally non-consensual in nature, since athletes have no other choice but to agree to whatever is contained in the statutes or regulations of their sports governing bodies"[76]. Admittedly, "[f]rom the point of view of the athlete concerned, it makes little difference whether he is bound to the jurisdiction of the arbitral tribunal by virtue of a statutory regulation or by virtue of a unilateral regulation imposed by a monopoly federation"[77]. In functional terms, CAS arbitration is analogous to mandatory arbitration imposed by the state.

b. The confession of the SFT in the *Cañas* case

In 2007, in its decision in the now famous Cañas case, the SFT carefully acknowledged this critique. The court was facing a question relating to the validity of a waiver of appeal of a CAS award signed by a professional ten-

17; Yamdjie, E. (2013), *Le consentement dans l'arbitrage des litiges sportifs*. Université Nice Sophia Antipolis, available at https://tel.archives-ouvertes.fr/tel-01215802/document, accessed 1 February 2017.

73 Mavromati, D. (2011), "Selected issues related to CAS jurisdiction in the light of the jurisprudence of the Swiss Supreme Court", *CAS Bulletin/Bulletin TAS* (1), 31–40, available at https://www.tas-cas.org/fileadmin/user_upload/Bulletin_1_2011.pdf, accessed 1 February 2017.

74 *Ibid.*

75 Rigozzi and Robert-Tissot, *supra* note 72, 59.

76 *Ibid.*, 60. Similarly, Steingruber, A.M. (2009), "Sports Arbitration: how the structure and other features of competitive sports affect consent as it relates to waiving judicial control", *American Review of International Arbitration* 20(1), 59–96, 73; Weston, M.A. (2009), "Doping Control, Mandatory Arbitration, and Process Dangers for Accused Athletes in International Sports", *Pepperdine Dispute Resolution Law Journal* 10(1), 5–50, 8; Yi, D.H. (2006), "Turning Medals into Metal: Evaluating the Court of Arbitration of Sport as an International Tribunal", *Asper Review of International Business and Trade Law* 6, 289–341, 312.

77 Haas, U. (2012), "Role and application of article 6 of the European Convention on Human Rights in CAS procedures", *International Sports Law Review* 12(3), 43–60, 45.

nis player.[78] It found that sporting competitions were characterized by a structural imbalance of power between athletes and SGBs due to the hierarchical structure of sports organizations and held that "[i]t is clear that an athlete's waiver of appeal against future awards will not generally be the result of a freely expressed desire on their part"[79]. In an interesting display of both honesty and self-critical reflexivity, the SFT recognized that its so-called liberal position regarding the validity of the consent to the arbitration clause could be perceived as "illogical"[80] in light of its reasoning in Cañas. Nonetheless, the Court justified this differentiated treatment of the consensual nature of the waiver of appeal and the CAS arbitration clause as a function of the need for a quick and knowledgeable resolution of sporting disputes.[81] In this context, it deemed that "maintaining the right to challenge an award is the proper counterbalance to the liberal approach underlying the examination of arbitration agreements in sports-related disputes"[82]. Since then the SFT continues to reaffirm its "benevolence"[83],

78 On this aspect of the case, see Krausz, N. (2011), "Waiver of Appeal to the Swiss Federal Tribunal: Recent Evolution of the Case Law and Compatibility with ECHR, Article 6", *Journal of International Arbitration* 28(2), 137–162, 144–146.

79 *Cañas. v. ATP Tour*, *supra* note 46, para. 4.3.2.2. The English translation used is available at http://law.marquette.edu/assets/sports-law/pdf/2012-conf-canas-english.pdf, accessed 1 February 2017).

80 "Qu'il y ait un certain illogisme, en théorie, à traiter de manière différente la convention d'arbitrage et la renonciation conventionnelle au recours, sous les rapports de la forme et du consentement, est sans doute vrai", *Ibid.*, 4.3.2.3. Festering on this acknowledgement, see Monheim, D. (2008), "Die Freiwilligkeit von Schiedsabreden im Sport und das Rechtsstaatsprinzip", *Sport und Recht* 15(1), 8–11.

81 "Toutefois, en dépit des apparences, ce traitement différencié obéit à une logique qui consiste, d'une part, à favoriser la liquidation rapide des litiges, notamment en matière de sport, par des tribunaux arbitraux spécialisés présentant des garanties suffisantes d'indépendance et d'impartialité [...], tout en veillant, d'autre part, à ce que les parties, et singulièrement les sportifs professionnels, ne renoncent pas à la légère à leur droit d'attaquer les sentences de la dernière instance arbitrale devant l'autorité judiciaire suprême de l'Etat du siège du tribunal arbitral.", *Cañas. v. ATP Tour, supra* note 46, para. 4.3.2.3.

82 *Ibid.*

83 *X. v. Y. & Fédération Internationale de Football Association (FIFA)*, *supra* note 46, para. 4.1; *Fédération International de Football Association (FIFA) & Cyprus Football Association (CFA)*, *supra* note 46, para. 3.2.2; *X. v. Y. sarl*, SFT Case 4A_246/2011, Judgment of 7 November 2011, para. 2.2.2; *A & B v. World Anti- Doping Agency (WADA) & Flemish Tennis Federation*, SFT Case 4A_428/2011, Judgment of 13 February 2012, para. 3.2.3.

"generosity"[84] and "liberalism"[85] in assessing the validity of a CAS arbitration clause. From the fact that a "CAS arbitration clause is typical of the sport requirements", it derived that "there is practically no elite sport without consent to sport arbitration"[86]. This is the closest the SFT gets to openly conceding that forced consent is, simply put, needed and that the free will of the athletes must be disregarded in the process.

As the realist critique started to bite, the SFT was forced to justify its position regarding the validity of CAS arbitration agreements. While the Pechstein rulings of the LG and OLG München clearly affirmed and problematized the forced nature of the consent to CAS arbitration agreements, the BGH decided to fall back to the SFT's contradictory position.

2. *The* Pechstein *rulings:* Consent, or no consent? That is the question

a. The ruling of the LG München: Not in Claudia Pechstein's name!

The question of the existence of a valid arbitration agreement between Claudia Pechstein and the International Skating Union (ISU) was decisive to affirm the competence of the LG München to hear the dispute. If recognized as valid, the agreement could preclude the jurisdiction of the German courts. Thus, the LG decided first to analyze the validity of the arbitration clause under Swiss law, while the applicable law was based on German private international law rules.[87] It found that the ISU was a monopolist and deprived Pechstein of any free choice. In other words, if she had opposed the signing of the clause, she would not have been able to compete in the 2009 World Championships.[88] Taking part in the competition

---

84 *A. v. World Anti-Doping Agency (WADA)*, *supra* note 46, para. 3.2.4; *Fédération International de Football Association (FIFA) & Cyprus Football Association (CFA)*, *supra* note 46, para. 3.2.2; *X. v. Y. sarl*, *supra* note 83, para. 2.2.2; *X. v. Y. & Fédération Internationale de Football Association (FIFA)*, *supra* note 46, para. 3.2.3.

85 *X. v. Y. & Fédération Internationale de Football Association (FIFA) supra* note 46, para. 4.1; *A & B v. World Anti- Doping Agency (WADA) & Flemish Tennis Federation*, *supra* note 83, para. 3.2.3.

86 *Ibid.*, para. 3.2.3.

87 LG München I, SchiedsVZ 2014, 100- 112, 104f.

88 "Ohne Unterzeichnung der Schiedsvereinbarung der Beklagten zu 2) wäre es der Klägerin nicht möglich gewesen, an dem Wettkampf am 7./8.2.2009 in Hamar teilzunehmen." *Ibid.*, 105.

of the ISU is the "sole possibility"[89] for Pechstein to exercise her profession. Due to the "structural imbalance" (*strukturelles Ungleichgewicht*) between the ISU and Pechstein, she is practically deprived of the ability to choose to submit to arbitration. This is not contradicted by the fact that Pechstein did not positively object to the arbitral clause.[90]

In the eyes of the tribunal, the lack of free consent is sufficient to invalidate the arbitration clause.[91] The LG reaches this conclusion, not un-controversially[92], on the basis of Article 27 paragraph 2 of the Swiss Civil Code. To this end, it openly disregards the "benevolent" (wohlwollende) interpretation of the SFT regarding the validity of CAS arbitration agreements.[93] The LG is of the opinion that this "benevolent" interpretation is contrary to Article 6 (1) European Convention of Human Rights (ECHR).[94] In fact, the difficulty posed by the reconciliation of forced consent to CAS arbitration with the Article 6 (1) ECHR has been previously highlighted in the literature.[95] I do not want to enter further into this debate, suffice to mention that many scholars believe that the forced

89 "Die Wettkampfteilnahme bei den Beklagten ist für die Klägerin angesichts deren Monopolstellung die einzige Möglichkeit, ihren Beruf angemessen auszuüben und gegen andere professionelle Konkurrenten anzutreten." *Ibid.*

90 "Entgegen der Auffassung der Beklagten zu 1) ist eine Freiwilligkeit nicht aufgrund des fehlenden Vorbringens von Einwänden oder der Abänderung oder Streichung der Zuständigkeit des Schiedsgerichtes anzunehmen." *Ibid.*

91 *Ibid.*

92 The LG München was widely criticized on that point in German scholarship, a criticism that might have led the OLG München to favour a competition law analysis. See, for example: Haas, U. (2014), "Zwangsschiedsgerichtsbarkeit im Sport und EMRK", *ASA Bulletin* 32(4), 707–734; Schulze, G. (2014), "Fortentwicklung des Schweizer Vertragsrechts und Präklusion bei der inzidenten Anerkennung eines CAS-Entscheids", *Sport und Recht* 21(4), 139–143, 140–141; Pfeiffer, T. (2014), "Rechtsgeschäftliche Entscheidungsfreiheit beim Abschluss von Schiedsvereinbarungen: Bemerkungen zum Pechstein-Urteil des Landgerichts München I vom 26 Februar 2014", *Zeitschrift für Schiedsverfahren* 12(3), 161–165, 163.

93 See references to the *Cañas* decision of the SFT at LG München I, *supra* note 87, 106f.

94 "Dieser Argumentation kann angesichts der Garantien der Art. 6 und 13 der Europäischen Menschenrechtskonvention (im Folgenden: EMRK) nicht gefolgt werden." *Ibid.*, 107.

95 Critical of the compatibility, see Lukomski, J. (2013), "Arbitration clauses in sport governing bodies' statutes: consent or constraint? Analysis from the perspective of Article 6(1) of the European Convention on Human Rights", *International Sports Law Journal* 13(1), 60–70, 70. Pointing at the difficulty, Besson, S. (2006), "Arbitration and Human Rights", *ASA Bulletin* 24(3), 395–416, 398; Steingruber, *supra* note 76, 74. See also, recently, Frumer, P. (2016), "L'arbitrage sportif, la lute contre

nature of CAS arbitration is not per se contradictory to Article 6 (1) ECHR.[96] In any event, the LG's decision shone a spotlight on the post-consensual nature of CAS arbitration, a view shared, though very differently, by the OLG München.

b. The ruling of the OLG München: Forced CAS arbitration as an abuse of ISU's monopoly

On appeal, the OLG faced the same legal question as the LG: does a valid arbitration clause between Claudia Pechstein and the ISU preclude its competence to hear the matter? It also answered this question negatively, but relied on very different reasoning, anchored in German competition law instead of the more classical private international law analysis conducted by the LG.[97] In fact, it expressly rejected the legal reasoning of the LG in its decision, and insisted that free consent is not a necessary condition for the validity of an arbitration clause under Article 6 (1) ECHR.[98] The thrust of the court's argument to find in favour of Claudia Pechstein lies in the finding that the ISU abused its monopoly position on the market for the organization of World Championships in speed skating by forcing her to agree to a CAS arbitration clause.[99] Indeed, the OLG concludes

---

le dopage et le respect des droits fondamentaux des sportifs professionnels : une incertitude peu glorieuse", *Revue Trimestrielle de Droit Européen* 27(108), 817–854. Asking a similar question in the US context, Gubi, J. (2008), "The Olympic Binding Arbitration Clause and the Court of Arbitration for Sport: An Analysis of Due Process Concerns", *Fordham Intellectual Property Media & Entertainment Law Journal* 18(4), 997–1024, 1011.

96 See Haas, *supra* note 92, 80; Haas, *supra* note 77, 51–52; Rigozzi and Robert-Tissot, *supra* note 72, 72; Muresan, R. and Korff, N. (2014), "Sportschiedsgerichtsbarkeit: Wie weiter nach dem "Pechstein-Urteil" des Landgerichts München?", *Causa Sport* 10(3), 199–211, 209–210.

97 On this argumentative shift, see Rombach, A. (2015), "The "Pechstein-judgment" of the OLG München: What does it mean for international sports and commercial arbitration?", *Zeitschrift für Schiedsverfahren* 13(3), 105–111.

98 "Entgegen der Auffassung des Landgerichts sind Schiedsvereinbarungen zwischen einem marktbeherrschenden Veranstalter internationaler Sportwettkämpfe und den daran teilnehmenden Athleten nicht schon deshalb generell unwirksam, weil es an einer freien Willensbildung der Athleten bei der Unterzeichnung fehlte." OLG München, SchiedsVZ 2015, 40–47, 43.

99 *Ibid.* On the competition law dimension of the case, see: Duval, A. and Van Rompuy, B. (2016), "Protecting Athletes' Right to a Fair Trial Through EU Competition Law: The *Pechstein* Case" In: C. Paulussen *et al.* (eds), *Fundamental Rights*

that a forced arbitration clause in favour of the CAS constitutes an unfair trading condition that would not have been agreed if ISU were not in a dominant position on the market for international skating competitions. The unfair nature of this clause derives from the OLG's finding of a lack independence of the CAS from the SGBs.[100] The forced nature of CAS arbitration as identified by the LG is thus re-casted in competition law terms.[101] Nonetheless, the underlying factual assessment remains identical: athletes (and clubs, officials, national federations etc) are forced by a global monopolist (ISU or any other SGB) to adhere to a CAS arbitration agreement if they want to participate in international competitions and exercise their profession. In other words, there is no alternative! The OLG, however, is not as radical as the LG and some authors[102], as it recognizes that a forced arbitration clause is not per se an abuse of a dominant position, nor necessarily contrary to Article 6 (1) ECHR.[103]

c. The ruling of the BGH: Saving the consensual foundations of the CAS

Finally, after two years of uncertainty with regard to the future of the CAS, on 7 June 2016 came the much-expected Pechstein ruling of the highest German civil court, the BGH. The court strongly sided with the CAS, by rejecting the reasoning of both the LG and the OLG. I have criticized the court elsewhere for its poor understanding of the institutional functioning of the CAS, and for not having considered the OLG's – in my view – legiti-

in International and European Law. The Hague: Springer, 245–276; Stancke, F. (2015), "Pechstein und der aktuelle Stand des Sportkartellrechts", *Sport und Recht* 22(2), 46–51.

100 For more details on this assessment, see Duval and Van Rompuy, *supra* note 99, 266–275.

101 A possibility envisaged (and discarded) early on by Netzle, *supra* note 32, 53–54.

102 See: Monheim (2008), *supra* note 80, 8–11; Monheim, D. (2014), "Das Ende des Schiedszwangs im Sport – Der Fall Pechstein", *Sport und Recht* 3, 90–94; Heermann, P.W. (2014), "Freiwilligkeit von Schiedsvereinbarungen in der Sportgerichtsbarkeit", *Zeitschrift für Schiedsverfahren* 12(2), 66–79.

103 On this rather favourable assessment of the validity of CAS arbitration by the OLG, see: Brandner, G. and Kläger, R. (2015), "Ein Sieg über (oder für) das System der Sportschiedsgerichtsbarkeit", *Zeitschrift für Schiedsverfahren* 13(3), 112–119; Scherrer, U. *et al.* (2015), "Pechstein ist kein "Bosman" der Sportschiedsgerichtsbarkeit", *Zeitschrift für Schiedsverfahren* 13(3), 161.

mate concerns with regard to its lack of independence.[104] Here, I will briefly analyze the BGH's holdings involving the consensual foundation of CAS arbitration in the Pechstein factual constellation.

The BGH in its judgment assessed whether the CAS arbitration clause was compatible with German competition law, in particular § 19 GWB.[105] Its main conclusion was that the "demand for an arbitration agreement which provides for the CAS as the arbitral tribunal, in any event, is justified by objective reasons and does not contradict the general statutory determinations"[106]. To reach such a conclusion, the court considered, and this is the most explicit and controversial argument regarding the free consent of Claudia Pechstein to CAS arbitration, that she "voluntarily and, thus, validly submitted herself to the arbitration agreement"[107]. In particular, the court added, it "has not been determined or argued that the Claimant was caused to do so by an illegal threat or deception, let alone by physical force"[108], thus, denying the fact that economic blackmail might have the same effect as sheer force or threats (which could be of an economic nature). Yet, the court, probably conscious of the "surrealism"[109] of this statement, qualified it in the following paragraph. The judges recognized that "if one of the contracting partners has such excessive power that he can de facto dictate contractual terms, this results in third party deter-

104 For the core elements of my critique of the judgment, see: Duval, A. (2016), "The Pechstein case: Transnational constitutionalism in inaction at the Bundesgerichtshof", *Verfassungsblog*, 10 June, available at http://verfassungsblog.de/the-pechstein-case-transnational-constitutionalism-in-inaction-at-the-bundesgerichtshof/, accessed 1 February 2017. A critical view widely shared by: Heermann, P.W. (2016), "Die Sportschiedsgerichtsbarkeit nach dem Pechstein-Urteil des BGH", *Neue Juristische Wochenschrift* 69(31), 2224–2227; Thorn, K. and Lasthaus, C. (2016), "Das Pechstein-Urteil des BGH – Ein Freibrief für die Sportsschiedsgerichtsbarkeit", *IPRax-Praxis des Internationalen Privat- und Verfahrensrechts* 36(5), 426–431; Rombach, A. (2016), "*Pechstein vs. CAS*: Game, Set and Match for Sports Arbitration?", *SchiedsVZ*, 276–279.

105 BGH, *supra* note 2, paras 42ff. The English translation of the BGH's ruling used is the one by Rombach, *supra* note 104, 268.

106 BGH, *supra* note 2, para. 48.

107 *Ibid*., para. 53.

108 *Ibid*. A view strongly supported by Haas, U. (2016), "The German Federal Court on Treacherous Ice – A Final Point in the Pechstein Case" In: C. Müller *et al.* (eds), *New Developments in International Commercial Arbitration*. Geneva/Zurich: Schulthess, 219–265, 258.

109 See Duval, A. (2016), "The BGH's Pechstein Decision: A Surrealist Ruling", *ASSER International Sports Law Blog*, 8 June, available at http://www.asser.nl/SportsLaw/Blog/post/the-bgh-s-pechstein-decision-a-surrealist-ruling, accessed 1 February 2017.

mination of the intent (Fremdbestimmung) for the other contracting partner"[110], and conceded that Pechstein "was determined by a third party"[111]. The clear contradictory nature of this finding with the previously claimed free consent of Pechstein to the clause, highlights the perilous and acrobatic nature of the BGH's legal reasoning. This acknowledgment leads the BGH to conduct a balancing exercise between Pechstein's rights and the interests of ISU in having a CAS arbitration clause, which in the end favours the latter.[112] Furthermore, the BGH claimed that the ECtHR would adopt a similar conclusion, for "the fact that the Claimant [Claudia Pechstein] was required to sign the registration for competition demanded by the Respondent 2 [ISU] in order to exercise her profession does not lead to an involuntary arbitration agreement which violates the convention"[113]. Finally, and rather unsurprisingly in light of the BGH's previous findings, it disavowed the LG's interpretation of Swiss law and recognized that it follows from the SFT's case law that "a professional athlete will sign the arbitration agreement only due to the fact that he is required to do so in order to exercise his profession, but that the arbitration agreement is nonetheless valid"[114]. It even mentioned the "theoretical contradiction in the treatment of the arbitration agreement and the waiver of legal remedies"[115].

The BGH's ruling, like the SFT's jurisprudence, on the consent to CAS arbitration is a perfect illustration of legal doublespeak. Doublespeak is a language that deliberately reverses the meaning of words, inspired by George Orwell's famous novel 1984. With regard to the consensual foundation of CAS arbitration, both the SFT and the BGH seem to be conscious of their slide towards doublespeak. I believe they fail to resist it because they are convinced of the necessity of preserving the CAS without fully embracing the alternative foundations that could be available to secure and legitimize its jurisdiction. Yet if the CAS is not truly speaking in the name of Claudia Pechstein, in whose name is it speaking then?

110 BGH, *supra* note 2, para. 55.
111 *Ibid.*
112 *Ibid.*, para. 62.
113 *Ibid.*, para. 65.
114 *Ibid.*, para. 70.
115 *Ibid.*

II. Speaking in the name of (…)?

The CAS faces a similar "foundational uncertainty"[116] as that bearing on other international courts. If the voluntary and consensual origin of the arbitrators' mission is an essential, quasi- ontological feature of arbitration[117], then it is difficult to accept that CAS arbitration agreements are valid.[118] CAS arbitration would go beyond the conceptual boundaries of the notion of arbitration.[119] The legitimacy of the CAS cannot be rooted in private autonomy; it must derive from somewhere else. The question is then, whether the CAS can be speaking in other names, no less legitimate than Claudia Pechstein's? The OLG München found that "important practical reasons" (gewichtige sachgerechte Gründe)[120] speak in favour of the necessity of forced CAS arbitration.[121] Four ideal-typical names, illustrating the "multifunctionality"[122] of the CAS, can be discerned in the literature to ground the legitimacy and the validity of CAS arbitration: state delegation, efficiency, proximity and equality.

---

116 Von Bogdandy, A. and Venzke, I. (2013), "On the Functions of International Courts: An Appraisal in Light of Their Burgeoning Public Authority", *Leiden Journal of International Law* 26(1), 49–72, 53.

117 "Quant à l'origine volontaire de la mission de l'arbitre, elle est, elle aussi, essentielle. Les arbitrages forcés ne sont donc pas de véritables arbitrages, mais une variété de juridictions d'exception, dont le pouvoir de juger procède, pour certains litiges spécifiques, d'une délégation de l'Etat, et auxquelles le législateur a souhaité appliquer tout ou partie du régime de l'arbitrage." Jarrosson, *supra* note 16, 19.

118 In other words: "[d]as ist aber doch denklogisch ausgeschlossen – ohne wirksame Schiedsabrede kann es keinen wirksamen Schiedspruch geben!" Monheim (2014), *supra* note 102, 93.

119 As: "s'affranchir de la volonté des parties pour le recours à l'arbitrage exclut la qualification d'arbitrage." Jarrosson, *supra* note 16, 20.

120 OLG München, *supra* note 98, 43.

121 Some commentators doubt that alternative names can be summoned to substitute the lack of free consent. Because, "so überzeugend diese Gründe auch sein mögen, so wenig sind sie doch isoliert betrachtet geeignet, das Erfordernis der Freiwilligkeit einer Unterwerfung unter die Sportschiedsgerichtsbarkeit in Frage zu stellen". Heermann, *supra* note 102, 75.

122 On multifunctionality, see Von Bogdandy and Venzke (2014), *supra* note 1, 5–17.

A. In the name of... the States

In some, especially American[123], contributions, reference is made to the adoption of the World Anti-Doping Code (WADC)[124] and the International Convention against Doping in Sport[125] to legally construct the jurisdiction of the CAS as a state delegation. The CAS jurisdiction would be based on the state consent doctrine traditionally used in the framework of public international law. However, there is no such clearly worded delegation included in the Convention[126], nor are the States party to the WADC, which includes a provision imposing CAS arbitration for international cases.[127] In fact, some States (France for example) specifically object to exclusive CAS jurisdiction in anti-doping disputes.[128] Neither is the World Anti-Doping Agency an international organization grounded in an international treaty. If there is a delegation it is very much implicit, through a soft endorsement, but it can hardly be the main source of an alternative legitimacy for forced CAS arbitration.[129] This soft endorsement, or "low visibility delegation"[130], could be used as an additional argument to support the validity of a forced jurisdiction of the CAS,[131] but it does not con-

123 See Ravjani, A. (2009), "The Court of Arbitration for Sport: A subtle form of international delegation", *Journal of International Media and Entertainment Law* 2(2), 241–284.

124 The latest 2015 version of the WADC is available at https://www.wada-ama.org/en/resources/the-code/world-anti-doping-code, accessed 1 February 2017.

125 The Convention was adopted in October 2005 and entered into force in February 2007. The full text of the convention is available at http://portal.unesco.org/en/ev.php-URL_ID=31037&URL_DO=DO_TOPIC&URL_SECTION=201.html, accessed 1 February 2017.

126 The CAS is not mentioned in the convention.

127 Though, Article 22.4 of the WADC symbolically indicates that "[e]ach government will respect arbitration as the preferred means of resolving doping-related disputes, subject to human and fundamental rights and applicable national law."

128 For example, Article L232–24 of the French *Code du Sport* foresees that appeals against decisions of the French Anti-Doping Agency (*Agence française de lutte contre le dopage*) can be lodged only with the administrative courts.

129 A point rightly highlighted by the OLG München in its *Pechstein* judgment. See OLG München, *supra* note 98, 43.

130 Ravjani, *supra* note 123, 260.

131 In 2003, the SFT referred to the Copenhagen Declaration on anti-doping that predated the UNESCO Convention to support its recognition of the CAS as an independent tribunal. It held: "Il faut y voir un signe tangible de la confiance que les Etats et tous les milieux concernés par la lutte contre le dopage accordent au TAS. On imagine mal que les intéressés aient pu consacrer de manière aussi éclatante le pouvoir juridictionnel de cette institution d'arbitrage, s'ils avaient eu

stitute a formal state delegation, nor can it stand as an isolated foundation to legitimize the binding jurisdiction of the CAS.

B. In the name of…efficiency

Another foundation often referred to in the literature is the so-called "utilitarian"[132] justification. The CAS is perceived, in cost-benefit terms, as the most efficient institution to solve sporting disputes.[133] It is touted as a faster and cheaper decision-making mechanism than national courts. This line of argument is supported by references to the painful experiences of athletes having tried to use national courts in sporting disputes.[134] Moreover, the need for a quick resolution is considered paramount in the sporting context, in order to ensure the smooth running of an on-going competition and in light of the short duration of an athlete's career.[135] In particular, the BGH and the SFT have mentioned the need for speed as an adequate rationale for CAS arbitration.[136] Whether the CAS can be consid-

---

le sentiment qu'elle se trouve sous la coupe du CIO." *A. & B. v. Comité International Olympique, Fédération Internationale de Ski and Tribunal Arbitral du Sport*, SFT Case 4P. 267/2002, Judgment of 27 May 2003, para. 3.3.3.3. Similarly, in its *Pechstein* decision, the BGH referred to Germany's signing of the Convention in its balancing exercise, see BGH, *supra* note 2, paras 59f.

132 See Rigozzi and Robert-Tissot, *supra* note 72, 68.

133 The identification of the CAS as an efficient venue to deal with sporting dispute is a very widespread view in the literature. See for some examples: Gubi, *supra* note 95,1016–1017; Reilly, *supra* note 21, 81; Blackshaw, I. (2003), "The Court of Arbitration for Sport: An International Forum for Settling Disputes Effectively 'Within the Family of Sport'", *Entertainment Law* 2(2), 61–83, 82; Findlay, H.A. (2005), "Rules of a Sport Specific Arbitration Process as an Instrument of Policy Making", *Marquette Sports Law Review* 16(1), 73–98, 74–76.

134 Faylor, *supra* note 66, 163–172. See also Nafziger, J.A.R. (2002), "Dispute Resolution in the Arena of International Sports Competition?", *The American Journal of Comparative Law* 50(3), 161–179, 172-177.

135 Netzle, *supra* note 32, 45–58.

136 The SFT held that "Il n'est pas certain que d'autres solutions existent, qui soient susceptibles de remplacer une institution à même de résoudre rapidement et de manière peu coûteuse des litiges internationaux dans le domaine du sport". *A. & B. v. Comité International Olympique, Fédération Internationale de Ski and Tribunal Arbitral du Sport*, *supra* note 131, para. 3.3.3.3. The BGH considered in its *Pechstein* ruling that "[t]he further advantages of international sports arbitration compared to the state courts also include […] the speed in making decisions which is of particular importance with regard to scheduled sports events […]" BGH, *supra* note 2, para. 59.

ered a cheap and quick judicial venue is a contested matter. In many instances, for example in doping cases, its costs are not necessarily lower than those incurred in front of national courts.[137] Furthermore, due to a fast-growing caseload, its celerity in deciding cases is not as pronounced as it once was. The recourse to ad-hoc mechanisms for international competitions (e.g. the Olympic Games or the FIFA World Cup), however, does offer the advantage of on-the-spot justice. Yet, could such a "utilitarian" foundation of the CAS truly replace free consent? This would imply that the sheer quantitative economy of justice, its cost and swiftness, would trump its qualitative component. It would also be blind to the fact that judges, or their alter-ego CAS arbitrators, are in the business of allocating economic and social opportunities and making distributive calls that are not automatic and contain a strong normative core.[138] Two parties might be allowed to decide freely to entrust the resolution of a private dispute (not affecting the public interest), and thus to make these distributive calls, to an arbitral panel of their liking. However, it would be abusive if one party, thanks to its monopolistic position, were allowed to decide unilaterally to do so. Hence, the fact that a mode of resolution of disputes is fast and cheap cannot be sufficient to justify the binding recourse to it. To be fair, the CAS's binding jurisdiction is almost never justified exclusively in those terms. Instead, the efficiency of CAS is often invoked in conjunction with its proximity to the sporting ethos and mind-set.

C. In the name of… proximity

A Swiss scholar, Gabrielle Kaufmann-Kohler, once qualified the CAS as a justice of proximity (justice de proximité).[139] She meant that the CAS, and in particular its arbitrators, was close to the social reality, the people and actions, it was supposed to rule over. In other words, the CAS is embedded in the global sporting community and best placed to solve the disputes arising between its members. In this perspective, it is not the quantitative

137 On the restrictive effect of the cost of CAS arbitration on access to justice for athletes, see Rigozzi and Robert-Tissot, *supra* note 72, 73–81.

138 For a discussion of the inevitable politicisation of private law constructs with regard to the *lex mercatoria*, see Zumbansen, P. (2003), "Lex mercatoria: Zum Geltungsanspruch transnationalen Rechts", *Rabels Zeitschrift für ausländisches und internationales Privatrecht* 67(4), 637–682.

139 Kaufmann-Kohler, G. (1998), "Nagano et l'arbitrage – ou vers une justice de proximité", *ASA Bulletin* 16(2), 311–324.

efficiency, speed and cost of CAS arbitration that is put forward, but its qualitative functional edge over territorially enshrined courts. In a way, it is building on the famous words of Lord Denning in the Enderby Town Football Club Ltd v. Football Association Ltd. case: "justice can often be done [...] better by a good layman than by a bad lawyer"[140]. In other words, "it may be doubted that ordinary judges are best suited to deal with specialized areas of sports discipline"[141]. Similarly, it is argued "national judges seldom have the opportunity to apply these regulations and thus may not always understand the ratio and spirit behind them"[142].

A more theoretical form of the same argument would identify the CAS as the natural tribunal of a *lex sportiva*, a transnational private legal system/order/regime of sport.[143] Its jurisdiction would stem from its institutional function inside the system.[144] From this point of view, "the very globalization of the sports movement and its high degree of cohesion, even to the point of recognizing the existence of an autonomous legal order, seem to justify a system of dispute resolution in support of this autonomy"[145]. By becoming the bouche de la *lex sportiva*, a CAS arbitrator metamorphoses into a judge embedded in a particular transnational community.[146]

He contributes primarily to the "consolidation"[147] and "coherence"[148] of the *lex sportiva* and no longer to the resolution of strictly individual disputes. In system-theoretical terms, the CAS is stabilizing the normative

140 Enderby Town FC v. the FA [1971] Ch 591, 605.

141 Paulsson, *supra* note 23, 361.

142 Steingruber, *supra* note 76, 67–70.

143 "Il n'est pas seulement l'organe chargé, selon la volonté commune des parties, de trancher leur différend; il est, au-delà la juridiction de tout un système." Latty, *supra* note 8, 288.

144 Maisonneuve, *supra* note 7; Latty, *supra* note 8, 288; Paulsson, J. (2010), "'Arbitration in three dimension", *LSE Legal Studies Working Paper* (2), 1–34, 24–25, available at http://papers.ssrn.com/sol3/papers.cfm?abstract_id=1536093, accessed 1 February 2017.

145 Steingruber, *supra* note 76, 68.

146 "Le passage de l'arbitre au juge est consacré lorsque le tiers s'exprime non plus au nom des parties, mais pour le compte d'une communauté plus largement comprise." Stone-Sweet, A. and Grisel, F. (2009), "L'Arbitrage International : Du Contrat Dyadique au Système Normatif", *Archives de philosophie du droit* 52, 75–95, 86.

147 See, in general, the excellent chapter on the function of the CAS in the *lex sportiva* in Latty, *supra* note 8, 257.

148 *Ibid.*, 261.

expectations in the system of global sport.[149] This is done, for example, through the development of a relatively stable jurisprudence.[150] The CAS becomes the judicial institution of a specific (private) transnational regime in whose name it acts.[151] The parallel is drawn with national legal orders and the forced nature of CAS arbitration is then a function of the fact that an individual is acting as a citizen/member of a specific transnational legal regime/system/order harbouring a particular functional rationality.

Can the binding jurisdiction of the CAS stem solely from it pertaining to a transnational regime/system/order regulating a specific sphere of world society? Is the pursuit of a functional rationality enough to support the CAS' forced jurisdiction? What if this functional rationality is contrary to other fundamental values (say for example the freedom to work)? The potential risk is that the "specific focus of an international court can easily lead to a strong orientation toward the 'regime interest' at the expense of other principles"[152]. An emphasis on the need for equality of athletes before the law tames this isolationist and functionalist perspective.

D. *In the name of… equality*

Finally, the mandatory jurisdiction of the CAS might stem from the need for equality in front of the (global) law. Synthetically, the much-rehearsed argument goes like this: if athletes are competing against each other on a singular global playing field, equality calls for any dispute resulting from these (global) competitions to be dealt with by a singular (global) court.[153] If not, this could lead to discrepancies of interpretation and nationalistic

149 This is a reference to Niklas Luhmann's theory of law. See also, for an identical analogy, Von Bogdandy and Venzke, *supra* note 116, 54.

150 "Au vu de la pratique du T.A.S., l'existence d'une jurisprudence arbitrale sportive est aujourd'hui un fait indiscutable. En ce sens, le Tribunal arbitral du sport détient un pouvoir 'prétorien' indéniable." Latty, *supra* note 8, 300. See also *supra* references in note 7.

151 On international courts as institutional actors of a specific regime, see Von Bogdandy and Venzke, *supra* note 116, 68–69.

152 Von Bogdandy and Venzke (2014), *supra* note 1, 97.

153 In other words: "Gerade bei internationalen Wettkämpfen ist jedoch das öffentliche Interesse besonders groß und damit einhergehend auch das Bedürfnis der Athleten nach entsprechender Chancengleichheit." Brandner and Kläger, *supra* note 103, 115–116.

favour.[154] From this point of view, one needs to preserve "a certain equality of treatment of athletes across borders"[155]. Thus, "the prospect of different national courts reaching inconsistent conclusions on the merits of Olympic and international sports disputes is a significant problem"[156]. Indeed, it ought to be "self-evident that international competition must be subject to a unitary international regime, lest national authorities yield to the temptation of indulgence for their own champions, thus leading to an uneven international playing field and, in some places, a race to the bottom"[157]. Hence, "[i]t is indispensable that all international competitors adhere to common rules, including reference to the same neutral mechanism for resolving disputes"[158].

Some national courts have endorsed this view. The SFT held for example that "an international development towards the CAS jurisdiction in doping matters is to be upheld with a view to ensuring compliance with international standards in this field"[159]. Similarly, the OLG München in its Pechstein ruling considered that "a uniform competence and procedure can preclude that similar cases be decided differently, and therefore safeguard the equal opportunities of athletes during the competitions"[160]. The BGH in its Pechstein decision also emphasized at numerous times the benefits of a unified sporting justice.[161] The underlying pragmatic logic is simple; "in order to be able to compare sports performances internationally, competitive sport must be performed in accordance with the same and uniform rules"[162]. However, "the risk to consistency increases with the number of fora before state courts and—as a consequence thereof—of national legal standards that apply"[163]. Thus, if "sport wishes to preserve its

154 This argument is raised by a plethora of authors. See, amongst many others: Haas, *supra* note 92, 722; Paulsson, *supra* note 23, 361; Steingruber, *supra* note 76, 70; McLaren, *supra* note 19, 381; Findlay, *supra* note 133, 96; McLaren, R.H. (2001), "Sports Law Arbitration by CAS: is it the Same as International Arbitration?", *Pepperdine Law Review* 29(1), 101–114, 102–103; Mitten and Opie, *supra* note 18, 284–285; Pfeiffer, *supra* note 92, 165.

155 Steingruber, *supra* note 76, 69.

156 Mitten and Opie, *supra* note 18, 284.

157 Paulsson, J. (2013), "Why Good Arbitration Cannot Compensate for Bad Courts", *Journal of International Arbitration* 30(4), 345–359, 357.

158 *Ibid.*

159 *A. v. World Anti-Doping Agency (WADA), Fédération International de Football Association (FIFA), & Cyprus Football Association (CFA)*, *supra* note 46, para. 3.3.1.

160 OLG München, *supra* note 98, 43 (our translation).

161 See BGH, *supra* note 2, paras 59ff.

162 Haas, *supra* note 77, 53.

163 *Ibid.*

global character and the principle of uniformity this is only possible by concentrating jurisdiction at a single forum in the form of arbitration"[164]. The emphasis of the argument is less about a specific sporting rationality enshrined in a particular system and more about the equality of global citizens in front of the law. It points out that in a transnational context, in which people of different countries are predominantly active on a common playing field constituted by a set of transnational rules, that only a single (global) court can warrant the equality of the participants. The significant difference with the proximity justification is that it does not focus exclusively on the specificity of sport, or its particular rationality, but on the need for common justice in a transnationalized social context.

This justice can, and in fact should, embrace fundamental values transcending the sporting rationale and including, for example, fundamental human rights enshrined in the ECHR.

The efficiency, proximity and equality justifications are often unconsciously bundled together in the literature and constitute the multifarious foundations of forced CAS arbitration recognized by national courts. Yet, once disentangled, one can clearly see that the first two are merely subservient to the latter. It is the call for equality between citizens engaging in a transnationalized field of human activity that ultimately convinces the courts that a forced CAS arbitration agreement must be deemed valid. This is an un-confessed acknowledgment that the CAS is exercising much-needed international public authority. Yet, with public authority should also come democratic legitimacy.

III. Conclusion: Democratize the CAS!

The CAS is definitely not speaking in the name of Claudia Pechstein. She never had a chance to commit freely to its jurisdiction.[165] Does this mean that the CAS should not have jurisdiction to decide her case as some[166] are suggesting? Probably not. Strong post- consensual (and post-national) rationales support the exclusive and mandatory jurisdiction of the CAS. Those potential Ersatz-names undersigning its jurisdiction are: efficiency,

164 *Ibid.*

165 Though one may argue that by submitting an appeal to the CAS and not challenging its jurisdiction she might have implicitly consented to it. This would be, as pointed out by the OLG, misreading the factual constraints that forced her in practice to take her chance at the CAS.

166 Heermann, *supra* note 102.

proximity and especially equality. Taken together, these constitute credible post-consensual foundations for the CAS, and are recognized as such by, for example, the highest German and Swiss courts.

The globalization of sport has, to paraphrase Gunther Teubner[167], broken the traditional frames of international arbitration and has led to the binding global jurisdiction of the CAS in many sporting disputes. In countless ways, it seems that the "facts on the ground are ahead of the theory"[168]. In this context, an excessive reference to consent might veil "the role of private law categories in the restructuring of post-national government"[169]. Thus, the contribution of private law "to the coagulation of sovereignty into new institutions with many state-like features remains all too often in the shade"[170]. The crisis of the consensual foundations of CAS arbitration unleashed by the Pechstein case brings these underlying political realities to the fore. The consensual myth was very useful "to accelerate the formation of highly political global institutions"[171], but holding onto it "unduly stifles political debate, and may mask profound redistributive implications"[172].

In their book, von Bogdandy and Venzke identify a similar dynamic at play in international law at large. International courts, which were traditionally seen as speaking in the name of the states, see their consensual foundations being eroded.[173] However, in general, consensual underpinnings remain a stronger basis for international courts than for the CAS. Still, this progressive shift away from state consent should, in their view, entail a democratization of international courts as "[n]o road leads past developing the democratic principle for international institutions"[174]. In

167 Teubner, G. (2002), "Breaking Frames: Economic Globalisation and the Emergence of *lex mercatoria*", *European Journal of Social Theory* 5(2), 199–217.

168 Paulsson, *supra* note 144, 26.

169 Caruso, D. (2006), "Private Law and State-Making in the Age of Globalization", *New York University Journal of International Law and Politics* 39(1), 1–74, 23.

170 *Ibid.*

171 *Ibid.*, 77.

172 *Ibid.*, 79.

173 In their words: "We do not deny that the consensus of the states continues to constitute an important resource of legitimacy; however, it alone no longer sufficiently sustains many of the decisions made in recent decades." Von Bogdandy and Venzke (2014), *supra* note 1, 3. See also Werner, W.G. (2016), "State consent as foundational myth" In: C. Brölmann and Y. Radi (eds), *Research Handbook on the Theory and Practice of International Lawmaking*. Cheltenham: Edward Elgar, 13–31.

174 Von Bogdandy and Venzke (2014), *supra* note 1, 98.

this regard, "[i]ndependence, impartiality, and legal expertise of the judges are not only requirements under the rule of law, but are also democratic necessities"[175]. This would require, in particular, ensuring the independence of judges[176] and the fairness and openness of the judicial process.[177]

Likewise, the post-consensual nature of its jurisdiction implies that a democratic lens should be applied to the CAS. Thus, the fairness of its procedures and the independence of its arbitrators must be assessed differently, and more strictly, than under traditional (consensual) international arbitration.[178] A lesser emphasis should be put on the parties to the arbitration and their consent to a particular procedural set-up and greater stress should rest on the respect of the procedural standards applied to other international and national courts, for example those enshrined in Article 6 (1) ECHR.[179] The CAS being embedded in a particular transnational legal regime/system/order, it is paramount that it be institutionally separated from the political authorities (the SGBs) of that same regime/system/order. In particular, the diversity of the people affected by CAS decisions must ideally be reflected in the selection process of the CAS arbitrators.

Here lies the point of re-entry for national courts. Their contribution to the democratization of the exercise of public authority by the CAS in the transnational realm will depend on the intensity with which they decide to supervise its procedural fairness. Contrary to the LG, the approach of the OLG in the Pechstein case is a paramount example of a reflexive control aimed at triggering a democratization process of the CAS. It is akin to a Solange position: the CAS should be allowed to operate even in the absence of a consensual foundation as long as it is truly independent from the SGBs.[180] In that regard, the latest decision of the BGH is a missed opportunity. The national court failed to understand its constitutional role and to properly check the democratic quality of the CAS.[181]

---

175 *Ibid.*, 159.

176 *Ibid.*, 158–170.

177 *Ibid.*, 170–176.

178 See for a different theoretical path to a similar conclusion, Schultz, T. (2011), "The Concept of Law in Transnational Arbitral Legal Orders and some of its Consequences", *Journal of International Dispute Settlement* 2(1), 59–85.

179 A necessity recognized by Frumer, *supra* note 95.

180 For an elaboration of this idea in the context of EU law, see Duval, A. (2015), "The Court of Arbitration for Sport and EU Law: Chronicle of an encounter", *Maastricht Journal of European and Comparative Law* 22(2), 224–255.

181 For a critique of the decision from this perspective, see Duval, A. (2016), "The Pechstein case: Transnational constitutionalism in inaction at the Bundesgerichtshof", *Verfassungsblog*, 10 June, available at http://verfassungsblog.de/the-pechstei

In a rapidly transnationalizing world, where private law constructs serve as a launchpad for much-needed transnational governance systems/regimes/orders, it is imperative that national (and regional) courts assume a new crucial constitutional function.[182] They ought to exercise a reflexive, but critical, review of the transnational private regulations and institutions that are born out of unbound private power.[183] Undoubtedly, "[i]f it is perceived that the important functions of control and enforcement are no longer carried out properly by the judiciary, the arbitral process may easily be manipulated for corrupt ends"[184]. In that regard, the OLG München's Pechstein ruling called for a necessary reform of the CAS.[185] There is certainly no need for "radical"[186] or utopian solutions, such as the creation of an International Sports Court by the states, but pragmatic fixes are in order to ensure that the CAS as an institution is not captured by the SGBs. Many proposals come to mind and here is not the right place to address them comprehensively.[187] Yet, one thing is certain, critically engaging with the CAS through a democratic lens has become more necessary than ever.

---

n-case-transnational-constitutionalism-in-inaction-at-the-bundesgerichtshof/, accessed 1 February 2017.

182 *Ibid.*

183 For a similar argument, see Benvenisti, E. and Downs, G.W. (2011), "National Courts Review of Transnational Private Regulation", 1–18, available at http://ssrn.com/abstract=1742452, accessed 1February 2017.

184 Paulsson, *supra* note 157, 352.

185 A reform also advocated previously in the literature, see Zen-Ruffinen, P. (2012), "La nécessaire réforme du Tribunal Arbitral du Sport" In: A. Rigozzi *et al.* (eds), *Citius, Altius, Fortius, Mélanges en l'honneur de Denis Oswald*. Basel: Helbing Lichtenhahn, 483–537. See also Downie, R. (2011), "Improving the performance of sport's ultimate umpire: Reforming the governance of the Court of Arbitration for Sport", *Melbourne Journal of International Law* 12(2), 67–96. And most recently by Frumer, *supra* note 95, 831–834.

186 On this I share the view of Veuthey, A. (2013), "Re-questioning the independence of the Court of Arbitration for Sport in light of the scope of its review", *International Sports Law Review* 13(4), 105–115, 114.

187 For some proposals, see Muresan and Korff, *supra* note 96, 208–211. See also Duval, A. (2015), "Three pillars for a reform of the Court of Arbitration for Sport: Independence, Transparency and Access to Justice", *Play The Game*, 4 December, available at http://www.playthegame.org/news/comments/2015/019_three-pillars-for-a-reform-of-the-court-of-arbitration-for-sport-independence-transparency-and-access-to-justice/, accessed 1 February 2017. And most recently Valloni, L (2016), "CAS Structure and Procedure – It is now Time for a Change!", *Football Legal*, 36–44.

Re-Imagined Communities: The WTO Appellate Body and the Communitization of WTO Law

*Geraldo Vidigal**

I. Introduction

The creation of the World Trade Organization (WTO), with its compulsory dispute settlement system, put WTO panels and the Appellate Body before a dilemma familiar to international adjudicators. Who do they adjudicate for, or, as Armin von Bogdandy and Ingo Venzke put it, *in whose name* do they adjudicate?[1] To an extent, the range of options is the same contemplated by these authors: "Is it in the name of the parties to the concrete case, in the name of the international community, or in the name of a functional regime?"[2]. In the case of the WTO, this question acquires specific contours. Should WTO adjudicators aim to "secure a positive solution" to bilateral disputes, as Article 3.7 of the Dispute Settlement Understanding directs them to? Or should they seek first and foremost to "provid[e] security and predictability to the multilateral trading system", as suggested by DSU Article 3.2? Perhaps adjudicators should not pursue any particular goal, and act merely to "preserve the rights and obligations of Members" by "clarify[ing] the existing provisions" of WTO law, as the same Article 3.2 immediately adds?

These questions are not of merely academic interest. The answers have significant implications for the diplomats and lawyers appearing before panels and the Appellate Body, since they determine which arguments will count as persuasive before these adjudicators. More importantly, the answers shape the very character of the WTO legal system. Do the WTO Agreements create a mere multi-party contract, establishing bundles of bilateral legal relations that sub-groups of WTO Members remain free to shape and reshape on the basis of mutual consent? Or do they establish a

* Assistant Professor in Public International Law and International Trade Law, Amsterdam Centre for International Law, University of Amsterdam.

1 Von Bogdandy, A. and Venzke, I. (2014), *In Whose Name? A Public Law Theory of International Adjudication*. Oxford: Oxford University Press.

2 *Ibid.*, 5.

community, a common legal system whose rules can only be modified pursuant to the legal regime's collectively agreed procedures? And should the approach of panels and the Appellate Body to adjudication aim first and foremost at protecting the multilateral trading system, leaving to other specialized regimes the tasks of ensuring the protection of non-trade values such as environmental protection and human rights? Or may adjudicators take into account developments that take place in other international decision-making fora in their interpretation of WTO rights and obligations?

This Chapter argues that, by establishing a common institutional framework for the negotiation of trade relations, the WTO Agreements set up a community in the sense of a forum in which decisions *can* be made collectively and affect all Members. On the other hand, the early years of the WTO saw a controversy with respect to what the specific features of this community would be. Here, the direction given by the Appellate Body to the jurisprudence has been decisive. The Appellate Body's reading of the function of adjudication and the institutional provisions of the WTO Agreements has resulted in a significant communitization of WTO law. Contrary to what some expected, this communitization did not result in a trade-focused regime. Instead, the approach adopted by the Appellate Body to the WTO Agreements puts on equal footing "trade" and "non-trade" goals. Trade-restrictive and even discriminatory measures are permissible as long as they find a justification in a non-trade goal that, according to the Appellate Body, the community of Members has determined to be legitimate. Crucially, the Appellate Body infers the views of this community not only from decisions of WTO bodies but also from multilateral decisions and documents adopted in other fora that, in its view, express a consensus or a common understanding regarding interpretations and are apt to legitimize non-trade concerns as justification for governmental action.

Following this introduction, Section 2 discusses two approaches to rule-making and adjudication, which we may call "societal-contractual" and "communitarian", arguing that the WTO Agreements themselves hesitate between the two. Section 3 demonstrates the adoption by the Appellate Body of a communitarian perspective, which has thwarted criticisms to the legitimacy of the WTO by incorporating non-trade values into the WTO Agreements and permitting a community-driven evolution of WTO rules. Section 4 discusses two problematic aspect of this approach. First, in the absence of a functioning legislator, the Appellate Body itself has become the arbiter of what constitutes the WTO community's views, an issue at the heart of the current Appellate Body crisis. Second, while the communitarian approach allows the incorporation of non-trade values that find a large degree of consensus within the community, it may hinder the evolution of trade rules on the basis of the societal-contractual method of agreements among some WTO Members only. Section 5 concludes.

II. Society and Community in the WTO Regime

A. Society, Community and International Institutions

The notions of "society" and "community" are borrowed from sociology, where they designate different models of relations between individuals and the group.[3] The notion of society implies voluntary association between individuals which have (in theory) willingly consented to engage in relations with other individuals. Relations between individuals in a society are voluntary, and therefore contractual in character (the social contract). In theory, given the voluntary character of their association, individuals could ultimately reject the contract and retain their original freedom. At the very least, in an ideal type contract-based society, consenting individuals are free to negotiate any agreements between them, as long as they do not impinge on other individual's rights. The notion of a community, on the other hand, implies an organic relationship between the group and its component individuals, which are seen as *members* of an entity that takes precedence over them and without which their individual existence lacks meaning. Members of a community do not adhere to its norms individually but co-develop the community's norms in their interaction with other community members. Within an ideal-type community, there is no freedom of sets of individuals to negotiate their mutual relations: interpersonal relations are governed by community norms.

International law was shaped, in the 18th and 19th Centuries, following a contractual-societal logic that still finds reflection in many of its rules. Pursuant to this logic, states are sovereign entities whose existence precedes the existence of any norms constraining their conduct.[4] While states are free to consent to restrictions on the exercise of their sovereignty,

3 Tönnies, F. (1935/2002), *Community and Society = Gemeinschaft und Gesellschaft*. Dover: Mineola. Tilman, R. (2004), "Ferdinand Tönnies, Thorstein Veblen and Karl Marx: From Community to Society and Back?", *European Journal of the History of Economic Thought* 11(4), 579–606.

4 The principle, expressed by the Permanent Court of International Justice (PCIJ) in *Lotus*, is that in the absence of consent "[r]estrictions upon the independence of States cannot... be presumed" (The case of the S.S. *Lotus (France v. Turkey)*, Judg-

sovereignty means that these restrictions are contractual in character: states remain free to leave these contractual engagements should they so wish and may, through mutual consent, modify between themselves any rule of purported general or multilateral application. The International Court of Justice traditionally operates under strong societal-contractual assumptions, recognizing the ability of pairs and groups of states to shape their mutual relations on the basis of consent.[5]

The narrative of an international society in which all obligations derive from consent is broken by two inter-related developments. First, the establishment of institutional fora of global reach, such as the United Nations institutions or the WTO, in which all states, or a significant number of them, may deliberate on the creation of new rules and norms, with such weight that there is little room left for those wishing to exercise their entitlement to individual rule-making outside the common normative framework.[6] Second, the creation – largely within these institutions – of broad consensus among states with respect to certain structurally relevant norms, some of which are considered to bind all states and not to permit any derogation on the basis of inter-state consent.[7] Whereas the latter norms are ordinarily considered to be the ones emanating from the "international community of States as a whole"[8] and therefore the most glaring example of the disruption to the societal-contractual model of rule-making, it is specific communities, created by treaties that establish legal regimes, creating institutional fora for deliberation and decision-making procedures, that have the largest potential to constrain states' ability to freely contract into and contract out of certain rules.

ment, 1927 PCIJ Series A No. 10, 18; *ELSI (United States of America v. Italy)*, Judgment, ICJ Reports 1989, 15, 42).

5 See, e.g., *Asylum (Colombia v. Peru)*, Judgment ICJ Reports 1950, 266, 277–278; *Fisheries (United Kingdom v. Norway)*, Judgment, ICJ Reports 1951, 116, 131; *Case concerning Right of Passage over Indian Territory (Portugal v. India)* Merits, ICJ Reports 1960, 6, 39; *Continental Shelf (Tunisia v. Libya)*, Revision and Interpretation, ICJ Reports 1985, 192, 219.

6 See, e.g., *Legal Consequences for States of the Continued Presence of South Africa in Namibia (South West Africa) Notwithstanding Security Council Resolution* 276 (1970), Advisory Opinion, ICJ Reports 1971, 16, 22; *Whaling in the Antarctic Judgment (Australia v. Japan: New Zealand intervening)*, Judgment, ICJ Reports 2014, 226, 257, 270–271; *Jurisdictional Immunities of the State (Germany v. Italy; Greece Intervening)*, ICJ Reports 2012, 99, 127, 147–148.

7 Vienna Convention on the Law of Treaties, Articles 53, 64.

8 *Ibid.*

B. Communitarian Institutions in the WTO Agreements

With the conclusion of the Uruguay Round of trade negotiations in 1994, the various multilateral trade agreements previously signed by contracting parties to the General Agreement on Tariffs and Trade (GATT 1947) were merged into the Agreement Establishing the WTO (AEWTO), to which all other WTO Agreements are annexes. The negotiation principle of single undertaking adopted during the Uruguay Round, under which the WTO Agreements constitute a "package deal" that must be adhered to in its virtual entirety or not at all, was incorporated into the AEWTO. Unless otherwise specified, all WTO Agreements are "binding on all Members"[9]. Reservations are prohibited unless explicitly permitted.[10]

Besides creating a single set of substantive rules, the AEWTO established what it calls a "common institutional framework" for the conduct of trade relations,[11] including an institutional structure and organs for collective decision-making.[12] AEWTO Articles IX (Decision-Making) and X (Amendments) set up specific procedures for adopting, within WTO decision-making organs, modifications to and authoritative interpretations of the rights and obligations of Members. Although the effectiveness of this proto-legislature to address the demands of the trade regime has been questioned,[13] the Ministerial Conference and subsidiary organs have adopted a number of waivers,[14] and various consensus-based decisions, some of which expand significantly on previous obligations, such as the 2015 decision to prohibit

9 Agreement Establishing the WTO, Article II:2. The exception were the four plurilateral agreements, two of which expired in 1997.

10 Agreement Establishing the WTO, Article XVI:5.

11 Agreement Establishing the WTO, Article II:1.

12 Nottage, H. and Sebastian, T. (2006), "Giving Legal Effect to the Results of WTO Trade Negotiations: An Analysis of the Methods of Changing WTO Law", *Journal of International Economic Law* 9(4), 989–1016.

13 Bartels, L. (2004), "The Separation of Powers in the WTO: How to Avoid Judicial Activism", *International and Comparative Law Quarterly* 53(4), 861–895; Ruiz Fabri, H. (2003), "La juridictionnalisation du règlement des litiges économiques entre États", *Revue de l'arbitrage* 3, 881–947; Von Bogdandy, A. (2001), "Law and Politics in the WTO – Strategies to Cope with a Deficient Relationship", *Max Planck Yearbook of United Nations Law* 5, 609–674.

14 See Feichtner, I. (2009), "The Waiver Power of the WTO: Opening the WTO for Political Debate on the Reconciliation of Competing Interests", *European Journal of International Law* 20(3), 615–645.

export subsidies on agriculture.[15] Although no formal authoritative interpretation has ever been adopted, in 2012 Members revised a plurilateral agreement (the Government Procurement Agreement),[16] in 2013 they agreed to a wholly new agreement (the Trade Facilitation Agreement),[17] and in 2017 the first amendment (to the Agreement on Trade-Related Aspects of Intellectual Property Rights) came into force.[18] At the margins, at least, WTO Members are able to create new rules and modify existing ones.

A core aspect of the WTO's institutional framework is its Dispute Settlement Understanding (DSU). Under the DSU, any WTO Member may bring a claim against any other Member with respect to any "measures affecting the operation of any covered agreement"[19]. The DSU all but ensures that a complainant can obtain a report which, once adopted, must be complied with by a Member found in breach.[20] To enforce reports, the DSU establishes a system of collective political surveillance of implementation by the WTO Membership[21] and, in case of persistent non-compliance, features a fall-back mechanism permitting the complainant to adopt trade retaliation against the recalcitrant state.[22]

C. *Communitarian Institutions and Bilateral Enforcement*

The existence of a dispute settlement system from which parties cannot withdraw provides the WTO with a strong communitarian element not usually found in international organizations. The DSU allows any WTO

15 WTO Ministerial Decision, "Export Competition", 19 December 2015 (WT/L/980). WTO organs can also adopt majority decisions, although these remain exceptional. Decision of the General Council on the accession of Ecuador (adopted in spite of the opposition of Peru), WT/ACC/ECU/5 (22 August 1995).

16 Revised Government Procurement Agreement, agreed 30 March 2012 (GPA/113), entered into force 6 April 2014.

17 Agreement on Trade Facilitation, General Council Decision of 28 November 2014 (WT/L/940), entered into force 22 February 2017.

18 Amendment to the TRIPS Agreement, 6 December 2005 (WT/L/641), took effect 23 January 2017.

19 DSU, Article 4.2.

20 DSU, Article 21.1. The current deadlock over Appellate Body appointments means that, since December 2019, the ability of Members to obtain a report has been compromised.

21 DSU, Article 21.6.

22 DSU, Article 22.

Members to obtain from an adjudicator an interpretation of another Member's WTO obligations. At the same time, there are no community organs tasked with enforcing the WTO Agreements, meaning that the agreements are only enforced to the extent that a Member takes issues with a violation. Additionally, despite trade retaliation for persistent non-compliance being collectively authorized, the only Members allowed to apply retaliation are those that have brought the complaint. The design of WTO dispute settlement subjects the WTO's institutionalized enforcement mechanism to the bilateral relations between the parties to a dispute.

In terms of law-making, the WTO Agreements not only establish decision-making procedures for the creation of new norms but feature two significant prohibitions on "contracting out". Article 11.1(b) of the Agreement on Safeguards prohibits WTO Members from agreeing to export-restrictive measures outside of WTO rules, including "voluntary export restraints, orderly marketing arrangements or any other similar measures". It specifies that the prohibition covers both actions taken by a single Member and "actions under agreements, arrangements and understandings entered into by two or more Members". This prohibition constitutes precisely the sort of collectively-determined restriction on contractual freedom that characterizes a community. It prevents resort to so-called "grey area" measures bilateral arrangements used prior to the creation of the WTO to circumvent GATT prohibitions on discriminatory and trade-restrictive measures on imports.[23] Authorization of trade-restrictions not warranted by WTO law must be given by the whole community, in the form of a waiver.

Additionally Article 3(5) of the DSU restricts the ability of parties to a dispute to agree to a mutually agreed solution that results in a violation of the WTO rules. It provides: "All solutions to matters formally raised under the consultation and dispute settlement provisions of the covered agreements, including arbitration awards, shall be consistent with those agreements and shall not nullify or impair benefits accruing to any Member under those agreements, nor impede the attainment of any objective of those agreements."

Article 3(5) applies to situations in which a matter is "formally raised" before the WTO dispute settlement organs. However, the DSU covers all "situations in which a Member considers that any benefits accruing to it

23 GATT Secretariat, "'Grey-Area' Measures – Background Note by the Secretariat", 16 September 1987 (MTN.GNG/NG9/W/6).

directly or indirectly under the covered agreements are being impaired"[24]. It therefore suffices for a Member to decide to bring a matter formally before the Dispute Settlement Body for Article 3(5) to apply, requiring "[a]ll solutions" to be consistent with the WTO Agreements. Article 3(7) provides that "solution[s] mutually acceptable to the parties to a dispute" are "to be preferred", as long as these solutions are "consistent with the covered agreements", and Article 22(1) provides that "full implementation of a recommendation to bring a measure into conformity with the covered agreements" is to be "preferred" to compensation of an aggrieved Member by the violator.

The language of "preference" is not unequivocal. Article 22(8), which governs the time after a dispute is over, presents as alternative possibilities the removal of the WTO-inconsistent measure, the end of the nullification or impairment caused by the measure, and the attainment of "a mutually satisfactory solution". While substantive provisions prohibit a violator from relying on the societal-contractual structure of the WTO to obtain the agreement of an aggrieved party to trade-restrictive measures, the bilateral structure of WTO dispute settlement, by which each Member may "exercis[e] its judgment" as to whether bringing a dispute "would be fruitful",[25] allows Members to tolerate non-compliance as well as to agree to bilateral arrangements that permit the persistence of measures found to be inconsistent with WTO rules. The WTO Agreements therefore feature some restrictions on the ability of Members to "contract out" of WTO rules, but entrust individual states with enforcing WTO rules and entering into understandings to settle disputes. The enforcement of the community-backed rules depends on bilateral relations between the Members.

III. The Appellate Body and the Establishment of a WTO Community

A. The Prospect of a Trade-Focused Community

In the early years of the WTO, it was unclear what effects the WTO's institutional structure would have for the continued ability of WTO Members to enter into "inter se" agreements – bilateral or "minilateral" agreements modifying WTO rules among some Members only – and have these agreements acknowledged by WTO adjudicators. Joost Pauwelyn argued that, in

---

24 DSU, Article 3.3.
25 DSU, Article 3.10.

case norms created outside the WTO system conflicted with WTO rules, these conflicts should be solved by recourse to the rules governing conflicting treaties in Articles 30, 41 and 59 of the Vienna Convention on the Law of Treaties. These rules have strong societal-contractual features, essentially permitting states to renegotiate their legal relations through *inter se* agreements as long as they do not interfere with the rights of third states. Pauwelyn summarized these rules as "the 'holy trinity' of (i) contractual freedom of states; (ii) *pacta sunt servanda*; and (iii) *pacta tertiis*"[26].

If this societal-contractual view were to prevail, panels and the Appellate Body adjudicating WTO disputes would be required to examine all the international agreements between the parties to a dispute and determine which rules prevail. In case they found the non-WTO agreement to prevail, they would then apply the norm contained in the non-WTO agreement rather than the WTO rule.[27] In other words, the WTO Agreements would not have established a community able to affect the freedom of WTO Members to enter into conflicting engagements and have them enforced within WTO adjudication. As Erich Vranes explains, this approach consists, in large measure, in "a restatement of the rules of general international law: *inter se* modifications of the WTO treaty are permissible in line with the principles of international law"[28]. In other words, state sovereignty, or their rule-making freedom under the societal-contractual assumptions of general international law, should prevail over communitarian provisions of the WTO Agreements.

The opposite view held that, while Members remained sovereign to sign any trade agreements, the provisions of the DSU governing adjudication did prevent panels and the Appellate Body from giving effect to norms established outside the WTO Agreements. Article 3.2 of the DSU provides that the WTO dispute settlement system serves to "preserve the rights and obligations of Members under the covered agreements, and to clarify the existing provisions of those agreements". Article 7.1 requires panels, unless

26 Pauwelyn, J. (2003), *Conflicts of Norms in Public International Law: How WTO Law Relates to Other Rules of International Law*. Cambridge: Cambridge University Press, 436.

27 Pauwelyn, J. (2003), "A Typology of Multilateral Treaty Obligations: Are WTO Obligations Bilateral or Collective in Nature?", *European Journal of International Law* 14(5), 907–951.

28 Vranes, E. (2008), "Comments on Joost Pauwelyn's Paper: 'How to Win a WTO Dispute Based on Non-WTO Law?'" In: S. Griller (ed.), *At the Crossroads: the World Trading System and the Doha Round*. Wien / NewYork: Springer, 83–100, 98. See also Vranes, E. (2006), "The Definition of 'Norm Conflict' in International Law and Legal Theory", *European Journal of International Law* 17(2), 395–418.

otherwise agreed by the parties, to examine disputes brought to the Dispute Settlement Body in light of the WTO Agreements only. And Articles 3.2 and 19.2 preclude panels and the Appellate Body from "add[ing] to or diminish[ing] the rights and obligations provided in the [WTO] covered agreements".

The arguments used to justify this deviation from the societal-contractual assumptions regarded not the substantive WTO rules, but the institutional provisions governing dispute settlement. Lorand Bartels proposed that, in case of conflict, DSU Articles 3.2 and 19.2 would ensure the primacy of WTO rules "in an indirect manner" by requiring adjudicators to consider the WTO rule as the "applicable rule" in the face of a conflicting external rule.[29] Gabrielle Marceau argued that an assessment of the relations established by the WTO Agreements should take into account "both the substantive and the procedural aspects of this relationship, i.e. the normative and jurisdictional dimensions"[30]. Panels and the Appellate Body would lack the "constitutional capacity to reach a conclusion that would lead *de facto* to an amendment of the WTO treaty"[31]. In case of a direct conflict that could not be avoided through interpretation, panels and the Appellate Body might recognize that a WTO obligation had been superseded. But these organs could at most issue a declaratory statement, refraining from adopting any rulings, findings or recommendations that would contradict their obligation not to add to or diminish the WTO rights and obligations of Members.[32]

Thus, this argument against "contracting out" of WTO rules does not amount to the claim that state sovereignty should be rejected, but instead argues that states would be able to employ, and in the case of the WTO had employed, their sovereignty to establish communitarian normative systems shielded from the general rules governing rule-making and rule-modification. In other words, through the institutional provisions governing rule-making and the tasks of panels and the Appellate Body, WTO Members had established a separate legal regime, a legal community with its own collectively agreed norms enforceable by these specialized adjudicators.

29 Bartels, L. (2001), "Applicable Law in WTO Dispute Settlement Proceedings", *Journal of World Trade* 35(3), 499–519, 507.

30 Marceau, G. (2001), "Conflicts of Norms and Conflicts of Jurisdiction – The Relationship between the WTO Agreement and MEAs and other Treaties", *Journal of World Trade* 35(6), 1081–1131, 1082.

31 *Ibid.*, 1095.

32 *Ibid.*, 1130.

These same norms could determine the extent to which modifications through external rule-making could impact the internal WTO regime.

Beyond its technical aspects, this debate was linked to concerns about a functional differentiation between the WTO's "trade regime" and other regimes protecting non-trade concerns, such as environmental protection or human rights. A communitarian WTO legal system, the reasoning went, would result in trade obligations prevailing over non-trade obligations. While these other concerns are protected in their own specialized regimes, none of these regimes can rely on the combination of nearly global participation, compulsory adjudication and enforcement through trade retaliation that makes the WTO system unique. If the "WTO community" were to be the community of specialized trade negotiators, deciding on the basis of the purely economic concerns negotiators sought to protect when negotiating trade agreements, leaving non-WTO rules outside the scope of adjudication could lead to the quasi-automatic condemnation before WTO panels of measures taken by WTO Members justified by norms developed in forums other than the WTO to protect non-economic concerns.

At the same time, rejecting the communitarian view would have implied a (re-)bilateralization of WTO legal relations. Any idea of a coherent WTO legal system would be lost in favour of a societal-contractual system in which each pair or sub-group of Members would be subject to particular legal relations. Pauwelyn noted that "WTO rules would apply differently to different WTO members depending on whether or not they have accepted other non-WTO rule", but considered this a means to avoid a more problematic scenario in which WTO adjudicators, finding themselves unable to take into account non-WTO rules, would make decisions purely on the basis of WTO rules and have the trade regime prevail over legal regimes that seek to protect non-trade values.[33]

These concerns appeared warranted by two disputes on environmental measures, one taking place immediately before, the other immediately after the entry into force of the WTO Agreements. In 1991, the GATT 1947 panel in *US – Tuna* examined a US measure prohibiting the importation of tuna products unless the tuna was caught using a mechanism to prevent the incidental capture of dolphins. The panel held that allowing this measure to be justified under GATT Article XX could threaten the entire "multilateral framework for trade" established by the GATT,[34] allowing a party

33 Pauwelyn, *supra* note 26, 476.

34 GATT, Panel Report, *US – Restrictions on Imports of Tuna* (DS21/R – 39S/155), 3 September 1991, para. 5.27.

to "unilaterally determine the conservation policies" of other parties.[35] This was followed, in 1999, by the WTO panel report in *US – Shrimp*, a dispute concerning a US prohibition on the importation of shrimp caught without a system for releasing turtles caught as by-catch. Following the GATT panel in *US – Tuna*, the WTO panel in *US – Shrimp* found that no WTO exception allowed the US to restrict trade in the pursuit of environmental goals outside US territory. Allowing a WTO Member to "condition[] access to its market for a given product upon the adoption by the exporting Members of certain policies, including conservation policies", the panel reasoned, would threaten the integrity of the multilateral trading system.[36] The reasoning used by these panels, grounded in the presumed objective of the WTO Agreements to promote trade liberalization and reject all discrimination, corroborated the narrative according to which the WTO Agreements established a trade-focused community, with WTO adjudicators privileging trade liberalization over the protection of non-trade concerns. It was the Appellate Body's intervention that challenged this narrative.

B. *From Trade Regime to Text Regime: The Appellate Body's Intervention in* US – Shrimp *and Beyond*

Despite its high profile, *US – Shrimp* was not the first dispute in which the conflict between trade and non-trade objectives appeared before WTO adjudicators. In its first report, in *US – Gasoline*, the Appellate Body famously declared that the WTO Agreements were "not to be read in clinical isolation from public international law"[37]. The *US – Gasoline* report also marked the first time the Appellate Body set aside a panel's trade-focused view of the WTO Agreements.[38] Instead, the Appellate Body developed what could be called a "text-centered" view of the WTO Agreements, putting on equal footing all the provisions of the WTO Agreements without making a distinction between trade and non-trade objectives. It

35 *Ibid.*, para. 5.32.

36 WTO, Panel Report, *US – Shrimp*, at 7.45, 7.61.

37 Appellate Body Report, *US – Gasoline*, 17.

38 Panel Report, *US – Gasoline*, para. 6.40. The panel linked the consistency of the US measure with Article III:4 to its compatibility with Article XX(g) ("affording treatment of imported gasoline consistent with its Article III:4 obligations would not in any way hinder the United States in its pursuit of its conservation policies under the Gasoline Rule").

found that the "purposes and objects" of the GATT included both "affirmative commitments", prohibiting discrimination and trade-restrictive measures, and the protection of the legitimate "policies and interests", made possible by the general exceptions of Article XX.[39]

The consequences of this shift in focus would become clear in *US – Shrimp*. The Appellate Body labelled the panel's reasoning, that Article XX simply could not allow a Member to condition market access on the adoption of environmental measures, "an *a priori* test" developed without a textual basis, stating that such a test would make "most, if not all", the GATT exceptions that allow the adoption of legitimate measures "inutile".[40] Crucially, the Appellate Body reversed the panel's statements of principle with respect to the object and purpose of the WTO Agreements, emphasizing instead that the WTO Agreements explicitly recognized "the objective of sustainable development"[41]. Thus, the Appellate Body considered the conservation objective pursued by the US measure not as an external interference from the environmental regime into the WTO regime, a "threat to the multilateral trading system" as the panel put it.[42] Instead, the Appellate Body incorporated the objective of environmental conservation into the WTO regime itself, expanding it from a trade-focused regime into a comprehensive legal regime that allows, and even encourages,[43] Members to pursue their public policy goals.

This logic, whereby "non-trade values" are not an external interference but an integral part of the WTO regime, was applied in subsequent cases in which the Appellate Body was confronted with a possible conflict between WTO obligations and supposedly external values that would have required Members to deviate from their WTO obligations. In *EC – Hormones*, confronted with the request that it adapt provisions of the SPS Agreement to the precautionary principle, the Appellate Body stated that the precautionary principle "finds reflection in" the various provisions of the SPS Agreement that allow Members to adopt SPS measures without full scientific evidence, so that there was no need to refer to external normative sources.[44] In *EC – Tariff Preferences*, the Appellate Body reversed the panel's

39 Appellate Body Report, *US – Gasoline*, 18.

40 Appellate Body Report, *US – Shrimp*, para. 121.

41 *Ibid.*, para. 129.

42 Panel Report, *US – Shrimp*, para. 7.61.

43 Appellate Body Report, US – Shrimp, para. 185 ("We have *not* decided that the sovereign nations that are Members of the WTO cannot adopt effective measures to protect endangered species, such as sea turtles. Clearly, they can and should.").

44 Appellate Body Report, *EC – Hormones*, paras. 120–124.

statement that the objective of trade liberalization was more relevant to the interpretation of the Enabling Clause than the objectives of promoting the trade of developing countries and fulfilling their development needs.[45] Instead, it found that these objectives coexisted on an equal footing, permitting the adoption of programmes that discriminate between developing countries on the basis of their development needs.[46] And, in *US – Clove Cigarettes*, the Appellate Body found that the obligations of the Agreement on Technical Barriers to Trade, which could limit Members' ability to regulate if such regulations restrict international trade, had to be interpreted in light of a recital of its preamble, which it labelled an "explicit recognition of Members' right to regulate in order to pursue certain legitimate objectives"[47].

C. Legitimate Non-Trade Values beyond the Four Corners: the Delegation of Authority and the Voices of the International Community

The Appellate Body's interventions have expanded the WTO legal system from a trade-focused regime into a broader legal regime in which "trade goals", i.e. the objectives of trade liberalization and non-discrimination, do not take precedence over but coexist with other goals. A legitimate objective, such as environmental conservation, the protection of consumer health or the fulfilment of development needs, may justify the adoption of trade-restrictive measures as well as discrimination between products, producers or countries.

How precisely these permitted grounds for discrimination are incorporated into the interpretation of WTO rules depends on the provision being examined, and the Appellate Body itself has provided different answers at different times. Under GATT and GATS, besides the obvious moment within the interpretative exercise for the consideration of legitimate grounds for the adoption of trade-restrictive or discriminatory measures (the General Exceptions of Article XX GATT/XIV GATS), the Appellate Body has occasionally found that legitimate grounds for distinguishing between products or services could justify not treating the imported product or service as "like" other products that otherwise compete in the same

45 Appellate Body Report, *EC – Tariff Preferences*, paras. 138, 170.
46 *Ibid.*, para. 173.
47 Appellate Body Report, *US – Clove Cigarettes*, para. 94.

market.[48] In *Dominican Republic – Cigarettes*, the Appellate Body also found that a measure that gives domestic products a competitive advantage over like imported products might not constitute less favourable treatment if the detrimental effect on imported products could be "explained by factors or circumstances unrelated to the foreign origin of the product"[49]. With respect to the Agreement on Technical Barriers to Trade, which does not feature an equivalent to GATT Article XX, the Appellate Body determined that the very finding of less favourable treatment involves an assessment of whether a measure's detrimental effects on imports are based on a "legitimate regulatory distinction"[50].

Expanding the possibility of fulfilling non-trade objectives opens the question of which policy objectives and which regulatory distinctions are "legitimate", permitting Members to adopt otherwise WTO-inconsistent measures. In this regard, the Appellate Body operated another crucial shift in the jurisprudence, "opening" WTO rules to inputs not only from WTO bodies but also from organs of the international community more broadly.

This shift first took place, once more, in *US – Shrimp*. The Appellate Body held that GATT Article XX(g) justified measures directed at the conservation of living resources, grounding this interpretation not only on the preamble to the WTO Agreement but also on a series of treaties, resolutions, declarations and reports signed or issued in connection with various international organizations and institutions. These documents, which did not in themselves create legal rights and obligations between the parties to the *US – Shrimp* dispute, were mentioned because they represented an "acknowledgement by the international community of the importance of concerted bilateral or multilateral action to protect living natural resources"[51] The "community determination" that shaped the Appellate Body's interpretation of a provision of WTO law was not a decision adopted by the WTO Membership following a procedure established in the WTO Agreements but the diffuse recognition, in various documents purportedly conveying the views of the international community, of a non-trade concern justifying the adoption of the US measure.

---

48 Appellate Body Reports, *EC – Asbestos*, para. 130; *Argentina – Financial Services*, paras 6.64, 6.70.

49 Appellate Body Report, *Dominican Republic – Cigarettes*, para. 96 (although the reason in this case was "the market share of the importer", the choice of words opens the door for other "factors or circumstances" to justify detrimental impact on foreign products).

50 Appellate Body Report, *US – Clove Cigarettes*, paras. 174, 181.

51 Appellate Body Report, *US – Shrimp*, para. 131.

Other decisions of the Appellate Body demonstrate a similar willingness to acknowledge the possibility for Members to enter into understandings outside the framework of the agreement being interpreted, influencing decisively the interpretation of WTO law. In *US – Cloves*, the Appellate Body noted that the assessment of what counts as a legitimate objective justifying detrimental effects on imported products could be done not only in light of the objectives explicitly recognized in the TBT Agreement but also by taking into account other objectives recognized in other WTO Agreements.[52] In *EC – Tariff Preferences*, the Appellate Body found that legitimate grounds for discrimination between developing countries in systems of preferences could be found in "[b]road-based recognition of a particular need, set out in the WTO Agreement or in multilateral instruments adopted by international organizations"[53]. In *EC – Hormones*, the Appellate Body found that a Member would be able to justify adopting a measure not ordinarily permitted by the SPS Agreement if there was a "clear textual directive" from the Membership authorizing it, but did not expand on who would be able to issue this directive.[54]

In *EC – Hormones*, while it is conceivable that only the organs specifically authorized to produce standards for food safety in the SPS Agreement[55] would be able to issue a textual directive affecting the outcome of the dispute, possibilities of collective "weighing in" are significantly broader. The notion that the formal procedure of Article IX:2 is required for Members to influence treaty interpretation was set aside in *US – Clove Cigarettes* and *US – Tuna II*. In the former, while recognizing that the Doha Ministerial Decision did not constitute an authoritative interpretation of the WTO Agreements (in the sense of AEWTO Article IX:2), the Appellate Body found that it constituted a subsequent agreement on the interpretation of WTO law by the Membership in the sense of Article 31(3)(a) of the Vienna Convention on the Law of Treaties.[56] In *US – Tuna II*, the Appellate Body found that it was sufficient for a decision to be adopted "subsequent" to the WTO Agreements and to "express an agreement between Members on the interpretation or application of a provision of WTO law"[57] for it to

52 Appellate Body Report, *US – Tuna II*, para. 313.
53 Appellate Body Report, *EC – Tariff Preferences*, para. 163.
54 *Ibid.*
55 See SPS Agreement, Annex A, para. 3.
56 Appellate Body Report, *US – Clove Cigarettes*, para. 262.
57 Appellate Body Report, *US – Tuna II*, para 372.

constitute a subsequent agreement, to be "read into the treaty for purposes of its interpretation"[58].

Panels have now caught up with the interpretative scheme applied by the Appellate Body and are willing to take into account multilateral non-trade documents to justify interpretations of WTO norms. In *Brazil – Taxation*, pointing to the United Nation's Millennium Development Goals, the panel recognized the legitimacy under Article XX(a) of Brazil's stated objective of bridging the "digital divide", even though characteracterizing this objective as part of "public morals" seems like a long shot, on the grounds that Brazil's stated concern was "internationally recognised as an issue confronting developing countries".[59] In *Australia – Tobacco Plain Packaging*, the panel accorded significant weight (without explaining its legal grounds for doing so) to the fact that Australia "pursue[d] its domestic public health objective in line with its commitments' under the Framework Convention on Tobacco Control", which the panel highlighted "ha[d] been ratified by 180 countries".[60] Both the existence of the convention and its broad ratification were found to be key to demonstrate why it would provide grounds for an interpretation of WTO rules permitting a Member to adopt a measure that could otherwise be found to impinge on other Members' rights.

D. *Delegated Authority and the Voice of the International Community*

From this jurisprudence, it appears that the "delegated authority" for influencing WTO interpretation is exercised effectively within multilateral fora and institutions, whether within or outside the WTO. Without multilateral or institutional support, on the other hand, Members may have a hard time influencing interpretations of WTO Agreements.

In the absence of institutions, Members have difficulty demonstrating the existence of multilateral consensus able to influence the interpretation of WTO rules In *Chile – Price Band System*, the Appellate Body noted that a "discernible pattern of acts or pronouncements implying an agreement among WTO Members" on the interpretation of a provision would amount to subsequent practice, decisively affecting interpretation under

58 Appellate Body Report, *US – Clove Cigarettes*, para. 269.
59 Panel Report, *Brazil – Taxation*, paras. 7. 563, 7.565.
60 Panel Report, *Australia – Plain Packaging*, para. 7.2596.

Article 31(3)(b) of the Vienna Convention on the Law of Treaties.[61] However, contrary to what is the case for subsequent agreements, demonstrating the "concordant, common and consistent"[62] practice required for this influence to take place is difficult. In none of the four disputes in which a party invoked subsequent practice did the Appellate Body consider that the relevant practice attained the degree of commonality required to influence interpretation.[63]

Similarly, non-multilateral agreements have been found to be irrelevant for the interpretation of WTO rules. In *EC – Poultry*, the Appellate Body refused to accord interpretative value to a bilateral understanding between the parties even though it had been approved by the GATT Contracting Parties.[64] In *Brazil – Tyres*,[65] *Mexico – Soft Drinks*,[66] *EC – Large Civil Aircraft*[67] and *Peru – Agricultural Products*,[68] the Appellate Body rejected claims that *inter se* agreements could *per se* influence either the rights and obligations of the disputing parties or the interpretation of the WTO rules in dispute.

Thus, following the guidance provided by the Appellate Body, WTO adjudicators have gotten into the habit of seeking authority or justifiable grounds for adopting a measure in principle contrary to WTO rules in documents that can credibly claim to express the view of the international community, either because they are adhered to by a vast number of WTO Members or because they emanate from an organization or institution to which a vast amount of Members are parties. This in turn creates an incentive for Members wishing to make an impact on the interpretation of WTO law to work towards building institutions and fora with legitimacy to make decisions in the name of the whole community, rather than agreeing to norms and interpretations individually or among small groups of Members, i.e. "minilaterally". The communitization of WTO rules therefore drives Members to develop other norms within community fora rather than in minilateral ones.

61 Appellate Body Report, *Chile – Price Band System*, para. 214.
62 Appellate Body Report, *Japan – Alcoholic Beverages II*, 13.
63 Appellate Body Reports, *Japan – Alcoholic Beverages II*, 13; *EC – Computer Equipment*, para 95; *Chile – Price Band System*, para. 214; *US – Gambling*, para 193.
64 Appellate Body Report, *EC – Poultry*, WT/DS69/AB/R, paras. 79–81.
65 Appellate Body Report, *Brazil – Tyres*, WT/DS332/AB/R, para 228.
66 Appellate Body Report, *Mexico – Soft Drinks*, WT/DS308/AB/R, para. 68.
67 Appellate Body Report, *EC – Large Civil Aircraft*, para. 845.
68 Appellate Body Report, *Peru – Agricultural Products*, para. 5.106.

IV. The Promise and Threats of Communitization

A. Communitization as a Legitimacy-Enhancing Approach

The Appellate Body's version of communitization, which includes the shift from a trade-focused regime to a text-focused regime open to influences that emanate from decisions representing the "community view", has permitted the WTO to deflect much of the early criticism directed at the organization. The Appellate Body's approach to interpretation, which put trade and non-trade goals on an equal footing, has thwarted fears that WTO rules would prevent Members from adopting measures to safeguard important societal values. Significantly, this approach has managed to do so while preserving the integrity of WTO law, that is, without permitting the fragmentation of the WTO Agreements into bundles of bilateral legal relations, each governed by a specific set of rules or by rules interpreted according to the specific relations between the parties to a dispute. As the Appellate Body put it in *EC – Large Civil Aircraft*, it sees its task as "ensuring a consistent and harmonious approach to the interpretation of WTO law among all WTO Members"[69].

This approach has ensured the "security and predictability"[70] of the WTO legal system and allowed the WTO to remain the "common institutional framework"[71] for decisions regarding multilateral trade relations. It has also secured the legitimacy of the WTO system vis-à-vis groups that would find it unacceptable for an international trade organization to prevent Members from adopting measures aimed at fulfilling legitimate social goals enshrined in documents emanating from the organs and bodies that speak in the name of the international community.[72]

On the other hand, the communitizing approach leads to two important consequences that have also raised questions regarding the legitimacy of the WTO. First, the focus on the interpretative unity of WTO law has led the Appellate Body to ascribe to its own reports an interpretative value that does not emerge clearly from the DSU. Second, the impossibility for Members to shape their own bilateral relations without multilateral

69 Appellate Body Report, *EC – Large Civil Aircraft*, para. 845.

70 DSU, Article 3.2.

71 AEWTO, Article II:1.

72 Weiler, J.H.H. (2001), "The Rule of Lawyers and the Ethos of Diplomats: Reflections on the Internal and External Legitimacy of WTO Dispute Settlement", *Journal of World Trade* 35(2), 191–207.

approval may still backfire, if non-trade values are enshrined in bilateral or minilateral rather than multilateral documents.

B. The Communitization of Interpretations

While the Appellate Body's approach to interpretation in principle opens the interpretation of WTO rules to input from organs and documents representing the voice of the Membership or the international community more broadly, it is simultaneously true that it has concentrated interpretative power – including the power to determine to what extent external input can be taken into account – in the hands of the Appellate Body itself.

In a sense, this is a consequence of the institutional structure of the WTO. The Appellate Body is tasked with reviewing "issues of law" and "legal interpretations" in panel reports.[73] The DSU ascribes to the dispute settlement system the function of providing "security and predictability" to the multilateral trading system,[74] something which arguably requires consistency among decisions. If it is to provide security and predictability to legal interpretations, the Appellate Body must necessarily seek interpretative consistency in its reports. Since every Member may ultimately obtain an interpretation from the Appellate Body that both itself and the respondent must unconditionally accept, any interpretation from an Appellate Body striving for consistency will eventually become the dominant interpretation. In this sense, the Appellate Body will always centralize WTO interpretations and determine what the "community interpretation" is.[75]

However, the Appellate Body has inferred from these institutional provisions an explicit hierarchy whereby its own reports become not just authoritative views but sources of law, not only guiding its own future decisions but also binding future panels and Members. In response to the statement of the panel in *US – Stainless Steel (Mexico)*, that it "felt compelled to depart from the Appellate Body's approach"[76], the Appellate Body stated that the DSU created a "hierarchical structure" between itself and panels. Only "cogent reasons" could justify a panel "depart[ing] from

---

73 DSU, Article 14.6.

74 DSU, Article 3.2.

75 See Stone Sweet, A. & Brunell, T.L. (2013), "Trustee Courts and the Judicialization of International Regimes: The Politics of Majoritarian Activism in the European Convention on Human Rights, the European Union, and the World Trade Organization", *Journal of Law and Courts* 1(1), 61–88.

76 Panel Report, *US – Stainless Steel (Mexico)* (WT/DS344/R), para 7.106.

well-established Appellate Body jurisprudence"[77]. In a subsequent case, *US – Continued Zeroing*, one Appellate Body member stated that since the Appellate Body had "spoken definitively" on zeroing, this statement "must prevail" in subsequent disputes.[78]

Thus, while the Appellate Body has made important steps towards expanding the legislative function in the "WTO community", it has also made itself – in the absence of agreement among the Members – the voice of this community, able to speak "definitively" where Members disagree. Since any attempt to reverse an interpretation by the Appellate Body requires the assent of the Member that requested adjudication in the first place, the "consistent and harmonious" interpretation of WTO law all too often boils down to the interpretation of WTO law *determined by the Appellate Body*. This centralization of interpretations in the hands of adjudicators constitutes a threat to the legitimacy of the Appellate Body – as seen in the present crisis on appointments – and, ultimately, to that of the organization itself.

C. Communitization and the Challenge of Value-Laden Regionalism

Given the difficulties of advancing at the multilateral stage, bilateral and minilateral trade agreements among small numbers of countries have grown significantly in importance and complexity since the WTO Agreements were negotiated. In late 2018, the 11-party Comprehensive and Progressive Trans-Pacific Partnership (CPTPP) entered into force.[79] Together with the Comprehensive Economic and Trade Agreement (CETA) between Canada and the European Union, which entered into force provisionally in September 2017, the finalized EU-Japan Economic Partnership Agreement, and the 2018 United States-Mexico-Canada Agreement, CPTPP marks a new stage in international economic dealings – an era of "mega-regional" agreements.

Mega-regionals are not necessarily new with regard to their scope. The range of topics governed by trade agreements has been expanding markedly since the early 2000s, with "Free Trade Agreements 2.0" establishing comprehensive disciplines for the regulation of themes such as intellec-

77 Appellate Body Report, *US – Stainless Steel (Mexico)* (WT/DS344/AB/R), paras. 304–313.

78 *Ibid.*

79 Hutton, J. (2018), "Trans-Pacific trade pact will go into force next month", *Straits Times*, 1 November.

tual property rights, financial markets, and electronic commerce, and including provisions relating to environmental regulation, labour rights and fisheries. Up until 2018, however, and with the exception of intra-regional agreements (the North American Free Trade Agreement and the European Union), FTAs 2.0 were restricted to the relations between the largest economies and their smaller trade partners. Relations between the world's largest economies across economic regions still took place essentially on WTO terms. The entry into force of mega-regionals changes that, with the result that significant portions of global trade will be governed by bilateral and minilateral agreements.

The communitization of the WTO legal system has prevented the use of FTAs to affect WTO legal relations, with the Appellate Body having acted decisively to prevent FTAs from being used to justify new trade barriers among the participants, new trade barriers vis-à-vis third WTO Members, and discrimination in favour of trade partners beyond the strict terms of Article XXIV. While so far this stance has strengthened the multilateral trading system by preventing the fragmentation of the WTO legal system, the same inflexibility may become a handicap once FTAs are both far wider in scope than WTO rules and a means of regulating relations between large Members (who still constitute the vast majority of the users of the WTO dispute settlement procedures).

The rejection of bilateralization of trade relations may become particularly problematic once the social or environmental chapters of FTAs 2.0 are invoked, either to bar trade in products whose production process or characteristics of production disregard social and environmental requirements or to justify trade barriers adopted in response to failure to comply with social and environmental clauses. While the Appellate Body's communitizing stance would permit justifying discrimination against a Member that is backed by a decision of a multilateral institution, such as the International Labour Organization or the Convention on International Trade in Endangered Species of Wild Fauna and Flora, the reasoning employed by the Appellate Body in *Mexico – Soft Drinks* and *Peru – Agricultural Products* would lead a panel to reject a trade-restrictive measure adopted in response to a failure to comply with environmental or labour provisions agreed on a bilateral or minilateral basis. The Appellate Body will then have to choose between its communitizing stance, which should lead it to reject restrictions based on bilateral deals, and its legitimacy-boosting stance of accepting that trade obligations should not prevent Members from adopting restrictions that fulfil non-trade objectives.

V. Conclusion

The transformation of the GATT regime into the World Trade Organization brought to the fore two dilemmas for the then new organization. First, to what extent did the WTO Agreements break with the societal-contractual model of trade relations that allowed GATT Contracting Parties to renegotiate agreements among them, and replace it with a communitarian system that requires collective approval for deviations from the general rules? Second, to the extent that the WTO regime is communitarian in nature, is this a trade-focused community or a branch of a broader international communitarian structure, capable of absorbing norms made by the international community outside the "four corners" of the WTO?

Through its jurisprudence, the Appellate Body provided answers to these questions through two significant shifts in WTO jurisprudence. First, the traditional approach to interpretation employed by GATT panels, which privileged an assessment of the presumed liberalizing intention of trade negotiators, was replaced with an assessment based on the text of the agreements and agnostic with regard to their overall purpose, recognizing different "purposes and objects" in different provisions of the WTO Agreements. Second, the Appellate Body views WTO law as a coherent legal system that emanates from a community of Members, and which is therefore simultaneously closed to renegotiation beyond the strict scope within which this community permits it and open to normative developments that carry the imprint of the community, be it within WTO organs that decide on the basis of consensus or outside WTO organs, through treaties, non-binding agreements and documents that have a credible claim to being the product of broad consensus within the international community.

While these two interpretative moves have shielded the Appellate Body, and the WTO more generally, from contestations to their legitimacy by external agents, they – together with the consequent centralization of interpretations in the hands of the Appellate Body – risk engendering "internal" contestation from WTO Members themselves. Some of the contestation of the centrality assumed by the Appellate Body in the development of the WTO legal system, in particular by the United States, has now reached an acute stage, with the blocking of the appointment of Appellate Body members and the consequent demise of the organ. But more contestation may be forthcoming if WTO adjudicators are faced with values-based trade restrictions justified on the grounds of an FTA. They may then be forced to choose between the closedness of the WTO legal system to bilateral deals, implied in the notion of communitization, and the openness to substantive developments to extent that they pursue the fulfilment of non-trade values.

These actual and potential contestations are evidence of a deeper challenge that faces international adjudicators. While the treaties providing them with jurisdiction may endow them with significant legal authority and direct them to preserve the integrity (or "security and predictability", as DSU Article 3.2 puts it) of the legal regime over which they adjudicate, international adjudication continues to take place within a broader system – the international legal order – that is characterized by decentralization, horizontality and the ability of states to enter into agreements among themselves, including the ability to change their minds with regard to what they previously found to be core principles in need of judicial protection. In these cases, adjudicators that had found themselves safely adjudicating in the name of a legal regime, or the multilateral governance system more broadly, may be confronted with the fact that their activity still takes place within the murky waters of the Westphalian international order.

The Democracy We Want: Standards of Review and Democratic Embeddedness at the Inter-American Court of Human Rights

Rene Urueña[*]

Reading *In Whose Name?* is like meeting an old schoolmate – that not-all-too interesting person who, in fact, turned out to be a rather fascinating character, full of ambition, achievements, and contradictions. That old acquaintance is, of course, the international court, whose adjudicative powers in the era of global governance are studied by Armin von Bogdandy and Ingo Venzke with the drive and gusto of a zoologist just made privy of a new species of tiger.

The result is kaleidoscopic. The public law theory of adjudication advanced by the text opens many fronts of fruitful engagement, particularly at the current moment of backlash against the book's central character.[1] In this contribution, I will focus on one such front. In Whose Name? puts forward the idea of political embeddedness as a source of democratic legitimacy of international courts. This chapter takes up that question and explores it in reference to the Gelman decision of the Inter-American Court of Human Rights (IACtHR).

* Associate Professor and Director of Research, University of Los Andes School of Law (Colombia).

1 On the backlash against international courts, see generally, Madsen, M.R., Cebulak, P. and Wiebusch, M. (2018), "Backlash against International Courts: Explaining the Forms and Patterns of Resistance to International Courts", *International Journal of Law in Context* 14(2), 197–220; Voeten, E. (2017), "Liberalism, Populism, and the Backlash against International Court", available at: https://global.upenn.edu/sites/default/files/voetenpaper.original.pdf; Posner, E.A. (2017), "Liberal Internationalism and the Populist Backlash", *Arizona State Law Journal* 49, 795. On the backlash against the Inter-American System of Human Rights, which will be discussed in this chapter, see Urueña, R. (2018), "Double or Nothing: The Inter-American Court of Human Rights in an Increasingly Adverse Context", *Wisconsin International Law Journal* 35, 398–425; Soley, X. and Steininger, S. (2018), "Parting Ways or Lashing Back? Withdrawals, Backlash and the Inter-American Court of Human Rights", *International Journal of Law in Context* 14(2), 237–257.

My central argument will be the following: the balance between the appropriate Inter-American standard of review and the democratic pedigree of the primary decision is fundamental for the democratic legitimacy of the regional court. Yet, in the context of human rights indeterminacy, such democratic balancing needs to be performed in reference to a regional (and not solely national) process of democratization, in which an Inter-American community of human rights practice plays a central role.

To advance that argument, this chapter explores first the issue of standard of review at the Inter-American Court of Human Rights, and then focuses, in the second section, on *Gelman* as an expression of the Court's no-deference standard. The third section, in turn, assesses the critiques of this decision, focusing on how its critics misrepresent both the indeterminacy of human rights, and the possibility of a regional, Inter-American, democratic process. The final section concludes, by proposing a good faith approach to the balancing between standard of review and the democratic pedigree of domestic decisions -- good faith as a way to achieve the democracy we *want* in Latin America, and not only to defend the democracy we *have*.

1. *Standard of review and the Inter-American Court of Human Rights:*

In Whose Name? argues that international adjudication can be made more democratically legitimate. International judges can be selected more transparently and representatively. The procedure before international courts can be made more transparent and participatory by allowing, for example, for *amicus curiae* interventions, or by establishing effective legal remedies. The international judicial decision itself can be used as a source of democratic legitimacy, if it is supported by solid legal reasoning.[2] Moreover, democratic legitimacy can be enhanced by a smart combination of international public authority and vibrant political processes. Thus, an appropriate standard of review, a self-critical use of soft law, and an increased politicization of the international system – all could, according to *In Whose Name?*, better embed international courts in the political process, thus enhancing their democratic legitimacy.[3]

2 Von Bogdandy, A. and Venzke, I. (2014), *In Whose Name?: A Public Law Theory of International Adjudication*. Oxford: Oxford University Press, 156–197.

3 *Ibid*., 199–206.

These venues of democratic legitimation, though, are deployed in a dense political context, both national and international. The selection of international judges, the procedure before international courts, and the adoption of their decisions, all occur in a political scenario that interacts with each of these sources of legitimacy – sometimes boosting, sometimes underlying them. For that reason, von Bogdandy and Venzke's treatment of international courts' embeddedness in the political process seems so crucial. Such embeddedness is, ultimately, not an alternative source of democratic legitimacy (as the authors suggest), but rather a prerequisite for the other sources of democratic legitimacy to begin operating.

Thought of as a prerequisite of democratic legitimacy, *In Whose Name?*'s notion of political embeddedness poses both a descriptive and a normative problem. Descriptively, it requires scholars to assess whether international adjudication has an impact on, or is impacted by, domestic political process. Much interesting work is being done at that descriptive level, particularly with regards to the Inter-American context.[4] At a normative level, political embeddedness poses the question of how much international adjudication *should* impact domestic political processes, if the objective is to enhance democratic legitimacy. In this contribution, I will focus on this latter normative question, and will explore it by discussing the appropriate standard of review used by the Inter-American Court of Human Rights in its political context.[5]

4 See the essays in Engstrom, P. (ed.) (2019), *The Inter-American Human Rights System. Impact Beyond Compliance*. Cham: Palgrave Macmillan. Also: Parra, O. (2017), "The Impact of Inter- American Judgments by Institutional Empowerment" In: A. von Bogdandy *et al.* (eds), *Transformative Constitutionalism in Latin America: The Emergence of a New Ius Commune*. Oxford/New York: Oxford University Press, 357–376. And Urueña, R., Sanchez, B. and Anzola, S. (2015), *Después del fallo: El cumplimiento de las decisiones del sistema interamericano de derechos humanos. Una propuesta de metodología*. Bogota: Uniandes, Series "Documentos Justicia Global".

5 It will be noticed that I will not discuss *In Whose Name?'s* emphasis on soft law. I am doubtful as to its potential as a source of democratic legitimacy, and the authors seem slightly dubitative as well. For the authors, "[t]he democratic content of (decisions by international political institutions) is not clear at all. Usually soft law is rather seen as an instrument of technocratic global governance. At this point, our theory walks a middle way between uncritical endorsement and categorical rejection" (Von Bogdandy and Venzke, *supra* note 2, 204). This caution seems well warranted. Soft law may be effective for advancing certain arguments or agenda, and thus read as legitimate in its effectiveness, but its democratic credentials, in basic terms of representativeness, transparency, or deliberation, are not beyond question. For an early argument in this sense, see Klabbers, J. (1998), "The Undesirability of Soft Law", *Nordic Journal of International Law* 67(4), 381. For an

A "standard of review" refers to the level of scrutiny that an adjudicator applies when reviewing the decision of a lower court or of another institution.[6] The notion comes from domestic judicial review, and is inspired by the appropriate balance of powers between high courts, lower courts, and institutions in other branches of power.[7] Put simply, a standard of review sets the questions asked of the primary decision. Thus, in domestic law, standards of review are often pictured as a continuum, with completely new review of the primary decision on one end and complete deference to that decision on the other.[8] Thus, when engaging in judicial review, a court has the option of applying a very strict level of scrutiny, considering and deciding the legal question anew—in effect substituting the primary decision-maker via judicial review. Alternatively, in the other extreme, the reviewing court has the option of adopting a highly deferential standard, under which it will give more weight to the primary decision-maker.

In this context, the connection between standard of review and democratic legitimacy emerges, in at least two senses. First, the primary decision may carry some kid of democratic pedigree, due to the way in which the decision-maker was elected, or to the process through which the decision was reached. In that case, such democratic pedigree may play a role into deciding the appropriate standard of review – most usually, by a triggering a more deferential approach towards a more democratic primary decision.[9] Second, the primary decision may *hinder* the democratic process. That is the case, for example, in John Hart Ely's argument for judicial review as a mechanism for "representation reinforcement": if the process of demo-

---

example of soft law as a tool for progressive social change with regards to internally displaced populations in Colombia (and no consideration of its democratic pedigree), see Sanchez, B. (2009), "Cuando los Derechos son la Jaula: Transplante rígido del soft law para la gestión del desplazamiento forzado", *Estudios Políticos* 35, 11–32.

6 The following description of standard of review is based on Urueña, R. (2016), "Subsidiarity and the Public–Private Distinction in Investment Treaty Arbitration", *Law and Contemporary Problems* 79(2), 99–121.

7 Peters, A. (2009), "The Meaning, Measure, and Misuse of Standards of Review", *Lewis & Clark Law Review* 13(1), 233.

8 For a discussion of US law, see generally Hofer, R.R. (1991), "Standards of Review – Looking beyond the Labels", *Marquette Law Review* 74(2), 231.

9 See Kavanagh, A. (2008), "Deference or Defiance? The Limits of the Judicial Role in Constitutional Adjudication" In: G. Huscroft (ed.), *Expounding the Constitution: Essays in Constitutional Theory.* Cambridge/New York: Cambridge University Press, 184.

cratic representation fails, then judicial review is in principle justified,[10] and hence, I would add, a stricter standard of review is justified.

In international law, the question of standards of review has taken on characteristics of its own.[11] International courts are often not reviewing a decision by a lower court, but they rather review the decision of one of the parties to the litigation—often, a state. Consequently, the issue of standard of review involves pondering the legitimate policy space of states, which risks being unduly restricted, hence triggering the problem of democratic legitimacy. Should international courts be deferential to the decisions of domestic institutions or, on the contrary, should they engage in *de novo* review of primary decisions? Exceptionally, in certain specialized regimes, the language contained in the relevant treaty answers this question.[12] Most international legal regimes, though, leave the question of standard of review open for the relevant court to decide. That is the case of the Inter-American Court of Human Rights, which has been reluctant to specify its own approach to standard of review. And this, in contrast with the European Court of Human Rights, which has developed, through its "margin of appreciation" doctrine, one of the few analytical tools in international law that explicitly discuss the level of scrutiny to be applied when assessing reviewing domestic measures[13].

---

10 See generally Ely, J.H. (1980), *Democracy and Distrust: A Theory of Judicial Review*. Cambridge: Harvard University Press.

11 The following discussion of standards of review in international law is based on Urueña, *supra* note 6.

12 Such is the case of dumping litigation at the World Trade Organization (WTO), for which the Article 17.6 Anti-Dumping Agreement provides a specific standard of review in anti-dumping proceedings. See Agreement on Implementation of Article VI of the General Agreement on Tariffs and Trade 1994 (Anti-Dumping Agreement), 1868 U.N.T.S. 201.

13 For an introduction to the doctrine, see Legg, A. (2012), *The Margin of Appreciation in International Human Rights Law: Deference and Proportionality* (1st ed). Oxford: Oxford University Press. The other explicit approach to the appropriate standard of review in international law can be found in international trade law. The General Agreement on Tariffs and Trade Article XX permits the adoption of certain exceptional trade-restrictive measures in order to protect public goals such as morality, security, or the environment. Such exceptional measures must be necessary to achieve the stated goal. Thus, when deciding whether the measure is truly necessary, the WTO panel and Appellate Body have developed a consistent body of case law that assesses whether the state has taken the least restrictive measure reasonably available that meets its permissible objective under General Agreement on Tariffs and Trade Article XX. To meet this standard, the defendant state must make a prima facie argument that the exceptional measure was necessary in its context. In that case, the panel or Appellate Body will have a deferential

As is well known, the margin of appreciation refers to the "'breadth of deference' that the Court is willing to grant to the decisions of national legislative, executive, and judicial decisionmakers".[14] The margin of appreciation is a form of standard of review under which an international court gives weight to the reasoning of the primary decisionmaker for reasons of democratic legitimacy, common practice of the states, or expertise.[15] The Inter-American Court, though, has not followed the European Tribunal's path on this point. While the former has used the expression "margin of appreciation" on certain occasions, it has in fact seemed to be referring to the traditional leeway international law gives states to configure their own domestic law to comply with their international legal obligations, and not to a deferential standard of review. Thus, in *Herrera Ulloa* and in *Barreto Leiva*, the IACtHR explicitly referred to a "margin of appreciation", but used the term as a shortcut to underscore states' sovereign right to regulate domestic remedies.[16] Similarly, in *Castañeda Guzmán*, the Inter-American Court also held that states had a "margin" in configuring their own electoral systems, as long as they were not in violation of the American Convention on Human Rights.[17] Even in cases where the facts would have been conducive to the application of a margin of appreciation doctrine, the Inter-American Court has declined to do so.[18]

---

attitude toward the primary decision-maker. Then the burden of proof shifts to the complainant, who must prove that the measure is unnecessary (mainly by proving the reasonable availability of a less trade-restrictive alternative measure). On the standard of review in the WTO, see generally Oesch, M. (2003), "Standards of Review in WTO Dispute Resolution", *Journal of International Economic Law* 6(3), 635–659. Investment arbitration, in contrast, is famously silent on the issue of the appropriate standard of review. See Urueña, *supra* note 6.

14 Burke-White and von Staden, 305.

15 Legg, *supra* note 13, 17.

16 *Herrera Ulloa v. Costa Rica*, IACtHR, Series C No 107, Judgment of 2 July 2004, para. 161; *Barreto Leiva v. Venezuela*, IACtHR Series C No 206, Judgment of 17 November 2009, para. 90.

17 See *Castaneda Guzman v. Mexico*, IACtHR Series C No 184, Judgment of 6 August 2008, para.162.

18 In *La Ultima Tentación de Cristo*, of 2001, the IACtHR had to decide whether Chile was in breach of the American Convention of Human Rights, by preventing the release of Martin Scorsese's 1988 film "The Last Temptation of Christ" on the basis of its alleged anti-Catholic message. The case had obvious coincidences with the case law that developed the margin of appreciation doctrine in Europe – in particular, *Otto-Preminger Institut v. Austria*, of 1995, which dealt with the criminal proceedings against a film institute that wanted to broadcast a series of satirical films on Christianity, and *Wingrove v. UK*, of 1996, which dealt with the prohibition of release of "Visions of Ecstasy", a movie derived from the life of St. Teresa of

Some scholarship in the region has argued that the Inter-American Court does adopt some level of a "margin of appreciation".[19] However, this observation seems questionable. While the IACtHR is interacting with domestic decision-makers in an increasingly close (and sophisticated) fashion, not all these interactions can be read as expressions of deference, or as a margin of appreciation doctrine. In particular, three distinctions need to be made. First, as was pointed out earlier, it is not uncommon for international courts to give states some discretion to configure their domestic law to comply with international legal obligations; this discretion, however, is different from a deferential margin of appreciation.[20] Second, there is an increasingly complex dialogue between the IACtHR and domestic courts,[21] and much of this dialogue implies a certain consideration of the reasoning of national courts.[22] This dialogue does not imply that the regional tribunal is giving primary decision-makers a "margin of appreciation" in their compliance with their human rights obligations. Finally, the Inter-American Court often frames its decisions as a problem of proportionality.[23] This framing often requires that the Court consider the primary decision-maker's own definition of a domestic measure's structure and

Avila. In its decision, the Inter-American Court decided not to use the margin of appreciation doctrine (despite quoting widely from other European human rights precedent), and adopted a strict standard of review, finding that "[Chile had] to amend its domestic law, within a reasonable period, in order to eliminate prior censorship to allow exhibition of the film "The Last Temptation of Christ", and must provide a report on the measures taken in that respect (…)." See *'La Última Tentación De Cristo' (Olmedo Bustos and others) v. Chile*, IACtHR Series C No 73, Judgment of 5 February 2001, para. 103.

19 See, for example, Barbosa Delgado, F.R. (2012), El margen nacional de apreciación y sus límites en la libertad de expresión: análisis comparado de los sistemas europeo e interamericano de derechos humanos. Bogota: Universidad Externado de Colombia.

20 See Nash Rojas, C. (2018), "La doctrina del margen de apreciación y su nula recepción en la jurisprudencia de la Corte Interamericana de Derechos Humanos", *ACDI – Anuario Colombiano de Derecho Internacional* 11.

21 Acosta Alvarado, P.A. (2015), *Diálogo judicial y constitucionalismo multinivel: el caso interamericano* (1st ed.). Bogota: Universidad Externado de Colombia.

22 See Neves, M. (2013), "Del Diálogo entre las Cortes Supremas y la Corte Interamericana de Derechos Humanos al Transconstitucionalismo en América Latina" In: R. Urueña, G.R. Bandeira Galindo and A. Torres Pérez (eds), *Protección multinivel de derechos humanos*. Barcelona: University Pompeu Fabra, 275–302.

23 See, for example, *Caso Kimel v. Argentina*, IACtHR Series C No 177, Judgment of 2 May 2008; see also *Caso Fontevecchia y D'Amico v. Argentina*, IACtHR Series C No 238, Judgment of 29 November 2011. Generally, see Clérico, L. (2018), *Derechos y proporcionalidad: violaciones por acción, por insuficiencia y por regresión.*

objectives, as elements of a test of proportionality. However, this consideration does not imply a particular standard of review as, even in the context of a strict proportionality analysis, a court can be more or less deferential.[24] In fact, the Inter-American Court has held that its analysis of proportionality *excludes* the relevance of a "margin of appreciation" doctrine.[25]

Why this reluctance towards deference? Despite the Court's formal silence, by Justice Cançado Trindade, former President of the Inter-American Court, has clearly stated the rationale behind this rejection of deference: "How could we apply [the margin of appreciation doctrine] in the context of a regional human rights system where many countries' judges are subject to intimidation and pressure? How could we apply it in a region where the judicial function does not distinguish between military jurisdiction and ordinary jurisdiction? How could we apply it in the context of national legal systems that are heavily questioned for the failure to combat impunity? [...] We have no alternative but to strengthen the international mechanisms for protection ... Fortunately, such doctrine has not been developed within the inter-American human rights system."[26]

Miradas locales, interamericanas y comparadas. Querétaro: Instituto de Estudios Constitucionales del Estado de Querétaro, Series "Constitución y Derechos", 156–186.

24 For an example of the different possible combinations of proportionality test and deferential/non-deferential standard of review in investment arbitration, see Henckels, C. (2012), "Indirect Expropriation and the Right to Regulate: Revisiting Proportionality Analysis and the Standard of Review in Investor-State Arbitration", *Journal of International Economic Law* 15(1), 223–255.

25 In *Artavia Murillo et al. ("In Vitro Fertilization") v. Costa Rica*, the IACtHR had to address an explicit argument of Costa Rica, according to which "a margin of appreciation [exists] to grant the status of child to unborn children" (para. 169). For the Inter-American Court, though, the fact that "the [Costa Rican] Constitutional Chamber based itself on an absolute protection of the embryo that, by failing to weigh up or take into account the other competing rights, involved an arbitrary and excessive interference in private and family life that makes this interference disproportionate. Moreover, the interference had discriminatory effects. In addition, taking into account these conclusions about the assessment and the considerations concerning Article 4(1) of the Convention (concluding *that* the embryo cannot be understood to be a person for the purposes of Article 4(1) of the American Convention – RU), the Court does not consider it pertinent to rule on the State's argument that it has a margin of appreciation to establish prohibitions such as the one established by the (Costa Rican) Constitutional Chamber" (para. 316).

26 Cançado Trindade, A.A. (2006), *El derecho internacional de los derechos humanos en el siglo XXI* (2nd ed.). Santiago de Chile: Editorial Jurídica de Chile, 390. The quote is originally in Spanish; this translation and text selection is quoted from Con-

Overall, then, the Inter-American Court of Human Rights has preferred to remain fuzzy about its own standard of review. This lack of clarity, though, in fact implies a very specific non-deferential standard of review. Despite a couple of somewhat haphazard uses of the expression "margin of appreciation", it seems clear that the Inter-American Court has preferred to steer clear of adopting a standard that would give explicit deference to the primary decision-maker, such as the European "margin".[27] As Cançado Trindade makes clear, in the context of a widely perceived failure to prosecute gross violations of human rights domestically, the primary decision-maker cannot enjoy much deference, a choice that, as we will discuss in the next section, gave ground to one of the most controversial decisions ever adopted by the Inter-American Court.

2. Gelman *and the no-deference standard*

Perhaps the clearest expression of the IACtHR's no-deference standard of review is the *Gelman* decision.[28] The case concerned Macarena Gelman, whose Argentinean parents were captured, tortured and killed by the Uruguayan military in 1976, in a joint Argentina-Uruguay action under "Operación Cóndor". Gelman's mother was seven-months pregnant when captured and gave birth in captivity. After the mother's forced disappearance, the infant was raised by a Uruguayan policeman and his wife, unaware of her real identity, until a paternal grandparent managed to track her down in 2000.

These facts are mostly undisputed, confirmed by an official "Peace Commission" report of 2003. However, a 1986 Uruguayan Law that granted amnesty to members and agents of the dictatorship (the "Expiry Law") prevented the prosecution of the perpetrators. The Uruguayan Supreme Court upheld the Law's constitutionality in 1988 by a three-to-

---

tesse, J. (2016), "Contestation and Deference in the Inter-American Human Rights System", *Law and Contemporary Problems* 79(2), 134.

27 With the same conclusion, see Duhaime, B. (2014), "Subsidiarity in the Americas: What Room Is There for Deference in the Inter-American System?" In: W.G. Werner and L. Gruszczynski (eds), *Deference in International Courts and Tribunals: Standard of Review and Margin of Appreciation*. Oxford/New York: Oxford University Press, 289–318. See also: Contesse, J., *supra* note 26.

28 *Caso Gelman v. Uruguay*, IACtHR Series C No 221, Judgment of 24 February 2011. The following discussion on *Gelman* is drawn from von Bogdandy, A. and Urueña, R. (2020), "International Transformative Constitutionalism", *American Journal of International Law* 114(3).

two majority vote. In 1989, a proposal to derogate its first four articles was rejected in a national referendum, with a 58 % percent voting in favor of the Law. Later on, in 2004, the Supreme Court denied a motion to have portions of the Law declared unconstitutional. However, in 2009, the Supreme Court finally held that certain elements of the Law were unconstitutional. Six days after this last decision, the proposal to derogate the same four articles of the Law was subject to a referendum for a second time. The Law stood by a 52 % majority.

Gelman provides a litmus test of the Inter-American Court's approach to deference. Congress adopted the Expiry Law t, which in three decades was reviewed thrice in its constitutionality by a relatively independent domestic Supreme Court. Moreover, it was subject to a national referendum not once, but twice. At a purely procedural level, it is hard to think of a domestic decision featuring a better formal democratic pedigree.

However, the Law openly collided with a consistent theme in Inter-American jurisprudence, especially in relation to the democratic transition, which emphasizes the obligation of states to ensure victims' right to the truth,[29] to a judicial process, and to full reparation for wrongdoing.[30] By the time of the *Gelman* case, the IACtHR had already rejected blanket amnesties in transitional justice processes in Peru.[31] Specifically, the roadblock for the Uruguayan Expiry Law was the 2001 decision in *Barrios Altos*[32] and the 2006 decision in *La Cantuta*[33], according to which amnesties constituted a violation of the American Convention on Human Rights and therefore "lacked legal effects"[34].

29 Antkowiak, T.M. (2002), "Truth as Right and Remedy in International Human Rights Experience", *Michigan Journal of International Law* 23(4), 977–1013.

30 See Pasqualucci, J.M. (2012), *The Practice and Procedure of the Inter-American Court of Human Rights*. Cambridge: Cambridge University Press, 230–288.

31 *Caso Barrios Altos v. Perú*, IACtHR Series C No 75, Judgment of 14 March 2001, paras 41–44.

32 *Ibid*. See generally Binder, C. (2011), "The Prohibition of Amnesties by the Inter-American Court of Human Rights", German Law Journal 12(5), 1203–30.

33 *La Cantuta v. Peru*, IACtHR Series C No 162, Judgment of 29 November 2006, para. 189.

34 In his separate opinion to *La Cantuta v. Peru*, Segio García Ramírez argues that domestic laws that violate the Convention are "basically invalid" (paras 4–5).

To be sure, such a non-deferential stance by the Inter-American Court implied an astonishing move,[35] and a first of its kind in international law.[36] However, the Peruvian amnesties, if understood in their context, prove to be a very different animal to the Uruguayan Law. The Peruvian amnesties were, in fact, "auto-amnesties", adopted by a Congress put in place by the same government responsible for the atrocities, after Fujimori closed the democratically elected Congress in his 1992 "auto-coup".[37] After Fujimori's fall from power, transitional Peruvian President Paniagua was opposed to maintaining the amnesties, but was bound by domestically valid laws, and lacked the political majorities in Congress to immediately overturn them.[38] In that context, Peru's agent put forward before the Inter-American Court the question of what to do with these formally valid amnesty laws,[39] thus opening the space for the IACtHR to strike down directly a piece of legislation that was not only contrary to Inter-American human rights law, but also inconvenient to the new administration.

The Uruguayan situation was quite different. Nevertheless, despite these important differences, the cards were already played at the Inter-American system when the *Gelman* case came about. With statements such as those in *Barrios Altos* and *La Cantuta*, the regional Court had already played its hand. It comes, therefore, as no surprise that it maintained its strict no-deference standard of review, and held that the Uruguayan Expiry Law, despite its democratic pedigree, was still in breach of the Inter-American Convention, and had to be reformed.

To do so, the Court drew a line between democratic support for a measure and its legality under human rights law, as the former does not imply the latter. Human rights, for the Court, belong to sphere of public decision-making that is, at last instance, immune from majoritarian rule. For the Court, "the fact that the Expiry Law of the State has been approved in a democratic regime and yet ratified or supported by the public, on two occasions, namely, through the exercise of direct democracy, does not auto-

---

35 See, generally, Huneeus, A. (2017), "The institutional limits of Inter-American constitutionalism" In: R. Dixon and T. Ginsburg (eds), *Comparative Constitutional Law in Latin America*. Cheltenham/Northampton: Edward Edgar, 300–324.

36 Cassese, A. 2002), "Y-a-t-il un conflit insurmontable entre souveraineté des États et justice pénale internationale?" In: A. Cassese & M. Delmas-Marty (eds), *Crimes Internationaux et Juridictions Internationales.* Paris: Presses Universitaires de France, 13–29, 16, quoted in: Binder, *supra* note 32, 1212.

37 See, generally, Levitsky, S. (1999), "Fujimori and post-party politics in Peru", *Journal of Democracy* 10(3), 78–92.

38 García-Sayán, D. (2017), *Cambiando el Futuro*. Lima: Lapix, 172–173.

39 *Ibid.*, 173.

matically or by itself grant legitimacy under International Law [...]. The bare existence of a democratic regime does not guarantee, *per se*, the permanent respect of International Law [...] The democratic legitimacy of specific facts in a society is limited by the norms of protection of human rights recognized in international treaties, such as the American Convention, in such a form that the existence of [a] true democratic regime is determined by both its formal and substantial characteristics, and therefore, particularly in cases of serious violations of [peremptory] norms of International Law, the protection of human rights constitutes a[n] impassable limit to the rule of the majority, that is, to the forum of the "possible to be decided" by the majorities in the democratic instance [...]."[40]

This line of reasoning has evident implications for the idea of democratic legitimation of international courts through political embeddedness, as suggested by *In Whose Name?* The Inter-American Court staked its legitimacy on a strategy that is the exact opposite of political embeddedness: by *not* being embedded in Uruguay's political process and *not* adopting a deferential standard towards domestic electoral decision-making, the Court justified its controversial decision. In a way, the Inter-American Court purposefully placed itself outside Uruguayan politics, and gave itself the role of drawing the external line of what can, and what cannot, be decided by local democratic processes. In *Gelman* the Expiry Law was "outside" what is decidable, and hence necessarily unlawful under the American Convention of Human Rights.

3. *Regional democracy, political embeddedness, and the Inter-American community of human rights practice:*

Gelman drew criticism from different fronts. To be sure, some of it came from states that see in a non-deferential Inter-American Court the risk of possible accountability for their own human rights violations. This line of critique, while politically relevant, is not particularly interesting in its substance. More interesting is the critique of scholars like Roberto Gargarella, who consider that the *Gelman* precedent is problematic in three senses. First, because the Inter-American Court overlooks that "reasonable and persistent differences of opinion persist with regards to justice and rights". Second, because the Court is not "sufficiently respectful to democracy or, more precisely, to what local communities democratically decide". Third,

40 *Gelman*, *supra* note 28, paras 238–239.

because the regional Tribunal seems biased towards a particular method of criminal punishment (prison) and fails to consider other alternatives that may provide a stronger basis for a democratic transition.[41]

In this section, I will discuss the thrust of the two first dimensions of the critique, and will assess them from the perspective of political embeddedness and from the democratic legitimacy of the Inter-American Court of Human Rights.[42]

The first critique, then, relates to the "fact of disagreement". For Gargarella, "we disagree over what [human] rights should be, and what their content and contours are" and, therefore, "we should not simply treat the idea of rights as isolated from or lacking any contact whatsoever with the

41 Gargarella, R. (2015), "Democracy and Rights in *Gelman v. Uruguay*", *AJIL Unbound* 109, 115–119. Expanding the argument: Gargarella, R. (2015), "La democracia frente a los crímenes masivos: una reflexión a la luz del caso Gelman", *Revista Latinoamericana de Derecho Internacional* 2, 1–15; Gargarella, R. (2016), *Castigar al prójimo: por una refundación democrática del derecho penal*. Buenos Aires: Siglo XXI, 91–124. For a similar critique, see Contesse, J. (2017), "The final word? Constitutional dialogue and the Inter-American Court of Human Rights", *International Journal of Constitutional Law* 15(2), 414–435; and Contesse, J. (2016), "Contestation and deference in the Inter-American human rights system", *Law & Contemporary Problems* 79(2), 123–145. Reviewing the critique from a criminal policy perspective, see Chehtman, A. (2018), "Amnistías, democracia y castigo en Castigar al prójimo", *Revista Jurídica de la Universidad de Palermo* 16(1), 155–165. The following discussion is drawn in part from Urueña, R. (forthcoming), "Democracy and Human Rights Adjudication in The Inter-American Legal Space" In: P. Zumbansen (ed.), *Oxford Handbook of Transnational Law*. Oxford: Oxford University Press.

42 The third dimension of the critique, namely, that of alternative forms of punishment and criminal reproach is, of course, relevant, but can be read as an example of the first two critiques, if considered as problem of standard of review and the (possible) deference that the Inter-American should show the primarily (national) decision-maker in this respect. If, on the other hand, it is not considered as a problem of deference, but rather as a substantive problem regarding the choice of punishment favoured by the Inter-American Court (as in, for example, Chehtman, *supra* note 41), then the critique becomes an intervention in the wider debate on the transitional governance framework preferred by the Inter-American Court. This debate, though, exceeds the scope of this chapter. On that latter issue, see Carvalho Veçoso, F.F. (2016), "Whose Exceptionalism? Debating the Inter-American View on Amnesty and the Brazilian Case" In: K. Engle, Z. Miller and D.M. Davis (eds), *Anti-Impunity and the Human Rights Agenda*. Cambridge: Cambridge University Press, 185–215. In the Colombian context, see Acosta-López, J.I. (2016), "The Inter-American Human Rights System and the Colombian Peace: Redefining the Fight Against Impunity", *AJIL Unbound* 110, 178–182.

notion of majority rule"[43]. This critique, while appropriate in targeting the Inter-American Court's definition of the "non-decidable" in the *Gelman* case, still misrepresents the implications of the indeterminacy thesis in human rights.

It is clear that human rights texts fail to define, in themselves, the outcome of a given conflict of rights. In their indeterminacy, human rights only find content in a contextual process of interpretation and decision-making. As Martti Koskenniemi pointed out almost two decades ago, "rights do not exist as such – 'fact-like' – outside the structures of political deliberation. They are not a limit, but an effect of politics"[44]. Ultimately, rights-talk "runs out", and finding appropriate solutions to specific rights-conflicts requires that the adjudicator turn to other tools of argumentation, outside the text establishing rights. Legal materials (such as the definition of a "right") *always* fail to provide a univocal outcome – a reality that opens the space to all sorts of strategic behavior on behalf of the interpreter,[45] often through argumentative devices such as rule/exception structures,[46] or proportionality analysis.[47]

The Inter-American Court plays down such indeterminacy of human rights in *Gelman*, where it fails to recognize that its application of the Peruvian amnesty jurisprudence is not the only possible outcome, but rather one of several reasonable possible answers. That is the thrust of Gargarella's "disagreement" critique, and he is right in pointing it out. But then again, *that is what courts do* – not only the Inter-American Court, but *all* court mobilize legal meaning in such a way that (dissenting opinions notwithstanding) they present their particular solution as the *only* possible answer.[48]

In terms of legal reasoning, *Gelman* is not different from any human rights case, as they all involve indeterminate rights whose interpretation is connected to the political context. Gargarella is wrong when he suggests

43 Gargarella, "Democracy and Rights in *Gelman v. Uruguay*", *supra* not 41, 118.

44 Koskenniemi, M. (2001), "Human rights, politics, and love", *Mennesker & Rettigheder* 4, 33–45.

45 See Kennedy, D. (2007), "A left phenomenological critique of the Hart/Kelsen theory of legal interpretation", *Kritische Justiz* 40(3), 296–305.

46 Koskenniemi, *supra* note 44, 33–35.

47 See Kennedy, D. (2016), "Proportionality and 'Deference' in Contemporary Constitutional Thought" In: T. Perišin and S. Rodin (eds), *The transformation or reconstitution of Europe: the critical legal studies perspective on the role of the courts in the European Union*. Oxford/Portland: Hart, 29–58.

48 See Kennedy, D. (1986), "Freedom and constraint in adjudication: A critical phenomenology", *Journal of Legal Education* 36(4), 518–562.

that the democratic pedigree of the Uruguayan Expiry Law makes *Gelman* so special that the Inter-American Court should not have posited a non-deferential standard of review as the only right answer. On the contrary, the mere fact that the Inter-American Court fails to draw attention to the contingency of its argumentative choices (and hence, to the latter's deep link to the wider political process) does not make *Gelman* a badly decided case, but rather makes it a squarely traditional human rights decision.

Legal operators (judges, litigants, academics, states) are aware of this indeterminacy. However, such an awareness does not imply that all outcomes are equally acceptable as a matter of fact. Indeterminacy does not simply mean that "law is politics – end of the discussion". On the contrary, certain outcomes are preferred, and the structural bias of institutions is mobilized to achieve those outcomes.[49] Which outcomes are preferred? In the context of human rights indeterminacy, the consensus of an Inter-American community of human rights practice selects acceptable outcomes;[50] a group of people that interact, in the framework of an Inter-American common law of human rights,[51] to push their own agendas and fulfill their mandates.[52] Civil society organizations that bring cases before the IACtHR, grassroots organizations that protect victims on the ground, clinics at law schools that file *amicus* briefs, domestic courts that interpret

49 This argument is made in Koskenniemi, M. (2005), *From Apology to Utopia: The Structure of International Legal Argument* (2nd ed.). Cambridge: Cambridge University Press, 605–607 ("the system still *de facto* prefers some outcomes or distributive choices to other outcomes or choices").

50 See Adler, E. (2005), *Communitarian International Relations: The Epistemic Foundations of International Relations.* London/New York: Routledge, 11. The following use of the notion of community of practice, as well as the idea of shared understandings, is influenced by Brunnée, J. and Toope, S.J. (2010), *Legitimacy and legality in international law: An interactional account*. Cambridge: Cambridge University Press. Brunné's and Toope's argument, though, seeks to unpack the notion of international legal obligation through a reinterpretation of the Fullerian criteria of inner morality of law. My interest is not in legal obligation, nor in compliance with international law; for that reason, I focus solely on their description of interactional international rule-making, and not in their effort to provide a normative basis for that process.

51 Such is the *Ius Commune Constitutionale en América Latina*, ICCAL. See von Bogdandy, A. (2017), "Ius Constitutionale Commune En América Latina: Observations on Transformative Constitutionalism" In: A. von Bogdandy *et al.* (eds), *Transformative Constitutionalism in Latin America: The Emergence of a New Ius Commune*. Oxford: Oxford University Press, 27–48.

52 This discussion of communities of practice is drawn from von Bogdandy and Uruea, *supra* note 28.

and apply that common law, civil servants that work on human rights for domestic governments, scholars writing and teaching Inter-American human rights law, and, the IACtHR itself, among others.[53]

All these participants have different, even conflicting, views of the Inter-American common law of human rights. The community of practice is not a top-down hegemonic regime, but rather a shared common understanding of what they are doing, and why.[54] Such is the function of decisions like *Barrios Altos/Cantuta*; beyond being statements of international legal obligation, they are expression of the consensus of a community of practice, around which that same community interacts. *Gelman* was a reiteration of the consensus of the Inter-American community of practice, crystalized by a legal utterance of the Inter-American Court that establishes a non-deferential standard of review when dealing with amnesties for gross violations of human rights. Thus, despite being textually free to consider other outcomes (in the sense that human rights texts are indeterminate), the Inter-American Court is restrained by the consensus of the Inter-American human rights community of practice, which is the community that, ultimately, will play a key role in implementing the Court's order. To be clear, there are few consensuses as clearly crystalized in that community as the non-deferential standard of *Barrios Altos/Cantuta* and now *Gelman*. The fact that the Inter-American Court is not explicit about its strategy to navigate the tension between textual freedom and adjudicatory restraint does not make it wrong. It makes it *accountable.*

To be sure, consensus in communities of practice are constantly changing, and it can be steered in one direction, or the other. The consensus (such as the non-deferential standard) influences the community's behavior, who tries to influence it back. *Gelman* itself is a crystallization of the current consensus and, at the same time, an effort to reinforce it. In this framework, each actor proposes its view of the Inter-American common law of human rights, and through continuous interaction with other

---

based on Urueña, R. (2013), "Global Governance Through Comparative International Law? Inter-American Constitutionalism and The Changing Role of Domestic Courts in the Construction of the International Law", *Jean Monnet Working Paper Series* 21(13), 1–36.

53 For the role of the domestic constitutional lawyers in what I call here the Inter-American community of practice, see Huneeus, A. (2016), "Constitutional Lawyers and the Inter-American Court's Varied Authority", *Law and Contemporary Problems* 79(1), 179–208 (note that Huneeus does not speak of a community of practice).

54 Adler, *supra* note 51, 22.

actors, settles the "norm" – which may be unsettled later again, by further interaction. It thus makes sense, that the Inter-American Court defends that the strict non-deferential standard as applied in *Gelman* (that is, as applied to a domestic decision with very high local democratic pedigree) is the *only* right decision allowed by human rights law. However, if one stands outside Court's position, it is also apparent that the *Gelman* non-deferential standards is part of an always-shifting consensus of the community of practice.

This constant interaction of the community of practice implies a second dimension of political embeddedness that escapes the critics of *Gelman*. The political context of the Inter-American Court of Human Rights is not only national politics, but also an Inter-American political process, that includes the Inter-American human rights community of practice. Through a constant process of interaction based on a common law of human right, human rights indeterminacy forges a political process that is distinct from domestic politics, and different to the principal-agent relation between the Organization of American States and its members.[55] In what remains of this section, I will focus on this other Inter-American political context.

As was hinted before, Gargarella's critique of *Gelman* focuses not only on the problem of reasonable disagreement, discussed above, but also on the appropriate consideration that the Inter-American Court should give to domestic democratic processes. In essence, Gargarella argues that the Uruguayan Expiry Law should be distinguished from prior amnesties (for example, those in Peru), due to its democratic pedigree. In his reading, the standard of review is in negative relation with the domestic democratic process of primary decision. This critique suggests a sliding scale, of the following kind:

55 Klabbers has suggested a similar third space with regards to the law of international organizations, as a result of functionalism's inability to dealt with the effects of the organization on third parties. See Klabbers, J. (2015), "The EJIL Foreword: The Transformation of International Organizations Law", *European Journal of International Law* 26(1), 9–82. The following discussion on *Gelman*'s variable standard of review is drawn from Uruena, *supra* note 41.

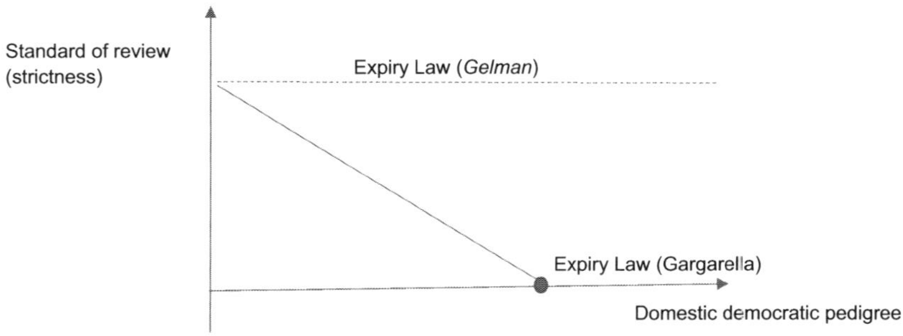

In this reading, the domestic democratic pedigree is the independent variable (as it is given, not decided by the Court, represented on the X axis), and the strictness of the standard of review is the dependent variable (as it is decided by the Court as a function of the democratic pedigree, represented on the Y axis). In the graphic, then, the higher the domestic democratic pedigree of the measure, the less strict the standard of review should be or, put otherwise, the more deferential the Inter-American Court should be towards the primary decision. Conversely, the lower the democratic pedigree, the stricter the standard of review.

Thus read, this view is not necessarily in conflict with the *Gelman* approach. *Gelman* does not give us evidence that the Inter-American Court rejects a movable standard of review, with democratic pedigree as the independent variable. A difference, though, does emerge with the Inter-American Court's approach to issues that are "non-decidable" through domestic democratic means. Regarding those cases (such as amnesties), the Court suggests that a strict standard of review is always applicable, regardless of the domestic democratic pedigree of the domestic measures (represented above by the dotted line). Critics, in contrast, argue that cases such as *Gelman* are not "non-decidable" but should be decided in reference to the same sliding scale: hence, *Gelman* should be subject to a low standard of review, given its high domestic democratic pedigree, represented by the "Gargarella" point in the graphic.

I find it difficult to agree with the Court's reasoning when drawing the line of the "non-decidable". *Gelman* builds a firewall around human rights adjudication, shielding it from democratic decision-making, that would require a much stronger justification than the Court provides. Such a firewall not only ignores that the indeterminacy of human rights implies a deep connection between the political process and adjudication, but is also ill-advised strategically, as it paints the Court as completely aloof from the democratic potential in the region. By adopting a non-deferential standard of review based on an alleged issue that is "non-decidable" at the domestic level, the Court tries to take a higher stand, and to extract itself from the domestic political process, but in fact ends up right in the middle of the Uruguayan political debate. As Duncan Kennedy has insightfully pointed out, a strict non-deferential stance is always "based on a simplistic distinction between legal interpretation and law-making. [The judge] cannot escape the usurpation charge simply by ignoring the role of politics in law."[56] Indeed, *Gelman's* critics charge the Court with of usurpation of the local democratic process.

The answer, though, is not adopting a deferent standard of review, as the critics suggest. *Gelman* serves an important function, as it sends a clear signal to the Inter-American human rights community of practice (particularly with an eye to future amnesties backed by plebiscites in other countries, such as Colombia or Venezuela). A deferential standard of review would imply yielding on this process of signaling, thus giving up on the Court's effort to maintain the current consensus of the community of practice concerning amnesties of gross human rights violations.

However, the Court's strategy of appealing to "non-decidable" issues seems too blunt an instrument for that purpose. It is unnecessary to create exceptions to the moving scale of the standard of review described above, and shield human rights adjudication from democracy, as the Court did. The Inter-American Court needs to ponder democratic legitimacy and the appropriate standard of review in all its decisions. However, it must consider not only the national democratic process, but also the Inter-American democratic process as a whole, in which the Inter-American community of practice engages daily.

Such is the limit of the critique to the *Gelman* decision. The Court's "non-decidable" issues argument is question-begging, and there should be a moving scale with regards to the appropriate standard of review. Critics focus solely on national political processes, and fail to take into account the regional process of democratization, in which the Inter-American Court plays a transversal role. It is true that the Court should be more deferential to a primary decision with a high democratic pedigree, but such a democratic pedigree needs to be considered regionally, not only based on national electoral processes, but also on the basis of the primary decision's potential impacts on the democratic process of the region as a whole. Even

56 Kennedy, *supra* note 48, 43. This discussion of democracy in the region is drawn from von Bogdandy and Uruena, *supra* note 28.

if the Uruguayan Expiry Law had sterling national democratic pedigree, it might have had lower *regional* democratic pedigree – particularly considering the potential impacts of a deferential Inter-American standard of review in the processes of democratization in other countries in the region, different from Uruguay. If that were the case, if the *regional* democratic pedigree is low, then it would have been perfectly reasonable for the Court to apply a strict standard of review – without having to use an ill-defined criterion of "non-decidable" issues.

Ultimately, Gargarella's second line of critique against *Gelman* depends on an extremely narrow national definition of democracy. Of course, thick electoral processes of representation only exist at a national level in Latin America. However, this approach seems to be too reductive, as if democracy were only possible at the level of the nation-state. If one is open to the idea of democracy beyond the state, then the Inter-American scale of the appropriate standard of review should consider that wider notion of democracy.

I am aware that calls for even the thinnest democratic process beyond the state are often met with skepticism.[57] However, the Inter-American common law of human rights is a democratic undertaking that, by definition, goes beyond the state and applies to the whole region – the Inter-American Court is embedded in that regional political process as well. This is not to say that Inter-American democracy is an extension of national democracies – it is, of course, different in character, institutions, and depth. However, it exists as part of wider regional political processes that is transnational. The common law of human rights in the region is, to borrow an expression from the global administrative law literature, a "democratic striving" undertaking.[58] *Gelman's* critics simply ignore this wider regional process, focusing solely on national electoral democracy. By

57 See generally De Búrca, G. (2007), "Developing democracy beyond the state", *Columbia Journal of Transnational Law* 46(2), 221–278. For a summary of the sceptical arguments, see Wheatley, S. (2011), "A Democratic Rule of International Law", *European Journal of International Law* 22(2), 525–548; Bohman, J. (2005), "From Demos to Demoi: Democracy across Borders", *Ratio Juris* 18(3), 293–314.

58 See Kingsbury, B., Vallejo, R. and Donaldson, M. (2016), "Global Administrative Law and Deliberative Democracy" In: A. Orford and F. Hoffman (eds), *The Oxford Handbook of the Theory of International Law*. Oxford: Oxford University Press, 526–544. The global administrative law literature has tried to unbracket the question of democracy by proposing a bottom-up deliberative "democratic striving" global rule of law. Other efforts focus on other possibilities for democracy beyond the state, for example, in Cohen, J. and Sabel, C.F. (2005), "Global democracy?", *New York University Journal of International Law and Politcs* 37(4), 763–798.

doing so, they end up depriving the Inter-American Court of its pivotal role as key promoter of a *regional* democracy, that complements and reinforces national democracies.

4. *Conclusion: Good faith in standard of review definition*

In whose Name? puts forward the idea of political embeddedness as a source of democratic legitimacy for international courts. This chapter takes up that question, and explores it in reference to *Gelman*. It argues that the balance between the appropriate standard of review and the democratic pedigree of the primary decision is indeed fundamental for the democratic legitimacy of the IACtHR. Yet, such democratic balancing needs to occur in reference to a regional (and not solely national) process of democratization, in which the Inter-American community of human rights practice plays a central role.

Part of the discussion in this chapter builds on an open recognition of the indeterminacy of human rights law. Such indeterminacy creates a deep link between adjudication and the political process, which in turn feeds back to the determination of the appropriate standard of review. The Inter-American Court is reluctant to underscore such indeterminacy, and is consequently reluctant to accept the contingency of certain legal outcomes over others. I argued in this chapter, in descriptive mode, that such reluctance is not surprising, as that is what courts often do when facing open-ended texts. In the context of *Gelman*, it is therefore not surprising that the Inter-American Court presented its non-deference stance as the only right legal answer to a difficult question.

Nevertheless, the normative question does emerge: how open should the Inter-American Court be when considering the tradeoffs of deference to the primary decision-maker? One alternative is to be aware of human rights indeterminacy, and still act as if a strict non-deferential stance is the only legal option available – for example, by deploying a "non-decidable" issue kind of argument. This is, though, a bad faith answer, and risks encouraging other actors of the community of practice to engage in bad faith interpretations of human rights texts, because they know that the Court's answer is contingent, and thus will act accordingly. This scenario would be characterized by a hermeneutics of suspicion, that seems undesirable in the region.[59] The Inter-American Court should develop a vocabulary that allows it to ponder the democratic pedigree of primary decisions transparently, without seeing its hands completely tied by domestic electoral processes. To that effect, the notion of *regional* democratization as correlation to a *regional* standard of review seems a useful starting point to unpack the Court's contribution to achieve the democracy we *want*, and not only to defend the democracy we already *have* in the region.

59 See Kennedy, D. (2014), "The hermeneutic of suspicion in contemporary American legal thought", *Law and Critique* 25(2), 91–139. Kennedy, against what is suggested in this chapter, in fact defends a certain measure of bad faith regarding deference and the appropriate standard of review. See Kennedy, *supra* note 47, 53–56.

In the name of the European Union, the Member States and/or the European citizens?

Freya Clausen[*]

In the well-known words of Judge Pescatore, the Court of Justice of the – then – European Communities had "une certaine idée de l'Europe" ("a certain idea of Europe").[1] The Court played a major role in the pursuit of that idea during the early years of the process of European integration. By virtue of the doctrine of direct effect,[2] another former member of that Court added, the latter "[took] Community law out of the hands of the politicians and bureaucrats and [gave] it to the people"[3]. The Court's self-perception was that of a Court embodied in a "new European *Volksgeist*"[4], acting as the "'conscience' of the peoples of Europe"[5]. Was the Court then deciding in the name of the (Member States' or Union's) citizens? My contribution shall address this very question in the light of the (recent) debate on the Court's (democratic) legitimacy.

Legitimacy can be defined as "the quality of a body that leads people to accept its authority"[6]. Incontestably, the Court of Justice of the European Union (CJEU) holds and exercises wide ranging judicial powers, which

---

* *Référendaire*, Court of Justice of the European Union. The views expressed are personal to the author.

1 Pescatore, P. (1983), "The Doctrine of Direct Effect: An Infant Disease of Community Law", *European Law Review* 8, 155–157, 157.

2 *Van Gend & Loos*, Case 26/62, Judgment of 5 February 1963, [1963] ECR 1.

3 Mancini, G.F. and Keeling, D.T. (1994), "Democracy and the European Court of Justice", *Modern Law Review* 57(2), 175–190, 186. The Court referred to the "[Member States'] nationals" in *Van Gend & Loos*, *supra* note 2.

4 Schepel, H. and Blankenburg, E. (2001), "Mobilizing the European Court of Justice" In: G. de Búrca and J.H.H. Weiler (eds), *The European Court of Justice*. Oxford: Oxford University Press, 9–42, 11.

5 *Ibid.*, 10, quoting Kakouris, C.N. (1995), "La Cour de Justice des Communautés européennes comme Cour Constitutionnelle: Trois observations" In: O. Due *et al.* (eds), *Festschrift für Ulrich Everling* (vol. 1). Baden-Baden: Nomos, 629–640, 632.

6 I owe this elegant definition to Ritleng, D. (2016), "The Independence and Legitimacy of the European Court of Justice" In: D. Ritleng (ed.), *Independence and Legitimacy in the Institutional System of the European Union*. Oxford: Oxford University Press, 83–124, 83.

must be legitimate: the CJEU reviews, *inter alia*, the lawfulness of acts and the conduct of the European Union (EU)'s legislature and executive, as well as those of the Member States. It develops EU law through dynamic interpretation; its decisions ultimately determine EU citizens' rights and obligations and have an impact on highly sensitive areas of (national) policy. While, undoubtedly, the two courts composing the CJEU, namely the Court of Justice (hereinafter the Court) and the General Court (GC), exercise these judicial powers, the need for legitimacy is stronger for the Court than for the GC and the threshold of legitimacy is set at a higher level.[7] That is certainly because, among the manifold functions conferred upon to the two courts, the most salient belong to the Court. It is the latter's case-law that is most frequently in the limelight, which might sometimes raise concerns about the impact of EU law on national (constitutional) law, the Member States' sovereign rights[8] and their domestic democracy.[9] Following this path, I shall limit my contribution to the legitimacy of the Court.[10]

It is a well-known fact that the Court developed its creative interpretation of the founding Treaties in a rather uncontroversial way during the 1960s and 1970s. The situation changed drastically in the course of the 1980s.[11] Ever since, both the legitimacy of the Court and its case-law have been subject to elaborate discussion and sometimes sharp criticism.

---

7 Epping, V. (1997), "Die demokratische Legitimation der dritten Gewalt der Europäischen Gemeinschaften", *Der Staat* 36(3), 349–380, 366–374.

8 Mancini and Keeling, *supra* note 3, 183.

9 Grimm, D. (2017), *The Constitution of European Democracy*. Oxford: Oxford University Press, 97–101, 105–115, 191–202.

10 Additionally, I shall exclude the legitimacy of national judges exercising their "European mandate" from the scope of my contribution. For a broader analysis of that issue, see Pernice, I. (1996), "Die Dritte Gewalt im europäischen Verfassungsverbund", *Europarecht* 34, 27–43; Roland, S. (2011), "La légitimité du juge comme auteur du/de droit. L'exemple du juge communautaire ou comment poser la question de la légitimité du juge communautaire? " In: L. Fontaine (ed.), *Droit et légitimité*. Brussels: Bruylant/Nemesis, 191.

11 On possible reasons for this change: Dehousse, R. (1997), *La Cour de justice des Communautés européennes*. Paris: Montchrestien, 129–150; Weiler, J.H.H. (1999), "The Least-Dangerous Branch: A Retrospective and Prospective of the European Court of Justice in the Arena of Political Integration" In: J.H.H. Weiler (ed.), *The Constitution of Europe*. Cambridge: Cambridge University Press, 188–206.

During the first peak of the debate on the Court's legitimacy in the course of the 1990s, democracy played a minor role.[12] While some authors addressed the democracy issue and pointed to its limits, they did so merely in the context of the selection of judges and their appointment to the Court.[13] Several former judges even opposed any attempt to make the Court more democratic,[14] as they considered that such attempts were liable to undermine the Court's necessary independence *vis-à-vis* the other EU institutions. They further rightly argued that a State-shaped democracy idea was unsuitable for the European Communities, today the Union. Accordingly, the Court's legitimacy was derived from other sources: the judges' independence, which was exceptionally identified as the source of the Court's "democratic legitimacy"[15], the judges' legal expertise or the persuasiveness of the Court's decisions, which might "compensate its democratic deficit"[16].

Nowadays, by contrast, scholars and judges explicitly address the issue of the democratic legitimacy of the Court[17] and discuss to whom it should respond[18] or in whose name it should decide (the Union, the Member

12 The Court's contribution to the rise of the democratic principle in the European Communities (Union) during that period was generally acclaimed: Mancini and Keeling, *supra* note 3; Pescatore, P. (1974), "Les exigences de la démocratie et la légitimité de la Communauté européenne", *Cahiers de droit européen* 10(5), 499–514, 511–513. For a more recent analysis, see Potvin-Solis, L. (2018), "La Cour de justice et la démocratie" In: C. Haguenau-Moizard and C. Mestre (eds), *La démocratie dans l'Union européenne*. Brussels: Bruylant, 148.

13 Epping, *supra* note 7; Mancini and Keeling, *supra* note 3, 176.

14 Kakouris, *supra* note 5, 637–638; Pescatore, P. (2000), "La légitimité du juge en régime démocratique", *Commentaire* 90, 339–349; Schockweiler, F. (1993), "L'indépendance et la légitimité du juge dans l'ordre juridique communautaire", *Rivista di diritto europeo* 33(4), 671–680, 674, 676–679.

15 Kakouris, *supra* note 5, 638.

16 Koopmans, T. (1993), "Judicial activism and procedural law", *European Review of Private Law* 1(1/2), 67–81, 79.

17 Hong, Q.L. (2010), "Constitutional Review in the Mega-Leviathan: A Democratic Foundation for the European Court of Justice", *European Law Journal* 16(6), 695–716; Tomuschat, C. (2006), "National Representation of Judges and Legitimacy of International Jurisdiction: Lessons from ICJ to ECJ?" In: I. Pernice *et al.* (eds), *The Future of the European Judicial System in a Comparative Perspective*. Baden-Baden: Nomos, 183–190, 187. *Contra*: Roland, *supra* note 10, 193–194.

18 De Witte, B. (2012), "Democratic Adjudication in Europe. How Can the European Court of Justice Be Responsive to the Citizens?" In: M. Dougan *et al.* (eds), *Empowerment and Disempowerment of the European Citizen*. Oxford: Hart, 129–144.

States or EU citizens).[19] A common understanding has developed that the judiciary of the EU – a *union of States and of citizens* – is to be evaluated no longer exclusively in its relation to the Member States and the legislative and executive branches of the EU, but also – if not predominantly – in its relation to EU citizens. In this regard, von Bogdandy's and Venzke's reading of Articles 9–12 TEU[20] opens the door for an in-depth analysis of the Court's practices in the light of a reshaped democratic principle.

Against this backdrop, in my contribution I shall give an overview of the debate on the ways in which the legitimacy of the Court is construed and how the democratic argument contributes to this debate. Bearing in mind that the concept of democracy shall not be overstretched and that the specific needs of the judiciary must be preserved, I argue that the Court's democratic justification largely relies on its very creation, its composition and its judicial functions in a Union "based on the rule of law"[21] (I). While I agree that the Court's legitimacy can be fostered by compliance with the requirements of fair trial, I do not believe that the democratic principles of transparency, openness, dialogue and participation should serve as a yardstick of the Court's (democratic) legitimacy (II). Finally, it is in the decision-making process, with regard to reasoning but also the definition of the level of judicial scrutiny, that the Court can generate authority, acceptability and, ultimately, legitimacy (III).

19 Wernicke, S. (2005), "In the name of the citizens! Art. I 1 of the Constitution and the European Court of Justice" In: I. Pernice and J. Zemanek (eds), *A Constitution for Europe: The IGC, the Ratification Process and Beyond.* Baden-Baden: Nomos, 235; Wernicke, S. (2007), "Au nom de qui? The European Court of Justice between Member States, Civil Society and Union Citizens", *European Law Journal* 13(3), 380–407; Perillo, E. (2018), "La justice européenne: au nom de qui?", *Revue des affaires européennes* (2), 319–332.

20 Von Bogdandy, A. and Venzke, I. (2014), *In whose name? A public Law Theory of International Adjudication*. Oxford: Oxford University Press, 135ff

21 *Les Verts v. Parlement*, Case 294/83, Judgment of 23 April 1986, [1986] ECR 1339, 1365.

I. Institutional and functional legitimacy

From an institutional and functional point of view, the Court's legitimacy is rooted in the Treaties[22] which created the Court, vested it with its judicial powers and entrusted it with its mission. Since the Treaties were ratified by all the Member States in accordance with their respective constitutional requirements (that is to say with the approval of their national parliaments), they confer an indirect democratic basis to the legitimacy of the Court as an EU institution. For the same reason, that legitimacy is attached to the Statute of the CJEU (hereinafter the Statute), which forms part of the primary law of the EU.[23] In an even more indirect manner, that legitimacy concerns the rules of procedures of the Court, which are established by the Court and approved by the Council.[24] The Court's legitimacy derives from its composition and judges' independence (A) as well as its mission (B).

A. The judges: judicial independence and composition of the Court

The legitimacy of the Court is classically derived from the appointment of its judges and their independence, their impartiality, as well as their legal expertise. In this regard, the debate mainly concerns the selection and appointment of the judges, since the latter's personal qualities – independence, impartiality and highest legal qualifications[25] – are not called into question and are guaranteed by a set of rules governing the office of the judge.[26] The Court's independence is well protected against court-curbing

22 Epping, *supra* note 7, 353; Everling, U. (1995), "Die Rolle des Europäischen Gerichtshofes" In: W. Weidenfeld (ed.), *Reform der Europäischen Union*. Gütersloh: Bertelsmann, 256–264; Molinier, J. (2004), "La légitimité du juge communautaire" In: J. Raibaut and J. Krynen (eds), *La légitimité des juges*. Toulouse: Presses de l'Université des sciences sociales de Toulouse, 151–161, para. 2.

23 Article 51 TEU; Article 281 TFEU.

24 Article 253(6) TFEU. For a critical assessment of the rules governing the establishment and modification of the Statute and the Court's rules of procedure, see Keppenne, J.-P. (2017), "Les procédures de révision du cadre réglementaire des juridictions de l'Union", *Cahiers de droit européen* 53(2), 343–370.

25 Article 19(2) TEU; Article 253 TFEU; Article 2 of the Statute.

26 Michel, V. (2010), "Les juridictions communautaires européennes" In: H. Ruiz Fabri and J.-M. Sorel (eds), *Indépendance et impartialité des juges internationaux*. Paris: Pedone 9–30, 16–20; Ritleng, *supra* note 6, 100–104. See also: Gaja, G. (2018), "Le rôle du juge ayant la nationalité d'un État membre intéressé à une

mechanisms.[27] It is also noteworthy that, nowadays, the Court itself pays great attention to the legality of its composition[28] and the lawfulness of appointment procedures[29] in order to guarantee the fundamental right to an independent and impartial tribunal.

A brief look at the historical evolution of the legal framework explains most of the controversy around the composition of the Court. Initially, during the negotiations that led to the creation of the European Coal and Steel Community, the Court was intended to become a rather typical international court. It was, therefore, to be composed of one judge per Member State and its members were to be appointed by a common accord of governments of the Member States. Yet, at a very late stage, the negotiations took a somehow unexpected turn and the Court was vested with powers of such original nature that it became a court of its own kind.[30] The "one

affaire devant la Cour de justice" In: V. Cannizzaro *et al.* (eds), *Liber Amicorum in onore di Antonio Tizzano. De la Cour CECA à la Cour de l'Union: le long parcours de la justice européenne*. Turin: Giappichelli, 371–375, 372.

27 Kelemen, R.D. (2013), "The political foundations of judicial independence in the European Union" In: S.K. Schmidt and D. Kelemen (eds), *The Power of the European Court of Justice*. London: Routledge, 43–58. It should be noted, in this context, that some authors have recently criticized the anticipated end of the term of the British members of the Court, in particular that of the Advocate General, as an attempt to the Court's independence (Halberstam, D., "Could there be a Rule of Law Problem at the EU Court of Justice? The Puzzling Plan to let U.K. Advocate General Sharpston Go After Brexit", available at https://verfassungsblog.de/could-there-be-a-rule-of-law-problem-at-the-eu-court-of-justice/, accessed 16 April 2020; Kochenov, D., "Humiliating the Court? Irremovability and Judicial Self-Governance at the ECJ Today", available at https://verfassungsblog.de/humiliating-the-court/, accessed 16 April 2020). However, in my view, this situation has to be seen as a mere direct consequence of the United Kingdom's withdrawal from the EU.

28 The Court examined whether the GC's composition, which heard the case in first instance, complied with the requirements of an independent and impartial tribunal: *Chronopost and La Poste v. UFEX and Others*, Joined Cases C-341/06 P and C-342/06 P, Judgment of 1 July 2008, [2008] ECR I-4777, para. 46.

29 See, to that effect, *Simpson v. Council* and *HG v. Commission*, Joined Cases C-542/18 RX-II and C-543/18 RX-II, Judgment of 26 March 2020, [2020] ECR.

30 Malenovský, J. (2011), "Les éléments constitutifs du mandat des juges de la Cour de justice à l'épreuve du temps: l'iceberg commence à fondre", *Il Diritto dell'Unione Europea* 4, 801–836, 801–813. On the negotiation leading to the Paris Treaty and the Rome Treaties, see Lagrange, M. (1979), "La Cour de justice des Communautés européennes du plan Schuman à l'Union européenne" In: *Mélanges Fernand Dehousse. La construction européenne* (vol. 2). Paris/Brussels: Nathan/Labor, 127–135; Pescatore, P. (1981), "Les travaux du 'groupe juridique' dans la négociation des traités de Rome", *Studia diplomatica* 34, 159–178.

judge per Member State" rule, which is still valid today,[31] and the appointment procedure remained unchanged at that stage. Under that procedure, candidates were at that time and continue to be designated by Member States pursuant to their own internal selection procedures. They were and continue to be appointed to the Court by common accord of the governments of the Member States for a renewable term of six years.[32] In practice, the accord amounts to a pure formality, given that the Member States generally do not call into question the candidates put forward by other Member States.[33] That procedure was subject to criticism: national selection procedures were regarded as executive-dominated and opaque, the judges' legitimacy derived exclusively from the appointment by governments – *i.e.* by the executive. Consequently, due to the proximity to national governments, the judges' independence and, ultimately, their legitimacy were called into question.

In response to part of that criticism, the Lisbon Treaty created an independent panel of experts, which hears the candidates designated by the Member States and issues an opinion on their suitability to perform their judicial duties.[34] While the panel's opinions are not binding, they are followed in practice. This procedure prevents purely political nominations.[35] Thus, the panel's creation has generally been welcomed, even though its functioning suffers from a lack of transparency.[36] Its creation and work had a significant side effect on the transparency of and parliamentary involvement in national selection procedures.[37]

Yet, the Court's composition is still subject to criticism in three regards.

---

31 Article 19(2 TEU. Currently, there are 11 Advocates General in the Court.

32 Article 19(2 (3) TEU; Articles 253 and 254 TFEU.

33 Epping, *supra* note 7, 362; Malenovský, *supra* note 30, 815; Michel, *supra* note 26, 14; Ritleng, *supra* note 6, 92.

34 Article 255 TFEU.

35 Ritleng, *supra* note 6, 95.

36 Alemanno, A. (2015), "How Transparent is Transparent Enough? Balancing Access to Information Against Privacy in European Judicial Selections" In: M. Bobek (ed.), *Selecting Europe's Judges: A Critical Review of the Appointment Procedures to the European Court*. Oxford: Oxford University Press, 202–221.

37 For a critical assessment of that issue, see Dumbrovský, T. *et al.* (2014), "Judicial Appointments: The Article 255 TFEU Advisory Panel and Selection Procedures in the Member States", *Common Market Law Review* 51(2), 455–482.

First, both scholars and judges claim that a non-renewable and longer term would further increase the judges' independence *vis-à-vis* their governments.[38]

Second, from a democratic viewpoint, some authors call for the direct involvement of the European Parliament in the appointment procedure[39] alongside national representatives. Such an amendment would reflect the dual nature of the European concept of democratic representation.[40] Both proposals are as old as the Court itself.[41]

Third, while it is indisputable that thanks to the "one judge per Member State" rule all domestic legal orders are represented in the Court, more recently authors have suggested that the Court's composition should be equally representative of EU citizens, in particular, in terms of gender balance and minority representation.[42] Nonetheless, under the current rules of appointment, where each Member State puts forward but one candidate and where the panel of experts hears the candidates individually, it is practically impossible to guarantee wider social diversity within the composition of the Court[43] even if, as authors have suggested, a set of objective eligibility criteria were developed.[44] That tendency might change if Member

38 Epping, *supra* note 7, 373; Léger, P. (2010), "Commentaire", in Ruiz Fabri and Sorel, *supra* note 26, 31–35, 34; Louis, J.-V. (2006), "The Court in the Constitution: How Federal?" In: Pernice *et al.*, *supra* note 17, 135–142, 137; Malenovský, *supra* note 30, 817–823, 828–829, 835; Pernice, *supra* note 10, 42; Ritleng, *supra* note 6, 98–100; Schockweiler, *supra* note 14, 676; Weiler, J.H.H. (2001), "Epilogue: The Judicial Après Nice" In: de Búrca and Weiler, *supra* note 4, 215–226, 225.

39 Pernice, *supra* note 10, 42; Ritleng, *supra* note 6, 100; Von Bogdandy, A. and Krenn, C. (2015), "On the Democratic Legitimacy of Europe's Judges: A Principled and Comparative Reconstruction of the Selection Procedures" In: Bobek, *supra* note 36, 162–180, 176–177. *Contra*: Schockweiler, *supra* note 14, 674.

40 Ritleng, *supra* note 6, 100; von Bogdandy and Krenn, *supra* note 39, 176–177.

41 Malenovský, *supra* note 30, 813. Later, in the 1980s, the Parliament attempted to play a role in selecting the judges (see, to that effect, Kenney, S.J. (1998–1999), "The Members of the Court of Justice of the European Communities", *Columbia Journal of European Law* 5(1), 101–133, 125–127).

42 That argument is based on the premise that "citizens are more likely to respect and trust courts whose personnel include people like themselves": Solanke, I. (2008–2009), "Diversity and Independence at the European Court of Justice", *Columbia Journal of European Law* 15(1), 89–121, 111; Shaw, J. (2001), "Gender and the Court of Justice" In: de Búrca and Weiler, *supra* note 4, 87–142, 116–118, 136f.

43 De Witte, *supra* note 18, 134–135.

44 Solanke, *supra* note 42, 102–111. I do not find the comparison, to this effect, with rules governing appointments to the CST particularly convincing (*Ibid.*, 106), since the centralised appointment procedure was specific to that court.

States were to put forward a list of several candidates[45] rather than one single candidature.

B. The functions of the Court

The (democratic) legitimacy of the Court is also based upon the latter's mission to safeguard the rule of law and to ensure legal protection within the European legal order. This legitimacy discourse is twofold. So are its shortcomings and counterarguments.

First, the Treaties conferred upon the Court the very broad mission to ensure the respect of the law,[46] vested it with wide-ranging judicial powers and created judicial remedies as well as a unique procedure of judicial dialogue with the national judges. The Treaties conferred upon the Court the exclusive power to render authentic interpretation of EU law. The Court's constitutional "duty" then is "to promote a Union based on the rule of law"[47]. The argument goes further in that as an EU institution, the Court is naturally called to pursue the aim of an "ever closer union among the peoples of Europe"[48] and to "promote [the EU's] values, advance its objectives, serve its interests"[49]. Here lay the foundations of the legitimacy of the Court in general and that of the latter's pro-integration case-law in particular.

The Court has built and strengthened that legitimacy by taking a leading role in the development and constitutionalisation of European integration:[50] thanks to an original method combining textual, teleological, sys-

45 As suggested by von Bogdandy and Krenn, *supra* note 39, 178.
46 Article 19(1) TEU.
47 Ritleng, *supra* note 6, 105.
48 Mancini and Keeling, *supra* note 3, 186.
49 Article 13 TEU. See, to that effect, Ritleng, *supra* note 6, 105.
50 Lecourt, R (1976), *L'Europe des juges*. Brussels: Bruylant; Kakouris, *supra* note 5, 638; Mancini and Keeling, *supra* note 3, 185; Ritleng, *supra* note 6, 108; Simon, D. (2006), "La légitimité du juge communautaire" In: *L'office du juge. Actes du colloque du Sénat des 29 et 30 septembre 2006*. Paris: Sénat, 447–468, 451–455, available at http://www.senat.fr/colloques/office_du_juge/office_du_juge42.html#toc419, accessed 21 August 2018; Vandersanden, G. (2004), "Mais où est la Cour de justice d'antan?" In: P. Magnette (ed.), *La Grande Europe*. Brussels: Editions de l'Université de Bruxelles, 237–246.

tematic and comparative interpretation,[51] the Court gave meaning to imprecise concepts laid down in the Treaties, constitutionalised the latter, went on – exceptionally, but legitimately[52] – to their "judicial revision"[53] and thereby promoted the integration process. It filled the gaps left open by the Treaties and/or the (paralysed) EU legislature,[54] it empowered (ordinary) national courts to fully apply EU law and recognised directly applicable rights, but also obligations of EU citizens.[55] Because of the *traité-cadre* nature of the Treaties and the lack of clear and complete legislation, the Court had no choice but to develop EU law consistent with its general mission and the objectives of the Treaties.[56]

However, the broad mission entrusted to the Court and the methods of interpretation it developed raised concerns of judicial activism and policy-making,[57] allegedly in favour of European integration and to the detriment

51 Poiares Maduro, M. (2010), "Interpreting European Law – On Why and How Law and Policy Meet at the European Court of Justice" In: H. Koch *et al.* (eds), *Europe: The New Legal Realism. Essais in Honour of Hjalte Rasmussen.* Copenhagen: Djoef, 457–478, 461–463; Ritleng *supra* note 6, 106–107.

52 Gaudin, H. (2001), "Introduction – De la détention d'une fonction constituante par la Cour de justice" In: T. Debard (ed.), *Les procédures de révision des traités communautaires: du droit international au droit constitutionnel.* Brussels: Bruylant, 25–52, 28–29, 40–45.

53 Jacqué, J.-P. (1986), "Note sous Partie écologiste Les Verts c/ Parlement européen", *Revue trimestrielle de droit européen* 22 (1986) 491–510, 503, on the standing of the European Parliament as a defendant.

54 Pescatore, P. (1983), "La carence du législateur communautaire et le devoir du juge" In: G. Lücke *et al.* (eds), *Rechtsvergleichung, Europarecht und Staatenintegration: Gedächtnisschrift für Léontin-Jean Constantinesco.* Cologne: Karl Heymanns, 559–580.

55 *Van Gend & Loos, supra* note 2; *Costa v. ENEL*, Case 6/64, Judgment of 15 July1964, [1964] ECR 585. On the importance of these cases, see Lecourt, R. (1991), "Quel eût été le droit communautaire sans les arrêts 1963 et 1964?" In: *L'Europe et le droit: mélanges en hommage à Jean Boulouis*. Paris: Dalloz, 349–361.

56 Mancini and Keeling, *supra* note 3, 186. During the first years of the European construction, only the Court was capable of pushing forward the process of integration: Cappelletti, M. (1979), "The 'Mighty Problem' of Judicial Review and the Contribution of Comparative Analysis", *Legal Issues of European Integration* 6(2), 1–29, 21–25.

57 Rasmussen, H. (1986), *On Law and Policy in the European Court of Justice: A Comparative Study in Judicial Policymaking*. Leiden: Brill. On the topic of judicial activism, see also: Dawson, M. *et al.* (eds) (2013), *Judicial Activism at the European Court of Justice.* Cheltenham/Northampton: Edward Elgar.

of the Member States' interests and sovereignty.[58] Yet, both that criticism and the legitimacy discourse reflect "differences of legal culture" with regard to the perception of the extent of discretion the courts enjoy.[59] Accordingly, they reveal "different conceptions of the role of courts and their legitimacy"[60]. It follows that an abstract discussion about the discretion enjoyed by the Court, its self-restraint or its activism is circular and somehow "misconceived".[61] Accusing the Court of activism often reflects a mere disagreement with the substance of the Court's decision.[62]

Second, scholars build and explain the Court's (democratic) legitimacy, by analogy to that of national constitutional courts, by reference to the Court's duty to ensure the respect of the rule of law and to theories of separation of powers or checks and balances.[63] Put in a nutshell, legitimacy amounts to a court's "independence and obedience to law [...], as a counterbalance to political power based upon democratic legitimacy" or, in accordance with a slightly different view, to "the rule of law [seen] as a constitutive element of a well-established democratic system" in which the judge, as the ultimate guardian of its respect, enjoys democratic legitimacy.[64] Regardless of the approach one choses, it will, to a certain extent, be transposable to the case of the Court, which is frequently compared to constitutional or supreme courts.[65] The CJEU forms indeed a "true third

58 See, for instance, the political reactions summarised by Weiler, J.H.H. (2008), "The Court of Justice in the limelight – again", *Common Market Law Review* 45(6), 1571–1579, 1571–1573.

59 Bengoetxea, J. (2010), "Reasoning from Consequences from Luxembourg" In: Koch, *supra* note 51, 39–56.

60 Poiares Maduro, *supra* note 51, 464.

61 Lenaerts, K. (2013), "How the ECJ Thinks: A Study on Judicial Legitimacy", *Fordham International Law Journal* 36(5), 1302–1371, 1310.

62 Simon, *supra* note 50, 449.

63 See, in particular, Epping, *supra* note 7, 353; Lenaerts, *supra* note 61, 1305.

64 Rodriguez Iglesias, G.C. (2004), "The Judge Confronts Himself as a Judge" In: R. Badinter and S. Breyer (eds), *Judges in Contemporary Democracy*. New York: New York University Press, 275–285, 281–282.

65 Azoulai, L. (2008), "Le rôle constitutionnel de la Cour de justice des Communautés européennes tel qu'il se dégage de la jurisprudence", *Revue trimestrielle de droit européen* 44(1), 29–45; Epping, *supra* note 7, 367; Gaudin, H. (2000), "La Cour de justice, juridiction constitutionnelle?", *Revue des affaires européennes* 10(3), 209–222; Ronse, T. and Waelbroeck, D. (2001), "La Cour de justice, juridiction suprême" In: P. Magnette and E. Remacle (eds), *Le nouveau modèle européen. Vol. 1: Institutions et gouvernance*. Brussels: Éditions de l'Université de Bruxelles, 89–103; Vesterdorf, B. (2006), "A Constitutional Court for the EU?" In: Pernice *et al.*, *supra* note 17, 83–90.

branch", which is "legally and institutionally bound into the framework of the European Union".[66] It interprets the Treaties and the system established by them in a sometimes creative and gap-filling manner. It reviews the lawfulness of the legal acts and the conduct of both the Member States and of the Union institutions. Thereby, it promotes the respect of the rule of law in the EU and exercises a democratic office.[67] The exercise of such judicial power is legitimate as long as it respects the constitutional constraints in which it is embedded; it is illegitimate when it encroaches upon the constituting power and/or the political decision-making power of the legislature or the executive.

The legitimacy of the Court also finds its source in the fact that the Court never has the final word.[68] Its case-law can always be corrected or overturned by more democratically accountable bodies: the EU legislature can correct any interpretation of secondary law by modifying the relevant legislative provisions. Where the interpretation is based on a treaty provision, the authors of the Treaties might overrule the Court's interpretation through a Treaty amendment.[69] So far, in practice, both the EU legislature[70] and the Member States as founding fathers have in most cases confirmed the Court's prior interpretations, even when those interpretations

66 Von Bogdandy and Venzke, *supra* note 20, 25.

67 Potvin-Solis, *supra* note 12, 150.

68 See, however, the vivid discussion on the identification by the Court of principles that even a formal treaty amendment cannot call into question: Boulouis, J. (1992), "Les avis de la Cour de justice des Communautés sur la compatibilité avec le Traité CEE du projet d'accord créant l'Espace économique européen", *Revue trimestrielle de droit européen* 28(3), 457–464, 462; Dutheil de la Rochère, J. (1992), "L'EEE sous le regard des juges de la CJCE", *Revue du marché commun* 35, 603–612, 607, 612; Bieber, R. (1993), "Les limites matérielles à la révision des traités établissant les Communautés européennes", *Revue du marché commun* 367, 343–350; Da Cruz Vilaça, J.L. and Piçarra, N. (1993), "Y a-t-il des limites matérielles à la révision des traités instituant les Communautés européennes?", *Cahiers de droit européen* 29(1–2), 3–37.

69 Gaudin, *supra* note 52, 37–38, 49–50. For a counter example, see Protocol 2 to the Maastricht Treaty, as mentioned by Dehousse, *supra* note 11, 132.

70 On the interplay between the Court and the EU legislature: Iliopoulou-Penot, A. (2015), "Réflexions sur la codification de la jurisprudence par le législateur européen" In: B. Bertrand *et al.* (eds), *L'identité du droit de l'Union européenne: Mélanges en l'honneur de Claude Blumann*. Brussels: Bruylant, 187–201.

were at odds with the exact wording of the provision at stake.[71] In other words, both the constituting power and the legislator appear to adhere to the Court's case-law thereby strengthening its legitimacy.[72]

That being said, however, there are critical voices to the effect that, while political overruling of the Court's case-law is theoretically possible, the practical hurdles are high and the prospect of a legislative or a constitutional overruling of the Court's decisions is rather remote. At the EU level, legislative procedures are arduous and apply without exception to the amendments of the existing legislation. The legislation often reflects difficult compromises reached after long negotiations between the Member States represented in the Council and, where the Treaty so requires, between the Council and the European Parliament.[73] Save for the simplified procedure provided for in Article 48(6) TEU, Treaty amendments require Member States' common accord and ratification, which "[make] the overruling of primary law interpretations almost impossible"[74]. The alleged *de facto* impossibility of contradicting the Court's decisions sometimes raises concerns about the Court's legitimacy.[75] Here again, "[t]he controversy is endless"[76].

Whilst the abovementioned arguments offer a strong basis of legitimacy for the Court *as a judicial body*, they have been criticised. In the recurring debate about the Court's legitimacy, they seem insufficient to appropriately address the voices that are raised not against the body as such, but against the exercise of judicial power. The answer to the de-legitimating discourse is, hence, to be found somewhere else. Turning to von Bogdandy's and Venzke's proposal, courts are capable of creating and building their own legitimacy through open, transparent, participatory and deliber-

71 Two striking examples can be mentioned in that context: first, the confirmation, in the Maastricht Treaty, of the Parliament's *locus standi*, as defined in *European Parliament v. Council*, Case C-70/88, Judgment of 22 May 1990, [1990] ECR I-2041, para. 27; and, second, the constitutionalisation of the Court's catalogue of the fundamental rights in the Charter of Fundamental Rights.

72 Simon, *supra* note 50, 467.

73 See the very strong objections to such reasoning by Weiler, J.H.H. (2013), "Epilogue: Judging the Judges – Apology and Critique" In: M. Adams *et al.* (eds), *Judging Europe's Judges. The Legitimacy of the Case Law of the European Court of Justice*. London: Hart, 235–254, 245–246.

74 De Witte, *supra* note 18, 142–143. Compare: Kelemen, *supra* note 27, 45–46.

75 Favoureu, L. (2001), "Rapport de synthèse: 'L'euroscepticisme du droit constitutionnel'" In: H. Gaudin (ed.), *Droit constitutionnel, droit communautaire: Vers un respect constitutionnel réciproque mutuel?*. Aix-Marseille: Economica, 379–390, 388.

76 Ritleng, *supra* note 6, 111.

ative procedures and sound decisions. I shall address both lines of argumentation.

II. Procedural legitimacy

The judicial process receives little or no attention in the debate about the Court's legitimacy. It is generally held that legitimacy flows from the respect of the requirements of a fair trial, openness, neutrality and independence.[77] The Court acts legitimately where it duly respects the applicable procedures and guarantees the parties a fair trial.[78] However, the question of whether the Court should "develop the judicial process in light of the democratic principle" as far as it pertains to openness, transparency and public dialogue or participation,[79] remains unanswered in the doctrine discussing the Court's legitimacy. In my view, regardless of their topicality or relevance, such considerations have limited potential for generating or fostering the Court's legitimacy.[80]

First of all, I have some difficulty in seeing how and to what extent such democratic principles as transparency, openness, dialogue and participation are intended to apply to the Court *in the exercise of its judicial functions*. It is true that Article 11 TEU, which calls for a transparent dialogue with EU citizens, is applicable to "the institutions", among which is the CJEU.[81] However, this fact "may be perceived as a sign of the arguable lack of reflection of the Treaty regarding the meaning and implications of participation as one of the foundations of democracy in the Union"[82]. This is all

---

77 Everling, *supra* note 22, 256.

78 With regard to procedural fairness requirements, see: Ritleng, *supra* note 6, 84.

79 Von Bogdandy and Venzke, *supra* note 20, 171.

80 Not to mention that the criticism the Court faces does not come from the citizens, but rather from the Member States, which accuse it of judicial activism (Ritleng, *supra* note 6, 112). Since Member States may plainly participate in all stages of all the proceedings both in preliminary reference procedures and in direct actions, I do not think that any possible improvements in that respect could adequately address that kind of criticism.

81 Von Bogdandy and Venzke, *supra* note 20, 152.

82 Mendes, J. (2011), "Participation and the Role of Law After Lisbon: A Legal View on Article 11 TEU", *Common Market Law Review* 48(6), 1849–1878, 1869. Scholars tend to establish a link between this provision and the policy making: Curtin, D. (2012), "The Role of Judge-made Law and EU Supranational Government: A Bumpy Road from Secrecy to Translucence" In: Dougan, *supra* note 19, 101–127; Grewe, C. (2007), "Article I-47" In: L. Burgorgue-Larsen *et al.* (eds), *Traité établis-*

the more true since the democratic principle sketched out in this article is further substantiated in Article 15(3) TFEU on access to documents, to which the Court is "subject [...] only when exercising [its] administrative tasks".

Second, it is necessary to strike a satisfying balance between any call for openness, transparency, public dialogue and participation with the requirements of the sound functioning and administration of justice. Judicial proceedings are different from political processes and do not offer an appropriate arena for a democratic, public, political debate. In other words, the need for transparency is less stringent in judicial proceedings compared to political and, in particular, legislative activities; the time-factor is important and the procedural rights of the parties to the proceeding must be guaranteed.[83] Among these, I shall mention the "right to defend their interests free from all external influences and, in particular, from influences on the part of members of the public" in direct actions.[84]

Finally, the proceedings before the Court involve a fair amount of transparency, openness and participation thanks to the publication of a notice on every case brought to the Court in the Official Journal of the EU, the organisation of a thorough debate in preliminary references procedures,[85] the admissibility of third party intervention in direct actions, the fact that hearings are public, the public delivery of the Court's decisions and, finally, the publication of judgments in 23 official languages of the EU. Having said that, there is always room for potential reforms. In particular, when it comes to the procedure: the national court's order for reference under Article 267 TFEU and written submissions could be made accessible to the general public in the course of or in the aftermath of the proceed-

sant une Constitution pour l'Europe: Commentaire article par article (vol. 1). Brussels: Bruylant, 624–633.

83 As stressed by von Bogdandy and Venzke, *supra* note 20, 178.

84 *Breyer v. Commission*, Case T-188/12, Judgment 27 February 2015, [2015] ECR, para. 119. The GC stressed that procedural documents are only served to the parties and are not to be made available to the public; it considered that the parties to the proceedings before it act unlawfully where they publish such documents on the internet. Upon appeal, the Court confirmed that position: *Commission v. Breyer*, Case C-213/15 P, Judgement of 18 July 2017, [2017] ECR, para. 62.

85 In accordance with Article 23(1) of the Statute, all parties to the proceedings before the referring judge, all the Member States, the Commission and the author(s) of the act the validity or interpretation of which is in dispute, are entitled to participate in the debate before the Court. An even larger debate is organised where one of the fields of application of the Agreement on the European Economic Area is concerned (Article 23(3) of the Statute).

ings. Upon the closure of proceedings in direct actions, public access to the record or even the case-file could be granted.[86] In cases of high social or political importance, oral hearings could be broadcast or webcast;[87] the report for a hearing might be re-introduced;[88] third party intervention in direct actions could be construed more openly[89] and, more generally speaking, the access of so called "non-privileged" applicants to court could be broadened.[90] Yet, these questions go beyond the (traditional) legitimacy debate.

When it comes to the decisions of the Court, whilst the judges' collegiate deliberations are secret by their very nature,[91] both judgments and Advocate Generals' opinions are public. "The public dialogue between the Court and its Advocates General plays an essential part in guaranteeing the transparency and intelligibility of the judicial process at the Court of Justice."[92] This, however, is deemed insufficient and scholars call for the

86 For further reading on this issue: Alemanno, A. and Stefan, O. (2014), "Openness at the Court of Justice of the European Union: Toppling a Taboo", *Common Market Law Review* 51(1), 97–139, 121–127.

87 *Ibid.*, 127–130, 132.

88 *Ibid.*, 130, 132–133. The virtues of the report for the hearing are at least twofold: on the one hand, since a paper/hard copy of the report is made available to the public before the hearing, the audience present in the courtroom has the means to grasp the gist of the case. On the other hand, the report for the hearing offers the parties a possibility to verify whether the judges have correctly understood the context of the case and their arguments.

89 By virtue of Article 40 of the Statute, whilst Member States and EU institutions have a right to intervene in any case before the Court, EU citizens, companies, non-governmental organisations *et cetera* fall into the category of "unprivileged" interested parties that must show "an interest in the result of a case submitted to the Court" and are not entitled to intervene in cases between Member States, between EU institutions or between Member States and EU institutions. Scholars call for a more open third party intervention: de Schutter, O. (2005), "Le tiers à l'instance devant la Cour de justice de l'Union européenne" in: H. Ruiz Fabri and J.-M. Sorel (eds), *Le tiers à l'instance devant les juridictions internationales.* Paris: Pedone, 85–104, 102.

90 On this difficult topic and on the implications of the Lisbon Treaty, see, *inter alia*, Lenaerts, K. (2009), "Le traité de Lisbonne et la protection juridictionnelle des particuliers en droit de l'Union", *Cahiers de droit européen* 45(5–6), 711–745; Coutron, L. (2010), "L'héritage de l'arrêt UPA", *L'actualité juridique: droit administratif* 10, 548–556.

91 Article 35 of the Statute.

92 Sharpston, E. (2009–2010), "Transparency and Clear Legal Language in the European Union: Ambiguous Legislative Texts, Laconic Pronouncements and the Credibility of the Judicial System", *Cambridge Yearbook of European Legal Studies* 12, 409–423, 420.

admission of dissenting opinions. [93] Such opinions by the judges in the minority, the argument goes, would result in the more discursive and more exhaustively reasoned decisions and would offer the public a better insight into all possible outcomes that have been discussed. The introduction of such opinions is, however, highly "unlikely" in practice.[94] This brings me to last aspect of the legitimacy debate: the grounds for the decisions.

III. Legitimacy through sound and reasoned decisions

Scholars insist on sociological legitimacy, *i.e.* the acceptance of the Court's case-law by Member States, EU institutions, citizens, litigants, *et cetera*.[95] The Court can generate such acceptance by adopting sound, persuasive, lawful, reasoned and acceptable decisions and, thereby, foster its own legitimacy.[96] A full and transparent reasoning allows for "democratic control"[97] or responsiveness[98] through public debate in the aftermath of proceedings. It is all the more important as the Court's rulings are not subject to an appeal and the Court cannot and shall not be held accountable for its case-law in front of any external body.[99]

93 In favour of the introduction of dissenting opinions: Höreth, M. (2011), "Richter contra Richter. Sondervoten beim EuGH als Alternative zum 'Court Curbing'", *Der Staat* 50(2), 191–226; Perju, V. (2009), "Reason and Authority in the European Court of Justice", *Virginia Journal of International Law* 49(2), 307–378; Weiler, *supra* note 38, 225. In order to avoid increased pressure on the independence of the judges, the call for such opinions usually goes hand in hand with proposals of a non-renewable and longer term of office. *Contra*: Schockweiler, *supra* note 14, 676.

94 De Witte, *supra* note 18, 141. See also: Alemanno and Stefan, *supra* note 86, 132.

95 For further reading: Pollack, M.A. (2017), "The legitimacy of the Court of Justice of the European Union", available at https://papers.ssrn.com/sol3/papers.cfm?abstract_id=2911836, accessed 17 August 2018, 1–56, 32–55.

96 The "quality of analysis […] is one of the very foundations of its legitimacy": Vesterdorf, *supra* note 65, 85.

97 Bengoetxea, *supra* note 59, 56.

98 Pernice, *supra* note 10, 40.

99 Be it in front of the Ombudsman, the Court of Auditors or the European Parliament: De Witte, *supra* note 18, 136–137.

The Court recognises the importance of the grounds for its decisions and elevates its duty to provide reasons[100] to a public policy rule.[101] The style of the Court's decisions has evolved over the years.[102] Nowadays, it can be seen as a middle path between the French elliptic style and the more discursive style found in decisions by the German Federal Constitutional Court.[103] Yet, in particular with regard to decisions on preliminary references, the Court faces criticism, for "[n]ot every judgment emanating from [it] is a model of lucidity and clarity"[104]. The Court's style of reasoning is sometimes perceived as giving the impression that "the outcome [of a case] is *inevitable*"[105]. Judgments, such as *Ruiz Zambrano*, *Mangold* or *Kücükdeveci*,[106] are said to be "too cryptic and apodictic"[107]. The interesting suggestions that judgments should be read not individually but in a broader context of cases, given that the case-law is built on a step-by-step basis,[108] are contested.[109] The Court is criticized for developing its case-law in a purely "self-sufficient manner"[110]. In other words, it is said that the Court should offer comprehensive and sound reasoning, provide a full analysis of all arguments put forward, explain all considerations that underlie an interpretation, maybe even its consequences, and engage in open discussion with academic and political voices and precedents.[111] The admission of dissenting opinion could ease the way towards more discursive judicial reasoning.[112]

---

100 Article 36 of the Statute.

101 On the GC's duty to state reasons: *Mindo Srl v. European Commission*, C-652/11 P, Judgment of 11 April 2013, [2013] ECR, paras 29–30; *European Ombudsman v. Claire Staelen*, C-337/15 P, Judgment of 4 April 2017, [2017] ECR, para. 85.

102 De Witte, *supra* note 18, 138.

103 Ritleng, *supra* note 6, 120.

104 Sharpston, *supra* note 92, 416.

105 De Witte, *supra* note 18, 138–139 (emphasized in the original text).

106 *Mangold*, C-144/04, Judgment of 22 November 2005, [2005] ECR I-9981; *Kücükdeveci*, C-555/07, Judgment of 19 January 2010, [2010] ECR I-365; *Ruiz Zambrano*, C-34/09, Judgment of 8 March 2011, [2011] ECR I-1177.

107 Ritleng, *supra* note 6, 120.

108 Lenaerts, *supra* note 61, 1350–1369. For further reading on this idea: Bertrand, B. (2012), "Les blocs de jurisprudence", *Revue trimestrielle de droit européen* 48(4), 741–770.

109 Weiler, *supra* note 73, 248–251 (in response to Lenaerts, *supra* note 61).

110 Without taking into consideration national constitutional law: Favoureu, *supra* note 75, 389–390.

111 See, *inter alia*: Bengoetxea, *supra* note 59; De Witte, *supra* note 18, 138–139; Kakouris, *supra* note 5, 639.

112 *Supra*, part II.

Furthermore, as a result of the manifold challenges and criticisms related to the Court's alleged judicial activism and self-sufficiency, scholars develop new methods of adjudication and reasoning with regard to the context in which the Court operates. Whether this context is analysed in terms of constitutional pluralism[113] or of the EU as a *Fédération*[114] or in a less determined manner, the general idea is that the Court should take into account not only the interests of the EU and its law, but also "the possible reception of its decisions in Member States" and "the broad spectrum of diverging social and cultural conceptions".[115] The Court's reasoning should "reflect the dialogical nature of European Constitutionalism" and the Court should "demonstrat[e] in its judgments that national sensibilities were fully taken into account".[116] In practical terms, these proposals have an effect not only on the reasoning, which should become "more discursive, analytic, and conversational"[117], but also on the level of scrutiny. It is said that the Court might show greater deference to Member States' constitutional identity and sensitivities and recognise a broader margin of their discretion (and their domestic courts). While this discussion barely refers to *democratic* legitimacy, it largely echoes von Bogdandy's and Venzke's proposals.

These proposals have found some response in the Court's recent case-law. The Court appears to show greater deference to considerations of national identity and to secondary law (reflecting compromises reached within the Council and with the Parliament) and grants both the Member States and the Union's legislator a rather large margin of discretion.[118] Whether the Court does indeed strike a satisfying balance between national and EU interests in every single case certainly depends on the

---

113 Azoulai, *supra* note 65; Poiares Maduro, M. (2007), "Interpreting European Law: Judicial Adjudication in a Context of Constituional Pluralism", *European Journal of Legal Studies* 1, 137–154; Poiares Maduro, *supra* note 51, 457; Ritleng, *supra* note 6, 118–124.

114 Roland, *supra* note 10, 222–230.

115 Timmermans, C. (2004), "The European Union's Judicial System", *Common Market Law Review* 41(2), 393–405, 398.

116 Weiler, *supra* note 38, 219, 225.

117 *Ibid.*, 225

118 Bailleux, A. (2018), "Du constitutionnalisme supranational au cosmopolitisme républicain? Citoyenneté, droits fondamentaux et libre circulation dans la jurisprudence de la Cour de justice" In: L. Potvin-Solis (ed.), *Le statut d'État membre de l'Union européenne*. Brussels: Bruylant, 177–203. See also Ritleng, *supra* note 6, 121–125.

assumptions on which different commentators base their analysis. I shall leave this question open at this point.

It follows from the foregoing that the legitimacy of the Court is strongly based on a combination of various factors pertaining to the Court's very creation, its composition, its mission, its functioning and working methods. While the Court actively contributed to strengthening this legitimacy over the years, it faces criticism which at times can be hostile, most often for its alleged pro-integration bias and activism. The most appropriate answer to such criticism is certainly to be found in the Court's working methods, reasoning, and balancing of all interests at stake.

The foregoing considerations, however, do not bring me any closer to answering the question in whose name the Court decides. On the basis of a natural reading of its case-law, one might simply observe that, in coherence with its status of an EU institution, the Court "serve[s the EU's] interests, those of its citizens and those of the Member States" (Article 13 TEU). From a substantive point of view, the Court decides, depending on the case, in the name of one of these three addressees, rather than any other.

If the Court's legitimacy is to be embedded in the EU's concept of democracy, I should stress the undisputed fact that the EU's democratic legitimacy rests with both the Member States and EU citizens.[119] Consequently, and following von Bogdandy and Venzke's approach, I should conclude that the Court decides in the name of both the peoples of the Member States and the EU citizens. Yet, the wording ultimately points to the very same group of individuals, *i.e.* the citizens of the Union.[120] As the Court put it itself, "Union citizenship is destined to be the fundamental status of nationals of the Member States"[121]. Is it then possible to conclude that the intention of the Court itself is to decide in the name of EU citizens in the first place? [122] While such a symbolic understanding of that case-law will, beyond any doubt, please the pro-integration public, it

119 Thus, Perillo, *supra* note 19, 332, considers that the EU Courts decide "in the name of the citizens and the Member States of the EU".

120 As Pernice, *supra* note 10, 30, put it, "Legitimationsbasis [und] Adressatenkreis hoheitlichen Handelns sind hinsichtlich der EG statt des Volkes eines Staates die Völker und *damit* die Bürger aller durch die Gemeinschaftsverfassung verbundenen Staaten" (emphasis added).

121 *Grzelczyk*, Case C-184/99, Judgment of 20 September 2001, [2001] ECR I-6193. This statement concerns the *mobile* citizens, which exercised their freedom to move.

122 To that effect, see Wernicke (2007) and (2005), *supra* note 19. While Wernicke mainly based his proposal on the Article I-1 of the Treaty establishing a Constitution for Europe, which provided that "*[r]eflecting the will of the citizens* and States

might encounter criticism emanating from a more Eurosceptic public. Ultimately, silence may then well be golden; it recognises that the point of reference for the Court's legitimacy is to some extent undetermined[123] and that, depending on the case the Court is called upon to decide, it draws in varying proportions from those mutually enhancing sources.

of Europe to build a common future, this Constitution establishes the European Union" (emphasis added), he also referred to the Court's case-law on EU citizens' rights and obligations. See also Epping, *supra* note 7, 357. That author argues that in the absence of a European *demos* the Court's legitimacy might well be constructed by reference to the EU citizens.

123 Roland, *supra* note 10, 229–230.

In the Name of the European Club of Liberal Democracies: On the Identity, Mandate and National Buffering of the ECtHR's Case Law*

*Armin von Bogdandy*** / *Laura Hering****

The ECtHR is under observation. The Copenhagen Declaration has called on the Convention States to evaluate its case law in order to decide on further reform. But what are the yardsticks for such an evaluation? We submit that they can be found in the source of the ECtHR's democratic legitimacy, one the one hand, and in the challenges it faces, on the other. Thus, the present contribution argues that the Court speaks *In the name of the European club of liberal democracies* and that its greatest challenge is continuing to do so in a credible manner.

---

* Translation by Fabian Eichberger. The text was published in German in Juristenzeitung 74 (2020), 53-63. A short version was published as an editorial in 58 Der Staat 2019, 1-5. It is based on a presentation given at the High-Level Expert Conference on the ECHR system, Kokkedal, 31 October - 2 November 2018. We would like to thank the Tuesday Round as well as Christina Binder, Raffaela Kunz, Angelika Nußberger, Mateja Steinbrück Platise and Ingo Venzke for their valuable criticism.

** Director, Max Planck Institute for Comparative Public Law and International Law; Professor for Public Law, Goethe University Frankfurt.

*** Senior Research Fellow, Max Planck Institute for Comparative Public Law and International Law.

I. Agenda

European human-rights protection and its most important institution, the European Court of Human Rights (ECtHR), face a wide range of challenges.[1] Of these, the procedural backlog may be the least. More importantly, the legitimacy of some judges is contentious: increasingly authoritarian governments are in power in a number of Convention States and many judgments are met with considerable resistance.[2] Moreover, well-established courts such as the German *Bundesverfassungsgericht* and the Italian *Corte Costituzionale* seek to limit the ECtHR's law-making authority.[3] In their Copenhagen Declaration of April 2018, the Convention States even formally stipulated that recent ECtHR case law should be evaluated.[4] It is not too far-fetched to interpret this announcement as an expression of dissatisfaction as well as a warning.

---

1 On the challenges, see e.g., Council of Europe Steering Committee for Human Rights (2016), "The Longer-Term Future of the System of the European Convention on Human Rights", available at https://rm.coe.int/the-longer-term-future-of-the-system-of-the-european-convention-on-hum/1680695ad4, accessed 27 October 2019; Çalı, B. (2018), "Coping with Crisis: Wither the Variable Geometry in the Jurisprudence of the European Court of Human Rights", *Wisconsin International Law Journal* 35(2), 237–276, 240 *et seq*.

2 On the attacks, see Madsen, M.R. (2016), "The Challenging Authority of the European Court of Human Rights: From Cold War Legal Diplomacy to the Brighton Declaration and Backlash", *Law and Contemporary Problems* 79(1), 141–178, 167 *et seq*.; Soley, X. and Steininger, S. (2018), "Parting ways or lashing back? Withdrawals, backlash and the Inter-American Court of Human Rights", *International Journal of Law in Context* 14(2), 237–257, 237 *et seq*.; Breuer, M. (ed.) (2019), *Principled Resistance to ECtHR Judgments – A New Paradigm?*. Heidelberg: Springer.

3 Italian Constitutional Court, Decision No. 49 (26 March 2015); BVerfG 148, 296 (*Bundesverfassungsgericht*); see *infra*, IV.

4 Copenhagen Declaration, passed at the High Level Conference of 12/13 April 2018, available at http://rm.coe.int/copenhagen-declaration/16807b915c, accessed 6 December 2019, para. 41. On the Declaration, see Polakiewicz, J. and Suominen-Picht, I. (2018), "Aktuelle Herausforderungen für Europarat und EMRK: Die Erklärung von Kopenhagen (April 2018), das Spannungsverhältnis zwischen EMRK und nationalen Verfassungen und die Beteiligung der EU an dem europäischen Menschenrechtskontrollmechanismus", *Europäische Grundrechte-Zeitschrift* 45(4), 383-390, 383 *et seq*.; Ulfstein, G. and Føllesdal, A. (2018), "Copenhagen – much ado about little?", *EJIL: Talk!*, 14 April, available at https://www.ejiltalk.org/copenhagen-much-ado-about-little/, accessed 6 December 2019.

Navigating through troubled waters requires steady orientation. One fixed star that has been underused thus far is the democratic legitimation of ECtHR rulings.[5] But democratic legitimation begs the following question: in whose name does the ECtHR actually decide? The core argument of this contribution is that the law and the Court's path thus far can be condensed into the postulation that the ECtHR speaks *In the name of the European club of liberal democracies*. At the same time, the Strasbourg Court's greatest challenge is for this postulation to remain credible.

The first part of this article explains why the democratic legitimacy of the ECtHR is an issue (II. A.). It then justifies the postulation *In the name of the European club of liberal democracies* as an answer (II. B.). The second part shows how this postulation materializes in the mandate of the Court. For many decades, the Court discharged this mandate by supporting the *rights revolution* in Europe, embedding constitutional courts in a European discourse and contributing to the transformation of post-authoritarian states (III. A.). In light of authoritarian tendencies in some Convention States, the mandate is now acquiring more dimensions, in particular the defense of the club's self-image as well as the need to support constitutional democracy in those States. This requires a new evaluation of the Court (III. B. 1.), in particular its jurisprudence on state of emergency (III. B. 2.), core rights (III. B. 3.), abuse of rights (III. B. 4.), and exhaustion of domestic remedies (III. B. 5.). Moreover, to secure its own future we argue that the Court should further develop its doctrine of the margin of appreciation (III. B. 6.). This, in turn, calls for a modification of its mandate and a buffering of its judicial law-making. The German *Bundesverfassungsgericht* and the Italian *Corte Costituzionale* provide ideas for this evolution (IV.).

5 On the various legitimacy-enhancing mechanisms, see von Bogdandy, A. and Venzke, I. (2014), *In whose Name? A Public Law Theory of International Adjudication*. Oxford: Oxford University Press, 156 *et seq*.

II. The Democratic Legitimacy of the ECtHR

A. The Issue

The ECtHR does not fit into the traditional role of an international court that serves merely as an intergovernmental dispute-settlement body. Its decisions regularly concern controversial domestic issues.[6] Moreover, it not only claims authority over the decided dispute but demands that all national courts follow its decisions.[7] Last but not least, the ECtHR is even reminiscent of a constitutional court, as it controls whether domestic legislators respect individual rights.[8]

The ECtHR wields no coercive power, but it nevertheless exercises public authority.[9] Its decisions exert considerable pressure. Thus, the Committee of Ministers of the Council of Europe monitors the implementation of ECtHR judgments under Article 46 para. 2 European Convention on Human Rights (ECHR), and the 14th Additional Protocol has added an infringement procedure under Article 46 para. 4 ECHR, which was recently invoked for the first time.[10] Other Convention States expect a losing State to abide by the judgments of the Court.[11] Even domestic law

---

6 See, e.g., *Hirst v. United Kingdom (No. 2)*, ECtHR Application No. 74025/01, Judgment of 6 October 2005, on the political rights of convicts; *Zaunegger v. Germany,* ECtHR Application No. 22028/04, Judgment of 3 December 2009, on child custody.

7 *Cf. Ireland v. United Kingdom*, ECtHR Application No. 5310/71, Judgment of 18 January 1978, para. 154; *Guzzardi v. Italy*, ECtHR Application No. 7367/76, Judgment of 6 November 1980, para. 86; *Rantsev v. Cyprus and Russia*, ECtHR Application No. 25965/04, Judgment of 7 January 2010, para. 197; *G.I.E.M. S.R.L. a.o. v. Italy*, ECtHR Application No. 1828/06, Judgment (Merits) of 28 June 2018, para. 252.

8 For the constitutional function, *cf.* Grabenwarter, C. (2015), "The European Convention on Human Rights: Inherent Constitutional Tendencies and the Role of the European Court of Human Rights" In: A. von Bogdandy and P. Sonnevend (eds), *Constitutional crisis in the European constitutional area*. Oxford: C.H. Beck / Hart / Nomos, 257–274; Nußberger, A. (2019), "Die Europäische Menschenrechtskonvention – eine Verfassung für Europa?", *Juristenzeitung* 74(9), 421–428; Walter, C. (1999), "Die Europäische Menschenrechtskonvention als Konstitutionalisierungsprozeß", *Zeitschrift für ausländisches öffentliches Recht und Völkerrecht* 59, 961–983, 962 *et seq*.

9 On the multiple functions and public authority of international courts, see von Bogdandy and Venzke, *supra* note 5, 5–18, 101–119.

10 *Mammadov v. Azerbaijan*, ECtHR Application No. 15172/13, Judgment of 29 May 2019.

11 Expressly mentioned in the Copenhagen Declaration, *supra* note 4, paras 19 *et seq*.

often requires compliance with the European human-rights system;[12] national courts, specific human rights institutions,[13] and an often-powerful public stand ready to scrutinize this compliance.

Such authority raises questions of legitimacy, including from a democratic point of view.[14] This is a particularly vulnerable flank of the Court, because it regularly opposes democratically elected institutions, i.e., institutions with the strongest possible legitimacy, whereas its own democratic mandate is not obvious. While many national courts claim democratic legitimacy in the first words of their judgments, which begin with *In the name of the people*,[15] the ECtHR remains silent.[16]

B. *The Club of Liberal Democracies*

Which prefatory expression could evoke a democratic legitimation similar to national courts' *In the name of the people*? In whose name does the ECtHR actually decide?[17] It could refer to the Convention and use *In the name of the European Convention on Human Rights* – which would be akin to a national court using *In the name of the law*. However, this would ignore the fact that it is not the law as such but the underlying parliamentary decision that provides the real source of democratic legitimacy.

This insight as to the real source leads to the national ratifications of the Convention. Accordingly, one could consider, following the classical understanding of international law, whether the ECtHR decides *In the*

12 For the position of the ECtHR in Member States' domestic law, see Keller, H. and Stone Sweet, A. (eds) (2008), *A Europe of Rights. The Impact of the ECHR on National Legal Systems*. Oxford: Oxford University Press, 31 *et seq.*

13 GA Res. 48/134 of 20 December 1993, U.N. Doc. A/RES/48/134.

14 On the importance of democratic legitimacy for the judiciary, Voßkuhle, A. and Sydow, G. (2002), "Die demokratische Legitimation des Richters", *Juristenzeitung* 57(14), 673–682. Critically, Torres, A. (2017), "In Nobody's Name: A Checks and Balances Approach to International Judicial Independence", *MPIL Research Paper* (3), available at https://papers.ssrn.com/sol3/papers.cfm?abstract_id=2924435, accessed 31 October 2019.

15 See, e.g., § 25 para. 4 BVerfGG (Act on the *Bundesverfassungsgericht*); Art. 101 para. 1 of the Constitution of the Italian Republic; Art. 454 of the French Code of Civil Procedure.

16 *Cf.* the fundamental critique of Bellamy, R. (2014), "The Democratic Legitimacy of International Human Rights Conventions: Political Constitutionalism and the European Convention on Human Rights", *European Journal of International Law* 25(4), 1019–1042.

17 Bellamy has also already tried to define the "constituency" of the ECtHR, see *ibid.*

name of the State parties to the dispute. This may be appropriate for the International Court of Justice. Yet it certainly does not apply to the Strasbourg Court where the litigants, as a rule, are not two States but one State and one individual, who is often also a citizen of the involved State. What then?

The democratic legitimacy of the Strasbourg Court is based first and foremost on the ratification of the Convention by *all* contracting parties. It accordingly decides *In the name of all the high contracting parties*. The holistic *all* expresses a fundamental feature: a judgment of the ECtHR not only adjudicates the disputed case, but also serves a common interest of all Convention States, to wit, "Human rights and the rule of law in Europe", as stated in recital 2 of the Copenhagen Declaration. The ECHR thus leaves the traditional bilateralism of international law far behind; its decisions pursue a community interest.

The expression, *In the name of all the high contracting parties* can be condensed further. The ECHR not only overcomes the traditional bilateralism of international law but also transcends that regime's traditional agnosticism with respect to the political system of States. A Convention State must be *liberal and democratic*.[18] Certainly not all the States met all the requirements when they joined. However, such States were accepted with the obligation to further develop their democratic and rule of law structures in accordance with the Convention.[19]

The demand to be liberal and democratic is not abstract but takes shape through its threefold opposition to the totalitarian systems of the Axis powers, Soviet communism,[20] and authoritarian regimes such as the Greece of the Obrists.[21] Today it rests on the consolidated practice of the

---

18 See the Preamble and Article 3 of the Statute of the Council of Europe. For the concept of democracy in the case law of the ECtHR, see Zand, J. (2017), "The Concept of Democracy and the European Convention on Human Rights", *University of Baltimore Journal of International Law* 5(2), 195–227; Lautenbach, G. (2014), *The Concept of the Rule of Law and the European Court of Human Rights*. Oxford: Oxford University Press, 193 *et seq*.

19 See, for example, regarding Russia: Parliamentary Assembly of the Council of Europe, Application by Russia for membership of the Council of Europe, Opinion 192 (1996), No. 7, available at https://assembly.coe.int/nw/xml/XRef/Xref-XML2HTML-EN.asp?fileid=13932&lang=en, accessed 31 October 2019.

20 Madsen, M.R. (2007), "From Cold War Instrument to Supreme European Court: The European Court of Human Rights at the Crossroads of International and National Law and Politics", *Law & Social Inquiry* 32(1), 137–159.

21 On the exclusion procedure against Greece in 1969 in accordance with Article 8 of the Statute of the Council of Europe, Richter, H.A. (2013), *Griechenland 1950–1974. Zwischen Demokratie und Diktatur*. Ruhpolding: Verlag Franz Philipp Rutzen, 323 *et seq*.

Strasbourg organs. It encompasses the effective protection of a broad range of fundamental rights, political pluralism and a functioning separation of powers, including independent courts.[22] This meaning of liberalism, it bears mentioning, has nothing to do with left leaning or neo-liberal ideologies. Instead, it contrasts with what Victor Orbán is projecting as an "illiberal democracy"[23].

The preamble to the Convention states that human rights and fundamental freedoms can best be safeguarded "by an effective political democracy". It even embraces a corresponding Europe-wide legal culture as "common heritage of political traditions, ideals, freedom and the rule of law". According to *travaux préparatoires*, the Convention was created not only to protect the people against dictatorships but also to strengthen the resistance against creeping attempts to undermine the democratic way of life – a significant objective in today's context.[24] As a result, we can replace "high contracting parties" with "liberal, democratic States". Thus we arrive at a more appropriate formula: the ECtHR, we submit, decides *In the name of European liberal democratic States*.

The Convention, furthermore, not only concerns the State apparatus and the formal organisation of public authority. It is also a groundbreaking treaty because it overcomes traditional international law in a third respect. By equipping individuals with rights and creating an individual complaint mechanism, it transforms private agents into transnational actors. Moreover, the Convention often addresses the individual as citizen and political subject. Securing democratic rights is one of the Court's most important lines of case law.[25] Just consider the Court's rulings on freedom of political association under Article 11 ECHR,[26] freedom of political expression

22 On the independence of the courts, *Campbell and Fell v. United Kingdom*, ECtHR Application No. 7819/77, Judgment of 28 June 1984, para. 78.

23 Orbán, V. (2018), "Speech at the 29th Bálványos Summer Open University and Student Camp", July 28, available at https://www.kormany.hu/en/the-prime-minister/the-prime-minister-s-speeches/prime-minister-viktor-orban-s-speech-at-the-29th-balvanyos-summer-open-university-and-student-camp, accessed 31 October 2019.

24 See Council of Europe (1979), *Collected edition of the "Travaux préparatoires" of the European Convention on Human Rights. Vol. 5: Legal Committee, Ad Hoc Joint Committee, Committee of Ministers, Consultative Assembly (23 June – 28 August 1950)*. The Hague / Boston / London: Martinus Nijhoff.

25 See *supra* note 18.

26 *Cf.* the case law on the ban of political parties, *Vona v. Hungary*, ECtHR Application No. 35943/10, Judgment of 9 July 2013, para. 58; *Freedom and Democracy Party (Özdep) v. Turkey*, ECtHR Application No. 23885/94, Judgment of 8 December 1999, para. 37.

under Article 10 ECHR[27] and the right to free elections under Article 3 of the First Additional Protocol,[28] as well as Articles 3 and 8 of the Statute of the Council of Europe. This inclusion of citizens is an important achievement of the Strasbourg system and should be manifested in the introductory formula. It is no coincidence that national courts do not adjudicate *In the name of the State* but in the name of *the people* or of *the republic*.

We can articulate this dimension by abbreviating the formula *In the name of European liberal democratic States* into *In the name of European liberal democracies*. Integrating *States* within *democracies* allows citizens to become part of that expression. One should note the grammatical plural *democracies*, moreover. It is significant because the Court does not speak in the name of some abstract idea of a political order. Rather, the formula underlines that the democratic legitimacy of the Court derives from the democratically organized peoples of the Convention States.

Finally, the formula should reflect the fact that the democratic legitimacy of the ECtHR is a common achievement of European democracies. It has an important collective dimension, not least because the Court's judges are elected by the Parliamentary Assembly of the Council of Europe.[29] This term *club* in the formula expresses, therefore, that European democracies have come together under the Statute of the Council of Europe and the Convention to pursue objectives that they cannot achieve on their own. The most important one is a regional human rights system that safeguards their concurrent constitutional systems.[30] To this end, the Convention States have established common, independent institutions vested with public authority, including the ECtHR, whose judges they

---

27 On freedom of expression, see *Handyside v. UK*, ECtHR Application No. 5493/72, Judgment of 7 December 1976, para. 49; also, Frowein, J.A. (2008), "Meinungsfreiheit und Demokratie", *Europäische Grundrechte-Zeitschrift* 35(2), 117–121.

28 See Natale, V. (2006), "Le droit à des élections libres ou la construction d'un véritable ordre démocratique européen", *Revue trimestrielle des droits de l'homme* 68, 939–972.

29 Von Bogdandy, A. and Krenn, C. (2015), "On the Democratic Legitimacy of Europe's Judges: A Principled and Comparative Reconstruction of the Selection Procedures" In: M. Bobek (ed.), *Selecting Europe's Judges*. Oxford: Oxford University Press, 162–180.

30 *Cf.* Bates, E. (2010), *The Evolution of the European Convention on Human Rights: From its Inception to the Creation of a Permanent Court of Human Rights*. Oxford: Oxford University Press, 5; Greer, S. (2006), *The European Convention on Human Rights: Achievements, Problems and Prospects*. Cambridge: Cambridge University Press, 56 *et seq*.

jointly elect in a parliamentary procedure. The term "*club*" is well established in this respect.[31]

III. *The Mandate to Protect the Democratic Rule of Law*

A. *The Development of the Mandate*

If the ECtHR speaks *In the name of the European club of liberal democracies*, what should it say? The answer can only be partially derived through the canon of legal methods with which the Convention is to be interpreted. These methods hardly ever determine a decision, especially in the case of open norms such as human rights.[32] What is more significant is how ECtHR judges, their national colleagues, other national and international authorities and, last but not least, the democratic public understand the mandate of the ECtHR. The current understanding of the mandate can be summarized as ascribing an active, sometimes even transformative role to the ECtHR in ensuring that the club is actually one of liberal democracies.

It can by no means be taken for granted, but is rather an outstanding and surprising achievement, that the ECtHR today has such a mandate to support and develop the *European club of liberal democracies*.[33] This becomes clear in retrospect. The ECHR was initially understood as a

---

31 The Council of Europe describes itself as "club of democracies", see Parliamentary Assembly of the Council of Europe (1995), *Official Report of Debates*. Strasbourg: Council of Europe Publishing, 45; *Cf.* also Carrillo Salcedo, J.A. (2003), *El Convenio Europeo de Derechos Humanos*. Madrid: Tecnos, 14; Weber, F. (2016), "Die Europäische Menschenrechtskonvention und die Türkei – Zum Notstand sowie zur Möglichkeit der Wiedereinführung der Todesstrafe", *Die Öffentliche Verwaltung*" 21(22), 921–929; Gioia, A. (2011), "The Role of the European Court of Human Rights in Monitoring Compliance with Humanitarian Law in Armed Conflict" In: O. Ben-Naftali (ed.), *International Humanitarian Law and International Human Rights Law*. Oxford: Oxford University Press, 201–249, 202.

32 Kelsen, H. (1929), "Wesen und Entwicklung der Staatsgerichtsbarkeit", Veröffentlichungen der Vereinigung der Deutschen Staatsrechtslehrer 5, 30-88, 31; Möllers, C. (2012), "Individuelle Legitimation: Wie rechtfertigen sich Gerichte?" In: A. Geis, F. Nullmeier and C. Daase (eds), *Der Aufstieg der Legitimitätspolitik*. Baden-Baden: Nomos, 398–418, 403 *et seq*.

33 On the development, see Bates, E. (2011), "The Birth of the European Convention on Human Rights" In: J. Christoffersen and M.R. Madsen (eds), *The European Court of Human Rights between Law and Politics*. Oxford: Oxford University Press, 17–42.

response to "Soviet-style communism"[34]. Since those States were not under the jurisdiction of the ECtHR, the Court had little to do. Its first president famously doubted whether it was relevant at all.[35] Jochen Frowein likened the ECHR of this day to a "sleeping beauty"[36].

Only gradually did the ECtHR assume a role in supporting what is described in the United States as the *rights revolution*: the substantial expansion of individual rights.[37] When individual rights protection became an important issue in Western societies, many Convention States did not have a good basis for this. They often lacked a modern catalogue of rights and had few institutions fit for constitutional adjudication. This gap provided an opportunity for the Court and the former Human Rights Commission to step in and begin supporting the *rights revolution* in a variety of countries, thereby taking on a task comparable to that of a constitutional court in this respect.[38] The legal instruments used to accomplish this task included the dynamic or evolutionary interpretation of the ECHR[39] and the authority of its decisions beyond the case at hand.[40] Once it had ventured onto this path, the Court gained the support of a large number of

---

34 Grabenwarter, C. and Pabel, K. (2016), Europäische Menschenrechtskonvention (6th ed.). Basel: Helbing Lichtenhahn Verlag, § 1 para. 1; Grote, R. (2013), "Entstehungs- und Rezeptionsgeschichte der EMRK" In: O. Dörr, R. Grote and T. Marauhn (eds), EMRK/GG Konkordanzkommentar (2nd ed.). Tübingen: Mohr Siebeck, para. 10.

35 Rolin, H. (1965), "Has the European Court of Human Rights a Future", *Howard Law Journal* 11, 442–451.

36 Frowein, J.A. (1984), "European Integration through Fundamental Rights", *Michigan Journal of Law Reform* 18(1), 5–27, 8.

37 *Ibid.*, 7: "legal revolution". Regarding the USA, see Epp, C.R. (1998), *The Rights Revolution. Lawyers, Activists, and Supreme Courts in Comparative Perspective*. Chicago: The University of Chicago Press.

38 See for Austria: Grabenwarter, C. (2008), "Österreich" In: A. von Bogdandy, P. Cruz Villalón and P.M. Huber (eds), *Handbuch Ius Publicum Europaeum. Vol. II: Offene Staatlichkeit – Wissenschaft vom Verfassungsrecht*. Heidelberg: C.F. Müller, § 20, paras 64 *et seq*.; for the Netherlands, Wessel, R.A. and van de Griendt, W.E., "Niederlande" In: *ibid*, § 19, paras 52 *et seq*.

39 Frowein, J.A. (2005), "Die evolutive Auslegung der EMRK" In: T. Marauhn (ed.), *Recht, Politik und Rechtspolitik in den internationalen Beziehungen*. Tübingen: Mohr Siebeck, 1–13; Bernhardt, R. (1999), "Evolutive Treaty Interpretation, Especially of the European Convention of Human Rights", *German Yearbook of International Law* 42, 11–26.

40 *Cf*. Copenhagen Declaration, *supra* note 4, paras 3, 8, 14, 26 *et seq*.; Arnardóttir, O.M. (2017), "*Res Interpretata*, *Erga Omnes* Effect and the Role of the Margin of Appreciation in Giving Domestic Effect to the Judgments of the European Court of Human Rights", *European Journal of International Law* 28(3), 819–843.

actors and thus acquired a key role for liberal democracy in Europe.[41] Today it is identified with this mandate, as is confirmed by the Copenhagen Declaration.[42]

The mandate is somewhat different for certain States like Germany or Italy, which have a proud and functioning constitutional court. These courts have independently developed the protection of individual rights that runs largely in parallel to the Strasbourg system. Accordingly, for these States the role of the ECtHR consists of embedding their courts in the European context.[43] Thanks to Strasbourg decisions, the German and Italian protections of fundamental rights are embedded in a Europe-wide human rights system which has a common vocabulary, a common doctrine and even first signs of a common legal culture.[44] This certainly creates a specific type of conflict, since it requires a visible control by the Strasbourg Court of the proud constitutional courts of these States in an area they consider the core of their mandate.[45] So far, however, such conflicts have been successfully handled. The key terms here are *dialogue* and *joint responsibility*.[46]

The third aspect of this mandate to promote liberal democracy arose after the fall of the Berlin Wall, when the Strasbourg Court began to accompany Central and Eastern European countries in their transformation.[47] New lines of jurisprudence emerged that restricted national autonomy far more intensively than before. One could point, for example, to the decisions on the structure of national judicial systems, to rulings on "tran-

41 *Cf.* Mowbray, A. (1999), "ECtHR and Democracy", *Public Law*, 703–725; on the transformation of the ECtHR system, see Roca, F.G. (2018), "La transformación del Convenio Europeo de Derechos Humanos", *Revista General de Derecho Constitucional* 28, 1–60.

42 Copenhagen Declaration, *supra* note 4, para. 2.

43 On embeddedness, see Helfer, L. (2008), "Redesigning the European Court of Human Rights: Embeddedness as a Deep Structural Principle of the European Human Rights Regime", *European Journal of International Law* 19(1), 125–159.

44 Häberle, P. (1991), "Gemeineuropäisches Verfassungsrecht", *Europäische Grundrechte-Zeitschrift* 18(12–13), 261–274.

45 Regarding this conflict, see Paris, D. (2017), "Allies and Counterbalances – Constitutional Courts and the European Court of Human Rights: A Comparative Perspective", *Zeitschrift für ausländisches öffentliches Recht und Völkerrecht* 77, 623–649.

46 See Copenhagen Declaration, *supra* note 4, paras 6 *et seq.*, 33, 36 *et seq.*

47 Hofmann, M. (2009), *Von der Transformation zur Kooperationsoffenheit?*. Berlin / Heidelberg: Springer, 86 *et seq.*, 182 *et seq.*, 248 *et seq.*, 315 *et seq.*, 395 *et seq.*; Motoc, I. and Ziemele, I. (eds) (2016), *The Impact of the ECHR on Democratic Change in Central and Eastern Europe*. Cambridge: Cambridge University Press.

sitional justice" or to pilot judgments that addressed structural deficits.[48] All this significantly increased the breadth and depth of Strasbourg's significance and influence. Nevertheless, most observers, as reflected in the Copenhagen Declaration, regard this case law as part of the Court's mandate.[49]

B. *The Mandate in Times of Crises*

The jurisprudence of the Court has successfully supported the *rights revolution* in European democracies, the European embedding of national constitutional courts and the transformation of Central and Eastern European countries. This means the ECtHR is in a position to credibly render decisions *In the name of the European club of liberal democracies*. However, this is by no means guaranteed and the club is at a crossroads. The Court must choose between two paths, both of which lead into difficult terrain.

In some countries, the human rights situation has deteriorated drastically,[50] to the extent that the credentials of some States as liberal democracies can be challenged. These States threaten the identity of the club. Of course, almost every club has difficult, even ill-suited members, without this endangering the club's identity. At a certain point, however, such members begin to shape this common identity due to their number, visibility, weight, strategy or influence on how the club is perceived externally. It is now becoming questionable whether the Strasbourg Court can continue to adjudicate *In the name of the European club of liberal democracies*.

At these crossroads, the club can, on one path, choose to defend its identity as a club of liberal democracies — although this would affect its identity, since its previous culture of consensus can hardly be maintained. On

48 The first pilot procedure concerned the so-called Bug River case from Poland: *Broniowski v. Poland*, ECtHR Application No. 31443/96, Judgment of 22 June 2004; See also *Broniowski v. Poland (friendly settlement)*, ECtHR Application No. 31443/96, Judgment of 28 September 2005. On the emergence see Sadurski, W. (2009), "Partnering with Strasbourg: Constitutionalisation of the European Court of Human Rights, the Accession of Central and East European States to the Council of Europe, and the Idea of Pilot Judgments", *Human Rights Law Review* 9(3), 397–453.

49 See Copenhagen Declaration *supra* note 4, paras 14, 17; *cf.* also Committee of Ministers, Resolution Res(2004)3 on judgments revealing an underlying systemic problem, (12 May 2004), available at https://search.coe.int/cm/Pages/result_details.aspx?ObjectId=09000016805dd190 (last visited 1 November 2019).

50 See, in this context, Copenhagen Declaration *supra* note 4, para. 16.

the other path, it could accept that those problematic members co-determine its identity[51] — in which case, the club would probably not dissolve but instead find itself with a very different identity. Without doubt, the Strasbourg institutions could continue to be useful. The United Nations Security Council, the United Nations Human Rights Council, and the International Court of Justice are certainly valuable, for instance. But they are not institutions of a club of liberal democracies.

If one understands the ECtHR's mandate as one of contributing to liberal democracy in Europe, then it should choose the first path. The Court's more recent jurisprudence, accordingly, should be evaluated in this light.

1. *Court Authority in Times of Crises*

Before analysing individual lines of case law, a preliminary point needs to be clarified. Every court must acquire authority, because only authority can help it fulfil its mandate.[52] Whether a losing State complies with its judgments is an important indicator about the authority of the ECtHR.[53] This means that the losing State not only pays any awarded compensation but also rectifies the established infringement and even adapts its internal legal situation to conform with the ruling. This process is often described as "implementation" or "compliance".[54]

---

51 Stewart, S. (2019), "Der Europarat und Russland. Glaubwürdigkeit verlangt konsequente Entscheidungen", *Stiftung Wissenschaft und Politik – Aktuell* 29(May), available at https://www.swp-berlin.org/publikation/der-europarat-und-russland/, accessed 1 November 2019.

52 On this challenge, Alter, K.J., Helfer, L.R. and Madsen, M.R. (2018), "How Context Shapes the Authority of International Courts" In: K.J. Alter *et al.* (eds), *International Court Authority*. Oxford: Oxford University Press, 24–56.

53 See Polzin, M. (2018), "Der verrechtlichte Ausnahmezustand – Art. 15 EMRK und die Rolle des Europäischen Gerichtshofs für Menschenrechte", *Zeitschrift für ausländisches öffentliches Recht und Völkerrecht* 78, 635–669, 650.

54 von Staden, A. (2018), *Strategies of Compliance with the European Court of Human Rights: Rational choice within normative constraints*. Philadelphia: University of Pennsylvania Press.

In this respect, the ECtHR has to contend with considerable difficulties.[55] The great importance it attaches to compliance with judgments, in particular the implementation of general measures, can easily lead it to be timid towards governments whose self-portrayal relies on their opposition to Europe. If one were to link judicial authority to this indicator first and foremost, one would place it in the hands of such governments and discourage the Court from intervening in what is probably the greatest challenge to European public order. This would make no sense. Therefore, evaluating the Court's operation requires a different approach.

This statement does not question that the implementation of the Court's rulings is legally mandatory. One should welcome, accordingly, that the Copenhagen Declaration leaves no doubt in this respect.[56] But while compliance and implementation remain the most important yardsticks for evaluating the losing State, criteria beyond compliance and implementation become important for assessing the Court. In particular, one should look at the *impact* of its case law.[57]

The focus on *impact* re-directs our attention to the question whether the Strasbourg Court's jurisprudence allows the club to maintain its identity as one of liberal democracies in a credible manner. It also entails inquiring into whether the case law supports domestic forces that are committed to liberal democracy in difficult States. An impressive example of this is the Inter-American Court of Human Rights (IACtHR). Although this court struggles with even greater problems of compliance,[58] its jurisprudence has given human rights an active role in often dramatic contexts of violence, exclusion and inequality. Today, political discourses and major disputes in Latin America are conducted in the language of human rights. This is from where the IACtHR draws its authority, and this is where it has found its

---

55 *Cf.*, e.g., Committee of Ministers (2019), *Annual Report 2018. Supervision of the execution of judgments and decisions of the European Court of Human Rights*. Strasbourg: Council of Europe, 71 *et seq*, available at https://rm.coe.int/annual-report-2018/168093f3da, accessed 1 December 2019.

56 See, in this context, Copenhagen Declaration, *supra* note 4, para. 19 *et seq*.

57 This approach was especially developed for the Inter-American system. See Parra Vera, Ó. (2017), "The Impact of Inter-American Judgments by Institutional Empowerment" In: A. von Bogdandy *et al.* (eds), *Transformative Constitutionalism in Latin America: The Emergence of a New Ius Commune*. Oxford: Oxford University Press, 357–376.

58 Anzola, S.I., Sánchez, B.E. and Urueña E. (2015), *Después Del Fallo. El Cumplimiento De Las Decisiones Del Sistema Inter-Americano De Derechos Humanos: Una Propuesta De Metodología.* Bogota: Universidad de los Andes (series "Justicia Global" 11).

mandate.[59] One should also remember the Helsinki Final Act, which since 1975 has supported Central and Eastern European human rights movements in their eventually successful struggle for freedom.

Today the Strasbourg Court can assist domestic forces through relevant decisions. This remains promising, not least since none of those States has turned totalitarian: there remain independent judges, opposition groups, and civil society forces.[60] The most meaningful yardstick for evaluating a human rights court in such a constellation is not the compliance of a government, therefore, but that court's ability to position human rights as a powerful argument in institutional procedures and public debates.[61] Supranational jurisprudence can thus promote national self-healing through domestic processes.[62]

Whether the Strasbourg Court is able to do so provides a yardstick for evaluating its jurisprudence. This applies in particular to the more recent case law on state of emergency (2), core rights (3), abuse of rights (4) and exhaustion of domestic remedies (5).

2. *Limits of the Case Law on State of Emergency*

The ECtHR has drawn red lines with its recent case law on state of emergency. Article 15 ECHR allows Convention States to suspend certain Convention rights in extreme situations.[63] In recent years, this Article has

59 See von Bogdandy, A. (2019), "The Transformative Mandate of the Inter-American System", *MPIL Research Paper* 16, 1–15, available at https://papers.ssrn.com/sol3/papers.cfm?abstract_id=3463059, accessed 6 December 2019; for a comparison of the European and the Inter-American system of human rights protection, see Vasel, J. (2017), *Regionaler Menschenrechtsschutz als Emanzipationsprozess*. Berlin: Duncker & Humblot.

60 On the ECtHR's influence on the developments in Eastern European States, see the references in *supra* note 47.

61 See Huneeus, A. (2016), "Constitutional Lawyers and the Inter-American Court's Varied Authority", *Law and Contemporary Problems* 79(1), 179–207.

62 With regards to Hungary: Sonnevend, P. (2017), "Preserving the *Acquis* of Transformative Constitutionalism in Times of Constitutional Crisis: Lessons from the Hungarian Case" In: von Bogdandy *et al.*, *supra* note 57, 123–145, 140 *et seq*.

63 On this, see Ashauer C. (2007), "Die Menschenrechte im Notstand", *Archiv des Völkerrechts* 47(3), 400–431.

gained considerable importance due to the derogation declarations of Ukraine[64], France[65] and Turkey[66].

The Court is certainly cautious in this sensitive area and allows the Convention States a wide margin of appreciation in assessing a dangerous situation and classifying it as an emergency.[67] It has begun to tighten the requirements,[68] however, in response to criticism.[69] The Convention States continue to have a wide margin of appreciation in the assessment of these exigencies, but the Court now conducts an increasingly detailed proportionality test.[70] This test takes into account the significance of the derogated right of the Convention, the general situation surrounding the state of emergency and its duration.[71] On several occasions, the ECtHR has found that the defendant State breached the requirements of Article 15

64 Council of Europe (2015), "Ukraine derogation from European Convention on Human Rights" (Press Release), 10 June, available at https://www.coe.int/en/web/portal/news-2015/-/asset_publisher/9k8wkRrYhB8C/content/ukraine-derogation-from-european-convention-on-human-rights, accessed 6 December 2019.

65 Council of Europe (2015), "France informs Secretary General of Article 15 Derogation of the European Convention on Human Rights" (Press Release), 25 November, available at https://www.coe.int/en/web/secretary-general/news/-/asset_publisher/EYlBJNjXtA5U/content/france-informs-secretary-general-of-article-15-derogation-of-the-european-convention-on-human-rights, accessed 6 December 2019.

66 Council of Europe (2016), "Secretary General receives notification from Turkey of its intention to temporarily suspend part of the European Convention on Human Rights" (Press Release), 21 July, available at https://www.coe.int/en/web/portal/news-2016/-/asset_publisher/StEVosr24HJ2/content/secretary-general-receives-notification-from-turkey-of-its-intention-to-temporarily-suspend-the-european-convention-on-human-rights, accessed 6 December 2019.

67 For the first application, see *Ireland v. United Kingdom, supra* note 7, para. 207. See also Krieger, H. (2013), "Notstand" In: Dörr, Grote and Marauhn, *supra* note 34, 417–443, para. 12.

68 See also Harris, D. *et al.* (eds) (2018), *Law of the European Convention on Human Rights* (4th ed.). Oxford: Oxford University Press, 821 *et seq*.

69 See, e.g., Chrysler, E. (1994), "Brannigan and McBridge v. UK: A New Direction on Article 15 Derogations under the European Convention on Human Rights?", *Revue Belge de Droit International* 27(2), 603–631, 628 *et seq*.; Gross, O. and Ní Aoláin, F. (2001), "From Discretion to Scrutiny: Revisiting the Application of the Margin of Appreciation Doctrine in the Context of Article 15 of the European Convention on Human Rights", *Human Rights Quarterly* 23(3), 625–649, 637 *et seq*.

70 For this assessment, see Polzin, *supra* note 53, 643 *et seq*.

71 *Brannigan and McBride v. United Kingdom*, ECtHR Application No. 14553/89, Judgment of 25 May 1993, para. 43; *Aksoy v. Turkey*, ECtHR Application No. 21987/93, Judgment of 18 December 1996, para. 68.

ECHR – such as in *Aksoy v. Turkey*[72], *A. a.o. v. United Kingdom*[73], as well as in *Altan v. Turkey*[74] and *Alpay v. Turkey*[75].

The current state of emergency in Turkey poses major challenges for the ECtHR.[76] Clearly, this is a situation when Strasbourg is most needed to stand up for the protection of human rights. However, the ECtHR risks its judgments not being observed or the Convention being denounced if it relies on a more progressive approach to Article 15 ECHR and imposes sweeping restrictions on the discretion of the Convention States. It also risks exposing itself to accusations of practicing politics instead of legal interpretation.[77]

The ECtHR has approached this dilemma firstly by exercising restraint. It did not make any general remarks on Article 15 ECHR, which was possible because the Turkish Constitutional Court had already issued the corresponding judgments. Particularly in the *Altan* and *Alpay* cases, the Court remained very cursory.[78] Secondly, the Strasbourg Court has drawn red lines by defining the limits of government restriction on freedom of expression: in the *Altan* and *Alpay* cases, the ECtHR for the first time examined Article 10 ECHR within the framework of a state of emergency. It is true that it did not expressly deal with the requirements of the exigencies of the situation under Article 15 ECHR. However, the explanations point to a narrow interpretation of the restrictions, one under which the right to freedom of expression pursuant to Article 10 ECHR can only be restricted in absolutely exceptional cases.[79]

Furthermore, the ECtHR recognizes that measures taken in a state of emergency might not only serve to address a threat but might also aim to weaken or even abolish democratic structures.[80] It emphasizes the impor-

72 *Ibid.*

73 *A and others v. United Kingdom*, ECtHR Application No. 3455/05, Judgment of 19 February 2009.

74 *Mehmet Hasan Altan v. Turkey*, ECtHR Application No. 13237/17, Judgment of 20 March 2018.

75 *Şahin Alpay v. Turkey,* ECtHR Application No. 16538/17, Judgment of 20 March 2018.

76 See Weber, *supra* note 31, 925 *et seq.*

77 *Ibid.*, 925.

78 *Altan v. Turkey*, *supra* note 74, para 140, 213; *Alpay v. Turkey, supra* note 75, paras 119, 183. However, in *A and others v. UK*, *supra* note 73, the reasoning comprised paras 182–190.

79 *Altan v. Turkey*, *supra* note 74, paras 206, 207; *Alpay v. Turkey, supra* note 75, paras 177, 178. See also Polzin, *supra* note 53, 667.

80 *Ibid.*, 654.

tance of freedom of expression for a functioning democracy and points out in an *obiter dictum* that a state of emergency must not serve as a pretext for restricting the freedom of political debate. Emergency measures must remain committed to the protection of democracy.[81] Moreover, it does not grant the Member States any margin of appreciation if they are accused of violating non-derogable rights through killings, torture or inhuman treatment.

3. *Core Rights*

The case law on freedom of expression likewise reflects the core rights case law of the ECtHR, which defines *essential* and therefore *red lines* of liberal democracies. The Court treats core rights differently from a doctrinal vantage point. While its mandate to support the *rights revolution* in Europe has led to a broad understanding of most Convention rights, the costs of this approach, combined with a context-open proportionality test, are well-known and have been countered by the concept of core rights.[82]

Accordingly, Convention rights consist of various elements, some of which are more important and therefore more worthy of protection than others.[83] This differentiation can be found not only in the case law of the ECtHR but also under the European Charter of Fundamental Rights[84] and in various national constitutions. When it comes to core rights, the Court draws red lines by dispensing with the usual balancing style of argumentation and instead adopts a more categorical reasoning.[85]

The protection of core rights is particularly evident in the prohibitions of torture (Article 3 ECHR) and slavery (Article 4 ECHR), where the ECtHR completely dispenses with balancing.[86] The prohibition of State killings (Article 2 para. 2 ECHR) is also interpreted in light of the protec-

81 *Altan v. Turkey*, *supra* note 74, para. 210; *Alpay v. Turkey*, *supra* note 75, 180.

82 *Cf.* von Bernstorff, J. (2011), "Kerngehaltsschutz durch den UN-Menschenrechtsausschuss und den EGMR: Vom Wert kategorialer Argumentationsformen", *Der Staat* 50(2), 165–190.

83 Leijten, I. (2018), *Core socio-economic rights and the European Court of Human Rights*. Cambridge: Cambridge University Press, 2, 11.

84 European Charter of Fundamental Rights, Article 52, para. 1.

85 Von Bernstorff, *supra* note 82, 172 *et seq*.

86 See *Gäfgen v. Germany*, ECtHR Application No. 22978/05, Judgment of 30 June 2008, para. 69.

tion of core rights, allowing for only narrow exceptions that cannot be part of proportionality assessments.[87]

Categorical forms of argumentation become more difficult for human rights that are subject to broadly defined exceptions, such as Articles 8 to 11 ECHR. But it is precisely here that the doctrine of core contents proves helpful. Expressions of opinion that are critical of the government can only be restricted if they constitute an incitement to violence.[88] Political debate is highly protected due to its key role in a democratic society.[89] The core rights oriented jurisprudence of the ECtHR thus constitutes a further element in the red lines that substantiate the *European club of liberal democracies*.

4. *The Abuse of Rights*

Another instrument to protect what is essential to the *club* and to respond to crises in the democratic rule of law is the prohibition of abuse of rights. Article 18 ECHR stipulates that restrictions may "only be imposed for the intended purposes".

For a long time, this provision appeared to be largely irrelevant,[90] and the requirements for presenting evidence regarding the motives of State authorities were strict.[91] This changed in 2004, however, when the ECtHR concluded for the first time that Article 18 in conjunction with Article 5 ECHR had been breached.[92] Further cases followed, mainly concerning

---

87 *McCann and others v. United Kingdom*, ECtHR Application No. 18984/91, Judgment of 27 September 1995, para. 150.

88 See, e.g., *Zana v. Turkey*, ECtHR Application No. 18954/91, Judgment of 25 November 1997; *Sürek and Özdemir v. Turkey*, ECtHR Application Nos. 23927/94 and 24277/94, Judgment of 8 July 1999.

89 According to the ECtHR's jurisprudence, the freedom of political debate is at the core of democratic societies, as envisaged by the ECHR, *Lingens v. Österreich*, ECtHR Application No. 9815/82, Judgment of 8 July 1986, para. 42; see Hinghofer-Szalkay, S. (2012), "Extreme Meinungen und Meinungsäußerungsfreiheit: Die Schranke des Artikel 17 EMRK", *Journal für Rechtspolitik* 20(2), 106–114.

90 Frowein, J.A. (2009), "Article 18" In: J.A. Frowein and W. Peukert (eds), *EMRK-Kommentar* (3rd ed.). Kehl am Rhein / Strasbourg / Arlington: N. P. Engel Verlag, para. 2; Keller, H. and Heri, C. (2016), "Selective criminal proceedings and article 18 ECHR: The European Court of Human Rights' untapped potential to protect democracy", *Human Rights Law Journal* 37, 1–10, 2 *et seq*.

91 On the pre-*Merabishvili* (Grand Chamber) case law, see Harris *et al*, *supra* note 68, 844.

92 *Gusinskiy v. Russia*, ECtHR Application No. 70276/01, Judgment of 19 May 2004.

countries in Eastern Europe and the Caucasus. The decisions often concerned measures that were symptomatic of authoritarian tendencies. Thus, the *Merabishvili*, *Tymoshenko* and *Lutsenko* cases concerned the imprisonment of prominent opposition politicians. In the *Jafarov* and *Mammadov v. Azerbaijan* cases, political dissenters were silenced by measures under criminal law.[93]

At the outset, however, the Court stressed that there was still a presumption that these Convention States were acting in good faith, i.e., that they were in principle complying with the treaty.[94] In procedural terms, this meant that the applicant not only had to bear the full burden of proof but that the Court also imposed strict requirements,[95] permitting neither *prima facie* proof[96] nor a reversal of the burden of proof.[97] After considerable criticism,[98] the Court then became more liberal: in the *Lutsenko*, *Tymoshenko* and *Mammadov* cases, the Court went for a more contextual approach and no longer required direct proof of a corresponding State motive.[99] In the *Jafarov* case, it took into account the general situation of human rights activists. The evidence of systemic problems in Azerbaijan thus facilitated the determination of a concrete violation of Article 18 ECHR.[100]

93 *Merabishvili v. Geogia*, ECtHR Application No. 72508/13, Judgment of 28 November 2017; *Tymoshenko v. Ukraine*, ECtHR Application No. 49872/11, Judgment of 30 April 2013; *Lutsenko v. Ukraine*, ECtHR Application No. 6492/11, Judgment of 3 July 2012; *Jafarov v. Azerbaijan*, ECtHR Application No. 69981/1, Judgment of 17 March 2016; *Mammadov v. Azerbaijan*, ECtHR Application No. 15172/13, Judgment of 22 May 2014; see also *Cebotari v. Moldova*, ECtHR Application No. 35615/06, Judgment of 13 November 2007; extensively Keller and Heri, *supra* note 90, 3 *et seq*.

94 *Mammadov v. Azerbaijan*, *supra* note 93, para. 137; *Lutsenko v. Ukraine*, *supra* note 93, para. 106; *Khodorkowski v. Russia*, ECtHR Application No. 5829/04, Judgment of 31 May 2011, para. 255.

95 *Lutsenko v. Ukraine*, *supra* note 93, para. 107; *Khodorkowski v. Russia*, *supra* note 94, para. 256; *Cebotari v. Moldova*, *supra* note 93, paras 52 *et seq*.

96 E.g., *Varnava and others v. Turkey*, ECtHR Application No. 16064/90, Judgment of 18 September 2009, paras 182–184.

97 *Khodorkowski v. Russia*, *supra* note 94, para. 256.

98 Tan, F. (2018), "The Dawn of Article 18 ECHR: A Safeguard Against European Rule of Law Backsliding?", *Goettingen Journal of International Law* 9(1), 109–141, 127 *et seq*.; Keller and Heri *supra* note 90, 8.

99 *Mammadov v. Azerbaijan*, *supra* note 93, para. 137; *Tymoshenko v. Ukraine*, *supra* note 93, para. 294; *Lutsenko v. Ukraine*, *supra* note 93, paras 104 *et seq*.

100 *Jafarov v. Azerbaijan*, *supra* note 93, paras 104, 159–163.

The Chamber decision in the *Mammadov* case also triggered the first proceedings under Article 46 para. 4 ECHR. In a recent decision rendered unanimously, the Grand Chamber of the ECtHR – in agreement with the Council of Ministers – stated that Azerbaijan had not implemented the judgment and thus had violated its obligations under the Convention.[101] The Court admitted that its first *Mammadov* ruling was declaratory and remained silent on the question of suitable individual measures. However, the absence of an explicit statement relevant for execution in the first *Mammadov* judgment was not decisive for the question whether Azerbaijan had breached its obligations under Article 46 para. 1 ECHR. In any event, the measures taken by the defendant must be "compatible with the conclusions and spirit of the Court's judgment"[102]. With this ruling, the Court sends a strong signal: even if a judgment is silent on individual remedies, this provides no defense for the defendant State. A *restitutio in integrum* in the form of release from custody cannot be refused if a conviction has been handed down on the basis of Article 18 ECHR and a Convention State has acted in bad faith.[103] Nevertheless, the judgment was subject to criticism: the added value of the proceedings was claimed to be minimal, while the risks to the legitimacy of the Court were considerable.[104]

The Court took a further step in its judgment in the *Merabishvili* case,[105] in which the Grand Chamber completely departed from the stricter requirements on proof under Article 18 ECHR. The Court held that the "usual approach to proof rather than special rules" "can and should" be applied.[106] Thus, the burden of proof is no longer borne exclusively by one party, and the Court can investigate *ex officio*.[107] This lowered standard increases the practical relevance of Article 18 ECHR.[108] Furthermore, the

---

101 *Mammadov v. Azerbaijan, supra* note 10.

102 *Ibid.*, para. 186.

103 Çalı, B. (2019), "No Going Nuclear in Strasbourg: The Infringement Decision in Ilgar Mammadov v. Azerbaijan by the European Court of Human Rights", *Verfassungsblog*, 30 May, available at https://verfassungsblog.de/no-going-nuclear-in-strasbourg/, accessed 3 December 2019.

104 De Londras, F. and Dzehtsiarou, K. (2017), "Mission Impossible? Addressing Non-Execution through Infringement Proceedings in the European Court of Human Rights", *International & Comparative Law Quarterly* 66(2), 467–490, 486 *et seq*.

105 *Merabishvili v. Georgia, supra* note 93. See Çalı, *supra* note 1, 267 *et seq.*; Tan, *supra* note 98, 133 *et seq*.

106 *Merabishvili v. Georgia, supra* note 93, para. 310.

107 *Ibid.*, para. 311.

108 See also Tan, *supra* note 98, 135.

Court strengthened the relevance of Article 18 ECHR by emphasizing the autonomous character of the norm. Although Article 18 ECHR still only becomes operative in conjunction with other provisions of the Convention, it now has autonomous significance insofar as it prohibits the Convention States from restricting Convention rights for purposes contrary to the Convention.[109] Here, the criterion of the "predominant purpose" of a measure introduced in the *Merabishvili* case appears to be problematic.[110] It seems as if the Court will tolerate abusive purposes as long as the legitimate purpose of the restriction of rights prevails.[111]

It will remain a challenge for complainants under Article 18 ECHR to make their case.[112] For example, in the *Navalnyy and Ofitserov* case,[113] the ECtHR established a new requirement regarding the application of Article 18 ECHR: in examining the violation of Article 6 of the ECHR, it acknowledged that there was an obvious link between the complainant's public activities and the decision of the investigative committee in bringing charges against him.[114] Nevertheless, it rejected the complaint as inadmissible, arguing that Article 18 ECHR cannot be asserted in conjunction with Article 6 and Article 7 ECHR.[115] This development of the case law was rightly received with disapproval.[116]

5. *The Exhaustion of Domestic Remedies*

It is a truism that red lines should be drawn as early as possible in order to have an effect. But the ECtHR must also respect its subsidiarity. According to Article 35 para. 1 ECHR, the ECtHR may only deal with a matter after

109 *Merabishvili v. Georgia, supra* note 93, paras 287–288.

110 *Ibid.*, para. 353.

111 For criticism in this regard, see the joint concurring opinion of Judges Yudkivska, Tsotsoria and Vehabović on *Merabishvili v. Georgia, supra* note 93, paras 1, 19, 37; also concurring opinion of Judge Serghides in the same matter, paras 3, 34; joint concurring opinion of Judges Sajó, Tsotsoria and Pinto De Albuquerque on *Tchankotadze v. Georgia*, ECtHR Application No. 15256/05, Judgment of 21 June 2016, para. 1.

112 On this jurisprudence, see Keller and Heri, *supra* note 90, 6.

113 *Navalnyy and Ofitserov v. Russia*, ECtHR Application No. 46632/13, Judgment of 23 February 2016.

114 *Ibid.*, para. 119.

115 *Ibid.*, para. 129.

116 *Ibid.*, separate opinion of Judges Nicolaou, Keller and Dedov; Keller and Heri, *supra* note 90, 6.

all domestic remedies have been exhausted. The corresponding dilemma can be seen clearly in the Court's reactions to the Turkish repressions that began in 2016. After receiving numerous complaints against repressive measures applied during the attempted coup, the Court initially dismissed such complaints as inadmissible in the *Mercan*[117], *Catal*[118], *Zihni*[119], and *Köksal*[120] cases. The complainants, the Court argued, had not exhausted domestic remedies[121] because the decisions of the Turkish Constitutional Court were still pending. This has likewise led to criticism.[122]

According to its case law, the Court may indeed decide if the legal remedy to be lodged is futile or ineffective.[123] The issue, therefore, hinged on the question of whether the Turkish courts – including the Constitutional Court – had remained functioning institutions. In the *Altan*[124] and *Alpay*[125] cases, the ECtHR, in agreement with the Turkish Constitutional Court, found that the detention of two journalists violated their rights under Articles 5 paras 1 and 10 ECHR. Under these circumstances, and in accordance with the principle of subsidiarity, the stance of the ECtHR seems plausible, especially as its cooperation with national courts is key to fulfilling its mandate.

6. *The Procedural Margin of Appreciation*

A club can only be strong and vibrant if its members act in its spirit. Accordingly, the procedures and doctrines that link supranational courts to national courts are key. Thus, the Court of Justice of the EU can avail itself of the preliminary ruling procedure as developed since *van Gend en Loos*, while the IACtHR benefits from the conventionality control introduced in

117 *Mercan v. Turkey*, ECtHR Application No. 56511/16, Decision of 8 November 2016.

118 *Catal v. Turkey*, ECtHR Application No. 2873/17, Decision of 7 March 2017.

119 *Zihni v. Turkey*, ECtHR Application No. 59061/16, Decision of 29 November 2016.

120 *Köksal v. Turkey*, ECtHR Application No. 70478/16, Decision of 6 June 2017.

121 Different in *Er a.o. v. Turkey*, ECtHR Application No. 23016/04, Judgment of 31 July 2012, paras 45 *et seq.*

122 Frowein, J.A. (2017), "Straßburg muss handeln", *Frankfurter Allgemeine Sonntagszeitung*, 3 March 2017.

123 On the exhaustion of domestic remedies, see especially *Vučković a.o. v. Serbia*, ECtHR Application No. 17153/11, Judgment of 25 March 2014, paras 69 *et seq.*

124 *Altan v. Turkey*, *supra* note 74.

125 *Alpay v. Turkey*, *supra* note 75.

Almonacid Arellano.[126] For a long time, the ECtHR lacked a comparable tool. However, the procedural *margin of appreciation* doctrine offers something comparable.[127] It could readjust the Court's mandate and substantiate its claim to speak the law *In the name of the European club of liberal democracies*.

The core idea is that the ECtHR will exercise restraint if the national decision at issue adequately considers the relevant case law of Strasbourg. This is based on the margin-of-appreciation doctrine,[128] according to which the Convention States have discretion concerning the interpretation and application of a Convention norm in many, albeit by no means all, case constellations. The doctrine is justified by the subsidiarity of the Convention system,[129] the greater democratic legitimacy of the Convention States' legislatures[130] and the greater proximity of the national authorities to the subject matter.[131]

---

126 See Weiler, J.H.H. (1991), "The Transformation of Europe", *Yale Law Journal* 100(8), 2403–2483, 2420 *et seq*.; Ferrer MacGregor, E. (2017), "The Conventionality Control as a Core Mechanism of the *Ius Constitutionale Commune*" In: von Bogdandy *et al.*, *supra* note 57, 321–336.

127 There is also the advisory opinion procedure under the 16th Additional Protocol which has, however, only been ratified by 13 States (Stand: 19.9.2019).

128 See *Marckx v. Belgium*, ECtHR Application No. 6833/74, Judgment of 13 June 1979, Dissenting Opinion of Judge Fitzmaurice, paras 27 *et seq*.; *Animal Defenders International v. United Kingdom*, Application No. 19010/07, Judgment of 22 April 2013, paras 102, 123; *X a.o. v. Austria*, ECtHR Application No. 19010/07, Judgment of 19 February 2013, para. 102; scholarship includes Bernhardt, R. (1983), "Internationaler Menschenrechtsschutz und nationaler Gestaltungsspielraum" In: R. Bernhard (ed.), *Festschrift für Hermann Mosler*. Berlin / New York: Springer, 75–88, 81 *et seq*.; Frowein, J. (1980), "Die Europäische Menschenrechtskonvention in der neueren Praxis der Europäischen Kommission und des Europäischen Gerichtshofs für Menschenrechte", *Europäische Grundrechte-Zeitschrift*, 231–237, 237; Spielmann, D. (2012), "Allowing the Right Margin: The European Court of Human Rights and the National Margin of Appreciation Doctrine; Waiver of Subsidiarity of European Review?", *Cambridge Yearbook of European Legal Studies* 14, 381–418; Binder, C. (2015), "The Concept of the Margin of Appreciation", *Journal für Rechtspolitik* 23(1), 56–66; Asche, J. (2018), *Die Margin of Appreciation*. Heidelberg: Springer.

129 Villiger, M. (2007), "The Principle of Subsidiarity in the European Convention on Human Rights" In: M. Kohen (ed.), *Promoting Justice, Human Rights and Conflict Resolution through International Law – Liber Amicorum Caflisch*. Leiden: Brill, 623–637, 632.

130 *S.A.S. v. France*, ECtHR Application No. 43835/11, Judgment of 1 July 2014, para. 129; Asche, *supra* note 128, 44.

131 *Handyside v. United Kingdom*, *supra* note 27, para. 48; *Jacubowski v. Germany*, Application No. 15088/89, Judgment of 23 June 1994, paras 26 *et seq*.

The margin of appreciation doctrine was of great interest to the ministers of justice in Copenhagen. In the first public draft of the Copenhagen Declaration of February 2018, the emphasis on the subsidiarity of the ECtHR read like a systemic criticism of its jurisprudence.[132] The harsh tone probably displeased many and obviously led to fundamental discussions. This is reflected in the Copenhagen Declaration which was adopted in April 2018 and underlines that a strengthening of the subsidiarity principle is not intended to restrict European human-rights protection.[133] But it nevertheless emphasizes, "[w]here a balancing exercise has been undertaken at the national level in conformity with the criteria laid down in the Court's jurisprudence, the Court has *generally* indicated that it will not substitute its own assessment for that of the domestic courts, unless there are *strong reasons* for doing so"[134]. This emphasizes how the margin of appreciation doctrine demands responsibility from the national institutions but at the same time preserves the ultimate responsibility of the ECtHR.[135]

Similar to the preliminary ruling procedure under Article 267 TFEU and the conventionality control of the IACtHR, the margin of appreciation can lead to a more intensive cooperation between the ECtHR and the national courts, thereby ultimately strengthening European human rights protection. In essence, it offers the national courts an incentive to recognize ECtHR jurisprudence as providing authoritative precedents for their decisions. Such a doctrine integrates ECtHR case law deeply into the national legal systems and thus increases its effectiveness. In doing so, it strengthens the club of European democracies and counteracts the criticism of an excessively invasive ECtHR. Of course, it diminishes the role of the ECtHR as a primary driving force in the development of human rights. However, such correction of its mandate seems appropriate because dynamic judicial protection of individual rights, a rarity in the 1970s, has become a regular occurrence in most European legal systems.[136]

---

132 See Draft Copenhagen Declaration, 5 February 2018, para. 22, available at https://menneskeret.dk/sites/menneskeret.dk/files/media/dokumenter/nyheder/draft_copenhagen_declaration_05.02.18.pdf, accessed 5 December 2019.

133 Copenhagen Declaration, *supra* note 4, paras 26 *et seq*.

134 *Ibid*., para. 28c (emphases added by the authors).

135 *Cf*. *ibid*., para. 10.

136 *Cf*. the contributions of von Bogdandy, A. / Grabenwarter, C. / Huber, P., Behrendt, C., Farahat, A., Tuori, K., Jouanjan, O., Bifulco, R. / Paris D., Besselink, L., Grabenwarter, C., Tuleja, P. and Amaral, M.L. / Pereira, R.A., Biaggini, G., Requejo Pagés J.L., Sólyom, L., Murkens, J. and Quint, P. In: A. von Bogdandy, C. Grabenwarter and P. Huber (eds) (2016), *Handbuch Ius Publicum*

This doctrine is also promising in view of the alienation of some Convention States from the jurisprudence of the ECtHR. These States often refer to the values of national identity, national diversity and national democracy. The margin of appreciation doctrine could take these values into account while at the same time protecting what is essential.

IV. Do the Bundesverfassungsgericht and the Corte Costituzionale frustrate the pursuit of this mandate?

But which ECtHR decisions have authoritative effects vis-à-vis national courts?[137] There are many possible gradations.[138] A controversial dialogue within the network of European constitutional courts has developed on this key issue.

The ECtHR has always claimed that its decisions are authoritative beyond the concrete case.[139] The Convention States expressly acknowledge such relevance in the Copenhagen Declaration.[140] However, the Court has recently adopted a particularly categorical position: "[t]he Court would emphasise that its judgments all have the same legal value. Their binding nature and interpretative authority cannot therefore depend on the formation by which they were rendered."[141] It does not distinguish between a decision of a single judge, a committee of three judges, a chamber of seven judges or the Grand Chamber of seventeen judges, nor between a new development and a doctrine that has been consolidated by several decisions in different formations. It bears mentioning, moreover, that EU law supports this stance of the ECtHR.[142] However, the German *Bundesverfas-*

Europaeum. Vol. VI: Verfassungsgerichtsbarkeit in Europa: Institutionen. Heidelberg: C.F. Müller.

137 On the general phenomenon, see the contribution in von Bogdandy, A. and Venzke, I. (eds) (2012), *International Judicial Lawmaking*. Heidelberg: Springer.

138 Jacob, M. (2014), *Precedents and Case-based Reasoning in the European Court of Justice*. Cambridge: Cambridge University Press, 218–219. Generally on the functioning of precedents, see Payandeh, M. (2017), *Judikative Rechtserzeugung. Theorie, Dogmatik und Methodik der Wirkung von Präjudizien*. Tübingen: Mohr Siebeck, 11 *et seq*.

139 *Ireland v. United Kingdom*, *supra* note 7, para. 154.

140 See Copenhagen Declaration, *supra* note 4, para. 26.

141 *G.I.E.M. S.R.L. a.o. v. Italy*, *supra* note 7, para. 252.

142 See recital 32 of the Dublin III Regulation (Regulation No. 604/2013 of the European Parliament and of the Council of 26 June 2013 establishing the criteria and mechanisms for determining the Member State responsible for examin-

sungsgericht and the Italian *Corte Costituzionale* take a much more differentiated view.

A. Domestic Buffering of the ECtHR's Authority

According to both these courts, Strasbourg's law making authority is subject to a number of prerequisites and limits. The ruling of the *Bundesverfassungsgericht* on the ban on strike action by civil servants is a landmark decision in this matter.[143] According to the decision, German law can only be interpreted in accordance with the Convention "[i]f German courts have latitude for interpreting and balancing within the scope of recognised methods of the interpretation of laws"[144]. German courts may not "schematically alig[n]"[145] individual constitutional concepts, but must integrate the ECHR "as carefully as possible into the existing, doctrinally differentiated national legal system"[146] by means of an "active process (of acknowledgment)"[147]. Cases in which the Federal Republic of Germany was not a party must be considered in a context-sensitive manner.[148] Moreover, not every Strasbourg decision has authority for German courts. Rather, they have to "identify statements regarding *principal values* enshrined in the Convention and address them"[149], but not more. This is

ing an application for international protection lodged in one of the Member States by a third-country national or a stateless person, OJ L 180/31, 29 June 2013).

143 On this judgment, see, e.g., Polakiewicz, J. and Suominen-Picht, I. (2018), "Aktuelle Herausforderungen für Europarat und EMRK: Die Erklärung von Kopenhagen (April 2018), das Spannungsverhältnis zwischen EMRK und nationalen Verfassungen und die Beteiligung der EU an dem europäischen Menschenrechtskontrollmechanismus", *Europäische Grundrechte-Zeitschrift* 45, 383–390, 385 *et seq.*; Jacobs, M. and Payandeh, M. (2019), "Das beamtenrechtliche Streikverbot: Konventionsrechtliche Immunisierung durch verfassungsgerichtliche Petrifizierung", *Juristenzeitung* 74(1), 19–26.

144 *Bundesverfassungsgericht*, *supra* note 3, para. 133.

145 *Ibid.*, para. 131.

146 *Ibid.*, para. 135, with reference to the decisions BVerfGE 111, 307, 327 and VerfGE 128, 326, 371.

147 *Ibid.*, para. 131.

148 *Ibid.*, para. 132; Kaiser, A.-B. (2017), "Streikrecht für Beamten – Folge einer Fehlrezeption?", *Archiv des öffentlichen Rechts* 142(3), 417–441, 432 *et seq.*

149 *Bundesverfassungsgericht*, *supra* note 3, para. 132 (emphasis added by the authors).

far removed from the precedential authority that the *Bundesverfassungsgericht* assigns to its own decisions.[150]

Similar limits can be found in the more recent case law of the Italian *Corte Costituzionale*. In 2015, it decided that the ordinary courts would only have to observe Strasbourg case law if Italy had been a party to the lawsuit or if the case law was "consolidated" or consisted of pilot judgments, since only these are generally binding.[151] Interpretation in conformity with the constitution must otherwise take precedence over interpretations in conformity with the Convention, and there is no obligation to initiate a judicial review proceeding before the Constitutional Court.

This jurisprudence has subjected the *Corte Costituzionale* to much criticism from scholars[152] as well as from the ECtHR itself.[153] If Italian courts now decide what is "consolidated law", this might have negative effects on Italian compliance with the ECHR and even on international legal certainty.[154] If all courts – and no longer just the *Corte Costituzionale* – can rule on the authority of Strasbourg's case law, ordinary courts might be overburdened,[155] as lower court judges usually do not possess enough knowledge about the case law of the ECtHR. Finally, the Constitutional Court threatens to remove itself from the dialogue between the ECtHR and national courts.

The *Bundesverfassungsgericht* does not make such a distinction. So far, it has dealt with relevant Strasbourg rulings regardless of whether they were issued by the Grand Chamber or only a Chamber.[156] However, its case law, which only binds German courts to pronouncements on *principal values* of

150 Extensively Payandeh, *Judikative Rechtserzeugung*, *supra* note 138, 373 *et seq*.

151 Decision No. 49 of 26 March 2015, para. 7; on this decision, see Paris, D. and Oellers-Frahm, K. (2016), "Zwei weitere völkerrechts 'unfreundliche' Entscheidungen des italienischen Verfassungsgerichtshofs aus dem Jahr 2015 (Nr. 49 und 50): Zur Frage der Maßgeblichkeit der Rechtsprechung des EGMR", *Europäische Grundrechte-Zeitschrift* 43(10–12), 245–252, 247 *et seq*.; Viganò, F. (2015), "La Consulta e la tela di Penelope", *Diritto Penale Contemporaneo* 2, 333–343.

152 Bignami, M. (2015), "Le gemelle crescono in salute: la confisca urbanistica tra Costituzione, CEDU e diritto vivente", *Diritto Penale Contemporaneo* (2), 288–302.

153 *G.I.E.M. S.R.L. a.o. v. Italy*, *supra* note 7, para. 252; see also separate opinion of Judge Pinto de Albuquerque, paras 57 *et seq*.

154 Paris and Oellers-Frahm, *supra* note 151, 249.

155 Tega, D. (2015), "La sentenza della Corte costituzionale n. 49 del 2015 sulla confisca: 'il predominio assiologico della Costituzione sulla CEDU'", *Quaderni Costituzionali* 2, 400–404.

156 E.g., *Bundesverfassungsgericht*, *supra* note 3, paras 163 *et seq*.

the Convention, leads to a similar buffering of the authority of Strasbourg's legal production.

B. Legitimacy through Control

At first glance, this case law of the *Corte Costituzionale* and the *Bundesverfassungsgericht* does not appear to be very Convention-friendly. It cannot be denied that it poses a considerable risk to the compliance with the ECHR and Strasbourg's case law.[157] Criticism and rejection of its judgments can damage the authority of the ECtHR, after all. At the same time, however, this case law also provides an opportunity to share the burden of legitimacy.

The ECtHR has a democratic mandate to not only resolve a dispute for the parties but also promote liberal democracy *In the name of the European club of liberal democracies*. Nevertheless, the democratic legitimacy of its decisions is often weak, especially when the Court uses open-ended human rights norms to adjudicate controversial or complex domestic issues in sweeping terms. The openness of the national legal systems not only to the abstract provisions of the ECHR but also to the ECtHR's judgments imposes an enormous burden on democratic legitimacy.

Against this background, the weakening of the ECtHR's authority through "buffering" national jurisprudence turns out to be a possible legitimatory asset that supports the pursuit of its mandate. If domestic courts are not strictly bound to Strasbourg precedents, they contribute their own democratic legitimacy when they refer to the ECtHR's decisions.[158] In addition, a genuine dialogue with the ECtHR, which all sides regard as indispensable, can only develop if the domestic courts can exercise control over the case law they choose to respect. By receiving and discussing Strasbourg's decisions, the national courts affirm the ECtHR's legitimacy.

---

157 See, for example, the problematic recycling of ECtHR-critical decisions from Germany and Italy by the Russian Constitutional Court (Decision of 14 July 2015, No. 21-P). Regarding this decision, Hartwig, M. (2017), "Vom Dialog zum Disput? Verfassungsrecht vs. Europäische Menschenrechtskonvention – Der Fall der Russländischen Föderation", *Europäische Grundrechte-Zeitschrift* 44, 1–23, 8 *et seq*.

158 On the legitimizing function of the highest national courts, see von Bogdandy, A., Grabenwarter, C. and Huber, P. (2016), "Verfassungsgerichtsbarkeit im europäischen Rechtsraum" In: von Bogdandy, Grabenwarter and Huber, *supra* note 136, § 95, paras 15, 17.

Of course, this mechanism only works if all institutions involved are aware of their shared responsibility for the European human rights system and understand themselves as good club members. In their dialogue with the ECtHR, all courts of the Convention States must continue to signal their principled support for the Convention system. This does not mean that they must always give their unqualified consent to Strasbourg's law making. But they must act as loyal members of the club of European democracies, in whose name the ECtHR is pursuing a very difficult mandate indeed.